PIMLI

762

HANS HOLBEIN

Derek Wilson is well known through his books, radio and TV appearances, frequent journalistic features and festival appearances as one of the UK's leading narrative historians. Among his critically acclaimed and best-selling books are *Sweet Robin: Robert Dudley, Earl of Leicester*; *Rothschild: A Story of Wealth and Power*; *The King and the Gentleman: Charles Stuart and Oliver Cromwell, 1599–1649* (Pimlico 2000); *In the Lion's Court: Power, Ambition and Sudden Death in the Reign of Henry VIII* (Pimlico 2002); *All the King's Women: Love, Sex and Politics in the Life of Charles II* (Pimlico 2004) and *Charlemagne: Barbarian & Emperor* (Pimlico 2006).

The Pope

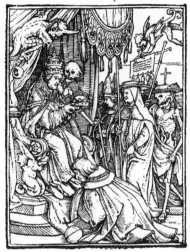

The Escutcheon of Death

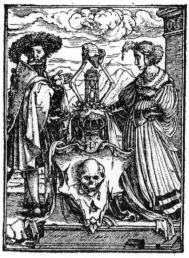

The Count

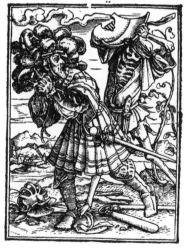

The Last Judgement

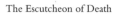

HANS HOLBEIN

PORTRAIT OF AN UNKNOWN MAN

DEREK WILSON

Revised Edition

PIMLICO

Published by Pimlico 2006

2 4 6 8 10 9 7 5 3

Copyright © Derek Wilson 1996 and 2006

Derek Wilson has asserted his right under the Copyright, Designs
and Patents Act 1988 to be identified as the author of this work

First published in Great Britain in 1996 by
Weidenfeld & Nicolson
Phoenix Paperback edition published in 1997

Revised Pimlico edition 2006

Pimlico
Random House, 20 Vauxhall Bridge Road,
London SW1V 2SA

Random House Australia (Pty) Limited
20 Alfred Street, Milsons Point, Sydney,
New South Wales 2061, Australia

Random House New Zealand Limited
18 Poland Road, Glenfield,
Auckland 10, New Zealand

Random House South Africa (Pty) Limited
Isle of Houghton, Corner of Boundary Road & Carse O'Gowrie
Houghton 2198, South Africa

Random House Publishers India Private Limited
301 World Trade Tower, Hotel Intercontinental Grand Complex
Barakhamba Lane, New Delhi 110 001, India

Random House UK Limited Reg. No. 954009
www.randomhouse.co.uk

A CIP catalogue record for this book
is available from the British Library

ISBN 9781844139187 (from Jan 2007)
ISBN 1844139182

Papers used by Random House UK are natural,
recyclable products made from wood grown in sustainable forests;
the manufacturing processes conform to the environmental
regulations of the country of origin

Typeset by SX Composing DTP, Rayleigh, Essex
Printed and bound in Great Britain by
Clays Ltd, St Ives PLC

CONTENTS

LIST OF ILLUSTRATIONS

FRONTISPIECE

Four images from *The Dance of Death,* Hans Holbein the Younger,
1538

DRAWINGS IN THE TEXT

PLATE SECTIONS

THE FOLLOWING ILLUSTRATIONS WERE SUPPLIED BY THE
BRIDGEMAN ART LIBRARY:

*Portraits of Two Youths, a Dwarf and a Townscape; De Vos van Steenwijk;
Ship of Fools; Madonna of the Burgermeister Meyer; The Dead Christ,*
Andrea Mantegna; *The Deposition,* Matthias Grünewald; *Erasmus;
Georg Gisze; Bonifacius Amerbach; Nicholas Kratzer; Thomas More;
Richard Southwell; The Ambassadors; Anne of Cleves; Christina of
Denmark; Henry VIII; Portrait of Edward VI as a child.*

PREFACE TO THE
REVISED EDITION

I am very grateful to Will Sulkin of Pimlico for encouraging me to make this revised edition. Over the last decade my own thinking, particularly about Holbein's religious affiliation, has moved on, helped not a little by a spate of specialist studies on the artist's work, Susan Foister's Ph.D. thesis, *Holbein and his English Patrons* (Courtauld Institute, University of London, 1989) is seminal. In 1997 the recently restored *The Ambassadors* went on display and the catalogue accompanying the exhibition by Susan Foister, Ashok Roy and Martin Wyld brought students up to date with the very latest thinking about this enigmatic painting. One of the abiding riddles of Holbein's portraiture – the identity of the sitter for *Lady With a Squirrel and a Starling* – was solved by David J. King in *Apollo,* May 2004, and the identification of Anne Lovell adds to our knowledge of the circle of Holbein's early English patrons. Ann Johnson very kindly gave me access to her paper, *From an analysis of Holbein's paintings can we discern where his religious sympathies lay?* Among other important recent publications are: Oskar Bätschmann and Pascal Griener, *Hans Holbein,* 1997 and Mark Roskill and John Oliver Hand, *Hans Holbein: Paintings, Prints and Reception,* New Haven, 2001. It has not been possible in this modest revision to reflect upon all the new insights provided by recent research but I hope what I have written below will encourage readers to further investigation of this remarkable man and his equally remarkable age.

INTRODUCTION

If any justification were needed for a new biography of one of the world's most accessible artists, whose paintings and drawings have always delighted, intrigued and informed, the 500th anniversary of his birth would provide it. In reality, the fascination of the Holbein story is its own vindication. His remarkable and varied talent has been recognized ever since Erasmus, Thomas More and Henry VIII sat for him. The royal tutor, John Cheke, reverently collected all the artist's drawings and sketches he could find, and the Swiss lawyer, Bonifacius Amerbach, eagerly bought up every available example of Holbein's work. Nicholas Hilliard described him as 'the most excellent Painter and limner . . . the greatest Master Truly in both those arts after the life that ever was'. Holbein was a coolly precise portraitist, capable of delineating nuances of personality with a flick of brush or pencil. His works in miniature were miracles of clarity. Yet he was also a master of the grandiose, who splashed gorgeously clad figures and prancing animals over large wall spaces.

Hans Holbein the Younger was the first European artist to provide later generations with a visual record of many of the most influential men and women of his day, and particularly the denizens of Henry VIII's court. When we call to mind the Tudor despot, or Anne of Cleves, the 'Flanders Mare', or the persecutor-turned-martyr Thomas More, or the scheming Duke of Norfolk or Thomas Cromwell, mastermind of the English Reformation, or scores of other politicians, churchmen and courtiers who were close to the centre of power in the 1530s, it is through Holbein's eyes that we see them. But he introduces us to many other men and women of contemporary importance and greater or lesser historical significance – German merchants, Swiss burghers, scholars, printers, diplomats, lawyers, doctors, princes and princesses.

Holbein is best known for his portraiture, which is perhaps a good reason for drawing attention once again to other aspects of his output. His influence on book design was revolutionary and his work with some of the great printers-publishers of the age has provided us with intricate title-pages and engravings, such as the unsurpassable *Dance of Death* series, which reveal him as a master of satire. Then there are his religious paintings, his Protestant propaganda pieces, his portrait miniatures, his designs for jewellery and stained-glass windows and his murals.

Whenever he had lived, Holbein would have been important as an artist who opened the shutters on his age, but what makes this artist especially important is the particular world he inhabited, the world of that spiritual and intellectual upheaval we call the Renaissance and the Reformation. Holbein was fifteen when Michelangelo completed the ceiling frescos of the Sistine Chapel. He was twenty when Martin Luther posted his ninety-five theses. He was thirty-four when the first great Protestant confession of faith was drawn up in his native Augsburg. He was thirty-eight when his patron, Thomas More, became England's most famous Catholic martyr. And it was in the year of his death (1543) that Copernicus published his heliocentric theory. No other epoch has experienced more seismic changes in the way people think about art, religion, science, politics and societal relationships. Holbein was at the centre of this disturbance, talking with radical thinkers like Erasmus and Melanchthon, listening to Oecolampadius and other preachers of reform, working both for upholders of the Catholic status quo such as More and for Cromwell, the builder of a new order. Holbein was a man who could not be indifferent to the issues which were tearing jagged holes in the fabric of Christian Europe. His was a spirit affected by the restlessness of the age. Until the last decade of his life he never settled anywhere longer than four years. Always he was searching – and not just for work.

As a young craftsman, trying to earn a living, Holbein sought commissions from wealthy ecclesiastics. He produced altarpieces and frescos celebrating Catholic doctrines and heroes, only to have them smashed and whited over by iconoclastic mobs. The art demanded by the new Protestant masters was propaganda denouncing papistry, and Holbein with no less skill produced paintings and woodcuts extolling a reformed faith. And through it all he had his own beliefs to find. As he rubbed shoulders with visionary poets, colporteurs of banned books, ambitious courtiers, men and women of high resolve, schemers, cowards, cynical temporizers, politiques who went in constant fear for their survival and those who were too absorbed in administration or money-making to concern themselves with principle, he was engaged in his own truth quest.

Truth above all else concerned Holbein. It obliged him to abandon existing conventions of religious art and increasingly to feast his imagination on Scripture. Truth would not permit him to make flattering portraits. When he satirized leaders of Church and state it was because their lives were at variance with what they claimed to believe and teach. Some of his more complex paintings he packed with signs and symbols which, rightly understood, tell us what he thought about the personalities and events he encountered. Holbein was no mere realist, dispassionately transferring to paper or canvas the outward appearance of things. When we stand before the haunting *Christ in the Tomb,* the puzzling *Ambassadors* or the seemingly straightforward *Anne of Cleves,* we are looking at a statement, or tract, that we can read once we have mastered Holbein's unique iconography and understood the circumstances in which it was created. What then emerges is a fresh, vibrant image of the man and his age, an image with many intriguing and surprising features.

We discover, for example, that the artist who is supposed to have turned his back on reformed Basel because of the destruction of religious art in the city was not even there when the iconoclastic outburst took place and that he had no interest in the preservation of traditional religious imagery. It becomes clear for the first time that his sympathy for Thomas More was expressed in the symbolism of *The Ambassadors* and that, despite this, he had a greater affinity with Anne Boleyn and was closely associated with her entourage. Most remarkable of all is what emerges about his relationship with Thomas Cromwell. Holbein's search for meaning ended when he entered the service of the systematic reformer who was introducing humanistic principles of religion and government by law backed with force. This was so far preferable to the peasant revolts and civil unrest which had convulsed parts of the continent that Holbein regarded England as the most favoured of countries and willingly became an agent in Cromwell's propaganda and espionage system.

Although an account of this extraordinary life, like good wine, needs no bush I ought, perhaps, to explain a little more fully why I consider this biography timely. It is over eighty years since the appearance of the last full-length study in English. A. B. Chamberlain's two-volume *Hans Holbein The Younger* (1913) is a splendidly detailed treatment of the subject, but it is not now easily available to students and admirers of the artist and, during the last eight decades, perceptions have changed and fresh information has come to light. Chamberlain drew heavily upon A. Woltmann's *Holbein und seine Zeit* (2 vols, Leipzig, 1874–6). These have remained the authoritative texts. Hundreds of books, monographs and articles have appeared dealing with various aspects of Holbein's *oeuvre*, many of which are noted in the bibliography of the present volume. They have enriched our understanding of the artist's work and working methods and enabled us more accurately to define his canon. This important concentration on artistic minutiae has not been accompanied by any attempt at a fresh overview of Hans Holbein which reinterprets him in the light of his age.

Yet, that age has come under particularly close scrutiny since the 1950s. Few movements have been more exhaustively researched, interpreted, reinterpreted and argued about during the last forty years than the Reformation. As a result we now have a far clearer perception than that enjoyed by earlier biographers of the world in which Hans Holbein lived. This, then, is a good moment to bring together the fresh insights about the artist and about his time. In doing this I believe we do see Hans Holbein more clearly.

Finally, I must confess to a personal reason for undertaking the present study. In a book published in 1950, Paul Ganz, the century's leading authority on Hans Holbein the Younger, declared that any attempt at a biography of the artist was doomed to be 'a dry recital of facts, revealing almost nothing of his personality, his character, his family life or his relations with his fellow-men in general'.[1] When I first read that assertion it seemed to me that, if irremediably true, it was very sad. I suppose I regarded it as something of a challenge – a challenge that eventually I had to take up. Hence this book, and specifically its title. After several years of reading, travelling, talking with experts and looking at every example of the artist's work I could find I feel that Hans Holbein is no longer for me an 'unknown man'. I hope the same becomes true for those who read this book.

One fact that will become obvious is the extent to which I am indebted to many specialists and experts who are more closely associated than I with Holbein's works. Among those from whom I have received unstinting help I would particularly like to record my gratitude to Dr Susan Foister, Miss Julia Lloyd Williams of the National Gallery of Scotland, the staff of the National Portrait Gallery, the Kunstmuseum and the Historisches Museum, Basel, the Musée d'Unterlinden, Colmar, the Historisches Museum, Augsburg, the British Library, the British Museum and the University Library Cambridge.

Chapter 1

AUGSBURG

1497–1515

In the year of Holbein's death the earth moved. It vacated its position at the centre of the universe and took up station as one of several planets circling the sun. Such was the drastic cosmological rethinking brought about by the publication, in 1543, of Nicolaus Copernicus's *De revolutionibus orbium coelestium*. No less metamorphic in another sphere was the beautifully illustrated book which Holbein's friend, Oporinus, printed at Basel for Andreas Vesalius in that same year. *De humani corporis fabrica* achieved for anatomy what Copernicus's treatise did for astronomy. Both set new courses for future scholars to steer because they questioned the accuracy of existing charts and shared with the old chartmakers a passion for truth. What links the works of these intellectual master mariners with the unremarked death of a Swiss immigrant artist in London is more than a date.

Copernicus insisted that the fundamental purpose of his hypo-thesizing was to 'save the appearances' of things. He challenged Ptolemy's understanding of the movement of heavenly spheres on the basis that heliocentric theory was at least equally true to observed fact. Vesalius accepted the same principle. He had a deep respect for the foundation texts of Galen, but he refused to follow the practice of medical professors who expounded those texts while disdaining to bloody their own hands by dissecting cadavers. When his own students asked for Vesalius's speculations about the nature and function of human organs the great anatomist told them actually to handle the tissue and to trust the evidence of their own fingers. Hans Holbein, himself the friend and companion of scholars, used the same compass. He has been called the 'master of realism' because he was committed to observing, understanding and portraying objects and people as they were, in their essential truth.

'Saving the appearances' of things was a process as much aesthetic as scientific and as much metaphysical as aesthetic. No sixteenth-century thinker doubted that all created phenomena were embraced within a divine order. The holy schema had several doors – theology, music, mathematics, art, astronomy, medicine, law. All gave access to the same truth, and that truth was beautiful. Thus Copernicus's cosmology, no less than Erasmus's *philosophia Christi,* claimed that its elegance and harmony testified to its validity.

Even the most cautious radical, respectful of ancient institutions, could not avoid the risk of being branded a heretic. Leonardo, Copernicus, Erasmus, Vesalius, Luther – all, in different ways, questioned received wisdom and challenged, explicitly or implicitly, existing establishments. They were far from being alone. The years through which Hans Holbein lived produced an unprecedented eruption of new ideas and innovative methodologies, propounded by self-confident teachers, preachers, writers, artists and statesmen. That is why they were years of spiritual and intellectual conflict and why Renaissance and Reformation must be seen as only different sides of the same coin.

The fascination and significance of Hans Holbein lie in his striving in this tumultuous world to find and speak with his own voice. As a thinking man and an artist he had to grapple with old certainties, new revelations and fashionable scepticisms, not merely for the benefit of his own soul, but so that he might express in his own way a truth that saved the appearance of things. Everything about his tumultuous life – his constant travels, his association with humanist scholars, his Catholic altarpieces, his vituperative Protestant engravings, his making and abandoning of friends, his forsaking of family, his involvement in court intrigue – has to be seen in this context. The age made the man. The man expressed the age.

Fame, like gunpowder, explodes to greatest effect when its three components are mixed in the right proportions. The incandescence of genius flares up only when the individual, the time and the place are correctly amalgamated in the mixing bowl of history. The chemical reaction which produced Holbein's breathtaking paintings, drawings, and engravings resulted from the bringing together of a powerful talent, a time of spiritual upheaval and a Europe in which there was a growing and changing demand for works of art. To understand the phenomenon that was Holbein the Younger we have to see him in relation to the people, ideas and events involved in the breaking up of western Christendom and the reshaping of European society.

Thus, to record that Hans Holbein was born in 1497, in Augsburg, and into a family of painters cannot be a merely conventional prelude to a consideration of the artist's life and work. We have to grasp something of what it was like to be reared in a painter's atelier in a thriving, south German city in the opening years of the sixteenth century. Augsburg was a special place, with an atmosphere which gave a valuable start to a unique career.

There is nothing new about Germany being the financial centre of the world. Today the streets of Augsburg bustle with brightly coloured Porsches and BMWs designed to proclaim their owners' wealth. Half a millennium ago, they were thronged with the garishly caparisoned horses and liveried retainers of another mercantile elite. The city dominated international banking and commerce. True, 'international' meant little more than European and Levantine. Trade contacts with the fabled Orient were limited and were anyway dominated by Islamic middlemen; long-distance sea routes were yet to be properly exploited; the New World was an unexplored wilderness whose auriferous riches were no more than the subject of optimistic legend. What men called Christendom was a small world, but it was wealthy, vigorous and, though it did not know it, poised for a period of expansion that would take its captains, entrepreneurs, missionaries and armies to every land mass on the planet.

In 1497 the proud, ancient, free, imperial city of Augsburg, some fifty kilometres north-west of Munich, already had a long history. Its cathedral, which still boasts Europe's oldest framed stained glass, had stood matriarchally at the centre of urban life for 500 years, its narrow twisting streets and cheek-by-jowl housing expanding ever outwards, like additional layers of skirts, over the plain between the Wertach and Lech rivers. It had enjoyed the liberties associated with its charter for 221 years. That meant that its internal affairs were governed by its own city council and that it owed allegiance to no prince of the Church and no territorial magnate save the Holy Roman Emperor.

Independence was all very well, but it implied vulnerability. Against kings and nobles who greedily eyed Augsburg's taxable potential and who were able to put sizeable armies in the field, a city of some 25,000 inhabitants (c.1497) could offer little resistance. That was why, for over a century and a half, Augsburg had been a member of the Swabian League. This recently reconstituted association of south German cities and hereditary rulers gave Augsburg's freemen a powerful stake in the turbulent politics of central Europe. They could promote their own interests and, if necessary, defend them with the league's militia of 12,000 infantrymen and 1,200 mounted troops.

Those interests were, predominantly, trade and finance. The city's goldsmiths and silversmiths had a reputation unsurpassed north of the Alps. Here dwelt Koloman Helmschmied, Europe's finest armourer. Exponents of many other crafts flourished in this thriving commercial centre. The modern visitor to Augsburg is soon made aware of the great names associated with the city's history – Holbein, Mozart, Diesel, Brecht – but in 1497 one family above all others dominated the life of the community. Jakob Fugger was nicknamed 'Jakob the Rich' by respectful and envious neighbours. He and his two brothers commanded a fortune which ran into millions of florins. The foundation of Fugger wealth had been the textile trade, but a century of steady and latterly spectacular expansion had seen them overtake wealthy rivals such as the Welsers and extend their interests into long-distance commerce, mining, manufacture and, on an increasingly grandiose scale, moneylending. From their palatial premises on what is now called Maximilianstrasse the Fuggers presided over a family empire with offices in most of Europe's commercial centres and outposts as far afield as Venice, Cracow, Seville, Lisbon and Antwerp. They held a virtual monopoly of silver and copper production. They provided credit to several territorial magnates, including the emperor, and their disposable income exceeded that enjoyed by any of the ancient ruling houses of Christendom, except the Medicis (and they, too, represented new money).

The Fuggers' relationship with the imperial house was of paramount importance. Jakob the Rich was the exact contemporary of Maximilian I, and mutual interest brought them close together. The emperor needed money but it was not just prestige and profit that inclined the Fuggers to lend. They had a stake in Maximilian's attempt to establish effective rule and efficient administration throughout the multitude of heterogeneous kingdoms, duchies, principalities and free cities which made up what was euphemistically called the Holy Roman Empire. In the end he failed to achieve what contemporary rulers in France, Spain, England, Muscovy, Poland and the Ottoman Empire were achieving – laying the foundations of strong, centralized states. Maximilian was a man whose creative and intelligent designs never quite seemed to come off. However, his instinct to bolster his government with well-disciplined finance was sound. One result of this was his relocating of his administrative activity. The empire's centre of gravity shifted from its traditional locus, Ulm, to Augsburg, Maximilian's favourite city.

Geography, naturally, played a part in this development, as it did in the rise of the Fuggers. Augsburg stood at the convergence of the most important north–south trade routes. From the Rotes Tor, roads led to Milan and Venice, to the Renaissance states of north Italy and the Mediterranean sea lanes which supplied the silks, spices, drugs, gem stones, gold, ivory, perfumes, sweet wines and the vulgar profusion of luxuries demanded by Europe's insatiable elite. It was not only goods and merchants which passed to and fro along the pack-mule roads. Ideas and fashions moved just as freely. German entrepreneurs learned more efficient ways of conducting business from their Italian counterparts who had pioneered double-entry bookkeeping, bills of exchange, commercial insurance, exchange-rate speculation and other capitalist tools and techniques. Further down the mercantile scale, pedlars wandered from town to town, fair to fair, bearing trinkets and the latest fashion news from the cities of Venice, Rome, Florence, and from the stylish princely courts south of the Alps. Fifteenth-century Europeans were no less xenophobic than their modern counterparts – though at the same time no less curious about what clothes, books, songs and gewgaws were in vogue among the arbiters of taste in the continent's fashion centres.

The minority with the wealth, leisure and status to enjoy imported luxuries were a thin crust covering the shifting sub-strata of society. Augsburg's increasing affluence ended up as coin in the purses of an elite minority. In 1475, 2–3 per cent of the population owned 61 per cent of the city's wealth, and the imbalance between haves and have-nots grew over ensuing decades. The rising burden of taxation to finance fortifications, imperial wars and other expenditure which seemed irrelevant to most of the citizenry shackled not the rich, who could afford it, not senior ecclesiastics or Augsburg's seventeen monastic foundations, who were exempt, not the lower orders, who did not own property, but the families of middle rank, who worked hard yet seemed destined never to enjoy the fruits of their labour.

These industrious artisans aspired to but seldom achieved a degree of influence over the affairs of their community. They were organized into eighteen guilds, and the guilds were represented on the two councils which controlled the city's affairs. But this apparent power sharing only sustained the ruling oligarchy. The small council which, effectively, ruled the city was dominated by the merchant guilds and Augsburg's ancient families. The larger council, on which all guilds had a voice, met irregularly and its functions were largely ceremonial. The majority of artisan families thus found themselves dependent for patronage on the fat cats of Augsburg and their contact networks in the wider world. These customers effectively controlled the prices guild members could charge for their wares. There was little that craftsmen could do to improve their lot. Civic authorities viewed with alarm any attempts at concerted protest and the Church denounced those who, impelled by avarice, threatened to disturb the divine ordering of society.

In 1476 Ulrich Schwarz, the guildmaster of the salt-producers, led a democratic revolt. He overthrew the smaller council and tried to replace it with a body on which all trade guilds would be represented equally. The rebellion was doomed to fail and did so as soon as the forces and, more effectively, the gold of the leading families were deployed. Some of Schwarz's supporters were bought off; he himself was arrested, tried and beheaded. But his name lived on. Among Augsburg's disfranchised majority he was revered as a popular hero. A generation later Hans Holbein's father boldly associated himself with the legendary hero when he not only painted the martyr's family kneeling in supplication for their ancestor but also represented their prayers as successful. In his picture, the revolutionary's descendants, supported by the intercessions of Christ and the Virgin, were shown persuading God to sheathe the sword of justice. The artist, though dependent on the leaders of Augsburg society, was yet loyal to his own class.

It was to the category of artisan–citizens – industrious, insecure, work proud, dependent on their betters and frequently resentful of that dependence – that the Holbeins belonged. They had been resident in Augsburg for a couple of generations, living at various addresses in Diepold, the craftsmen's quarter of the city, between Maximilianstrasse and the old wall (marked now by the line of Oberer Graben). Michael Holbein, the grandfather of Hans the Younger, was a leather dresser who sired at least six children before dying, around 1484, while his two sons Hans and Sigmund were still minors. His widow struggled to bring up her family and, probably, to continue running her husband's business. She did not remarry, as women in her position usually did, and frequent moves from house to house, including a spell in the poor quarter outside the city wall, suggest reduced circumstances.

Hans and Sigmund were not, it seems, apprenticed to their father's craft, perhaps because Michael was dead before he could begin their training or because their talents very obviously lay in a different direction. We do not know when the brothers were born. Historians and biographers have suggested a variety of dates between 1460 and 1475 for Hans's birth, and most nowadays tend to favour the earlier part of that period. Sigmund's will makes it clear that he was born between 1477 and 1481. Taking the first proposed birth date for each boy places seventeen years between them, which seems unlikely. The earliest authenticated painting by Holbein the Elder was created in 1493 and the first reference to him as a householder occurs in 1494. A guild member usually acquired property and a wife in order to qualify as a master and it is improbable that an artist of Hans's talent would not have qualified until he was well into his thirties. A self-portrait sketch of 1516 seems to clinch the matter. Behind the mass of hair and beard is a face that cannot be much more than forty years old. In the absence of unequivocal data we are justified in placing Hans's birth in the first half of the 1470s and his brother's five or six years later. The most important point about the Holbein boys is that they were both gifted painters.

Just along the street from where the Holbeins lived in the 1480s was the house of the Burgkmairs. Today the Vorderer Lech is a quiet street of fashionable apartments overlooking the conduited stream and away from the bustle of the city centre. It was less salubrious five centuries ago but it was far from being down-at-heel. Thomas Burgkmair was a popular and successful painter – in fact he was the most celebrated artist in Augsburg. His son Hans, who was destined to outshine him, was born in 1473, and was thus a close contemporary of his namesake, Hans Holbein. The two must have been playmates along the banks of the stream which flowed past their front doors on its way to the Lech. They were in and out of each other's houses and it would have been odd indeed if Thomas had not spotted the talent of his neighbour's boys. When Michael Holbein died it would have been both charitable and intelligent of Burgkmair to take Hans and Sigmund into his atelier, while their mother struggled to keep the leather business going. An early, undocumented legend asserts that Hans Holbein the Elder married one of the daughters of his master and benefactor.

In the years when Hans was learning the rudiments of his profession in Augsburg, the eyes of all young German artists were upon Colmar, 250 kilometres to the west, beyond the Danube, the Swabian Alps and the Schwarzwald. It was there that 'Hübsch' Martin ('Pretty' Martin) Schongauer held court. Intellectual centres such as Basel, Heidelberg and Strasbourg were taking over from war-torn Venice in the art of printing. It was the north that produced, over the next few decades, the great masters of the fine-drawn line. Engraving would be Germany's most stunning contribution to the Renaissance. Schongauer was the pioneer. This master, who had earlier gorged his imagination on the works of Jan van Eyck, Rogier van der Weyden and other Flemish Renaissance painters, stood out as the most exciting and innovative modern artist. His representations of microscopic detail combined with complex composition and astonishing breadth of imagination drew pupils and admirers from far and near to the upper Rhine. It was Schongauer's engravings rather than his paintings which spread his fame and his ideas. The new craft of printing provided unprecedented opportunities for artists. Publishers wanted illustrations for their books and pamphlets, and this in turn generated a demand for separate prints. Schongauer developed a remarkable technique which demonstrated how the lines, textures and tonal contrasts of monumental frescos and large altarpieces created for wealthy patrons could be translated into small-scale copperplate and wood engravings affordable by men and women of modest means – and by apprentices.

Schongauer had particularly close associations with Augsburg. His family originated in the city. His father Casper had been a goldsmith there and, though his sons moved their base of operations, the commercial links were retained. Paulus and Georg followed the family trade in Colmar and Basel respectively, and Ludwig worked as a painter in his brother Martin's studio. These two Schongauer brothers were neither the first nor the last to forsake the jeweller's tools in favour of brush and pigment. It was an easy, even an obvious, transition. The painters' and goldsmiths' guilds worked closely together. Metalworkers were constantly in need of artists to design trinkets, sword hilts, reliquaries, ecclesiastical plate and precious items for the secular and religious markets. Given the strong family connections, it is not surprising that Holbein's friend, Hans Burgkmair, should travel to Colmar in the late 1480s to sit at the feet of the master during Shongauer's last years (he died in 1491).

Art historians discussing the influence of 'Hübsch' Martin on the work of the elder Holbein have speculated that he, too, may have travelled to the upper Rhine. It seems more probable that Hans and Sigmund were tied to Augsburg and its environs in these years. They were the only breadwinners in the family. Like other young artisans, they would have been eagerly seeking customers, ready to take on any commissions, no matter how small, in order to sustain themselves and their dependants. The fifteenth-century painter was not a 'pure' artist, attendant on his muse and disdainful of prostituting his genius by undertaking projects which did not permit him to express his individual talent. The concept of the creative genius as fêted prima donna had yet to spread from north Italy. When, a few years later, Albrecht Dürer visited Venice and was pressed by the government to enter the service of the state he was struck by the different status he enjoyed in the Serene Republic. Bitterly he commented, 'Here I am a gentleman, at home a parasite.' North of the Alps the opportunities to specialize in creating magnificent altarpieces, church frescos, religious or allegorical subjects for the walls of noblemen's houses, portraits of the rich and powerful or illustrations for their devotional books were difficult to come by and had to be hard earned. Even successful artists were kept firmly in their place as servants of their wealthy patrons. That we know little about Hans Holbein the Elder, and much less than we would like to know about his son, is a reflection of their perceived value in contemporary society. The deeds and words of popes, princes and prelates were deemed worthy of record; not so those of their more talented social inferiors. We lack even the names of some of the finest painters of the age. For the artist to draw attention to himself when depicting holy events or his social betters by adding his signature would have been regarded as presumptuous. As a result later ages must rest content to know some late-medieval geniuses simply by their works – the Master of Flémalle, the Master of the Augustinian Altarpiece, and so on. It was the growing popularity of cheap engravings which, as we shall see, gave artists their first real opportunity for self-advertisement.

In the 1480s and 1490s the beginner, wanting to leave his master's atelier and strike out on his own, had to accept any commission that was going – jewellery designs, signboards, painted furniture, decorated house fronts, title-pages for printed books, and whatever hackwork could be turned into rye bread, beer, sausage or salt herring. It is probably no coincidence that Hans's elder son, Ambrose, was born about 1494, which is around the time that he was beginning to receive important commissions. It suggests, as we would certainly expect, that Hans Holbein was able to contemplate marriage only when his income had reached a respectable level.

The elder Hans was an affectionate and responsible family man – that much seems obvious from the slender records. As well as his wife and the two sons she bore him, he found room under his roof for his widowed mother and his unmarried brother Sigmund. He had four married sisters, living with their families in and around Augsburg, who might have taken a share of these responsibilities, but he seems to have shouldered willingly the burden as head of the family. This seriously strained his resources and he constantly found it difficult to make ends meet. In 1508 he received 325 gulden for an altarpiece for St Moritz's church in Augsburg, but because the fee was smaller than the total of his debts it was divided up between various of his creditors. This was all too typical. Old Hans was always having arguments about money – money borrowed, money owed, money advanced against work promised. He was no stranger to the courts or to confrontations with impatient creditors. On one occasion his butcher sued him for an unpaid bill of one gulden. Life for the Holbeins was a struggle, as it was for many artisans. The painters' guild was one of those professional associations which had many members and little power. Augsburg's artists competed hard for whatever work was available. Theirs was a buyers' market. They were mere artisans to be hired and fired at will. Yet, when every allowance has been made for the harsh economic imposts of the time it is hard to avoid the conclusion that Hans Holbein the Elder was a poor manager of money.

By the time he was in his thirties he was certainly a man whose work was in demand. In 1502, when the Abbot of Kaisheim, near Donauwörth, ordered decorative improvements to the church, the monastery records noted that the three best available craftsmen had been employed. These were Kastner the joiner, Erhart the sculptor and Holbein the painter. Hans's growing reputation enabled him to demand higher prices for his work, but that does not seem to have done much to improve his predicament. Restlessness and insecurity were his constant companions. In this he was no different from other craftsmen, most of whom worked hard for modest returns and had to travel a great deal. They might have to travel to seek out work when there was little to be found close to home, or to present themselves to distant patrons to whom they had been recommended, or to make an artistic pilgrimage – a *Wanderjahr* – which meant jobbing around far regions in order to see the work of other artists, talk with them and visit their studios. Holbein had insufficient leisure or financial independence to indulge this last kind of culture-tour. Unlike Burgkmair, whose period in Colmar was followed by an extended stay in Strasbourg and who later spent time in Venice and Lombardy, Holbein's known absences from Augsburg – in cities such as Ulm and Frankfurt – were connected with major painting jobs.

Holbein's second son, christened Hans, was born in 1497. The records reveal no other children, and it seems likely that Ambrose and Hans did have other brothers and sisters but that none of them survived infancy. The reconstructed sixteenth-century house on Vorderer Lech signposted for the modern visitor as Hans the Younger's birthplace was only one of several in which he grew up as lack of money made successive moves desirable. From his earliest years there was imprinted on the boy's mind a determination above all things to avoid poverty. Ambrose and Hans gave early evidence of talent, yet it was the younger son who stood out as a truly precocious genius. Like Leopold Mozart, two and a half centuries later, the elder Hans recognized something truly remarkable in his boy's gifts. He could not parade the child prodigy around the courts of Europe, but he certainly did all that he could to draw attention to him.

He made a clear statement of this in one of his finest paintings. Veronica Welser, a member of the banking family, was also secretary to the Convent of St Catherine in Augsburg, a stone's throw from the Holbeins' front door. In 1504, to decorate the chapter house, she commissioned the artist to execute a large, three-part panel depicting incidents from the life of St Paul (see plate section). Holbein had provided other works for the convent, but this was his best work for the patron and one of his finest religious paintings. Scenes from the saint's life, from conversion to martyrdom, crowd the painted space, but two remarkable features form a link between the biblical events and the viewer. The focal point of the painting is occupied, daringly, by the back view of a seated woman. This intimate portrayal, reminiscent of Netherlandish interior pictures of the period, creates an aura of peace in the midst of the stirring events taking place around it. The figure is identified as St Thecla, who according to legend was a follower of St Paul. She is depicted absorbed in the apostle's preaching. The message would have been obvious to the nuns of St Catherine: they, too, should hang upon Paul's doctrine and be content to lose their identities in meditation on holy things.

Yet it is the left-hand panel that interests us more in the present context. In a corner of the scene presenting the saint's baptism Holbein has introduced himself and his two sons. That in itself was a bold though not unique stratagem, and it was one which must have had his patroness's approval, but the arrangement of the group tells us still more about the Holbein family. All attention is focused on young Hans. The father gazes out of the picture as if to catch our attention. One hand rests on the boy's head. The other actually points at him. Ambrose holds his brother's hand and simultaneously clasps his shoulder. Even Hans's own right hand seems to point to his face, and with his other (he was left-handed) he holds what looks very much like a paintbrush. We might interpret these gestures as signs of affection, but that would be to attribute to the late-medieval world the emotions and social attitudes of a subsequent age. The painter is not betraying the kind of sentimentalism we might find in a Victorian family group. The sixteenth century had a much harsher attitude towards children. Infancy was a necessary biological prelude to the serious business of adult responsibilities and relationships. Old Hans had a very clear purpose – an economic purpose – in portraying himself and his two boys in these specific poses. He was bringing his son to the attention of a wealthy patron. And not his *elder* son. By their gestures Ambrose and his father are acknowledging that young Hans has a talent greater than theirs. They are commending the seven-year-old as one whose gifts are already remarkable. In this painting Holbein the Elder is putting down a marker for the future.

The Holbein workshop was a busy one. When old Hans painted the St Paul panel he was at the height of his fame and had to employ many helpers. Several of his apprentices spent much of their time in making designs for stained-glass windows, which became something of a speciality of his atelier. Holbein's major commissions and virtually the only ones designed for semi-permanence, came from ecclesiastical patrons. Most of the studio's output has not survived because it was not intended to do so. Late-medieval artists were not painting for posterity. The distinctions we make between creative artist, commercial artist and decorative artist would have been meaningless to old Holbein and his colleagues. They performed all these roles indiscriminately, making designs for Augsburg's goldsmiths, painting furniture, polychroming religious statues and producing the decorative murals and distempered panels on cloth with which wealthy citizens adorned their walls.

The angel of prosperity which hovered over the Holbein atelier around the dawn of the new century fluttered away to bestow his favours elsewhere towards the end of the first decade. For a few radiant, hectic years the artist was in his prime, was widely acclaimed as the leading exponent of the Augsburg school and was much in demand throughout Swabia and beyond. Then patrons began to drift away. Other painters were in vogue. Men and women with commissions to bestow sought out artists who could express fresh ideas in new ways. Money troubles began to multiply from about 1507. Holbein's establishment dwindled in size and within nine years he had left his native city for good. This traumatic move had nothing to do with declining health or failing talent and everything to do with intellectual and spiritual upheaval.

In 1501 the young humanist Thomas More wrote to a friend, 'You ask how I am doing in my studies. Wonderfully, of course; things could not be better. I have shelved my Latin books, to take up the study of Greek.'[1] More was only one of hundreds of young scholars throughout Europe who were responding excitedly to what they called the New Learning. The intellectual elite were exulting in the rediscovery of classical texts. Medieval scholastic theology was being questioned, ridiculed and abandoned by a wave of students intoxicated by purer texts of the 'plain word' of Scripture. Emancipated thinkers believed that rediscovery of Christianity's foundation documents coupled with a simple, direct, affective faith would bring about a revitalization of the Church, cleansing it of corruption and mismanagement; expurgating from it accretions of doctrine and

custom that had grown up over more than a millennium of
ignorance. By the second decade of the century – when Erasmus was
emerging as the doyen of European scholarship – such views were
widely held by Church leaders and educated laymen throughout
western Christendom. Cardinals were patronizing radical writers and
translators. Licensed preachers were expounding the Bible in a fresh
way. Enlightened priests were training their parishioners in the
technique of mystical devotion. When it came to ordering a new
altarpiece or a set of panels for a private chapel more and more patrons
looked for artists who could express new truths, or old truths in new
ways. In art, in religion, in politics, in the ordering of society,
everything was being questioned and re-evaluated.

The world of international humanism was a close-knit, excited,
trend-setting sub-culture, a fellowship of brave-new-worlders who
had rediscovered among the rubble of Europe's classical heritage the
architectural principles upon which a better future could be built.
Here and there groups of scholars and would-be intellectuals gathered
around great teachers, writers and preachers such as Sebastian Brant,
Jakob Wimpfeling, Geiler von Kaysersberg, Jacques Lefèvre, John
Colet, Marsilio Ficino and scores of other advocates of innovative
thinking. They were self-conscious literati who wrote to each other
frequently, filling their letters with allusions to ancient authors and
signing themselves with latinized names. Increasingly, as time went
by, they commended themselves to each other and to their patrons by
sending painted or printed portraits. It was important for evangelists
with a civilizing mission that they should be recognized. The
acknowledged leader of this brotherhood was Desiderius Erasmus,
the Rotterdam-born scholar who, having escaped the cloister, lived a
restless life, teaching, writing, exposing the shortcomings of traditional scholarship and Church leadership, amusing his disciples with
his brilliant satire while at the same time exhorting them to greater
piety and love of learning.

Nor were revolutionary ideas confined to that tiny minority of
young men being turned out by the European universities. *Nouveaux
riches* merchants, farmers and artisans were on the whole slower to
forsake traditional ways of thinking, but they tended to take their cue
from their social superiors, who were themselves coming under new
religious influences. Indeed, it would be wrong to think of those
wellsprings which we identify in 'Renaissance' and 'Reformation' as

issuing from the upper social strata and seeping downwards. Springs were bubbling up from below and had been doing so for years with increasing vigour. The year of Holbein's birth was also the year in which the fiery reformer Girolamo Savonarola held his bonfire of the vanities in Florence's Piazza della Signoria. Bands of children and young people, stirred by the friar's preaching, paraded the city streets, knocking on doors and demanding the surrender of carnival costumes, games, lewd books and all other kinds of *anathemae.* They built a pyre twenty metres high and eighty metres in circumference. Then, when the citizenry had gathered to hear a sermon and to sing songs of devotional penitence, the symbolic fire was lit and Florence was cleansed of its godlessness. This conflagration was the best-recorded and probably the most spectacular demonstration of communal piety, but it was not the only one. In towns and villages throughout Europe wandering preachers summoned the inhabitants to declare their rejection of the world, the flesh and the devil by fasts, vigils, ritual flagellation and dramatic destruction of 'vanities'.

Many parts of the continent were experiencing religious revival. Alpine villages sheltered groups of renegade Franciscans, Waldensians, *fraticelli* and other zealots, whom Church leaders dubbed heretics. Religious radicals were at work in southern France, England, the Low Countries, Bohemia and northern Germany. In an age of sporadic and intense revival, European Church life was both vibrant and hetero-geneous. No less than the modern Americas or Asia or Africa, turn-of-the-sixteenth-century western Christendom possessed an abundance of prophets, evangelists, gurus, holy men and women and leaders of charismatic sects. Some of the Church's leaders they revered as saints; others they burned as heretics or tolerated uneasily. Still others they did not know what to do with. The proclaimers of new truth and radical insights varied from sophisticated intellectuals such as Sebastian Brant, whose *Ship of Fools* attacked contemporary evils with pious cynicism, to uneducated innocents like Hans Beheim, the Drummer of Nicklashausen, who prophesied an egalitarian apocalypse 'when pope, emperor, princes, barons, knights, squires, citizens, farmers and the common man will be the same . . . and all will work'.[2]

Augsburg had its share of restless, uncomfortable men and women. There were known groups of Waldensians and Hussites in the city who, despite occasional protests from Rome, were tolerated as long as they behaved themselves. It was otherwise with the 'cellar people', religious enthusiasts and social malcontents who met in secret to listen to unorthodox and – so city officials believed – inflammatory sermons. But it was not just working-class rabble-rousers who caused concern. Popular Franciscan friars often joined their voices to the chorus of protest against social inequality and the ostentation of the rich. Then there were the humanist scholars, serious-minded academics who criticized the doctrinal framework on which the existing order was based and argued, from pulpit and printed page, for sweeping reform in Church and state.

What made the ferment of ideas particularly disturbing and potentially dangerous was the speed of their dissemination. Between the development of movable type in the middle of the fifteenth century and the year of Holbein's birth, some six million volumes rolled from printing presses set up in most of Europe's leading towns and cities. Where books were made, scholars and men burning to share their convictions tended to congregate. And Augsburg was one of the principal centres of book production.

Whether they couched their novel ideas in elegant classical hexameters or boisterous vernacular prose, academics and socio-religious radicals appeared to be saying – and in many cases were saying – the same things. Both groups were indignant with a Church hierarchy widely perceived as corrupt and with local clergy who were spiritually and intellectually ill-equipped to meet the needs of their people. Both questioned the relevance and efficacy of masses, pilgrimages, relics, indulgences and the complex penitential para-phernalia by which earnest souls were urged to seek – but could never be assured of finding – eternal salvation. Both believed in the rediscovery and propagation of a pure, biblical faith (scholars were studying Hebrew and Greek to achieve a more accurate text). Erasmus wanted the labourer to read Scripture as he trudged behind the plough. Ordinary people who attended sermons at the market cross or gathered around 'gospellers' in clandestine candlelight discovered a holy text which did not exist to support elaborate official doctrines or the power of the priestly caste. The prevailing wish among many who cared deeply about religious things was for honesty, simplicity, immediacy. Those are always powerful advocates of change.

There had to be a corresponding change in the images that religious enthusiasts could identify with. Gothic painting, like the mysterious, cavernous interiors of great churches, gleaming with gilded polychrome and radiant glass offering glimpses of heavenly glory, would no longer serve. The religious focus had shifted. It was no longer a matter of bringing paradise down to earth but of exalting earth to paradise. The fiery Savonarola inveighed against the serene madonnas and saints of traditional conventions: 'You fill the churches with vain things. Do you think that the Virgin should be painted as you paint her? I tell you that she went clothed as a beggar.'[3] Ardent Christians – those, that is, who saw any virtue at all in the carved or painted image – wanted down-to-earth realism and drama in their religious art.

'Realism', a term applied frequently to the 'Italian Renaissance' and the 'Northern Renaissance', is one that needs unpacking. No great painter of the period regarded his task as simply the faithful replication of natural objects in two-dimensional terms. Capturing varied textures, depicting the interplay of light and shadow and bringing out spatial relationships were challenges to an artist's virtuosity, and new techniques for achieving these ends were being explored with heightened enthusiasm. Yet there was always more to the act of creativity than the representation of things as they are and for their own sake. Objects in a picture have significance. The fifteenth-century Netherlands painters exulted in recreating the paraphernalia of everyday life (and it is no coincidence that the Low Countries had long been a fertile seedbed of affective religion). When Robert Campin executed a *Virgin and Child in an Interior* he surrounded the holy figures with familiar objects – a laundry basket, fire irons, a length of cloth hanging over a rail, a candle in a sconce, a bowl of water set warming before a fire. The wealthy burgher who commissioned such a devotional piece would have been utterly at home in the kind of room in which the infant Saviour and his mother were depicted. He would have marvelled at the loving precision with which Campin had reproduced all its components. But he would have understood that they were objects enjoying an *enhanced* realism. By giving ordinary things an increased vividness, by presenting each to the beholder as something mundane yet at the same time precious, the artist was investing them with spiritual significance. The heavenly had come into the worldly. Human habitats as well as human life were suffused with the divine.

The realism displayed by contemporary Italian painters was of a different order. Their increasing concern was to discover and make plain the inherent significance of material objects. Thus a portrait existed not just to show what the sitter looked like, nor to display him in a pious pose, but 'to find the mind's construction in the face'.[4] The rediscovery of classical architecture and sculpture led to investigation of the mathematical principles of harmony. Painters studied human and animal anatomy to understand the divine ordering of things and to portray it with greater clarity. And when Raphael painted a religious group, such as the *Alba Madonna*, closely observed plants and flowers appeared in the foreground and a mountainous, misty landscape in the background to anchor the Virgin and the infants Jesus and John the Baptist in this world. The sense of serene holiness came from the arrangement of the figures and the pastoral peace of their setting. There was no need to invest the ordinary with the numinous. The created order *was* holy. The significance of the Incarnation lay not in the temporary indwelling of the human by the divine but in the fact that Mary and Jesus were real people. By observing and representing in pigment the perfection of nature the artist was actually sharing in the work of creation.

One way of emphasizing the interaction of heaven and earth was by introducing portraits into religious pictures. It had long been standard practice to depict devout patrons (or patrons who wished to be thought devout) in kneeling adoration on the wings of altarpieces. Thus presented, they were essentially observers of the holy dramas being enacted on the centre panels. Now, real people were increasingly incorporated in the action. When an anonymous Netherlands artist painted the *Feeding of the Five Thousand* around 1500 he included portraits of many royal and noble personages among the multitude. About the same time, Carpaccio depicted his patron, Cardinal Bessarion, as St Jerome and set the scholar–saint in a very Renaissance interior. We have already seen how Holbein the Elder put himself and his sons in a narrative religious painting. Perhaps the most astonishing fusion of the worldly and other-worldly is the self-portrait Albrecht Dürer made in 1500. In a painting which remained among his most treasured possessions until the end of his days, the artist adopts the pose of the *Vera Ikon*, the image of Christ. He appears full-face against a black ground. The composition is perfectly symmetrical, the expression searching and compassionate. The painting makes a statement that is intensely personal and religious. It transfers to another medium the teaching of Thomas à Kempis about the imitation of Christ. The mystic urged the believer to identify, through devotional discipline, with the Saviour. This is the ideal which Dürer represents. It may be that he goes a stage further, claiming for the artist as creator recognition of a special relationship with the supreme Creator who laid down the universe according to those laws of harmony and mathematical principles which painters, sculptors and musicians in their several ways sought to discover and apply.

South German artists were subject to all these influences at the turn of the sixteenth century and to the general confusion of cultural and spiritual impulses. Painters responded by abandoning old conventions, intensifying the dramatic content of their works and emphasizing their relevance to the contemporary world. There were more portraits painted. Traditionally, Church teaching about the sin of pride had inhibited this particular art form. Painters who put their patrons into altarpieces or made portrait sketches for larger works were not in the business of creating individual character studies. It may be significant that Hugo van der Goes (died c.1482), whose portraits did achieve a greater sense of personal identity than those of his contemporaries, spent his last years in a monastery on the verge of insanity, grappling with profound feelings of mankind's sinfulness.

The artist's observation of the world was also changing. Dürer, the greatest of the elder Holbein's German contemporaries, can claim among his many trophies the title Father of European Watercolour Drawing. During his travels away from his native Nuremberg, he made hundreds of sketches and finished studies of landscapes, townscapes, animals and plants. The majority of them were not done as preparations for major works and certainly were not for sale. They were exercises in training his eye and hand, as well as personal mementoes of places to which he had been, things he had seen. Above all they were sheer, exultant expressions of Dürer's delight in God's creation.

Dürer was a prodigy and he also had strong ideas about the honour which should be accorded to artists. On both counts he was fêted wherever he went by his fellow painters, though doubtless the green pennants of jealousy were evident amid the professional bunting which welcomed him when he entered an artistic community such as that at Augsburg. The other acknowledged new master who made an impression on his fellows in southern Germany was Mathis Nithart

Gotthart, now known as Grünewald. The Nuremberg genius possessed the technical brilliance and breadth of vision to amalgamate influences from both sides of the Alps, but it was Grünewald who, supremely, captured the age's intensity of religious passion. What little is known about this artist's life confirms that he was a man of deep personal conviction. He enjoyed the patronage of humanist ecclesiastics but in his later years moved in the direction of Luther and became so involved in the social and religious upheaval of the 1520s that he fell from favour, abandoned his palette and is last to be glimpsed making a back-breaking living in the saltworks at Halle. Thus the painter who, more than any other before or since, depicted with searing realism the horror of Christ's physical suffering himself made great sacrifices for his faith.

The large gaps in our knowledge of Grünewald's life coupled with some technical similarities that have been detected between his work and that of Burgkmair and the elder Holbein have led some scholars to suggest that he spent a few years in Augsburg, perhaps even in the Holbein atelier. Certainly, any comparison reveals that Grünewald achieved effects which his Augsburg contemporaries could only strive for. Within a few months of one another (1501–2) Holbein the Elder and Grünewald completed studies of Christ's Passion: for the collegiate church in Aschaffenburg Grünewald portrayed the mocking of Christ; some fifty kilometres down the Main at Frankfurt Holbein depicted the arrest of Jesus on an altarpiece for the Dominican church. In both paintings the tormentors are grotesque, but that is where the similarity ends. Holbein's Christ, betrayed, deserted, roped and spat upon, yet retains his dignity. Standing and elaborately haloed, he occupies the centre of the composition. Grünewald's Saviour is forced into the bottom left corner. There he sits, bedraggled and blindfolded, subjected to a savage beating by thugs who are stirred to even greater frenzy by a colleague with pipe and drum. Grünewald's panel surges with movement. Muscles strain. Bodies balance themselves to strike the next blow. If we blink we might miss seeing that upraised fist crash down on Christ's head. Holbein's figures are inhibited by Gothic didacticism. He faithfully portrays every element of the story – Judas's greeting, the fleeing disciples, Jesus healing the servant's severed ear, the torchlight cleaving the darkness. The artist wants us to understand this Gospel incident. Grünewald, by contrast, invites us to enter into an experience, to feel and share the sufferings of his Lord. He goes beyond the strict Bible text to engage our participation. The man in charge, responding to a whispered comment from the bearded figure behind, seems to be about to restrain the tormentors, even as the musician urges them on. We are meant to take sides. We cannot be neutral.

Dürer and Grünewald, in their very different ways, expressed the changing religious sensibilities of the age. Other artists wanting to please patrons with humanist or mystical leanings strove to capture something of their directness, their immediacy, the power of their images. The elder Holbein failed and, in failing, saw the decline of his business. It was not that he was insensitive to changing requirements or that he was unwilling to learn. During the second decade of the century he experimented with new concepts and techniques. Southern influences were increasingly evident in his output. The St Sebastian Altarpiece, painted for his old patrons at the Convent of St Catherine (1516), reveals an artist for whom harmony was becoming a dominant concern. Holbein shuns the attempt to convey the full horror of the saint's martyrdom. He concentrates on the movements of the circle of archers loading, aiming and firing their crossbows. The old stiffness has gone. So has grotesqueness; the faces of the persecutors are those of real people, based on portrait drawings. Foreground plants and background buildings are painted in careful detail. The scenes depicted on the various panels are enclosed not by Gothic arches, but by Tuscan columns. Yet the work manages to fall between the stools of Italian bravura and German angst.

Even while Holbein was working on this project troubles were piling up. He had to break off his work on at least three occasions to face his creditors in court. Before the end of 1516 the bailiffs were in. The artist was totally ruined. His house and his few pieces of furniture were sold. His workshop was dismantled and his last remaining apprentices released to seek other masters. All Hans salvaged from the wreck was his painting materials, and he then had to borrow thirty-four florins from his brother to convey them to Issenheim in Alsace. Humbled by misfortune, his family also left their home town, their friends and the artistic community of Augsburg. His brother Sigmund settled in Berne. Prosy (Ambrose) and young Hans went to Basel. Some indication of the bitterness engendered by their losses is recorded in court documents. In January 1517 Sigmund sued his brother for the thirty-four florins, which had not been repaid.

Old Hans could not help his sons any further, and his remaining days were spent staving off destitution. There is great poignancy in his Issenheim sojourn. The cultured Austin canons of the Anthonite monastery were engaged in the refurbishment of their church. Eagerness for new artistic and religious insights impelled them to scrap existing paintings and sculptures and replace them with works by a new generation of artists. Schongauer's high-altarpiece was among the casualties. His lovingly observed figures were replaced by an image unrivalled for brutal ultra-realism. Grünewald's uncompromising *Crucifixion,* its figures harshly distorted by pain and grief, was the most powerful representation of the Passion created in the pre-Reformation years. Many consider it the most arresting ever painted. Grünewald completed it in 1515 before moving to Brandenburg and a new patron. Holbein arrived a few months later to undertake other work for the Anthonites and thus had to live in the shadow of this masterpiece, which expressed religious feelings he could never experience. He was still engaged at Issenheim in October 1517 when, at the other end of Germany, Martin Luther posted his ninety-five theses. The tremors which had played their part in loosening the foundations of Holbein's professional life were becoming more regular and more violent. It was his son's fate to live through the years when the cultural earthquake was at its most devastating.

This was the atmosphere of insecurity and busy creativity in which the Holbein boys grew up. Their childhood was of short duration. They were pressed into service in the workshop as soon as they could make themselves useful – clearing up, running errands, mixing pigments, applying layers of gesso to wooden panels in order to build up painting surfaces. From early days Ambrose and Hans absorbed rather than learned their craft. They watched their father's assistants at their desks making intricate designs for the goldsmiths. They delivered drawings to the blockmakers and noted the painstaking transference of drawn line to wood or copper plate. In the clattering printshops they could watch the cumbersome presses which multiplied the pictures that had begun on the drawing board. Like all children, they eavesdropped when their father and their uncles chatted among themselves, conferred with clients, or discussed technicalities with visiting artists such as the exuberant Dürer and the introverted Grünewald. Although they must have been cuffed when they got in the way and soundly thrashed when some accident or prank made extra work for one of their elders, they were nevertheless encouraged to try their own hand with brush, pen or silverpoint pencil, and the day arrived when they were actually permitted to contribute to the output of the atelier. Some of the large paintings executed by Hans the Elder included brushstrokes laid on by his sons.

Then there was the other side of a craftsman's life – business. Commissions had to be sought. That meant writing letters to potential patrons couched in terms of grovelling flattery. There were accounts to be sent and follow-up demands when those accounts were not settled. There were painting materials to be ordered, books to be kept, taxes to be paid, apprentices' wages to be negotiated, guild dues to be met. If the head of a studio did not take care of the money side of things efficiently – and Holbein probably did not – then he and his dependants lived under constant financial pressure. It was incumbent on Ambrose and Hans to contribute as soon as possible to the atelier's income. It was, therefore, a matter of relief as well as of parental pride when the boys, and especially Hans, showed obvious talent.

Was it, perhaps, in portraiture that the extraordinary ability of old Hans's younger son first manifested itself? Drawing and painting faces was a standard part of the artist's repertoire. Models, often taken from the city's poorer residents who were grateful for a few easily earned pfennigs, were used to provide the features of saints and the anonymous members of crowds. Such representations did not need to be accurate and, indeed, were often 'improved' on by being rendered beatific or grotesque. Greater discipline was required when patrons were to be displayed in a votive altarpiece. Yet portraiture was still to emerge as an art form in its own right. If young Hans displayed a particular gift for it, no one could then have prophesied that posterity would remember him primarily as a limner.

It was while he was maturing as an artist that those philosophical changes occurred which prepared the way for the output of Holbein's later years. In the first half of the sixteenth century the recording of the features of living people developed rapidly throughout Europe as an art form in its own right. The urge freely to explore human personality was becoming stronger. The growing class of wealthy merchants and artisans, eager to copy the sophisticated manners of their betters, provided a growing market for the straight portrait, though the frequent incorporation of a *memento mori* in the paintings indicated a lingering awareness of the dangers of hubris. When Dürer visited Augsburg in 1505 one of his tasks was to paint likenesses of Georg and Ulrich Fugger. More and more German artists studied the faces of men and women, not to use them as vehicles for conveying religious impressions but to make honest statements about real people.

'All men, whatever be their condition, who have done anything of merit, or which verily has a semblance of merit, if so be they are men of truth and good repute, should write the tale of their life with their own hand.'[5] So wrote Benvenuto Cellini in 1558. Half a century before, such a sentiment would have been widely regarded as monstrous vanity bordering on blasphemy. In 1486 the first printed version of Thomas à Kempis's *De Imitatio Christi* rolled off an Augsburg press and became an immediate best-seller. By the end of the century it had gone through dozens of editions and had appeared in all the main European vernaculars. The *Imitatio* concentrated in an easily assimilable form the affective, interiorized spirituality of the mystic tradition. The heart of the matter was:

> Let this be thy whole endeavour, this thy prayer, this thy desire: that thou mayest be stripped of all selfishness, and with entire simplicity follow Jesus only; mayest die to thyself, and live eternally to me. Then shalt thou be rid of all vain fancies, causeless perturbations and superfluous cares.[6]

Since this life was transitory, a mere preparation for the greater life beyond the grave – as the garish 'dooms' painted or carved in every church reminded worshippers – what mattered human accomplishments or transitory beauty? Self-renunciation and contempt for the world were the signposts on the path to heavenly bliss. Such inhibitions go only part of the way towards explaining the reluctance artists felt about embarking on character portraits. This kind of painting was undervalued, even despised. On his travels Dürer made drawings of prominent people that he met, in order to impress them with his skill, but he recorded on at least one occasion that the recipients frequently did not bother to pay him. The ability to capture another's features on paper, it seems, was regarded with passing admiration, as though it were a mere party trick. Several artists adopted a similarly dismissive attitude. Michelangelo would not demean himself by making portraits. Some of his contemporaries resented having to earn their bread and butter by painting the likenesses of vain patrons. Giorgio Vasari, whose *Lives of the Most Excellent Italian Architects, Painters and Sculptors* first appeared in 1550, was dismissive of portraiture, which in his opinion owed nothing to 'artistic power and design'. Karel van Mander, who performed the same biographical function for the northern artists, deplored the economic necessity that had diverted several talented men into the bypath of portrait painting – 'Thus many a fine and noble mind has remained without fruit and quenched, to the great detriment of art.'[7]

Hans Holbein the Elder was an excellent portraitist. Over 200 of his silverpoint drawings have survived. They reveal a delight in the display of character as also of details of dress. In his finished portraits he showed that he could capture features and expressions by subtle colour shading as well as by delineation. He recorded with great affection the features of family members and friends. Yet he did not take this aspect of his work very seriously (see plate section). As far as we know, he produced very few finished portraits and he was not commissioned to 'counterfeit' any of the great men and women of his age. Painting lesser mortals was simply not economical.

No doubt Holbein's boys soon discovered their skill in drawing faces. Perhaps they sat in a corner of the workshop with charcoal or chalks, doing lightning sketches and caricatures of the apprentices and of the self-important patrons who came in to discuss commissions. There is a likeness of a young Augsburg woman which may be by Holbein the Younger. If the attribution is correct it is the artist's first known work. As the brothers grew up there were fewer opportunities for moments of self-indulgent amusement. They worked hard to master a wide range of techniques – designs for goldsmiths, drawings for the engravers, frescos for wealthy burghers, illustrations for the book printers and, at last, backgrounds and figures in the great church pieces.

Someone who had an even greater influence on the younger Holbein than his father was Hans Burgkmair, in all probability, Holbein's uncle. He returned home in 1507 or 1508 from an extended visit to Italy. His nephew Hans was then entering his most impressionable phase, ready to appreciate the new influences apparent in Burgkmair's work and to listen eagerly to his stories of the new ideas and techniques current in Venice.

Voluptuous, vice-ridden, self-confident, wealthy Venice, gorged on its trade with the East and execrated for making commercial pacts with the Muslim Turks who had overrun eastern Christendom and constantly threatened Europe, attracted fortune-hunters and free-thinkers of all kinds to its bustling Rialto and its sumptuous *palazzi*. Yet it was as an artistic and intellectual centre that the Queen of the Adriatic attracted Dürer, Burgkmair and a procession of northern painters. Scores of private schools and colleges offered residents and visitors a grounding in humanistic studies, especially classical art and literature. Venice could boast more printing houses than several other Italian cities put together. It was here that Aldus Manutius, the scholar-turned-printer, had perfected a revolutionary development on a par with the invention of the paperback. He devoted himself with missionary zeal to making the works of Greek and Latin masters available to students and others of modest means in small, cheaply bound pocket editions. Aldus set himself to publish all the significant works of the Greek philosophers, dramatists and poets, and he attracted several of the leading contemporary scholars to assist in this work. It was for this purpose that the great Desiderius Erasmus spent most of 1508 in Venice. Intoxicated as the humanist idol was with disseminating to an ever widening readership the works of the world's most elegant and original writers (and his own ideas about them), Erasmus laboured at the printworks throughout the daylight hours and long into the lamplit nights, writing, correcting and proof-reading before retiring to his lodgings in the home of Aldus's father-in-law. It may well be that Burgkmair met Erasmus in Venice, thus providing the first link between the scholar and Hans Holbein.

Burgkmair certainly met Giovanni Bellini, the king of the Venice ateliers, now in his seventies but still very active and always hospitable to visiting artists. Though he and his brother Gentile had dominated the cultural life of the city for decades, there was no sense in which their school had become stuck in a rut. It was their encouragement of talented painters experimenting with new ideas and techniques which made Venice such an exciting place for fellow craftsmen from distant lands. Here the inventive Giorgione and the monumental Carpaccio were daring to innovate. Experts with an eye for young talent had already marked out Titian as a prodigy. What most enthralled and sometimes shocked northern artists like Burgkmair was the way Venetian art was struggling to free itself from moral and religious didacticism. The delight in brilliant colours, seductive silken draperies, lavish costumes, imposing architecture, sylvan landscapes and well-fleshed nudes found expression in classical and allegorical subjects but was increasingly invading the biblical scenes painted for Venetian nobles and ecclesiastics. The process was by no means complete, but even in religious works there was an emphasis on humanity and its this-worldly setting. One commentator has said of the murals in the ducal palace, 'one has the curious impression that the Doge and the Deity met on equal terms'.[8] The religious intensity many northern artists felt and sought to express was inimical to their Venetian contemporaries. They preferred (or perhaps it was their patrons who preferred) to treat those aspects of the Christian faith that had to do with gentleness (the Nativity, the Virgin and Child) or triumph (the Transfiguration, the Assumption of the Virgin). In technical terms the main difference between north and south lay in loving attention to detail as against exuberant breadth of conception. It would be an exaggeration to speak of Flemish and German 'drama' and Italian 'theatricality'; but certainly the painful, tortured, sometimes grotesque images of late Gothicism spoke to a different kind of piety and a different kind of worldview than did the sumptuous, rhythmically flowing compositions of the Venetian Renaissance. Between Grünewald's Issenheim *Crucifixion* and Titian's *Assumption* in Santa Maria dei Frari, completed within four years of each other, there was a great gulf fixed. It was a gulf about to widen and separate rival Christianities.

This did not mean that there could not be borrowing and cross-reference. Burgkmair was intoxicated by the Venetians' use of colour and their creation of gorgeous effects. In the altarpieces he painted during the decade after his return, dramatic lighting and treatment of landscape indicate the lessons he had learned in Italy. He also brought back new ideas about portraiture. The citizens of Venice were less inhibited about having themselves painted. This gave artists the opportunity to experiment with technique and also to probe character. Giovanni Bellini's depiction of Doge Leonardo Loredan is in the idiom of the official icon – it is reminiscent of a sculpted bust – but the colours, texture and pattern of the brocade cape and cap are opulent and precise and the face expresses both severe resolve and warm humanity. Within a few years Titian was achieving a more relaxed, and therefore more revelatory, style of portraiture. Giorgione's moving and expressive painting of an old woman (c.1509) shows that the moralizing portrait was still not dead south of the Alps.

Burgkmair had always loved portraiture and taken it seriously. A devout man himself, he was particularly attracted to religious personalities as subjects for fully developed paintings, and especially to advocates of reform. Early in his career, when he was working in Strasbourg, he painted the lined, intense features of the city's preacher Johannes Geiler von Kaysersberg. Geiler, whose stirring addresses were much in demand throughout Germany, came to Augsburg in 1515. Burgkmair was a friend of the radical Bishop Friedrich van Zollern of Augsburg, whom he painted in 1490. Zollern engaged in a long (and ultimately unsuccessful) battle with the cathedral chapter to establish a funded preachership for the purpose of spiritual renewal. Jakob Fugger, whom Burgkmair also painted, took up this particular cause and, with papal backing, forced the clergy to accept a preaching post in 1517. In the same year, Burgkmair was much impressed by the ascetic visionary Anna Laminit. Hundreds of Augsburgers and even members of the imperial court were drawn to this prophesying ecstatic who, so she claimed, consumed no food but the consecrated host. Burgkmair convincingly captured the drawn, ethereal features with their hint of fanaticism. Doubtless he was as disillusioned and angry as most of her devotees when Anna was exposed as a fraud. Soon after his return to Augsburg he painted the imperial councillor and humanist author, Sebastian Brant, whom he had known since Strasbourg days. Brant's satirical *Ship of Fools* (1494), which was still a best-seller, was seminal. He was the radical humanist who, more than any other, paved the way for Erasmus, and deeply influenced the self-perception of a whole generation.

Burgkmair's fortunes improved dramatically when he attracted the patronage of Maximilian I. He was for several years the emperor's principal wood engraver. This brought him into contact with many of the leading writers and artists who thronged Maximilian's cultured court. He made a death-portrait engraving of Germany's greatest humanist scholar, Conrad Celtis, the finest native poet before Goethe. He pioneered the engraved portrait in Germany, producing duplicated likenesses, among others, of Maximilian, Jakob Fugger, Hans Paumgartner (another wealthy merchant) and Pope Julius II (whom he drew when accompanying the emperor to the Council of Pisa in 1511). In these and other portraits Hans Holbein's uncle was part of a movement which not only merged Italian and northern traditions, but also created a new climate of acceptability for this secular art form.

Burgkmair, friend of scholars, habitué of the imperial court, supporter of radical religious thinkers, was in tune with the new age. He was one of a group of German craftsmen eager for change in art, in Church life, in society. In his attitudes on all these matters he shared much with Dürer, the elder Cranach, Grünewald, Hans Baldung (often known as Grien) and other artists who, a few years hence, would willingly lend their support to the Lutheran revolution. Burgkmair's brother-in-law was not of this intellectual, well-connected circle. It was inevitable that the adolescent Ambrose and Hans Holbein, seeking their own identities, rebelling against old ways, growing more aware of the challenging ideas radiating like seismic shocks from many of Europe's intellectual centres, should have been stimulated by their uncle and his circle of friends.

If Hans sought a younger role model he may well have found it in Hans Baldung Grien, a prodigy only four or five years his senior who, by 1512, was taking the German art world by storm. He came from an intellectual background in Strasbourg. His closest friends were humanist scholars, and his brother was a professor at Freiburg. He spent some years as Dürer's pupil before returning to his home town, getting married and setting up his own workshop. His first explosion of youthful creativity demonstrated both the religious intensity of his native land and the ideas of beauty and harmony emanating from Italy. He was equally at home treating religious and secular subjects. He could paint great altarpieces while, at the same time, producing character portraits. From his studio came moralizing studies of death and the vanity of human wishes and also classical allegories featuring voluptuous nudes for the new humanist market. Possessing the absorptive capacity old Holbein lacked, Baldung prospered. By 1510 he was wealthy enough to donate an expensive camel-hair altarcloth to the cathedral.

In 1512 Baldung moved to Freiburg-im-Breisgau to begin work on his finest masterpiece, a great polyptych for the cathedral. Two years later Grünewald had arrived in nearby Issenheim. A few kilometres up the Rhine was the Mecca of German-speaking free thinkers – Basel, whose university and liberal city administration had attracted a variety of humanists and radicals. Situated at the convergence point of Swiss, German and French territory and commanding excellent road and river communications, Basel was a cosmopolitan city and one where men of dangerously independent opinions not infrequently sought refuge from their persecutors. Here Ulrich Zwingli studied in the opening years of the century and controversial printers like Johannes Froben and Johannes Amerbach published books for followers of the New Learning. Several humanist intellectuals came to Basel for shorter or longer periods. In 1515 Oswald Myconius of Lucerne was teaching there and in the same year the preacher Wolfgang Capito and the scholar Johannes Oecolampadius arrived. Within a few years, they would become Reformation leaders in Switzerland and southern Germany. Above all Desiderius Erasmus, who had arrived to supervise the publication of his Greek New Testment, came to Basel in 1515. He was the toast of the town, being feasted and flattered by intellectuals from far and wide who had come to see Europe's most famous scholar. Here, in that same year, the eighteen-year-old Hans Holbein and his brother arrived seeking work and eagerly expecting intellectual and artistic stimulus.

Chapter 2

BASEL

1515–1517

St Martin's church in Basel once rang with the conviction preaching of the Reformation. We know the names of some of the prominent citizens who were enthralled by the new teaching because their memorials remain, attached to walls and pillars. One records in meagre detail the life of Sebastian Spoerlin, who died in 1544 at the age of eighty. This city father, who lived through the most tumultuous years of Basel's history, selected the following words to be placed upon his funerary tablet: 'ΈΜΟΙ ΤΟ ΖΗΝ ΧΡΙΣΕΣΤΟΣ', 'To me to live is Christ'. In that brief quotation from St Paul's letter to the Philippians we catch a glimpse of the religious and intellectual enthusiasms which made this municipality on the Rhine such a remarkable place. Spoerlin, an affluent burgher whose life was in trade, was a man who knew his Bible, had some grasp of New Testament Greek and, like Paul, believed in the inwardness of religion.

Today old Basel on its steep hill above the fast-flowing river breathes an air of sweet reasonableness. The wide square before the cathedral and the solid Romanesque–Gothic building itself, with its massive arches bathed in light, symbolize an unfussy, no-nonsense faith. The quaint west-front statue of St George and the dragon might be seen as an allegory of truth vanquishing error. Even in 1515 the atmosphere here was very different from that of claustrophobic Augsburg. In Basel men were – notoriously – free to preach, publish and debate novel, exciting ideas. This was one of the city's attractions for the Holbein brothers. Ambrose deliberately aped humanist scholars by using the latinized form of his name, Ambrosius.

Arrangements had been made for the boys to enter the atelier of Hans Herbst. This master remains a less than shadowy figure in the Holbein story. However, we do know what he looked like. Ambrosius did a portrait of him in 1516 which shows him as a man with astute features fringed with luxuriant brown hair and beard. From the bare records in official archives we know that Herbst was born in Strasbourg in 1468, that he was enrolled in the Basel painters' guild in 1492 and died, full of years, in 1550. This artist of the elder Holbein's generation was a member of the upper-Rhineland school, but no existing works have been attributed to him with much conviction. However, other evidence connects him firmly with reformist-humanist circles. He was related to another Johannes Herbst who, in the 1490s, was a professor at Heidelberg and who wrote a poem in praise of printing. His son became a prominent humanist scholar in Basel, where he taught Latin and Greek and took the latinized name of Oporinus. Later, he opened his own printing house and pursued a publishing policy which, at least once, landed him in jail. This was an experience to which his father was no stranger. In 1524, Hans Herbst fell foul of the authorities for publishing a diatribe against the mass and was detained for several days.

Basel, and its sister municipalities on the upper Rhine – Heidelberg, Strasbourg, Freiburg-im-Breisgau, Colmar – were the places where substantial burghers and transient students read and listened to reforming humanists such as Sebastian Brant, Geiler von Kaysersberg and Jakob Wimpfeling in the closing decades of the old century. By 1515 several first-generation humanists had died. Those who remained were angry old men, but their influence was undiminished. New advocates of change were appearing in the humanist heaven burning with a more lustrous, potentially devastating brilliance. Oecolampadius, Capito, Philip Melanchthon and Ulrich Zwingli were among those who studied at Heidelberg, Freiburg and Basel and greedily devoured the avant-garde teachings of their masters and the Herbsts were among the many satellites circling the major planets of the Rhineland humanist system.

Hans Herbst's studio introduced the Holbeins to the printing houses on which artists relied for a steady flow of work. But Hans and Ambrosius were busy making their own contacts. They had letters of introduction to various of Basel's intellectual luminaries and they would have lost no time in frequenting the taverns and printshops fronting the narrow streets around the cathedral and the university which crisscrossed the hill climbing from the Rhine to the Pfalz.

Very rapidly the young men from Augsburg were accepted into the humanist fellowship of Basel. Hans in particular made many friends among the avant-garde, and this can only have been because of his obvious genius and his sympathy with advanced ideas. He did not have the education that would have qualified him for intimacy with the scholars of the university and their students. His own schooling had been basic. His grasp of Latin was and would remain weak. Of Greek he was wholly ignorant. Yet he was soon the companion of men whose lectures, sermons and writings were changing the world.

As for Ambrosius, one piece of evidence survives which places him firmly in the humanist camp. In Basel's Kunstmuseum there hangs a remarkable little devotional painting labelled, *Christ as Intercessor to the Father*. The Man of Sorrows is depicted seated upon a rainbow over the world. In the clouds around him angels exhibit symbols of human sin and folly – guns, whips, swords, instruments of torture. From within a heavenly nimbus the Father accepts the sacrifice, holding up a hand in blessing and sending forth the Holy Spirit, in the form of a dove. Although it makes use of some elements of traditional iconography, this is a highly individualistic piece of pictorial theology. It depicts the central theme of Christian humanism: Christ as the sole and all-sufficient intermediary between man and God the Father. It is a positive, optimistic avowal of divine grace. However, like the Erasmian Christology which informs it, it carries negative implications: if the Son of God is the only divinely appointed and adequate intercessor, then such accretions to the faith as invocations to the saints, the Church's treasury of merit, indulgences and requiem masses have limited value or no value at all.

Such thinking was gaining ground in intellectual circles but nowhere was it more dominant than in Basel.

I feel entitled to hope with confidence that not only the moral virtues and Christian piety but also the true learning, purified of corruption, and the fine disciplines will revive and blossom forth. All over the world, as if on a given signal, splendid talents are stirring and awakening and conspiring together to revive the best learning. For what else is this but a conspiracy, when all these great scholars from different lands share out the work among themselves and set about this noble task, not merely with enthusiasm but with a fair measure of success, so that we have an almost certain prospect of seeing all disciplines emerge once more into the light of day in a far purer and more genuine form?[1]

So Erasmus enthused to Capito in 1517. At that time the two men
were firm friends, sharing common ideals, a relationship which did
not survive the imminent crisis. Wolfgang Köpfel, who took the
latinized 'Capito' as his humanist pseudonym, was the cathedral
preacher in Basel and a teacher at the university. He was one of the
early sixteenth-century scholars who mastered Hebrew as well as
Greek, and Erasmus found his assistance with his New Testament text
invaluable. Johannes Hüszgen, or Oecolampadius, was also involved
in the editorial process while pursuing his own studies of early
Church fathers. For intense and happy months they and others
worked together in Johannes Froben's printing house, zealous sharers
of the common vision proclaimed by Erasmus in the preface of the
Novum Instrumentum.

> Christ wished his mysteries to be published as openly as possible. I
> wish that even the weakest woman should read the Gospels –
> should read the epistles of Paul. And I wish these were translated
> into all languages, so that they might be read and understood, not
> only by Scots and Irishmen, but also by Turks and Saracens. To
> make them understood is surely the first step.

Erasmus loved Basel, although he had not come there on purpose.
He had been on his way back to Italy, where he intended to supervise
new editions of his writings. Those plans changed when he experienced a rapturous welcome and, particularly, when he met Johannes
Froben (Frobenius in humanist circles), who persuaded the itinerant
scholar to let his printing house undertake the work. Erasmus needed
little bidding. He wintered in Basel and was delighted to discover
there not only the professional competence of Froben's workers, but
also a brotherhood of enthusiastic scholars, the Sodalitas Basiliensis,
dedicated to the New Learning. He called the city *amoenissimum
museum,* 'a most delightful precinct of the muses'. Soon he was
writing to his correspondents fulsomely extolling the virtues of his
new friends and celebrating his good fortune at having fallen in with
them:

> They all know Latin, they all know Greek, most of them know
> Hebrew, too; one is an expert historian, another an experienced
> theologian; one is skilled in the mathematics, one a keen antiquary,

another a jurist. . . . I certainly have never before had the luck to live in such a gifted company. And to say nothing of that, how open-hearted they are, how gay, how well they get on together! You would say they had only one soul.[2]

Apart from a brief visit to England in the spring of 1515. Erasmus stayed in Basel for eighteen months. It was the first step to his adoption of the Swiss city as his home.

The vision that Erasmus, his Basel colleagues and most of their humanist friends throughout Europe shared was that of reformation on the basis of Scripture. The Bible was the key to the revival of morals and manners in public and private life. A pure text, good vernacular translations and books to expound its message would transform society and purge the institutionalized Church of abuses.

Erasmus did not, as we might suppose, find his soulmates in the university of which the Basel fathers were so proud. In fact, the faculty masters tended to be very conservative. It was in the print-shops and the neighbouring taverns lining the steep streets falling from the cathedral down to the Rhine that radical students, authors, proof-readers and copy-editors gathered. In these establishments the Holbeins touched the hem of fashionable humanism. And among this coterie of people who gathered to make books, read books and talk about books, Erasmus was at home.

Among the score or more printing–publishing houses in the city, those of Amerbach, Petri and Froben, widely known as 'the guild of three', were the most important. Like the Holbeins, the founders of these enterprises were all from south Germany. They were men of culture as well as business acumen. They provided works of ancient scholarship and new interpretation for a rapidly growing market. The name that figures most prominently in the Holbein story is that of Amerbach. When he arrived in Basel in the 1480s Johannes Amerbach's mind was already as well filled as his purse. He took care to give his three sons the best humanist education available. When the father died the brothers sold the printing business to Froben and became men of independent means on the proceeds. But they remained passionately committed to the dissemination of Christian truth and understanding. Erasmus regarded himself as much indebted to this family as to his hosts and principal publishers, the Frobens. When he had first come to Basel one of the projects he was involved in was a new edition of Jerome. The Amerbachs not only sponsored it but oversaw the editorial work, as Erasmus acknowledged in a letter to the pope.

> Our most important assistants are the brothers Amerbach, at whose expense and efforts the work is mainly undertaken. One may well believe that this family has been raised up by Fortune to be the means of bringing Jerome back to life. Their father, the best of men, had his three sons instructed in Greek, Hebrew and Latin for this purpose. When he died, he bequeathed to his children a legacy, dedicating his fortune to its fulfilment. These excellent young men are diligently discharging the commission imposed on them by their father.[3]

Basel, and indeed the art-loving world, is indebted to the Amerbachs. Old Johannes counted collecting among his cultural activities. He accumulated several works of art and antiquarian curios. On his death these passed to his youngest son, Bonifacius, who was, in his own right, something of a connoisseur of paintings and goldsmiths' work. Bonifacius was about the same age as Ambrosius, a sensitive and intelligent man whose student years were spent at the feet of some of the finest masters of the day. He became a lawyer and was eventually professor of jurisprudence at Basel. He was one of Erasmus's very closest friends and was nominated by the philosopher as his heir. What is more important is that he was a close friend and committed patron of Hans Holbein. It was probably Amerbach who brought Hans and Ambrosius into contact with the Erasmian inner circle. He was certainly one of the first collectors to appreciate the talent of the young man from Augsburg. He avidly acquired the artist's drawings and some of his paintings over the years. When he died he passed the augmented Amerbach collection to his son, Basilius. Basilius made the family treasures available for public display and this Amerbach Kabinett subsequently became the basis of the Basel Kunstmuseum and Historisches Museum collections. Thus it was that Holbein's adopted city became the proud possessor of an incomparable range of the master's works, especially his drawings and sketches.

Johannes Froben, whose contract brought Erasmus to Basel in 1514, was a businessman as well as an idealist. The editorial and production costs involved in publishing Erasmus's Greek New

Testament were considerable and, though it would have a good sale among scholars capable of reading it, it would never be a best-seller. Therefore, the deal that he struck with his author included the right to produce editions of some of Erasmus's other books, especially the *Encomium Moriae*. The new *Praise of Folly* came off the presses in the middle of 1515 and the first copies were eagerly snapped up by Erasmus's friends and admirers.

One copy was bought by Oswald Molitar, a schoolmaster and theologian from Lucerne, who preferred to be known by the latinized soubriquet Myconius. This ardent disciple of the great Desiderius had come to Basel for an extended stay in order to meet his hero and to be a part of the highly charged atmosphere that Erasmus's presence created. He earned his living teaching at the St Theodor and St Peter schools. When he had read the satire, Myconius decided to add to the jest. He would have a series of marginal drawings done in his copy and present it to Erasmus. He probably wished to draw himself to the attention of the master, for he was not at this time a member of the humanist inner circle. His decorated copy of the *Moria* (as the book was commonly referred to within the Erasmian fraternity) was conceived as an in-joke. Whatever the exact circumstances surrounding the creation of Myconius's little presentation volume, the important fact for Hans Holbein was that the schoolmaster chose him and his brother to do many of the drawings.

The idea may actually have come from the Holbeins. One aspect of the illustrated *Moria*'s whimsicality was that it was a parody of another book which had just been issued in a limited edition in Augsburg. In 1513 Johannes Schönsperger had embarked on the publication of a prayer book for the emperor and had commissioned Dürer, Burgkmair, Baldung and other artists to produce marginal drawings. This magnificent – and expensive – volume came from the presses in 1515. It was a major piece of prestige publishing and one Hans and Ambrosius knew about from its inception. Similarly to embellish the *Moria* would be a jest well appreciated by the Basel humanist circle. Froben might even consider printing it for a wider clientele.

The importance of the project for the newcomers was that it involved them closely with Myconius, Froben and their friends. The schoolmaster discussed the book in detail with the young artists and doubtless provided translations of passages he had specifically marked for illustration. The Holbeins appreciated the witty flavour of the text

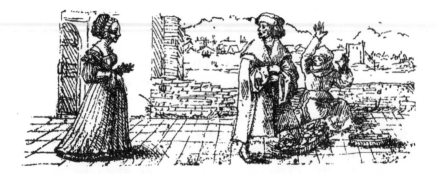

Marginal drawings from the *Praise of Folly: A distracted young man stumbling into a basket of eggs* (British Museum, London)

and translated it into a series of drawings which underlined rather than overburdened the satire. It is impossible to look at this book, now one of the Basel Kunstmuseum's most treasured possessions, without recognizing the gleeful delight with which Hans and Ambrosius undertook their task. There are few art forms in which the executant more immediately and clearly displays his own feelings and opinions than in the lampoon. In their whimsical or cruel or outraged caricatures Breughel, Cruickshank, Goya, Daumier, Thurber appear before us heart-on-sleeve. Hans Holbein's *Moria* illustrations (he did most of the eighty-two drawings) are not in the same league, but they are the first pictures that can, without controversy, be attributed to him and they immediately tell us much about his outlook on life.

They show us a young man who is a keen observer of the human scene. The sketches were completed within a few days, yet Holbein crammed his tiny drawings with numerous details. All manner of men and women have their place in Folly's cavalcade. Holbein shows us a woman at her loom – her movements very clear. He depicts scholars engrossed in their studies, nuns at their devotions, kings and prelates richly attired, ragged peasants, gluttons, women accoutred in the height of fashion and gullible church congregations. His figures are placed in varied architectural or outdoor settings, delineated or suggested with complete assurance. Here is the disciplined artist, fascinated by but detached from his world and therefore able to display it in a series of tiny drawings which enable us to recognize the denizens of that world half a millennium later.

The sketches speak to us of a young man with a ribald sense of humour. Holbein caught the author's emphasis on incongruity, his ridiculing of a world gone mad, although he was not equal to all the scholar's subtleties. Erasmus's book was a monologue by Stultitia, represented by the author as the unacknowledged queen of the entire human race. He poked fun – or, rather, Folly poked fun, for Erasmus was wont to deflect criticism by insisting that the opinions expressed in the *Moria* were not his own – at all sorts and conditions of men and at most human institutions. Human behaviour is absurd: war, love, philosophy, scholarly disputation – all are vanity. Happiness and true wisdom lie in accepting this simple fact. Holbein exuberantly illustrates this hypothesis. A group of men arguing theological niceties are as deformed as their specious debating points. A young man is so intent on ogling an attractive woman that he steps in a basket of eggs. And when Stultitia finally descends from her pulpit she leaves the congregation, like herself, kitted out with caps and bells.

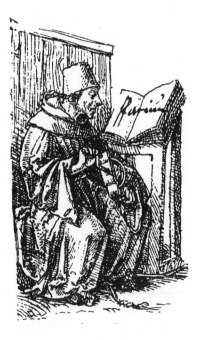

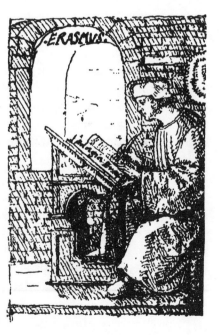

Nicolas De Lyra   *Erasmus at his Desk*

One aspect of Holbein's humour which first appears in these drawings and was to be apparent throughout his life was his love of puns and all manner of wordplay. It was a delight he shared with most Renaissance thinkers. The very title of the *Encomium Moriae* was a *double entendre*. The work had been inspired, during a recent visit to England, by Thomas More, described by Erasmus as 'by far the sweetest friend of all'. The latinized form of More's name was 'Morus' but that also meant 'fool'. Thus *Encomium Moriae* was – and was intended to be – both a tribute to a much loved fellow humanist and an elegant exposé of the ills of contemporary society. We find Hans Holbein fully entering into the spirit of the thing. Thus he showed the early fourteenth-century biblical exegete Nicolas of Lyra simultaneously studying Scripture and playing a stringed musical instrument. Basel's printers were early attracted as much by Holbein's ready wit as by his technical facility. When called upon by the publisher Christopher Froschauer to conceive a new printer's mark for his books and his trade sign, Hans drew a child playing with frogs in a glade. The word 'Froschauer' means literally 'One who lives in frog meadow'. It was sure to attract attention and laughter – an excellent advertisement. The young man had a remarkable immediacy of perception. He quickly grasped the effect he wanted to create and then transferred it to paper with pen or silverpoint speedily and precisely. Froben and his publishing rivals soon realized that what they heard about this young man from his father, his brother and Hans Herbst was true. Hans brought a completely fresh mind to the designing of title-pages and book illustrations. He provided drawings that were complex yet clear and elegant. From very early on he created title-plates that were dramatic or humorous. One objective of the *Moria* drawings was to attract the attention of the printing fraternity to a remarkable new talent. It succeeded.

Yet there was a harder edge to the book which could also be felt in the pictures. Notwithstanding Erasmus's protestations to the contrary, the *Moria* had a serious purpose. It projected reformist indignation against the shortcomings of organized religion – the corruption of the clergy, the encouragement of superstitions, the sale of indulgences and all those practices which kept people from abandoning themselves to divine folly, which, according to Stultitia, was true Christianity. In the front line of Erasmus's enemies were those diehards and obscurantists who opposed freedom of debate and the advance of pure scholarship.

One case in particular had been running, on and off, since about 1510. The leading Hebrew scholar of the age, Johannes Reuchlin, had fallen foul of the Inquisition over his contacts with Jews and his books on the language of the Old Testament. He was acquitted by an episcopal court in 1514 but his persistent Dominican enemies appealed the case to Rome, where it dragged on for several more years. Reuchlin's tribulation was a *cause célèbre* among humanists, and those who read the *Moria* saw it as an indictment of the kind of reactionary stupidity which had armed itself against the scholar.

The illustrations captured the mood of the barbed jest and sometimes went further. Monks were depicted as lustful and money-grubbing. Nuns at their devotions were either simple or deceived. Uneducated peasants were shown blindly worshipping religious images. If there was ever any suggestion of publishing an illustrated version of the *Moria,* the ribaldry of the drawings would have prevented it. The *Moria* was a controversial work. Several members of the Church hierarchy who did not take kindly to having their self-importance pricked had already complained about Erasmus's irreverence, his mockery of 'holy things', even his alleged contempt for Scripture. The scholar's enemies had their eventual triumph years after his death when a strait-laced Pope Paul IV branded the *Moria* and all Erasmus's works as heretical and put them on the Index of banned books. In the years before the storm Erasmus was able to take cover behind the ambiguity (or alleged ambiguity) of his text. But pictures were far less open to rival interpretations. Myconius's jest was altogether too pointed. It made very plain a degree of cynicism and anger that would have alarmed critics still more. To have published lampoons graphically pointing up elements of Folly's anti-clericalism might have invited trouble.

These painstaking yet carefree drawings from the pen of an eighteen-year-old prodigy also made an impact on the Erasmus circle. Hans was soon very much at home in the company of humanists, most of whom were his intellectual superiors. He became firm friends with Myconius, the families of Froben and Amerbach and others of their circle. He grew particularly close to Bonifacius Amerbach, the printer's youngest son, and, more importantly, came to the attention of Erasmus, the humanist 'king', the nearest thing sixteenth-century Europe had to an international celebrity. The great man appreciated Holbein's drawings, though he did see through one piece of sycophancy. One of the sketches depicted a very young Erasmus seated at his desk beside a window. When the scholar saw it he burst out laughing; 'If I really looked like that I'd be searching for a wife,' he jested. The young artist never became an intimate of the middle-aged scholar, but he could call himself a friend and was the closest thing Erasmus ever had to a 'court painter'. All this had been achieved by Hans within a few exciting months of leaving home.

It could not last. Early in 1516 Erasmus set off on his travels once more. The court disbanded. Myconius moved to the monastic school in Zurich. Young Amerbach resumed his studies in Freiburg. Oecolampadius took a sabbatical after his intense editorial labours, returning to his home town of Weinsberg, near Heidelberg. He was also nursing a bruised ego. There had been complaints about his preaching in Basel. People said his sermons were too earnest and joyless. Unlike many of the friars who indulged in all manner of pulpit buffoonery, the thirty-four-year-old scholar declined to entertain his congregation with ribald tales or dramatic accounts of saintly miracles. Life in Basel returned to normal, and the journeymen Holbeins concentrated on their bread-and-butter work.

This involved, in addition to designs for the printers' blockmakers, the usual internal and external house murals, painted furniture, shop and trade signs – anything that members of the thriving Basel community were prepared to commission. One item of Hans's from the early months in Basel that has fortuitously survived (though its attribution to Holbein is not universally accepted) reveals more of his sense of humour and his delight in showing off his technical mastery. In June 1515 Hans Baer, a leading citizen, married Barbara Brunner, who came from another wealthy burgher family. The couple them-selves or a close relative had the idea of providing as the centrepiece of the new household a painted dining table. Hans was commissioned to cover the wood and slate top with an exuberance of painted detail. Such items were not uncommon in the homes of the well-to-do, but Holbein's *tour de force* provided the Baers and their guests with a stimulating conversation-piece. The borders displayed sporting scenes: knights jousted; hunters pursued their quarries; fishermen plied rod and net; falconers loosed their hawks; young men and women picnicked, danced and played games in a grassy glade. These were probably the sort of pastimes that the newlyweds enjoyed in their leisure hours. Baer held an honoured military position as standard-bearer to a troop of Swiss mercenaries, which would explain the tournament scene.

The table's centre is devoted to two jokes. A pedlar sleeps by a roadside while a troop of monkeys plays havoc with his stock in trade. And St Nobody, a popular figure of German mythology, sits dejectedly among broken household items, his lips padlocked. Any parent will know how the eternally mute 'Nobody' traditionally shoulders the blame for domestic mishaps. Very probably these two scenes represented private jokes known only to the immediate family circle. Holbein still had one more jest. He littered the table's surface with a profusion of objects – a seal, a carnation, scissors, tools, a letter, a pen, a playing card, spectacles and many other articles. These *trompe-l'oeil* decorations were made to appear real, as though the items had been untidily left strewn across the table. It was the kind of visual witticism which had been popular with painters and workers in marquetry ever since the techniques had spread from Italy in the fifteenth century. It enabled them in a good-humoured way to show off their virtuosity, and in all art forms virtuosity always impresses people. The story of this table has a dark conclusion. Three months after his wedding, Hans Baer marched proudly at the head of his troop across marshy ground at Marignano, to join battle with a French force advancing on Milan. When the Swiss mercenaries were at last forced from the field the Basel standard-bearer was among the slain.

Another utilitarian piece which has survived from the early Basel years is a sign which Hans and Ambrosius executed for a local schoolmaster. The hanging board, painted on both sides, depicted adults and children at their letters, assisted by the teacher and his wife. The legend informed passers-by that instruction was available:

> For whoever wants to read and write German in the shortest possible time, even those who cannot read a single letter, who want to be able to write down and be able to read their debts. Satisfaction guaranteed. Will take on burghers, journeymen, women and maidens, whoever needs to learn. Reasonable prices for instruction. Young boys and girls only accepted after the ember day fast.

It has been suggested that Myconius commissioned this piece of commercial art and that Holbein's friend is portrayed upon it. There is no supporting evidence for this identification and, on balance, it

seems unlikely. Myconius left Basel in 1516. There were other
pedagogues in Basel and a growing demand for their services. In the
circles in which Hans and Ambrosius moved they encountered many
men dedicated to the spread of education.

This is more significant than the identification of the customer.
Although we should not overemphasize the point it is further
evidence that the brothers were at home among intellectuals with a
social mission. These were men who believed in the extension of
literacy as a principle. Some of them went further: they were
evangelists who wanted to use the spread of education to advance
their own devotional, theological and political ideas. Erasmus was a
blatant, if naive, advocate of social engineering. He looked to
vernacular Scriptures and religious tracts to reform society. He had
many allies, most of them devout churchmen, who did not realize
that Amalthaea's horn would also be Pandora's box. Renaissance
humanists were neither the first nor the last idealists to believe in the
benevolent effects of universal education. Mystics, devotional writers
and monastic reformers had long encouraged ordinary people to learn
to read so that they could feed their souls on approved texts. The
invention of printing had been welcomed as an exciting means to this
end. But, as books proliferated in their thousands and as tradespeople
and artisans clamoured to join the ranks of the literate, the control of
education slipped from ecclesiastical fingers. Town and city councils
set up their own schools. Independent entrepreneurs, like Holbein's
unknown patron, hawked their wares to passers-by.

Intellectual freedom and the restraints that might reasonably be
placed upon it were among the topics earnestly discussed in humanist
circles during Hans Holbein's adolescent years. In 1487 the papacy
had made a belated and vain attempt to control the output of the
presses by insisting that all books should carry an imprimatur. In 1521
the emperor put the weight of secular power behind this edict by
bringing the publication of proscribed texts within the common law.
These efforts at censorship were – as such efforts usually are – largely
counterproductive. Students demanded the freedom to read whatever
they wanted and to make up their own minds. Advanced thinkers,
whether theologians, alchemists, mathematicians or geographers,
resented the fear of persecution that inhibited them from airing their
hypotheses. Yet there could be no question of unbridled licence.
Europe's market places and printing houses were magnets for heretics,

unemployed academics, disaffected monks, charlatans and 'miracle-workers'. Such men who used the mystique of education to ensnare Christian souls had to be curbed. These were the years that gave birth to the Faust legend, which emphasized the perils as well as the excitements of free-thinking. The wide-ranging debate about the uses and abuses of literacy and education was becoming more urgent and more decisive in the second decade of the century. Hans Holbein was a part of that debate.

The arguments extended to the graphic arts – what subjects were suitable for representation and how might they legitimately be presented? It is difficult to see what stance Holbein took on religious painting during his first Basel period because there is little work in this genre which has, without dispute, been attributed to him. Six paintings or groups have some connection with young Hans but, of these, two versions of the Virgin and Child have been claimed for Ambrosius and the elder Hans respectively, some Passion scenes have been designated as Herbst workshop pieces, and only two small works – an Adam and Eve (see plate section) and a fragmentary treatment of saints' heads – are, without dispute, awarded to Hans the Younger.

Yet, if we only possessed the Adam and Eve, we would still have a powerful testimony to Holbein's thinking and his methods of conveying his ideas. It was a private commission, in oils on paper, painted for his friend Bonifacius Amerbach in 1517. The student lawyer wanted it for his private devotions, hanging it in his Freiburg lodgings as a reminder of fallen human nature and of the temptations of the flesh which lay in wait to beguile a young man away from home. The painting is as eloquent for what it omits as for what it contains. Holbein evinces no interest in the nude form, which for virtually every other contemporary artist was an integral part of the treatment of this subject. Similarly he eschews Renaissance delight in foliage and the symbolism of birds and animals. Even the serpent is missing. The painting is a head-and-shoulders study. The man is darker-complexioned than the woman, true to current convention, and has his arm draped rather awkwardly around her shoulder. Eve holds between them the apple, which forms one apex of a triangle which links it with the couple's eyes. Yet, although it is her left hand that is depicted in well-observed detail, its colour has taken on some of the brownish tint of Adam's flesh: man and woman are united in tragedy. It is that realization which haunts the faces in what is, in reality, a double portrait. Adam and Eve seem to have been caught at the moment when the full realization of what they have done has dawned upon them. Their eyes are about to shed tears of remorse. Adam's down-curved, whispy moustache accentuates his melancholy. The message is underlined by the only piece of symbolism Holbein permits himself – a maggot wriggles its way out of the apple.

In this deceptively simple, early work Hans Holbein clearly states what was to be his guiding principle throughout his career. He has been called the painter of realism. That oversimplification obscures his relationship with the changing cultural conventions of his age. No more than any other Renaissance artist did Holbein eschew symbols, signs, codes and metaphors. Quite the reverse; he exulted in the mythological allusions, allegories and visual puns beloved of the humanist brotherhood. He was concerned with the 'hidden meaning deep down things'. Whether painting a religious subject or a portrait he sought to convey essential truth as he saw it. Where he differed from most forerunners was in insisting that the road to that truth lay through the immediate appearance of people and objects, and was not a dogma or theory to be imposed upon his subject matter. This attitude goes to the very heart of Reformation thinking.

It was this love affair with unadorned truth that made Holbein at one with the Erasmian circle. As linguistic scholars strove to discover the best early classical and biblical texts and offer the world 'pure' versions of the Hebrew, Greek and Latin; as the translators and printers strove zealously to make available accurate vernacular versions of holy Scripture; as theologians cut away the ivy of dogma and superstitious custom from the trunk of Christianity; as reformers called clergy back from their warring, wenching and political intrigues to their spiritual responsibilities; as political thinkers were measuring contemporary practice by the yardstick of classical principles of government – so the young Hans Holbein wanted to free his paintings and drawings from outworn conventions and doctrinal accretion so that the subjects could speak for themselves.

There is an element of this in the Passion paintings of the early Basel period. Five scenes from a larger series on canvas were probably created about 1516 as temporary decorations for the use of a local church during holy week. After Easter they would have been taken down and stored away until the following year. When, in 1529, the Basel council banned religious imagery, the paintings were left to moulder. Fortunately, Bonifacius Amerbach acquired a couple of them for his Holbein collection, and an unknown person rescued three more. The subject matter is fully in tune with current trends in Rhineland devotion. Heavenly visions of triumphant madonnas and apocalyptic dooms had given way to a closer concentration on the humanity and suffering of Christ. The style of these paintings is very much in the Germanic tradition. The figures and lighting effects particularly show the influence of Grünewald and Baldung. In Holbein's treatment of Christ's agony in Gethsemane we can see how far the young man has travelled emotionally since the days in his father's workshop. The elder Hans's arrest scene was a composite of didactic detail. For his son, as for Grünewald, mood is everything. An agonized Christ almost screams to the heavens his entreaty, 'Let this cup pass from me!' The disciples sleep, their faces betraying weariness. The posse enters by the garden gate, lamps and torches highlighting their lurid intent, led by Judas the bounty-hunter clutching the bag of blood money to his bosom. In all this, the artist is concerned to convey the impact of a dramatic moment. Conventional symbols pregnant with spiritual significance are kept to a minimum. An angelic hand in the top right-hand corner holds the chalice containing the cross which the humanity in Christ rejects. Otherwise, this is a terrestrial scene. Holbein seeks to portray it as it happened. The narrative needs no embellishment.

A painting of Christ carrying the cross, now in Karlsruhe, if indeed by the younger Holbein, is the first signed and dated (1515) work from his hand. It is a crowded and not very accomplished piece, and, though it was executed only months before the Passion series just referred to, the contrast is marked. It lacks the direct impact of a single narrative line. It follows earlier tradition in being crammed with biblical and legendary allusions. Simon of Cyrene, the weeping Virgin, St John, Joseph of Arimathea, St Veronica with her handkerchief – all are represented along with the brutal soldiery and the jeering crowd in a rocky landscape outside the city wall. The work certainly has the feel of Holbein the Elder. If by his son, it represents a master still struggling to escape from convention in order to say things his own way. When Holbein returned to the subject at a later stage of his career his treatment of it was very different; for example, he omitted the non-biblical figure of Veronica. One intriguing inclusion in the composition is the figure of Sebastian Brant shown just above the cross. It is modelled on the portrait made by his uncle. By including the author of *The Ship of Fools,* Holbein is making his own observation: this tragic rejection of the Son of God was the supreme human folly. If Holbein had already begun work on the *Moria* illustrations, or if the project had, at this stage, only been mooted, such ideas would certainly have been running in his mind.

In 1516 Hans received a commission that was to prove more important for his career (certainly in financial terms) than orders for religious paintings. The brother-in-law of the late Hans Baer, for whom Holbein had decorated the 'St Nobody' table, was the moneylender and self-made entrepreneur Jakob Meyer. Like Baer, he had strong military connections and had fought on campaigns in Italy as a young man. In all probability this was how he had accumulated the capital to start up his business. Sixteenth-century warfare depended on mercenaries. Professional armies with no ideological or emotional stake in the conflicts they were engaged in served their paymasters faithfully as long as their terms of employment were honoured (theoretically, at least). They were better trained, better equipped and often better motivated than contingents of conscripted peasants and townsmen dragged from their fields and workbenches. Certainly they were better paid. They were in a position to dictate terms to their employers and after battle they were well placed to secure a major share of booty. No troops had a better reputation than the Swiss pikemen. Like the German *Landsknechte,* whom Holbein depicted in *Christ Carrying the Cross,* they were well-drilled bands and more than a match for cavalry and other infantry forces. In a few campaigning seasons fighting for the emperor, the King of France or some Italian prince, a young citizen of Basel could, if he survived the attendant risks, accumulate a sizeable capital sum.

Jakob Meyer was one of the more successful. He combined professional and military activity and was as adventurous and positive in business as in battle. By his mid-thirties, he was a significant figure. He gained admission to the city council. In 1513 he made a rich second marriage (Magdalena Baer had died in 1511) with Dorothea Kannengiesser, daughter of an imperial tax collector. In 1515 he was fortunate enough to return from Marignano not only alive but with an honoured reputation. In 1516, he reached the apex of his career when he became the first member of Basel's non-patrician class to be elected to the top civic position of burgomaster.

It was a triumph worth trumpeting and the *arriviste* was not the sort of man to be reticent about proclaiming his pre-eminence. As one of the celebrations of his new-found dignity, Meyer *zum Hasen* (Meyer at the Hare – a reference to the signboard outside his house) commissioned Holbein to paint a double portrait of himself and his second wife. For Hans this was a vitally important contact. It introduced him to the civic aristocracy, not only of Basel, but of other cities which had political and commercial links with it. It is possible that Meyer recognized the talent of this young man and decided to give him his big break. He was familiar with the table Holbein had painted for the Baers and, doubtless, with other pieces of his handiwork which have not survived the centuries. Meyer was a man of forthright and independent mind. During his three periods as burgomaster he initiated many reforms, the effect of which was to shift the balance of political power from the Church and the nobility to the merchant community. In the troubled years which followed he stuck to his principles, preferring prison and public humiliation to any compromise of his convictions. So he might well have vigorously championed a young artist in whom he happened to believe. But the new leader of Basel society was also a shrewd businessman. It will certainly have been a part of his calculation in employing a relative unknown, rather than one of the city's established painters, that the young Augsburger came cheap.

Hans made silverpoint drawings of the couple before setting paint to his prepared limewood panel. This became his established *modus operandi* throughout his career. It served two purposes. It enabled him to record quickly all the essential elements of his customers' features without subjecting them to long sittings. It also provided preliminary work which he could show his patrons so that they could decide whether they wished him to move to the next, more expensive stage. This was a vital precaution for a portraitist. Wealthy and powerful clients were not noted for prompt payment of their bills or, indeed, for paying at all if they could avoid it. An artist might spend days or weeks on a painting only to wait in vain for his fee or to be told that his customer did not like the picture. The drawings for this first, undisputed Holbein portrait have fortunately survived and they reveal an artist who, at the age of nineteen, was already a self-assured master of expression and detail. The structure of the heads was delicately and precisely laid down on paper, and red chalk was used to touch in the moulding of the surfaces. Concerned not to try his patrons' patience, Hans added scribbled notes on colour and texture to his hasty sketches. Once assured of Jakob zum Hasen's approval, he returned to the Herbst workshop to complete this excitingly important commission.

The two small panels, designed as a diptych, proclaim opulence. They show the burgomaster and his wife against a background of elaborate classical pillars and carved friezes, in the Italian style. This locating of his sitters within a sumptuous architectural setting, as well as being fashionable, heightened their importance. The first impression we get is that, in his concern to show himself a master of detail, Holbein has almost overpowered the two figures. As we look longer we realize that this robust sumptuousness is intentional. Holbein uses colour and texture to reinforce the effect. The warm flesh tones, the gilding, the glowing browns and red, the soft sheen of velvet – all combine to make a simple statement. Cleverly, Holbein has achieved his objective without making the Meyers self-assertively overdressed. Jakob's fingers are heavily ringed and clutch a coin, which shows the nature of his business and provides a further hint about his wealth. Otherwise, the man's accoutrements are modest. He wears no chain or badge of office, merely a scarlet cap and a black gown over a gold-embroidered shirt. Dorothea is more richly clothed, without being ostentatious. She wears necklaces of gold and pearls. Her velvet-trimmed dress is cut low to reveal an elaborate under-bodice embroidered with gold thread. The simple cap which covers her hair has a long fall draped round her right shoulder and curled back beneath her arm.

The faces of husband and wife are serious and composed. They reveal no spiritual quality, such as that which Holbein conveyed in his portrait of Amerbach three years later. The painter has done what his patron wanted him to do: he has left the observer in no doubt that his subjects are people of substance, while yet depicting them as sober, intelligent and responsible citizens, not consumed with hubris. There is no doubt that the burgomaster was pleased with the work. He had Holbein make a drawing of his thirteen-year-old daughter Anna (if this was worked up into a painted portrait it has not survived). He commissioned other works over the ensuing years. And he recommended Hans to friends and colleagues.

The Holbeins had been only a couple of years in Basel, but already they were becoming known beyond the city. The next two years would see them working for customers in other towns. The period 1517–19 also provided Hans with the nearest he ever came to a *Wanderjahr*.

Chapter 3

LUCERNE AND NORTH ITALY

1517–1519

If we had some hint of the relationship between the Holbein brothers we would get appreciably closer to understanding what sort of a man Hans was as he emerged into manhood. It might have been a classic situation of resentment and mistrust: the elder son jealous of a brother who was not only their father's favourite but also more talented. This would have caused a growing rift between the young men after they arrived in Basel and Hans rather than Ambrosius attracted the attention of the printers, the intellectual elite and the city's civic leaders; ill-will would have mounted between the boys and, at the first opportunity, they would have gone their separate ways. Such an interpretation of events receives some support from civil documents. In 1517 Ambrosius joined the Basel painters' guild and Hans became a member of the Brotherhood of St Luke, the equivalent body in Lucerne.

One problem with such an analysis is that Ambrosius did not trail far behind his brother in technical skill. There are several works of the early Basel period which experts cannot agree to assign to Hans or Ambrosius. The elder brother was an accomplished portraitist. He depicted Johannes Herbst in 1516, the goldsmith Jörg Schweiger two years later, and other men now anonymous but of obvious substance, and he also made some charming paintings and drawings of children. Bonifacius Amberbach thought sufficiently highly of Ambrosius's work to acquire examples for his collection. Ambrosius appears not to have wanted for commissions from printers. He made engravings for several of the top Basel publishers. Illustrations from his designs appeared in Erasmus's *Novum Instrumentum*. He produced classical and religious subjects, title-pages and initial letters to order. His best-known work in this field is the illustrations for Froben's edition of Thomas More's *Utopia*. Yet, for all his skill, Ambrosius lacked Hans's flair and must have been painfully aware of that. And he never gained the really important commissions which came his brother's way.

Both Holbeins had the vitality, vigour and, sometimes, the arrogance of youth. They pursued their careers with boldness and enthusiasm, not slow to make and grab opportunities. They were exuberant too. In the summer of 1516 Ambrosius's carousing with some of his friends led to an altercation with neighbours which ended up in court. Seventeen months later Hans was heavily fined by the Lucerne authorities for brawling in the streets with one Caspar, a goldsmith. Neither was the sort of man to suffer slights and indignities passively and it would be strange if fraternal rivalry did not sometimes turn to friction.

The opportunity to put some distance between himself and his brother came when Hans was offered a long-term project in Lucerne, a couple of days' journey to the south-east. Lucerne was Myconius's home town, and the reformist schoolmaster may have used his influence in high circles to secure the commission. However, since his new patron was the chief magistrate and ex-mayor of the city it seems more likely that the introduction was effected by Jakob Meyer or someone in his circle. Jakob von Hertenstein was of an ancient family whose imposing castle was perched above the lake not far from the city. Though from a different social class, he was of a similar age to Meyer and also had a military reputation. He had led the Lucerne contingent across the quags and marshes of Marignano. Like Meyer, his fortunes were in the ascendant. He had made no less than four advantageous marriages and had held the top civic post in 1515. To mark his augmented dignity, Hertenstein built himself a new, four-storey townhouse at Kappelplatz, in the city centre. He decided that this residence should be richly decorated, inside and out, with wall paintings. The exterior splendour of the Hertenstein house would compel citizens and visitors alike to stop and stare, and, since some of the scenes to be depicted were of ancient legends and improving tales, they might have a beneficial effect on morals. The internal paintings were to be no less splendid but were designed to be of a more intimate nature.

Wall paintings were not a novelty for Lucerne but their role there was not usually to mark out a patron of substance. There were few precedents for such a project in the city or, indeed, north of the Alps. It was in the warmer climate of Italy that grandiose murals were applied not only to churches and public buildings but to *palazzi* and substantial private dwellings. Visitors marvelled at the breathtaking effects Raphael and Michelangelo were achieving in the Vatican, at Correggio's *sotto in sù* cupola paintings in Parma, at Giorgione's decoration of the doge's palace in Venice. A direct link between north and south was provided by the latter artist's external frescos on the Fondaco dei Tedeschi, the Venice headquarters of the German merchant community. Observers could not fail to be impressed by the vastness of conception and the technical skills which created the illusions of walls and ceilings opening on to terrestrial or heavenly landscapes, of outside walls affording glimpses of interior scenes. Hertenstein was intent on making a fashion statement. By incorporating these in-vogue Italian features in his new house he would proclaim to the world that here lived a cosmopolitan sophisticate, a man of cultured taste.

But there was a problem. He could not afford, or did not choose to afford, to employ one of the leading Italian masters. When Hans Holbein was brought to his attention it seemed that a possible solution had been found. Here was a young man of prodigious talent who had yet to establish a reputation, who was looking for work and who would therefore be cheap. However, the gifted novice also had to project himself. He did so with the bluff and arrogance born of monumental self-confidence. He was only twenty years of age. He was only a journeyman and not a guild member. He had never undertaken a project of such size. He had never directed the work of other artists, and the Hertenstein house decorations would certainly demand the labours of a team of craftsmen. Furthermore, he had not been to Italy to see at first hand the best examples of mural painting. Yet he convinced Hertenstein that he was the man for the job. Holbein was certainly not short of audacity, and it paid off.

He arrived in Lucerne fairly early in 1517 and worked first on the room decorations of his client's house. According to later accounts the subjects he employed were richly varied. In the chamber which served the family as a chapel Holbein treated his material in a very traditional manner. The Hertensteins were depicted in attitudes of modest devotion before Lucerne's patron saint and other holy figures. Another scene displayed a pious legend from Bamberg in Franconia concerning a vision of the Christ-child vouchsafed to a fifteenth-century peasant, presumably a favourite story in the Hertenstein household. A religious procession occupied a third wall. Since we can no longer see how Holbein handled these subjects we can draw no conclusions, but the choice of subject matter certainly indicates no preference for new concepts of devotion. The young painter was doing a job for a traditionally minded burgher. As with the Baer table, his main concern was to depict his virtuoso skills.

The family recreations that Hans had illustrated for the Baers were repeated here in expansive painted tableaux. The Hertensteins were depicted hunting stags, hares and duck with their impressive hilltop fortress in the background. The only other subject of which we have a detailed description takes us back to the world of the *Moria*. For one of the rooms Holbein painted an elaborate joke, illustrating the folly of human aspirations. This was the popular legend of the fountain of youth: a cavalcade of more or less ludicrous aged individuals make their way to the gushing geyser, there to be restored to health, beauty and vigour. It may be that in this chamber the artist was given *carte blanche*. The theme of human vanity had a great appeal for Holbein. The Fountain of Youth was one way of presenting a subject to which he later returned in the black-comedy engravings of the *Dance of Death*.

During the months Holbein spent on these interiors the eldest son of the household, Benedikt von Hertenstein, having recently come of age, was elected to the Lucerne great council. The portrait of the young man Holbein was commissioned to execute to honour this important dynastic event shows Hans at pains to emphasize his understanding of Italian style. He chose the three-quarter-face pose currently in favour but, less conventionally, he showed the eyes gazing straight out at the spectator. This combination presents considerable problems for the artist. Someone looking out of the corners of his eyes almost inevitably appears uncertain, haughty or shifty. It was no doubt for this reason that Holbein subsequently abandoned this pose almost completely. When he did use it, for example in the picture of Sir John Godsalve, it was in order to make very pointed statements about the personality of his subject. Here the unsatisfactory treatment is probably the result of painterly ambition unmatched by experience. Benedikt von Hertenstein betrays a diffidence out of keeping with everything else the portrait is saying about him. His dress is rich. He wears a gold chain and several rings on his fingers. His left wrist rests on the damascened pommel of his sword. His social standing and his military connections are evident.

Benedikt von Hertenstein was yet another young man of good family who sought battlefield laurels. He had served under his father at Marignano and had every prospect of following Jakob by attaining both civic and military honours. Such ambitions were not destined to be fulfilled. Five years later he led a Lucerne contingent in the pay of the King of France during the campaign in north Italy. 'Bicocca' has entered the Castilian language to describe something splendid and unexpected. For the Swiss the name of this Italian village signified unmitigated disaster. In the annals of warfare it marked a major turning point. The Swiss pikemen made their usually irresistible assault upon an entrenched imperial position. For the first time they came under well-regulated fire from trained arquebusiers. Despite their thinning ranks they marched right up to the enemy positions before being finally repulsed. Jakob von Hertenstein's heir was among those not to survive the carnage.

However, that was well in the future when Holbein painted his portrait in 1517. To emphasize his sitter's martial prowess and his own skill he set Hertenstein in a room with a sculpted frieze depicting a Roman triumph. The inspiration for this came from engravings of paintings by Mantegna. The Mantuan artist, who had died in 1506, was a painter's painter. His range, his inventiveness, his intellectual brilliance were admired by practitioners of his own and later generations, who studied and tried to emulate his techniques. Particularly striking were Mantegna's delight in illusion and his use of grisaille to create the impression of relief sculpture. It was this that Holbein copied in a complex design of marching soldiers, prancing horses and cheering crowds.

It is extremely unlikely that Benedikt was the only member of the family to have been painted at this time. A nineteenth-century source refers to a portrait of Jakob von Hertenstein dated 1517, and Holbein would almost certainly have painted the old man's wife as a pendant to it. Since his depiction of Jakob and Dorothea Meyer the young Augsburger's fame as a limner had gone before him. The arrangement between Holbein and his new patron would have included a series of portraits emphasizing the importance of the Hertensteins – portraits which Jakob could, and in all probability did, have copied as gifts for friends and business associates.

Making preliminary drawings, discussing them with the client, marking out the designs on the walls and working up the finished murals took months of hard work. But, under pressure to give satisfaction, Holbein completed the interior before the end of 1517. It was not Holbein's only project in Lucerne. As well as Benedikt's portrait he worked on book engravings and patterns for stained-glass windows. Then there was the exterior of the Hertenstein house to be planned. He could not achieve all this single-handed. He employed two or three journeyman assistants. Ambrosius came over from Basel to help and Hans's father may also have lent a hand. Doubtless, they both needed the money. The elder Holbein received few major commissions in his later years (or, if he did more, no evidence of them has survived). He was still dogged by financial problems and shortly after the visit to Lucerne he fell out with his patrons at Eisenheim. Either he failed to produce the work they had commissioned or what he did paint was not wholly acceptable. Not only was the old man dismissed, but the Eisenheim monks confiscated his painting materials. Hans was later involved in a long and probably fruitless battle for the restoration of his father's property. As for Ambrosius, he seems to have been afflicted with a similar lack of business sense. The records reveal that he had difficulty paying his guild dues. Bit by bit it was Hans who was taking over the responsibility for the family.

Winter approached. Work on the house exterior was suspended. Holbein took the opportunity to cross into north Italy. In order to create the desired effect on the frontage of the Hertenstein mansion he needed to study the frescos of the great masters. He must have been longing to see the innovative wonders which had, till now, been available to him only in copies and engravings; to observe the techniques Burgkmair and visitors to his father's studio had enthused about. No record survives of this visit. Any attempt to construct an itinerary of Hans's travels in 1517–18 relies on tracing in his own work the influence of what he saw beyond the Alps.

This was not a *Wanderjahr* in the usual sense of the word – a lengthy period devoted to studying with and working for the best contemporary masters. Holbein had neither the money nor the time for such luxury. His character suggests that he also lacked the inclination to spend long months listening to other men's ideas and admiring their talent. Some creative artists need the comfort and stimulus provided by their peers. Others not only work better alone, they are temperamentally unable to submit to tutelage. Everything we know about Hans Holbein suggests that he was, as far as his profession was concerned, a loner. From the time he left his father's atelier he was bent on developing an individual career and pursuing his own ideas. His sojourn with Hans Herbst was brief and was endured only for as long as it took the self-assured young artist to establish his own contacts. Inevitably, Holbein's style was fashioned by his Augsburg training. Yet, though he admired the technical accomplishments of other artists and was not averse to learning how they achieved their effects, he did not crave the company of his fellows. He belonged to no school and he founded no school. Not one of his surviving paintings or drawings depicts a brother member of the craft. At a time when artisan guilds were achieving greater power within civic constitutions, Holbein was no political champion of artists' rights. He was not likely to have been a denizen of the artists' *quartier* in Lucerne or Basel, carousing with other painters and sculptors in their own adopted taverns or arguing late into the night about the latest theories. Holbein's chosen friends were intellectuals and educated business-men. He enjoyed the company of adventurers, those who explored the expanding world in search of profit or launched themselves upon the ill-charted waters of speculative thought.

His foray into north Italy seems to have been very limited in scope. Holbein headed south from Lucerne and traversed the mountains via the St Gothard pass before the winter snows set in. Throughout the following months his travels took him no further afield than Lom-bardy. Milan, until 1499 the most powerful state in Italy after Venice, had close ties with its transalpine neighbours. Swiss arms had restored the ancient ruling house of Sforza in 1516 but, after the disaster of Marignano, the dukedom had reverted to French rule. Thereafter, it was merely a counter on the board of Habsburg–Valois rivalry. This did not prevent it being an Aladdin's cave of beautiful things. Enlightened princes such as Lodovico Sforza had carried out extensive building works in Milan and brought in artists of the stature of Bramante and Leonardo to embellish palaces, churches and public buildings. Where an enlightened ruler led, his wealthier subjects followed. Commissions abounded, in the towns of the region, for painters, sculptors, carvers and architects. There was, therefore, much for Holbein to see, much to make notes and sketches of. In Milan, there was the *Last Supper* which Leonardo had executed for the abbey of Santa Maria delle Grazie. To the south was the Certosa di Pavia, a Carthusian monastery exuberantly adorned with Gothic and Renaissance motifs and containing some of the finest examples of funerary architecture. In Treviglio, Holbein could gaze at the glowing polyptych, painted about the time of his own birth. In several churches of the region he admired and noted the brilliant, enamel-like surfaces which made religious paintings glow as though lit from within.

Valuable as all this was for Holbein's collection of technical information, it was not what he had come specifically to see. The emerald city at the end of his particular yellow-brick road was Mantua. Here he could admire and analyse the work of a master with whom he felt a true rapport. Andrea Mantegna had been one of those innovative geniuses who had unlocked a cupboard full of new possibilities, which it took a whole generation of artists to examine fully. Mantegna was a passionate antiquarian fascinated by classical sculpture and architecture. He pioneered the techniques for translating the monumentality and gracefulness of stone and bronze into paint. He mastered perspective and foreshortening. His achievements in the art of fresco created astonishing three-dimensional illusions. But the grandiose was only one aspect of his accomplishments. His small devotional paintings were luminous masterpieces of well-observed detail. Mantegna realized the importance of printing and did more than anyone else south of the Alps to transform copperplate engraving into an art form.

Yet what Holbein may have appreciated most about Mantegna was his cool appraisal of his subject matter. The Italian was a thinking artist employed for much of his life by one of the most cultured Renaissance princes. Lodovico Gonzaga presided over a humanist court where scholars and artists were his constant companions. He collected ancient manuscripts of Latin authors. He set up one of the first Italian printing presses and from it came works by Virgil, Dante and Boccaccio. Mantegna thrived in this atmosphere, which encouraged the exploration of new ideas and the detached discussion of ancient wisdom. He achieved a reputation as a thinker as well as an artist. At his house outside Mantua, modelled on a Roman villa and crammed with antiquities, he received visits from poets, men of letters and even from Lorenzo de' Medici. Mantegna's understanding of classical culture and philosophy informed his work, which combined loving attention to detail with the calm dispassion of the intellectual. From such a master Hans Holbein could readily learn.

However, Holbein lacked the leisure for an extended stay in Italy. He had to get back to Lucerne to finish his commissioned work for Hertenstein. He adorned the exterior of Jakob's house with a variety of classical motifs which demonstrated his versatility and his under-standing of the Italian masters. By the skilful use of *trompe-l'oeil* effects, the painter created the illusion at some points of looking outwards at a passing cavalcade (based on Mantegna's *Triumph of Caesar),* while at others interior scenes appeared to be opened up to the spectator. In the top section of the composition Holbein depicted moralizing tales drawn from ancient legend. Columns, pilasters and decorated cornices 'supported' and 'enclosed' these painted narratives, some modelled on the Certosa di Pavia. Simulated sculptured friezes created by the use of grisaille completed what must have been an ebullient façade.

Hans did not lack for work in and around Lucerne. The Her-tensteins used their influence on his behalf. When they wanted to present a stained-glass window or a statute of the Archangel Michael to churches within their patronage it was Holbein who provided the designs. Important commissions came from religious bodies. Hans executed an altarpiece for the Lucerne Augustinians, although it is known now only from partial later copies. When there were no major projects to challenge his creative talent he had plenty of bread-and-butter jobs to keep him busy. There were designs for stained-glass windows. There were pennants and banners to be painted for the guilds and civic authorities for use on festival days. As well as the projects of which some trace has survived there must have been many other commissions, large and small, which came to his studio. From a professional point of view there seems to have been no obvious reason for Holbein to bring to an end his stay in Lucerne.

Before we consider the possible reasons for Holbein's return to Basel in the summer of 1519 we need to set that event against what was happening in the wider world. The hounds of scepticism, criticism and fearless enquiry which Erasmus and the humanists had unleashed had begun to sink their teeth into the more vulnerable parts of western Christendom's anatomy. As the Reuchlin case showed, the Church's lawyers and theologians were already dividing into liberal and reactionary camps. Despite the verdict of 1516, the Dominicans had not given up their pursuit of the great Hebraist. They attacked Reuchlin in print and through the influence of their friends in Rome, Champions of the New Learning responded with satire. *Letters of the Obscurantists* (1513; new extended edition 1517) poked fun at the Dominicans as head-in-the-sand bigots who were terrified of unfamiliar ideas.

If Reuchlin's encouragement of Hebrew studies provoked discord, this was as nothing compared with the impact of Erasmus's *Novum Instrumentum*. As fast as copies rolled off Froben's press from 1516 onwards, scholars all over Europe hastened to buy them. No one read the book more avidly than a monk in Wittenberg and a parish priest in Einsiedeln. Luther took the book as his basic text for preaching and lecturing in the university. It confirmed his growing suspicion that the Church had, over the centuries, progressively obscured the Gospel behind a wall of doctrine and obligatory ceremonial. It became clear to him, for example, that when Jesus spoke of 'repentance' he was referring to a change of heart and not to the mechanical performance of 'penance' in return for priestly absolution. It was on the basis of this understanding that Luther challenged the hawking of indulgences in his ninety-five theses of October 1517, the challenge which, simplistically, has often been regarded as the 'beginning' of the Reformation. The author had no intention of starting a new movement. Rather, he believed that he was aligning himself with the Erasmians in calling for a purification of Church doctrine and practice. He wrote fulsomely to the great scholar, extolling his learning and his clear exposure of error. Luther identified himself as a member of the humanist brotherhood, and to demonstrate it he assumed a Latin name, Eleutherius – the free man.

While the mantle of humanism was hopelessly stretched across Luther's massive shoulders, it fitted much more snugly around those of Ulrich Zwingli. To all outward appearances the priest of the Alpine village of Einsiedeln, snuggled up to the walls of an ancient Benedictine abbey, was a conventional servant of the Church. Coming from peasant stock himself, he understood his people. Although better educated than most parish clergy, he was content to make his way methodically up the ladder of preferment, showing due loyalty to his superiors. It was in the privacy of his study that a different man might have been observed. He had accumulated a library far more extensive than was warranted by the requirements of preaching to a rural congregation. Having mastered Greek as well as Latin, he avidly sought out the latest offerings from the humanist presses on both sides of the Alps. He was excited and inspired by the thrust of new thinking emanating from Erasmian circles and was among those who hurried to Basel in 1515 or 1516 to obtain an introduction to the great man. He exchanged letters with Erasmus. He corresponded with Myconius, Froben, Amerbach, Capito, Reuchlin, Oecolampadius, Wimpfelling, Pellican and other international humanists, excitedly debating issues arising from his reading. The *Novum Instrumentum* was a revelation to him. The purified Greek text with its Latin commentary exposed the shortcomings of the Vulgate and the weak foundations upon which parts of the Church's doctrinal edifice rested. He heard for the first time the siren song of Scripture, free from extraneous noises and distorting echoes. And he was completely seduced. One of the young priest's closest friends was Oswald Myconius and it was he who later described the relationship which changed Zwingli's life:

> For his personal use, he copied out all the Pauline letters, to soak himself in them. . . . Later, he did the same with all the other books of the New Testament. . . . And in order not to err, or lead others astray with a false picture of the Spirit, he compared scriptural passages with each other. . . . Thus knowledge of the Scriptures, so long suppressed to the detriment of men's souls, was reinstated in the happiest possible way.[1]

Studying and preaching the unadulterated word of God – it was exactly what Erasmus had long been advocating. Zwingli was clearly destined for better things than the relative obscurity of Einsiedeln. His humanist friends wanted him to have a more public platform. At the end of 1518 Myconius, who seems to have been something of a 'fixer', was among those who secured his appointment as priest and preacher in the minster at Zurich.

During the second half of Holbein's stay in Lucerne the intellectual world of Europe was in a state of high excitement. It seemed that the humanist revolution of which Erasmus had spoken to his intimates was about to break forth. Other writers and preachers had weakened the ramparts of convention and prejudice but it was Luther who opened up the first breach. The Wittenberg monk's earliest published works took up three aspects of the Erasmian manifesto: they advocated inward religion; attacked ecclesiastical abuses; and set forth the basics of Christian faith in straightforward vernacular that anyone could understand. The impact in humanist circles and beyond was immediate. Martin Bucer, the Strasbourg reformer, spoke for many when he observed, 'That which Erasmus insinuates [Luther] speaks openly and freely.'[2]

Printers clamoured to publish the works of this new best-selling author. Froben brought out an edition in 1518 of the ninety-five theses and a longer theological exposition of Luther's teaching on indulgences, but it was Adam Petri who, because he specialized in popular rather than scholarly literature, became Luther's principal Basel publisher. He printed the Wittenberger's version of *A German Theology*, written originally by an anonymous fourteenth-century mystic. This struck a common chord with hundreds of devout lay men and women. Seldom before had a religious teacher appeared who appealed so immediately to readers in the ivory tower, the counting house and the farm kitchen. Luther's instant appeal prompted other radicals to rush into print. Within months treatises, pamphlets and polemical tracts were jostling each other on the printshop stands. Basel became the centre for the dissemination of Lutheran literature throughout Switzerland and southern Germany.

This was intolerable to the forces of reaction. The pope instructed Luther's order to bring their errant son under control. In April 1518 he was summoned to Heidelberg to appear before the Augustinian chapter. His enemies gloated, asserting that he would end up on the stake – if he was not assassinated *en route*. But Luther's superiors dealt leniently with him, and the whole episode only provided more publicity for Brother Martin's ideas. Several of Holbein's friends travelled down the Rhine from Basel to see this new phenomenon. Yet more of the artist's acquaintances caught a glimpse of the monk six months later when he was bidden to Augsburg to explain his conduct to the pope's representative.

Meanwhile, the pamphlet war grew hotter. Luther's more intemperate supporters did not hesitate to draw from the controversy the logical conclusion that he had so far avoided: if the pope rejected the judgement of Scripture, he could not be accepted as God's vicar. There were few informed men and women in the empire who did not take sides in this *cause célèbre*, particularly as it rapidly assumed a nationalist complexion. Luther became a symbol of the German Church and people standing up to a degenerate Italian papacy whose financial exactions and political demands were becoming more intolerable year by year.

In Zurich, Ulrich Zwingli was in no doubt about which side of the argument he stood on. Soon after his appointment indulgence-mongers appeared in the city. Zwingli denounced them. He had the support of the council, who had no desire to see Wittenberg's problems duplicated within their jurisdiction. On this occasion there were no confrontations, no pulpit disputations or pamphlet campaigns. The Vatican simply ordered the indulgence-sellers to leave the city. It was a non-event, but it had established a precedent: the leading citizens had challenged ecclesiastical authority on a spiritual issue and they had won. At the same time many of them were responding warmly to their new preacher. Zwingli was attracting growing congregations with his straightforward biblical exegesis, his insistence on personal faith rather than reliance on the ministrations of the clergy, and his fearless attacks on moral and political abuses in the life of the state. There were others, particularly among the cathedral clergy, who found the radical drift alarming. They complained that Zwingli was not showing due respect for religious images or the Virgin Mary; that he was casting doubt on the doctrines of purgatory and intercessions for the dead; that he was raising disputed matters with the laity which were best kept within professional circles; that he was denouncing the mercenary system. The battle lines were being drawn.

Each city made its own response to the new ideas. Everything depended upon the balance of parties among the clergy and civic leaders. Lucerne had long been and would remain the standard-bearer of papal authority among the Swiss cantons. Myconius, who returned to his home town in 1519, wrote to Zwingli to report on the growing hostility there to religious change. Lucerne's economy was based more on agriculture than trade. Mercantile and craft guilds were less prominent in government. Ancient landholding families, like the Hertensteins, held sway and ensured the dominance of tradition and conservative values. The social and economic differences between Lucerne and the cities of the plain reinforced normal rivalries and ensured that the intellectual fashions in one would be resisted in the other. After two or three years vainly attempting to introduce humanistic reform, Myconius was dismissed from his post (1522). He turned his back on the city of his birth for the more congenial atmosphere of Zwingli's Zurich. Before then, and perhaps for not totally dissimilar reasons, Holbein had made his way back to Basel.

Chapter 4

BASEL

1519–1523

The city to which Hans now returned was, like much of German-speaking Europe, in a state of increasing intellectual turbulence. The movement which had begun as an academic critique of medieval Catholicism was rapidly becoming one of heretical revolt. Rome had responded violently to Luther's *95 Theses* and the reformer had been excommunicated in the papal bull, *Exsurge Domine*. Thereafter the quarrel was taken up via a multitude of books, pamphlets, broadsides and propagandist prints which poured from the presses all over Europe.

All this meant that for artists there was work aplenty. As well as paintings expressing traditional devotion for churches and pious lay donors there were illustrations to be provided for items of religious polemic. During the years 1519–23 Holbein produced a range of religious paintings and engravings. This has led some art historians to suggest that Holbein lacked deep commitment or, at least, that he was not partisan. Such a view cannot be sustained if we understand something of the milieu in which the artist worked. He was a thoughtful young man trying to find his own religious and philosophical way in a world buffeted by several winds of change. His own developing ideas were reflected in his work.

Let us first consider three dramatic woodcuts commissioned from him in connection with the theological disputes of the day. The first is called *The German Hercules* and it is a very violent depiction of Martin Luther. It depicts the polemical monk as the ancient hero. He is laying about him with a spiked club and has vanquished scholasticism in the persons of Aristotle, Aquinas, Occam, Duns Scotus and Nicholas of Lyra. He is about to despatch Jakob von Hochstraten, the leading opponent of Reuchlin. All the while, the pope, like a hanged felon, is suspended from the reformer's nose. The accompanying text drives home the point:

See how mightily he hits out at the mad sophists, and how his stout club punishes the savage dogs . . . acknowledge him as a brave man and a master, your equal as an opponent to whom once before, when you were hit, you surrendered in defeat . . . enough errors have been committed. Be wise; purify yourself or the unclean serpent of Lerna [the Hydra] awaits you with its hellish flame.[1]

The engraving might at first sight seem to be a piece of pro-Lutheran propaganda but that is not how contemporaries viewed it in the 1520s. Many of the reformer's friends were, in fact, incensed by the likening of their leader to the classical hero who overcame by brute force the triple-bodied giant Geryon (here represented by the triple-tiaraed pope). It seemed to support the language of the 1520 papal bull, *Exsurge Domine*, which condemned Luther as a wild boar in the vineyard. Where, then, did the picture and its anonymous accompanying text originate? One leading Lutheran had little doubt.

I do not know if Erasmus himself is the author. I only know that the proverb 'to suspend by the nose' [coined by Horace] was once mentioned in his company; that this tag stimulated him to depict the tragedy of it in words; and that in addition one of those present drew a rapid sketch. But I hear that the whole outrage is being laid at Erasmus's door, a suspicion which is strengthened by the press which issued it.[2]

The message of the picture fits well with Erasmus's current attitude towards the German reformer. Their paths, once running parallel, had separated, not because they differed in their concern to purify the Church, but because Erasmus deplored Luther's aggressive language and because Luther accused Erasmus of being a faint-hearted fence-sitter. The occasion for this mini-pamphlet may have been the election of Adrian VI in August 1522. Adrian Florenszoon Boeyens, the last non-Italian pope for four-and-a-half centuries, was an old friend and tutor of Erasmus from Louvain. He was an earnest reformer who fully recognized the corruption of the Vatican and its unpopularity north of the Alps. He was the kind of pope who might see the wisdom of the course of action recommended in the 'German Hercules' engraving. 'Look,' the lampoon seems to say, 'Luther is fully justified in most of his complaints and it is useless to hurl anathemas at him. Instead, it would be wise to treat him with respect; to address the abuses to which he has drawn attention; to learn from the wrong tactics of the past.' Unfortunately, if the appeal was made to an eirenically-minded pope, it failed of its purpose; Adrian VI was dead within the year.

The second engraving could also be regarded as illustrating a humanist agenda. *Christ as the Light of the World* was in praise of the open Bible. On the left of the picture Jesus pointed peasants and simple townsmen to a brilliant candle flame representing the Gospel. On the other side, the pope, scholars and monks, having turned their backs on this light, were following Plato and Aristotle into a black pit. There was nothing revolutionary in the idea. Christian humanists had long complained about the Aristotelianism of the scholastics and, while welcoming the benefits of classical studies, had warned against pagan philosophy. In a little treatise on Bible study written in 1522 Zwingli used the same imagery: philosophy was a pale, uncertain human light which flickered feebly beside the radiant torch of revealed truth. What was new was the illustration of such ideas. When criticism of spiritual and intellectual leaders was made pictorially vivid, and therefore accessible to a wide audience, it became potentially much more disruptive than elegant Latin diatribes designed for an intellectual elite.

The other picture, *The Sale of Indulgences,* went much further. Again the viewer was presented with a stark contrast. To the left an open-handed God was seen freely forgiving the repentant figures of King David (an adulterer), King Manasseh (an apostate) and an anonymous supplicant labelled 'Flagrant Sinner'. The other half depicted a busy scene of indulgence-hawking, the pope having authorized a rapacious crew of Dominicans to sell heavenly favours for cash. What made this lampoon particularly subversive was the clear identification of the pontiff as Leo X. The Medici arms were represented no lesss than ten times on the walls of the hall where the scandalous transactions were taking place.

Erasmus would never have sanctioned this blatant attack on Leo X. As early as May 1519 he had admonished Luther,

It is more advisable to scream out against those who abuse papal authority than against the popes themselves. . . . We should not so much disdain the schools as call them back to a more sensible form

of scholarship. . . . On all occasions one must be cautious not to say
or to do anything with arrogance or a party spirit[3]

The scholar who only months before had forecast an anticyclone
of enlightenment now read the meterorological signs very differently.
Fervid storm clouds were gathering. Vigorously he set about
detaching himself from the men who, a decade later, would be called
Protestants. Erasmus was afflicted with that naivety, not rare among
highly intelligent men, which prevented him from foreseeing the
results of his own words and deeds. He genuinely believed that
contemporary life and manners could be transformed by reasoned
debate. He was convinced that corruption in Church and state could
be cut out by the silver sickle of sharp, elegant prose. He rejected the
warnings of those who said that the excitement of an open Bible and
simple Gospel-teaching would go to men's heads and that doctrinal
error could not be challenged without provoking anger against those
responsible for it.

It is unfortunate that we cannot tie *Christ the Light of the World* and
The Sale of Indulgences to specific tracts. However, we can relate both
visual images to Lutheran propaganda. The German monk was as
forthright as the humanist scholars in denouncing the sterile methods
of the medieval schoolmen and their blind following of Aristotle. In
theological treatises and printed sermons he frequently contrasted the
obscure and convuluted teachings of the philosophers with the clear
light of Scripture which testified to Christ. Luther's condemnation of
indulgences was, of course, the launchpad for his attack on the whole
Catholic system. In a pamphlet of 1521 against *Exsurge Domine* he
specifically drew on the example of King Manasseh, whose
repentance drew forth free divine forgiveness in contrast with the
pope who claimed to have grace for sale.[4] In making the drawings for
these woodcuts Holbein was, of course, following the instructions of
printers and patrons but he was also displaying his own clear grasp of
the issues at stake.

In considering these polemical works as a group we have got
slightly ahead of our story. When Hans returned from staid, conservative Lucerne in the summer of 1519 it was to take up residence
once more in a city where there was a stimulating intellectual climate
as well as friends and patrons who would help him to acquire new
commissions. But such considerations did not provide the immediate

occasion for his move. That had something to do with his relationship with his brother.

Hans's reappearance in Basel coincided with Ambrosius's 'departure' from the city. What became of the elder Holbein is a mystery. The last mention of his name in official records was in June 1518, when he took out citizenship. At that time he was in straitened circumstances for he could find only a quarter of the necessary fee: the remainder was supplied by Jörg Schweiger, who is described in the records as a goldsmith but who almost certainly included money-lending among his business activities. The portrait Ambrosius made of the sharp-featured Schweiger is likely to have been a part payment of this debt. We know that, later in 1518, he was working for the publisher, Adam Petri, on a set of engraved plates for a forthcoming book but he never completed the commission. When the volume was published the following April only four of the illustrations were by Ambrosius.

It is traditionally supposed that Ambrosius died some time in late 1518 or early 1519. That is the simplest explanation for the young man's disappearance but we should not rush to accept it. Ambrosius Holbein is not the only Renaissance artist whose name vanishes abruptly from the record. In some cases this is because art did not, for some, remain a lifetime avocation. Some abandoned it for reasons of principle. Grünewald turned his back on painting out of religious conviction. So, probably, did Hans Herbst. Such craftsmen were far from being alone in an age when many men were involved in deep soul-searching. More artists gave up for economic reasons; they simply could not make a living. Ambrosius may have been one such, lost to history simply because he laid aside his brushes and pencils. His attempt to establish his own atelier in Basel had failed. Unlike Hans, he did not attract any major commissions and he had even been reduced to going to Lucerne to work for his brother. He never became an independent master. For full guild membership marriage and citizenship were both required. Ambrosius, with difficulty, met the latter qualification but he never took a wife. Unable to afford a domestic establishment he could not be regarded as a substantial member of the community. A sense of failure may well have forced upon the young man the necessity of doing something else with his life in a new location or, perhaps, back in Augsburg.

Even if we accept death as the best working hypothesis we do not know how Ambrosius came by it. All manner of diseases were rife and few sixteenth-century men and women survived beyond what we consider as middle age. Yet who is to say that an intense young man, depressed by failure, did not die by his own hand? Every year scores of suicide and murder victims were fished out of the Rhine.

However we account for Ambrosius's abrupt departure from Basel, it certainly opened the way for his brother's return. The alacrity with which Hans now established himself adds weight to the suggestion that bad blood had existed between the siblings. As soon as the elder was out of the way, the younger hurriedly abandoned his self-imposed exile in order to take up again the life in Basel he had abandoned in 1517. He joined the painters' guild. Within a year he had taken out Basel citizenship and become an independent chamber master of his confraternity working from his own house. He had also married.

Elsbeth Schmid was a few years older than Hans. Since the Battle of Marignano she had been a widow bringing up an infant son and running her late husband's tanning business. Possibly the elder Holbein, with his own knowledge of the leather trade, knew the family and, anxious to see his son settled, used his influence to bring about a match. The marriage was certainly a very suitable business–domestic arrangement. Outside the convent, manlessness was a difficult state for a young woman to sustain. It inevitably carried a measure of insecurity and the possibility of scandal. A husband brought regularity, both domestic and social, into Elsbeth's life. For his part, Hans obtained a partner for bed and board, a cash dowry and the income from the tannery, all of which were of considerable help for an artist setting up his own studio. All this is not to say that there was no affection between the newlyweds. Hans painted his wife's portrait in 1523 or 1524 (the painting in The Hague is accepted by most scholars as being of Elsbeth Holbein, although some demur). The pose was not far removed from that of Leonardo's *Gioconda* and was suffused with a similar tranquillity. Hans saw his bride as a serene and kindly woman and that is what he painted. Within the first year of their married life the Holbeins had a son, who was named Philip.

Once Hans was resettled his old friends and patrons commissioned more paintings, engravings and designs and were influential in introducing the artist to new customers. Even the percentage of Holbein's sketches and finished works which survive must have kept him and his assistants very busy during the early years of his return to Basel. It is significant that one of the very first paintings he undertook was a portrait of his friend and ardent supporter, Bonifacius Amerbach (see plate section). This charming study of a man Holbein knew and liked very well is freer, more closely observed and altogether more accomplished than the portraits of the Meyers, executed three years earlier. The background is less elaborate – writhing vine leaves and a suggestion of distant mountains. The jurist's dress is simple – a black cap and academic gown over a green brocade doublet. This enables attention to be fully focused on the refined, 'poetic' features of Amerbach and the tablet hanging on the tree beside him. The portrait inscription was a convention more common in northern art than in that of Italy and was used to identify sitters, add information or provide moral comment. In this instance the Latin legend, provided by Amerbach, extols the skill of the artist. Playing on the word *picta*, which can mean both 'painted' and 'unreal', it reads: 'I may be painted/unreal but I am not inferior to life. I am my master's true likeness as he was at eight times three years. In me the skill of art truly describes what nature has formed. Bon. Amerbach, painted by Holbein 1519, the day preceding the ides of October [the 14th].'

The young lawyer was impressed with his friend's commitment to the humanist principle of seeking out and representing objective truth. He had already committed himself to collecting Holbein sketches and finished works. It must have been due, in part, to Amerbach's enthusiasm that Hans painted other members of the scholar's circle, including Johannes Froben (1522), and made various studies of Erasmus himself (to which we shall return). Members of the international humanist brotherhood, as well as maintaining a vigorous correspondence with each other, had taken to exchanging keepsakes. Sometimes this included portraits drawn on paper or painted on small panels and box lids. There was rather more than the expression of friendship to such gestures: by commissioning a likeness of himself a humanist scholar was abandoning the old shibboleths denouncing vanity and was making a positive statement, not about his own importance, but about the purposes of a God who delighted in his creation. Several of Holbein's finished works and sketches were ordered for presentation gifts.

However, the type of painting for which the artist is most remembered formed a very small part of his output in the 1520s. What the wealthy burghers of Basel most clamorously wanted of Holbein was the showy decorative frescos he had produced in Lucerne. As soon as he returned, he got down to work on the façade of the Amerbachs' house in Rheingasse, *zum Kaiserstuhl*. Within months its plain exterior was resplendent with *trompe-l'oeil* classical columns and a representation of the enthroned Emperor Charlemagne. Similar commissions followed. The goldsmith Balthasar Angelrot wanted his residence down by the Rhine bridge embellished. So successful was Holbein in creating a vigorous combination of architectural fancies and human figures that the name of the house was permanently changed in local parlance. Part of the décor was given over to a frieze depicting an energetic *Kermesse* or peasant dance. This immediately caught the imagination of the Baselers, who thereafter dubbed *chez* Angelrot the *Haus zum Tanz*.

The fashion for elaborate painted exteriors caught on rapidly. The wealthy quarter of Basel took on a colourful and lively appearance as Holbein and his assistants, as well as rival ateliers, covered previously bare walls with exotic designs. There were no limits to the subject matter which might be treated in these murals. Classical and biblical stories, legends, religious subjects, moralizing tales, scenes from contemporary life – all were grist to the painters' mill. The only obligatory requirement was that of deceiving the eye of the beholder – of turning blank surfaces into verdant glades, classical façades, elegant ruins or sumptuous interiors inhabited by seemingly real people. These painterly conjuring tricks enabled artists to flaunt their virtuosity – their grasp of perspective and foreshortening, their use of line and colour to create spatial illusions. The sixteenth-century originals have long-since faded and peeled. Most of the buildings they adorned have become victims of redevelopment. But the techniques can still be observed on the exterior of Basel's town hall and on other structures in the towns of Switzerland and south Germany where civic authorities have preserved or recreated something of the glories of the past.

The originals may have disappeared but, thanks largely to Bonifacius Amerbach, several of Holbein's preparatory drawings have been preserved in the print room of the Basel Kunstmuseum. These are the designs that he showed to prospective clients. A few of them are monogrammed, which suggests that the artist sold or gave to friends items with which he was particularly pleased. It is astonishing how much time, effort and skill Holbein expended on large-scale works such as these which, as well as being poorly paid, were open to the elements and visibly deteriorated unless frequently touched up.

He seems to have particularly enjoyed executing *tours de force* and was engaged on such projects throughout his career. He who could prepare intricate detailed drawings for blockmakers and jewellers with eye-straining diligence could unleash himself when he had several square metres of wall at his disposal. Yet there was certainly no loose-ness of treatment in Holbein's larger paintings. Every feature was delineated with care; every figure was well observed.

His intriguing pen and watercolour drawing of the ship of drunkards – perhaps a version of the traditional ship of fools – is a case in point (see plate section). The vessel is smaller than reality in relation to its passengers but its rigging, planking and accoutrements are faithfully itemized. Each member of its carousing crew is presented as an individual. A drummer and piper play martial music. Soldiers strike bellicose attitudes or engage in dalliance. Some sailors swill wine, fight or vomit and lookouts neglect their duty while a couple of more sober colleagues haul on ropes in an attempt to trim the sails. Beneath the stern, rowers strain to bring a boat alongside the disaster-bound ship but whether to restore sanity or join in the party is not clear. The spirit of this absurdly laden barque is reminiscent of the *Moria,* but in this case no words are needed to embellish the cynical lampoon of human folly.

Whether making fun of his fellow creatures or simply observing them, Holbein was more at home upon the terra firma of human behaviour than in the ethereal blue of theory and speculation. This emerges increasingly strongly in his religious subjects. After his return to Basel Hans was much employed by Church officials and pious individuals to make paintings and window designs as aids to worship and devotion. His changing treatment of orthodox truth was, in part, a reaction to the quickening pace of Reformation in Switzerland.

At the same time that Holbein was taking up his life in Basel something much more significant occurred in Zurich. If the posting of the ninety-five theses was the overture of the Reformation, this event was the dramatic conclusion of Act I: Ulrich Zwingli was saved from death by, as he believed, divine intervention. Performing his priestly duties in the plague-visited city, he succumbed to the disease which was carrying off a quarter of the population. On what was likely to be his deathbed, he invoked no saints. He did not seek the Church's traditional ministrations. He cast himself solely upon God's mercy. When the crisis passed, he knew that he had been spared for a divine mission and that the one who had drawn him back from the very brink of the next world would protect him in all mere worldly perils (a conviction probably fortified when a brother died of plague only a few months later). This paroxysmal experience was his call to prophecy. It confirmed his determination to preach only from the Bible. It ranged him squarely alongside Luther, whose followers were now being openly threatened with the stake.

Conservative clergy were not slow to react. Zurich pulpits rang with denunciatory oratory. Congregations listened with increasing levels of commitment to evangelical and traditionalist sermons. In 1520 the council, in an attempt to smother the flames of controversy, decreed that preaching must be based upon the Bible and should avoid debate of contentious novelties. It was too little, too late, and, in that it was an incursion by the civil authority into spiritual matters, this edict in effect played into the hands of the reformers.

Basel's city government did not take a similar step until 1523. In the months prior to this decision, it had been facing other, though not unrelated, problems. Power politics in the city states of Europe always had a religious dimension and this was certainly the case in Basel. Episcopal control had been declining for decades and, in 1521, the council shook itself free from the final vestiges of outside influence when it decreed that the bishop should henceforth have no say in civic elections. But this by no means marked the end of Basel's power struggle. The very fact that it enhanced the authority of the Little Council, representing the city's mercantile elite, aroused the discontent of those who felt that their interests were not being represented. In 1521 the craft guilds (including the painters' guild, the Zunft zum Himmel) held a series of angry demonstrations. They campaigned against the powerlessness of the Great Council, which was little more than a rubber-stamp for the decisions of the legislative body. They protested about the economic privileges enjoyed by the clergy and by members of the gentlemen's guilds. And they angrily denounced government corruption.

The main targets of their indignation were the *Kronenfresser,* the 'crown-eaters'. In the shifting boardgame of Habsburg–Valois rivalry the Swiss Confederation was a vitally important counter. France and the empire both needed the cantons' mercenary forces, and tried to draw the league into military alliance. The French embarked on a crude policy of vote-buying. Gold flowed into the purses of influential councillors and, as a result, all the Confederation members except Zurich voted, in the spring of 1521, for the Valois alliance. In Basel this decision was vastly unpopular. Most guild members were sympathetic towards the emperor and furious with sleazy oligarchs who had ignored public opinion and what they perceived to be the best interests of the city for the sake of lining their own pockets. This gave rise to more angry protests. So fierce was the opposition that the Little Council bowed to it. The offending *Kronenfresser* were indicted and made to yield up their corrupt gains. One of those whose career took a hard knock was Holbein's enthusiastic patron Jakob Meyer. Since 1516 he had been elected for further terms as burgomaster in 1518 and 1520. Now, he not only suffered financially, but he served a short prison term, and was barred from public office. Meyer was not the sort of man to accept meekly such a humiliating reverse. Over the ensuing years he fought bitterly against 'extremist' and 'jealous' enemies and eventually emerged as the leader of the Catholic party on the Little Council.

There was a religious colour to all these disputes. Top ecclesiastics and citizens who enjoyed positions of political power were in favour of the status quo and tended to conservativism in matters of faith as well as civic policy. Struggling artisans were more likely to join the groundswell of support for change. They were contending, not for abstract political and theological ideas, but for their livelihoods and against 'unfair' privileges claimed by the often 'unworthy' leaders of Church and city. Such radicals were temperamentally inclined towards 'Lutheranism' (as all religious innovation tended to be labelled in the early 1520s) and the emancipating emphasis upon personal salvation without the need for priestly mediation and rejection of spiritual pressures to support ecclesiastical institutions. These lower orders of Basel life could not be ignored. In order to preserve peace and order, the Little Council were obliged to take their complaints seriously. This was seen not only in the drawing up of new trading regulations and the punishment of corrupt officials but in the injunctions about biblical preaching.

But the turbulent waters of dissent were now in too much turmoil to be calmed by application of the oil of moderate reform. The people had developed a taste for protest and demonstration. Inspired by the growing number of evangelical preachers, groups of extremists disobeyed the lenten rules in 1522 and attempted to break up church processions. On the feast of Corpus Christi, the parish priest of St Alban's church, instead of displaying holy relics, as was customary, elevated the Bible for the congregation to gaze upon. Such small acts of defiance assumed a cumulative significance, particularly when seen against the background of more rapid and turbulent change else- where. The Little Council were at a loss how to strike a balance between concession and discipline. They removed the evangelical Tilman Limperger from his cathedral preachership in favour of a safe traditionalist, but they were lenient in punishing those who disturbed the peace on religious grounds. Baselian toleration was too firmly entrenched for the civic leaders to resort to those hard measures which, elsewhere, were provoking more violent reform.

It was the comparative peace of Basel which brought Erasmus back to the city in 1521. The last three years, spent at Louvain, had been years of mounting pain and anguish. He was profoundly disturbed by the conflict between Wittenberg and Rome, with partisans of both sides pestering him to join in the fray.

> Hear me, knight of Christ, ride out beside the Lord Jesus Christ. Defend the truth and earn for yourself the martyr's crown. . . . I have heard you say that you have allowed yourself two more years in which you will be fit enough to work. Spend them well in the service of the Gospel and true Christian faith. . . . Take your stand on this side, so that God may be proud of you.

So Albrecht Dürer exhorted Erasmus in May 1521 on hearing a false report of Luther's death (though only in the privacy of his diary). Erasmus was increasingly bitter about former friends and colleagues who were abandoning the middle ground of *philosophia Christi* for the embattled heights of Lutheranism or Catholicism. And he resented having to defend himself against the charge that it was his challenges to orthodoxy that had started the whole war. Now this lover of a quiet life came to seek respite among old friends in an atmosphere of moderate scholarship. He lived with the Frobens, who provided him with the facilities for peaceful study. But Basel was not the haven Erasmus was seeking, and his very presence there transformed it into a focal point of the Reformation. As the troubled 1520s advanced, combatants watched to see which way Basel and its most famous resident would move.

One of the Dutchman's first visitors was Ulrich Zwingli. The Zurich reformer was scrupulously and painstakingly working his way from biblical first principles towards a radical position which would take him beyond Luther. When he arrived in Basel early in 1522 he had either just married or was about to do so. This defiance of Catholic precept was based on the conviction that the Church had no right to decree a celibate priesthood which had no scriptural justification and that honest marriage was the only way to avoid adding to the sexual scandals which were already rife. Zwingli eagerly sought his hero's support for this and for other innovations. He tried to entice Erasmus to settle in Zurich with an offer of free citizenship. But the humanist was determined to distance himself. He had not escaped the Lutheran frying pan in order to leap into the Zwinglian fire. At first he held the Swiss reformer politely at arm's length but, by the end of the year, he was roundly upbraiding him, dismissing his latest anti-papal publication as 'another piece of nonsense, utter rubbish. . . . If all Luther's party are like this, I wash my hands of the whole lot of them. I never saw anything more mad than this foolish stuff.'[5]

By this time a very changed Oecolampadius had returned to Basel. Erasmus's erstwhile proof-reader and humanist colleague had gone through various intellectual and spiritual adventures and had emerged a convinced Lutheran. He now came back to occupy a chair in the theology faculty and to preach in St Martin's, a church in the very heart of Basel's business quarter. His theological pilgrimage was still not complete: he was very soon involved in a vigorous correspondence with Zwingli. Another old colleague who started teaching at the university around the same time was the Franciscan, Conrad Pellican. Erasmus was particularly fond of him but the friendship was not sufficiently elastic to stretch across a widening theological gulf as Pellican, too, came under the spell of Ulrich Zwingli (he moved to Zurich in 1526). Erasmus felt keenly the 'desertion' of men he had once regarded as dedicated disciples and heralds of the humanist dawn. His references in letters to those whose consciences impelled them towards more extreme views became ever more bitter: they were 'pseudo-evangelists', 'rabble pleasers', 'utterly seditious', 'lacking in sincerity', 'mangy men', 'savage tyrants'. For the moment he resisted all entreaties to venture into print against the 'disturbers of the Church', but his position on the fence grew increasingly uncomfortable by the month.

All this made him appreciate more and more the company of Basel friends who, whatever their opinions, believed in tolerant debate rather than public denunciation. He drew even closer to Johannes Froben, Bonifacius Amerbach and their circle – a circle of which Hans Holbein was now an established member. And in 1523 the artist joined the company of Massys and Dürer, contemporary masters who had been permitted to paint the likeness of Desiderius Erasmus (see plate section). So began one of the most remarkable relationships between artist and sitter in the history of portraiture.

It extended over a decade. Holbein made several painted and engraved portraits of the philosopher between 1522–3 and his final departure for England. The first dated examples known from surviving originals or copies were executed in 1523. They are revealing on several counts. Sketches preserved now in Basel suggest that Holbein worked particularly hard at these commissions. He made especially careful drawings of the scholar's hands – those precious hands that were constantly engaged in the production of wise, elegant prose both in books and in tireless correspondence. The depiction of character is masterly. Only in Holbein's representations of Erasmus and Thomas More can we test the artist's perception against what the subjects themselves have revealed through their writings. The 1523 portraits augment with astonishing accuracy the impression we gain from reading Erasmus's literary legacy. The hands are delicate, resting lightly on book and paper, or holding a pen with relaxed yet purposeful grip. The lips are thin with the faintest suggestion of a superior smile. The facial flesh of the fifty-seven-year-old academic is beginning to tighten over the skull beneath, suggesting a man of abstemious habits rather than indulgence. There are few lines etched in its surface and the eyes look from it with shrewd detachment. Holbein shows us a fastidious, withdrawn man, wrapped in a thick, fur-trimmed gown to keep the draughts at bay during the long hours spent standing at his desk. Erasmus was delighted with the likenesses. Though, in describing them to a friend, he came close to damning with faint praise – reporting that they had been produced by 'a not unskilful artist' – he demonstrated his admiration of Holbein's talent by commissioning further portraits and portrait engravings. He certainly thought more highly of Holbein than of Dürer as a limner.

Yet the most interesting impression given by these 1523 studies is

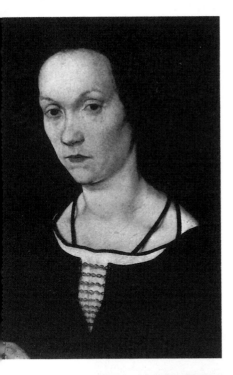

(*left*) *Portrait of a Woman*, Hans Holbein
the Elder, *c.*1520
(Musée d'Unterlinden, Colmar)

(*below*) *The Basilica of St Paul*, detail,
Hans Holbein the Elder, 1504
(Staatliche, Gemaldegalerie, Augsburg)

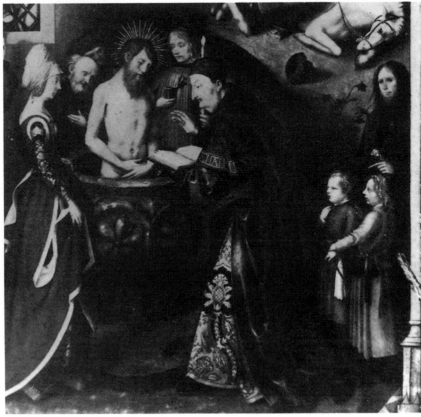

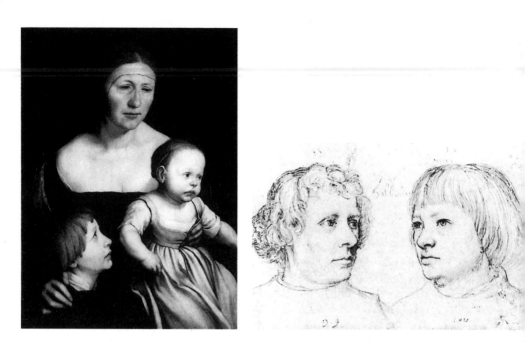

(*left*) *Portrait of the Artist's Family*, *c*.1528 (Öffentliche Kunstammlung, Basel)
(*right*) Ambrosius and Hans Holbein, drawing, Hans Holbein the Elder, 1511
(Staatliche Museen, Berlin)

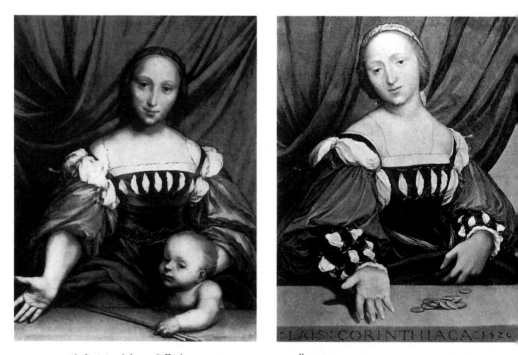

(*left*) *Magdalena Offenburg as Venus*, *c*.1526 (Öffentliche Kunstammlung, Basel)
(*right*) *Magdalena Offenburg as Lais Corinthiaca*, *c*.1526
(Öffentliche Kunstammlung, Basel)

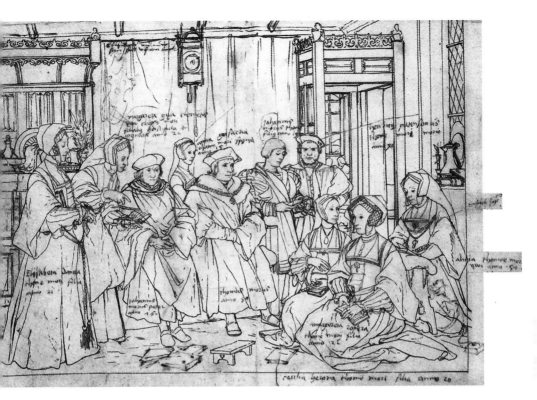

(**above**) *Thomas More, his Father and his Household*, drawing, *c*.1527
(Kupferstichkabinett, Basel)
(**below**) *Thomas More, his Father and his Household*, signed 'Rowlandas Lockey 1530'
(Nostell Priory, Wakefield; National Trust)

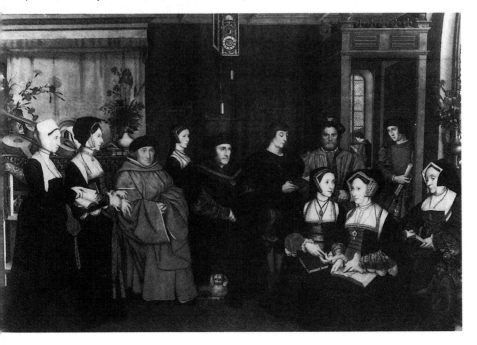

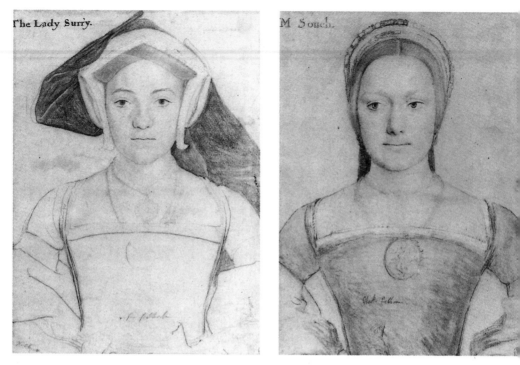

The Lady Surry.

M Souch.

(*left*) Frances, Countess of Surrey, drawing, *c*.1532 (The Royal Collection
© H.M. the Queen)
(*right*) Mary Zouch, drawing, *c*.1532 (The Royal Collection © H.M. the Queen)

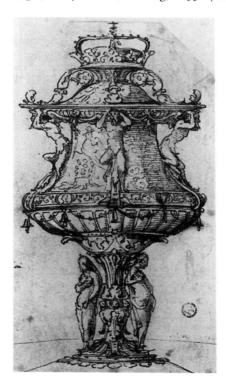

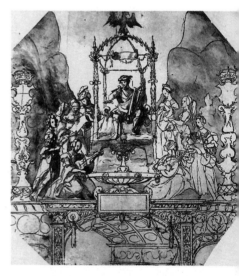

(*left*) Ceremonial cup designed for
Anne Boleyn, *c*.1533
(Kupferstichkabinett, Basel)
(*right*) Triumphal arch designed for Anne
Boleyn's coronation procession, 1533
(Staatliche Museen, Berlin)

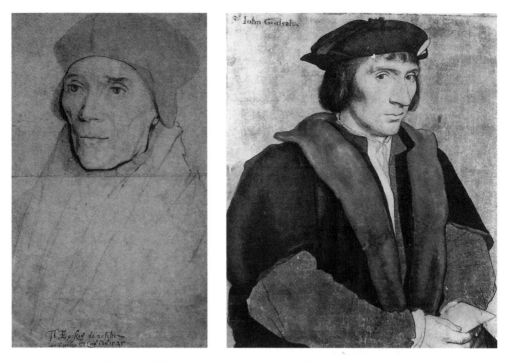

(*left*) John Fisher, Bishop of Rochester, drawing, 1535 (The Royal Collection
© H.M. the Queen)
(*right*) John Gonsalve, drawing, *c.*1536 (The Royal Collection © H.M. the Queen)

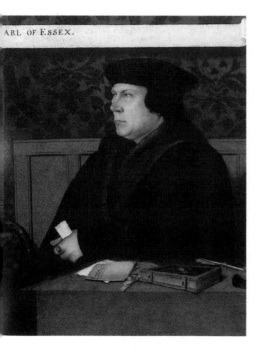

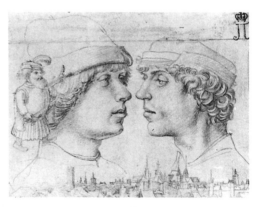

(*left*) Thomas Cromwell, 1st Earl of Essex,
after Hans Holbein the Younger, *c.*1530
(National Portrait Gallery, London)
(*right*) Portraits of Two Youths, a Dwarf
and a Townscape, drawing, *c.*1514
(The Hermitage, St Petersburg)

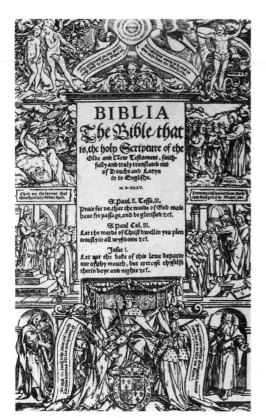

(*left*) Title-page of Coverdale's English translation of the Bible, first printed in 1535 (British Museum, London)

(*below*) *The Tudor Dynasty*, Remigius van Leemput, after Hans Holbein the Younger, 1537 (The Royal Collection © H.M. the Queen)

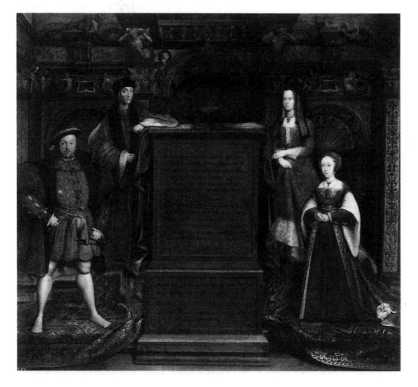

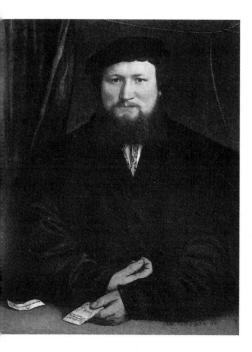

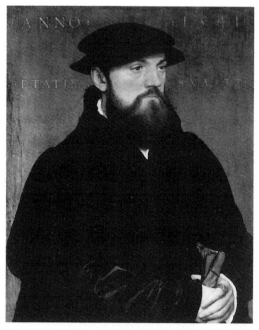

(*left*) Derich Berck, 1536
(Metropolitan Museum of Art,
New York; the Jules S. Bache
Collection)
(*right*) De Vos van Steenwijk, 1541
(Staatliche Museen, Berlin)

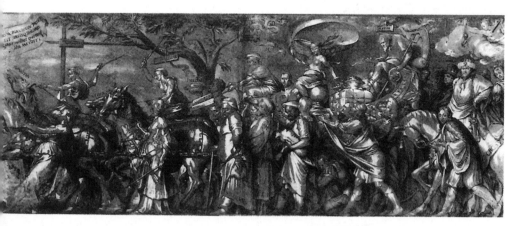

(*above*) *The Triumph of Riches*, Lucas Vorsterman the Elder, after Hans Holbein
the Younger, n.d. (Ashmolean Museum, Oxford)

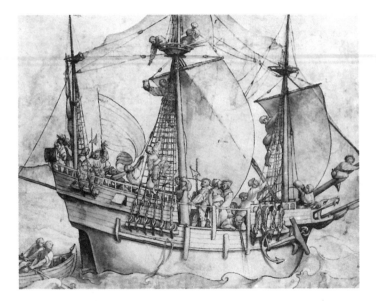

(*top*) *Ship of Fools*, watercolour, n.d. (Kupferstichkabinett, Basel)
(*bottom*) *The Old and the New Law*, c.1535 (National Gallery of Scotland, Edinburgh)

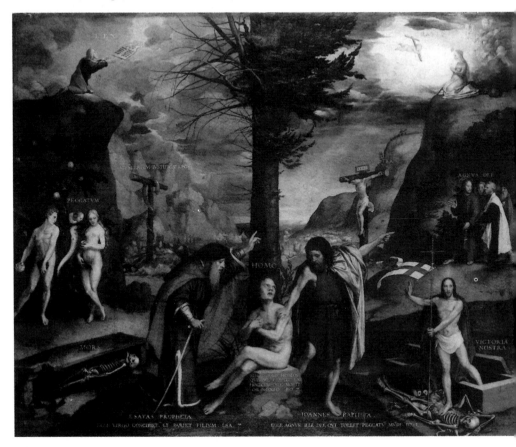

of a certain intimacy between artist and sitter. The sense of having been admitted to the great man's inner sanctum is not entirely due to Holbein's skill. There is about these portraits a feeling of relaxed informality. It is most marked in the version now in the Louvre. The spectator seems to be standing at the scholar's elbow, permitted to look on as he works at his paraphrase of Mark's Gospel. This is not a representation of Erasmus as he wished to be seen by the world; it is Erasmus supposedly caught off-guard as he wished to be remembered by the unknown English friend to whom it was despatched.

How close were the scholar and the artist? There was certainly a link of mutual admiration, and perhaps one of fellow feeling. One of the portraits contains Latin lines composed by Erasmus in praise of the painter. Erasmus, seemingly, was prepared to endorse the arrogance of an up-and-coming artist. In despatching portraits to his friends he was not only advancing his own cause; he was also drawing attention to the painter. In addition he was prepared to write elegant lines to commend the young man's talents. We do not know who had belittled those talents but it is commonplace for creative geniuses to provoke opposition and for them to be particularly sensitive to that opposition. Holbein would scarcely have been human if he had not resented the gibes of his detractors. No one felt more keenly than Erasmus the pain inflicted by the barbs of enemies and jealous rivals. Doubtless, this made him sympathetic towards the struggling Holbein and explains the sentiment expressed in the inscription on a painting soon to be sent to England. The lines devised by Erasmus – using wordplay, which the humanists loved – include letters that have become illegible, but they seem to read:

> Ille ego Joannes Holbein, en, non facile ullus.
> Tarn mini mimus erit quam mihi momus erat.
> (I am none other than the celebrated Johannes Holbein.
> My critics will become my emulators.)

But the respect Erasmus and Holbein afforded each other had no basis in professional equality. There was no question of the painter being able to enjoy comparable status with a scholar whose years of study and mastery of classical style had made him an intellectual giant. Holbein, according to the social evaluation of the time, was a mere technician, a man who, far from expressing his own ideas through his chosen medium, was paid to paint house fronts, execute costume designs and undertake routine jobs for the printers. He was not the sort of companion upon whom Erasmus could sharpen his wits, who would understand arcane classical allusions and applaud clever wordplay. Yet he shared many conversations on those days when he climbed the narrow staircase from the printworks to the Frobens' private quarters for another session with his sitter. Erasmus was not the sort of man to suffer fools gladly and we may be sure that Holbein would never have been able to complete his sequence of portraits if the great scholar had found his presence tedious. Not only did Erasmus make personal use of Holbein's talents, he also recommended him to friends.

The scholar had good reasons for commissioning portraits at this particular time. He felt himself to be growing old and his letters frequently harped on the imminence of death. He was in his late fifties at a time when three score years and ten was a generous allocation allowed to few. He wanted to leave mementoes for his friends – paintings which could be multiplied by copyists and engravers and thus enjoy a wide circulation. But distributing his likeness served another end. It was useful propaganda. The printing houses of Europe were the armaments factories of the ideological war. Pamphlets and pictures were produced in ever growing numbers to be bought by Reformation partisans. Luther's engraved images became something of an icon throughout much of northern Germany. Along with ribald lampoons, they were displayed in private houses and public places to inspire devotion or to reinforce opprobrium. One German doctor, incensed by the religious changes sweeping his country, bought an engraving of Erasmus so that he could pin it up in his house and spit at it every time he passed it.

Erasmus, openly at least, refused to enter the battle of words but he was increasingly concerned about the propaganda conflict, which only favoured the extremists of both sides. Let there be an end, he constantly urged, to insults, threats and bitter controversy. Let the pope declare an amnesty for all past offences. He wanted to hold together the humanist caucus; to keep in men's minds – and particularly in scholars' minds – the moderate option of gentle Catholic reform. This was the eirenic purpose behind his large, daily volume of correspondence. And he knew that if his programme was to be taken seriously he had to maintain a high personal profile.

Despite his frequent protestations of indifference to the opinions of men, he resented his declining influence. 'I, who was formerly described in innumerable letters as "the greatest hero of all", "the prince of letters", "the star of Germany", "the bright light of scholarship", "the high priest of good learning", "the champion of genuine theology", am now passed over in silence or far differently described.' So Erasmus complained to the pope in March 1523.[6] But he was not content to grumble, and the Holbein portraits were part of a positive programme of self-publicity.

As already indicated, we should not be persuaded by Holbein's closeness to Erasmus to label him an Erasmian. Art historians wanting to distance the artist from the more extreme elements of the Reformation, and certainly from those who vented their anti-Catholic spleen in violent iconoclasm, have tended to over-emphasize this connection. This enables them to portray the artist as a moderate and, therefore, as someone more to their taste. Thus, for example, Oskar Bätschmann and Pascal Griener, discussing the philosopher and the artist, insist, 'Both men refused to be drawn into the confessional controversy and to make their position clear.'[7] Erasmus, in fact, *was* drawn into the controversy – albeit reluctantly – and attacked Luther on the central theological issue of human free will and its relationship to divine grace. Holbein, too, developed his own religious perspective and it would take him steadily away from Erasmian detachment.

Various portraits of Erasmus done by Holbein have survived. Like the well-known painting of Thomas More, they speak volumes about the characters of this intellectual giant. But we must always remember that the examples of Holbein's work we can see today are merely those that, often by chance, have survived the ill-usage of time. The fact that we have physical evidence of Holbein's closeness to the Erasmian circle does not, of itself, indicate that he was a disciple of the humanist philosopher.

In any case, this 'circle' was not a brotherhood of totally like-minded souls. We need look no further than Johannes Froben. He was Erasmus's friend and host. The scholar stood godfather to one of his children. Yet, while Erasmus was deploring the spread of Lutheran polemic and boasting that he had not read any of the German's writings, Froben was reporting to Wittenberg that the reformer's books were selling as fast as they came off his presses; that major consignments were being exported; and that Zwingli had ordered several hundred for dissemination in Zurich. Froben's house, far from being the Erasmus campaign headquarters, was a centre of free debate. However much Holbein admired Erasmus and felt privileged to enjoy his company, he was no slavish follower of all the scholar's ideas.

Theological controversy accounted for only a small part of Holbein's output. Much of his time was devoted to painting and designing religious subjects for altarpieces, windows, books and items for private devotion. Art historians have scanned these works for evidence of transition from Gothic to Renaissance handling of subject matter. If we would learn something of the artist's understanding of religious verities we have to probe rather deeper. What was more important to Holbein than the techniques he learned in Augsburg and on his subsequent travels was the way he could use everything he knew to express what he felt about the sacred. When we look at what survives of his entire religious *oeuvre* between 1519 and 1523 we discover some remarkable facts about what moved him and how he was responding to early Reformation impulses.

Like any artist worth his salt, Holbein, while obliged to work within the prevailing conventions, strove to expand the boundaries of those conventions, both technically and emotionally. The more deeply he felt about the subject matter the more intensely he committed himself to its representation.

In most of his designs for stained-glass windows he was grappling with the problems of setting religious figures against classical architectural backgrounds and distant landscapes. Holbein was content to display saints with their traditional emblems and to use accepted stereotypes of Catholic devotion. But even in such subjects where the artist was given little room for originality we can detect new thinking. For example, if we compare his *Crowning of the Virgin* (c.1520) with Hans Baldung Grien's altarpiece of the same subject in Freiburg-im-Breisgau cathedral (c.1516) we can note significant conceptual differences within what was a highly conventionalized northern format. Baldung places the heads of the three main figures on the same level and has the Holy Spirit dove hovering above. Holbein rejects this elevation of Mary to visual equality with the Father and the Son. His members of the Trinity are on the same level and the Virgin, in a suitably humble pose, takes a lower station. Baldung's Christ, crowned and richly robed, holds the terrestrial globe as a possession. Holbein shows us the thin, scarred body of the Saviour. In his version it is God the Father who holds the world and also a cross, signifying his acceptance of the Son's sacrifice. For Holbein the exaltation of the Virgin has to be set within the divine scheme of redemption if it is to have any devotional impact.

Holbein made several studies of the Virgin and Child and the Holy Family for windows and for wall paintings in grisaille. He is not seen at his happiest in some of these attempts to depict simple, homely scenes against massive classical pillars and soaring arches. The most successful is a charming drawing in which the artist does not use an impressive architectural setting. This is one of the few sketches that Holbein signed and dated, which probably suggests that he was particularly pleased with it. It shows Mary as a young woman with long, windswept hair, teaching her son to walk. The mother and her child are not invested with hagiographic significance. A feathery halo is the only concession to conventional iconography. Mary and Jesus are warmly human. In his passion for *veritas*, Holbein declares, 'This is how it was or must have been: this is the simple truth before theologians and pietists got hold of it.'

Like other northern visitors to Italy, Holbein was impressed with Leonardo's already famous representation of the Last Supper. Soon after his return to Basel he painted a version, presumably for one of the city churches, of which only the central panel has survived. This is the first painting on panel in which we can see how well Holbein mastered the techniques perfected by Mantegna for achieving glowing colours. The composition is more compressed than the original which inspired it, and Holbein, constrained by the space at his disposal, has brought some figures into the foreground. But what is more important is the painting's theological schema. Leonardo's fresco was a disquisition on the Eucharist and the conventional scholastic interpretation of the words of institution. This was to become the central doctrinal controversy of the Reformation. Dürer's 1523 woodcut of the same scene gives it a Protestant gloss by drawing attention to the bread *and* wine (a reference to administering communion to the laity in both kinds as opposed to the Catholic practice of only giving bread). Holbein is not involved in these speculations: he wants to convey to us the biblical moment, the moment of truth. Christ has just uttered the words of institution. The disciples react in a variety of ways: they gaze in adoration or consternation; they debate the meaning of what their master has said. But the most arresting figure in the group is the semi-grotesque Judas. Isolated in brooding scepticism, he ponders his course of action, but the right hand braced against the bench seat indicates that he is on the point of deciding to leave the room. However intricately men may debate the central truths of the Gospel, those truths must ultimately be either accepted in faith or rejected.

In the late summer of 1522 Holbein made contact with these truths in a fresh and dynamic way. The text of a new book which had been long and eagerly awaited reached Basel. It was Luther's German translation of the New Testament. The printer, Adam Petri, acquired copies as soon as they came off the presses in September. Within three months he had rushed his own edition on to the market. Holbein provided the illustrations.

The impact must have been powerful. Holbein had, by now, spent some years in the company of men who studied the Scriptures in Latin, Greek or Hebrew. He had heard Oecolampadius and other preachers expound the lively oracles of God in straightforward and challenging ways. But (although vernacular Bible fragments did exist) it is unlikely that he had until now been able to read for himself the writings which lay at the heart of the Reformation. The title-page for the new book, depicting Peter and Paul and the symbols of the four evangelists, was one of Holbein's finest engraving designs. The clamour for the German New Testament was intense. Within months Petri ran off two new editions, and a rival, Thomas Wolff, had also climbed on the bandwagon. Both publishers wanted fresh pictures from Holbein and he illustrated over thirty scenes and subjects, most of them quite distinct from the stereotyped images of Annunciation, Nativity, Passion sequences and Last Judgement which were staples of religious art. At no time before had he been so thoroughly steeped in the Bible. He was able to experience its narrative sweep more completely and his fascination with what he read is indicated by his attention to the details of the episodes he was called upon to illustrate.

Inevitably, it was the central events of the Christian story that Holbein depicted most frequently. Equally inevitably, his paintings and drawings presenting Christ's Passion were the most emotionally charged. However, it was not just the subject matter which dictated the level of pathos he introduced. It is clear that he studied the biblical narrative believing that fidelity to the Word of God would enable him

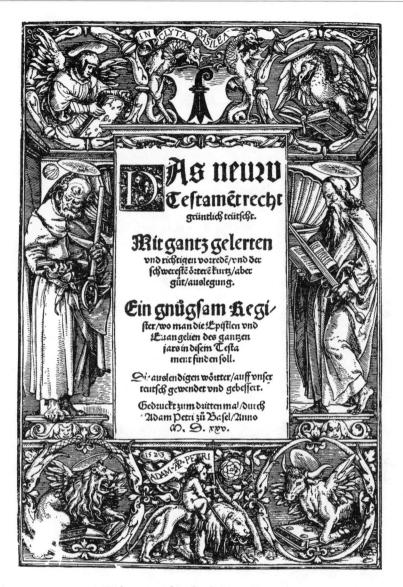

Title-page of Luther's New Testament

to communicate truth more accurately and, therefore, more effectively. Between 1523 and 1525 he treated the Passion narrative in designs for a series of windows and also in four painted panels, probably for an altarpiece. He approached the same problem through different media: how to balance dramatic effect, faithfulness to Scripture and the relevance of the message to the beholder. Earlier

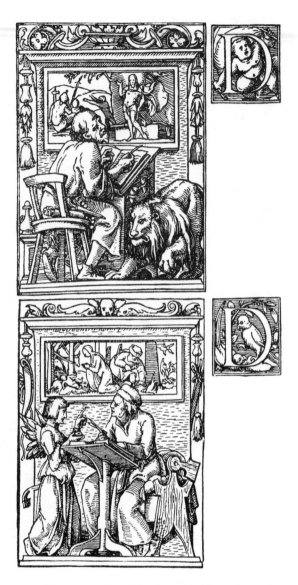

Two evangelists from Luther's New Testament
(*British Museum, London*)

northern painting, culminating in Grünewald, had tended to heighten
the drama by means of exaggerated movements, distorted faces and
vivid lighting effects. The results could be powerful and shocking but
also ran the risk of seeming to locate the action in an unreal world.
Italian masters had solved the technical problems of representing

human forms in realistic spatial relationships but could lose spiritual significance in their concentration on naturalistic detail, or confuse it with mere monumentality. In steering between this Scylla and Charybdis Holbein took the Bible as the chart for his imagination.

The painted version was probably the first of the two Passion cycles to be completed. It is vivid in its use of colour and dramatic lighting. The turbulent fluidity of movement heightens the violence of Christ's tormentors. The amazing skill with which Holbein crams crowds of people into a small space while yet presenting dozens of individual cameos creates the impression of significant events in the midst of frenzied activity. But it is the detail which is most telling. The Crucifixion panel is the one in which we would expect to see the most graphic presentation of physical suffering and mental anguish. Holbein was familiar with the Issenheim Altarpiece. The clenched hands and grief-stricken face of St John are reminiscent of Grünewald's presentation. But here the figure of the disciple is almost entirely masked by that of the Virgin and we are denied a view of her anguished face. Issenheim's drooping, emaciated, scarred Christ is replaced by a more robust body partially supported by ropes. The Saviour's face is hidden from the viewer. Holbein rejects exagg-eration and distortion as a means of saying 'Look, how dreadful this is'. He concentrates not on labouring the significance of the event but on capturing a moment of biblical time. Joseph of Arimathea has arrived with the document permitting him to take possession of the body. Christ has just died and the only people interested in the tragedy, apart from Mary and John, are Joseph, the soldier beside him whose spear thrust has just verified death and the centurion behind who is observing, 'This really was the Son of God.' Otherwise the event takes place amid bustling indifference. A mounted troop ride away from the execution site, their work done. Soldiers throw dice for Christ's cloak. And the foreground is dominated by a group of splendidly clad officers engrossed in their own conversation. Holbein is trying to tell us not 'This is what it means', but 'This is how it was'. Like Erasmus, Luther, Zwingli and other reformers, who believed passionately in the open Bible, Holbein was convinced that divine truth was capable of speaking for itself, leaving the individual free to respond with commitment or indifference.

The attitude he adopted in the drawn sequence was slightly different. Taking as his model a series of engravings by Schongauer and, like Schongauer, setting the events and personalities involved in the contemporary world, he nevertheless made several significant changes. He removed the – non-biblical – Veronica from the depiction of Christ carrying the cross. He introduced anonymous observers into some of the scenes, to suggest a link with the spectators. And he added details of telling realism. As Christ is nailed to the cross he is gagged to stifle his screams. A soldier holds his arm down and another sits on his legs to stop them thrashing about. This Saviour, Holbein points out, is fully human. He is likely to struggle, as any man would, when subjected to such painful torture. The drawings, like the painted panels, are frozen moments of time. The Crucifixion in this series represents an earlier stage of the execution. A soldier descends from the ladder having just nailed up the inscription over Jesus' head. His colleagues raise their hands in mock salute to the 'King of the Jews' and invite him to descend from the cross. Once again, what emerges most strongly is Holbein's avoidance of overt emotionalism, on the one hand, and of virtuosity for its own sake, on the other. He incorporates everything that will bring to life the biblical moment.

There is one painting above all others that makes quite clear his attitude to Christian imagery and, therefore, to Christian faith. It is, in the view of many, the most remarkable work that ever came from the brush or pencil of Hans Holbein. Dostoyevski exclaimed *of Christ in his Tomb* (1521), 'This picture could rob many a man of his faith,' and in doing so he missed the point entirely. No other picture expresses more eloquently the faith of the Reformation, the Christocentric faith of many humanists, the faith of those for whom the Bible had become a living book (see plate section).

Holbein had seen other representations of the dead Christ, including Grünewald's Issenheim predella and, probably, Mantegna's version in Milan (see plate section). These images ignited something deep inside him which smouldered away until he could no longer put off attempting the subject for himself. It has been suggested that he had to wait until he could find a cadaver to use as a model – perhaps a drowned man fished out of the Rhine. But dead bodies, even disowned dead bodies, cannot have been all that uncommon in Basel. It is much more likely that this was a project undertaken out of passionate compulsion. It was not, as was once thought, part of an altarpiece, and there is no evidence that it was executed as a private commission. The *Dead Christ* is a signed piece in every sense of the term, a statement of what Holbein believed it important to say about the Christian religion. It is not an essay in objective realism lacking spiritual values. It is an affirmation of truth from which non-essentials have been stripped in order to make the truth self-evident.

All the representations of the descent from the cross and the entombment that Holbein knew tried to bring home the awfulness of Christ's death by emphasizing his wounds and the anguish of his followers. This was certainly true of Grünewald's treatment of the subject. Even Mantegna, who was preoccupied with the technical problems of foreshortening and who shunned Gothic grotesquery (his dead Christ reposes in what could be sleep), introduced grieving disciples as code-breakers for his painting's emotional message. Holbein would have none of this. He wanted as far as he was able to represent the truth as it was. The Bible spoke of the Word of God becoming flesh. That flesh suffered death. In the black secrecy of the tomb that flesh began to decay. Grasp this, Holbein says, and you begin to understand what Incarnation is about. Grasp this and the miracle of Resurrection will strike you with full force. *Christ in his Tomb* is the testimony of a man who has had long discussions with humanists and evangelicals and has come to share their commitment to the unvarnished word of God and to personalized faith.

It is also the first and the most powerful demonstration of Holbein's concentration upon death. He may recently have lost his only brother and he would soon certainly be mourning the passing of his father. These experiences only increased an already present tendency to reflect upon mortality. Within a few years he was labouring at his *Totentanz* woodcuts, which were to be among his more important works. But his was no morbid preoccupation. With Erasmus he accepted,

> if with our whole heart we believe the things that God has promised us by his son Jesus, all the delectations of this world should soon be little regarded, and death which sets us ever unto them with a painful (but yet a short) passage, should be less feared.[8]

What minimizes that fear is the knowledge that the God-man has passed this way before us. According to the earliest inventory of the Amerbach collection this item originally bore a very simple label: 'Jesus Nazarenus Rex'.

Chapter 5

BASEL

1524–1526

'Oecolampadius is reigning here.' So Erasmus complained at the beginning of 1524. 'Old Nosey', as the radical preacher and teacher was known because of his beak-like organ, was taking Basel by storm. As well as cramming St Martin's Sunday after Sunday, he was attracting large audiences to his more demanding university lectures. When he spoke on the book of Isaiah to the theological faculty, 400 citizens crowded into the hall along with the students and clergy. The preceding August he had, despite the opposition of the city council, staged a public disputation on four explosive topics – that the writings of philosophers and theologians are not authoritative; that men are justified only by faith in Christ; that the invocation of saints is valueless; and that all Christians, whatever their social status, are 'brothers, kings and priests'. Nor did Oecolampadius confine himself to strictly religious comment. He demanded socio-economic reform, based on Gospel principles, of sensitive issues such as care for Basel's poor. The humanist who had once exhausted congregations with his earnest, humourless sermons had found a new fire, a new vision. His mix of egalitarianism, moral and political outrage and theological conviction was potent. Public opinion became increasingly polarized as a growing majority demanded radical reforms and the city fathers, backed by the senior clergy and the wealthier merchants, were forced into becoming a reactionary 'party' committed to the defence of the status quo. Erasmus, therefore, was not guilty of much exaggeration when he made his complaint.

He had, by this time, finally responded to the many entreaties to enter the sawdust ring: the sheaves of a new book, *De libero arbitrio,* were piling up in his study. *On Free Will* was an attack on the very bastion of Luther's theology, as the reformer himself admitted. Erasmus broke his silence, in part, from his concern over the violence of all kinds that was breaking out like a fever rash all over Europe: 'I see from this emerging much that is ruinous and seditious. I see the destruction of good letters and learning. I see the severing of friendships, and fear the outbreak of cruel tumult.'[1] Basel had not escaped the contagion. As well as the heated scholarly debates and the thunderings of rival sermoneers, there was the impact of visiting partisans, trying to draw Basel into the Reformed or Catholic camp. In 1524 William Farel blustered in from Paris, where he had already set the ecclesiastical dovecotes fluttering. He spent several argumentative weeks in the city, raised the temperature of the conflict, had a furious row with Erasmus and was hustled out of town.

The council were at a loss to know how to react. When should they be tolerant and when should they take a firm stand? They asked Erasmus's advice on the issues that were troubling civil calm – flagrant breaking of lenten rules, priests and monks marrying, inflammatory publications, attacks on the mass, rejection of images and ancient ceremonies. They had good reason to be nervous: not only were their counterparts in other cities facing similar problems, these were but the twitchings of a more widespread convulsion. For years apocalyptic preachers and writers had pointed to 1524 as a year of doom. In the autumn of that year all the planets would coalesce in the constellation of the fish, and that could only mean general chaos and destruction. The prophecies fulfilled themselves. Old social and economic discontents, fresh-honed by religious conviction, were taken out of the armoury and widely distributed. The result was the Peasants' War.

This umbrella term describes a series of agrarian and urban risings of varying severity. For all that, they were none the less frightening to the political establishments who found themselves faced with demands for reform backed by force of arms. Trouble began in the late summer of 1524, a mere fifty kilometres up the Rhine from Basel at Waldshut. It spread through the towns and villages of the Schwarzwald. By the following spring an arc of revolt extended from Zurich to Freiburg. Brandishing swords, scythes, sickles and axes, bands of peasants attacked monasteries, towns and castles, egged on by wild-eyed 'prophets' posing as harbingers of the Third Age – the era of divine retribution and the rule of the saints. There was little coherent common policy throughout this concatenation of local protests, but all the rebels insisted on their loyalty to pope and emperor. Their arguments were with subordinate rulers.

By April 1525 it was known that the tide of insurgency was running towards the walls of Basel. Peasants from the dependent territory around the city were gathering to the north. But this was far from being the council's only problem. Social unrest and political protest had not come to an end after artisan guilds' demonstrations in 1521. In the highly stratified society of the city there were always some who considered themselves to be discriminated against. In 1524–5 it was the turn of the poorest members of the community. Encouraged by egalitarianism preached from the pulpit and the triumphs of militants out in the countryside, the inhabitants of the Steinenvorstadt slum suburb organized themselves for protest. The weavers took the lead, demanding redress of grievances, some of which, such as the requirement placed upon their guild of maintaining an altar lamp in the cathedral, were religious. The Little Council temporized, but time was not on their side. On 30 April riots broke out. The preacher at St Leonard's denounced the city leaders. Revolutionary articles demanding, among other things, that the Little Council be purged of Catholics were widely circulated. On 3 May the peasant army arrived at the gates of Basel.

The establishment were probably saved – for the time being – by Basel's now settled tradition of moderation and reasoned debate. The city leaders were able to talk themselves out of trouble. They received deputations, listened to complaints, discussed the insurgents' demands and promised redress. Satisfied, the peasant host struck camp, its members returning home to tend their crops and herds. Within the city the council set up *ad hoc* committees designed to allow the poorer guilds more participation in government – or, at least, the illusion of more participation. If the leading burghers allowed themselves a sigh of relief, they also recognized that the respite was temporary. Pressures within and without the city were steadily increasing. Socio-religious issues were becoming more complex, the protagonists more turbulent.

The effects of disturbance on the artistic community were little short of catastrophic. For at least three very pressing reasons the flow of commissions was dwindling to a trickle. Economic insecurity inhibited expenditure on luxuries. Radicals were openly questioning the propriety of religious images and this made potential patrons nervous about adding to the embellishment of churches. As for secular painting, the leading citizens, under the envious scrutiny of the lower orders, were reluctant to initiate new works which might be interpreted as ostentatious self-display. The competition for prestigious house painting among wealthy families came to an abrupt end. In all probability portraits and other status symbols were also less in demand.

Holbein was obliged to abandon the major project on which he had been engaged. In 1521 the stonemasons and carpenters who had been working on a prestigious building right in the heart of Basel for a dozen years finally departed. The city's new Rathaus overlooking the market square was now revealed in all its glory. Or not quite all; it still needed to be decorated. One of the last acts of Jakob Meyer during his reign as burgomaster was to secure the commission for Hans Holbein to paint the walls of the long council chamber (approximately eleven metres by twenty-two), where all important decisions affecting the city were taken. After a pause of three months to allow the walls to dry out, the artist had made a start. Within ten months he and his apprentices had completed two walls, for which he had received substantial stage payments. He even asked for and was granted a bonus.

The humanist community, and perhaps Erasmus himself, must have been consulted over the subject matter, which gave evidence of close knowledge of ancient history and legend. The scenes chosen contained a strong moral message: they were designed to remind councillors to legislate impartially, to embrace justice and not to neglect mercy. Although the stories were old, the settings and the dress of the characters were contemporary. Allusions to recent events and the current situation cannot have been lost on Basel's ruling elite. The Roman general Curius Dentatus is shown cooking a simple camp meal and turning his back on a group of Sammite ambassadors who have come to bribe him into an alliance. Pointing to the vegetables in his cauldron the incorruptible soldier observes, 'I would rather have these in my pot and rule over those who have gold' – a warning to potential *Kronenfresser*. Even more pertinent was the depiction of the Persian King Saphur (Sapor), using the conquered Emperor Valerian as a human mounting block. This, the greatest humiliation Rome ever suffered, happened to a ruler who had carried to its worst extreme the persecution of Christians and the confiscation of Church property. Holbein emphasized the suggestion that councillors should exercise caution and moderation in religious causes by setting 'Sapor and Valerian' in the Marktplatz right outside the proud, new Rathaus. Five single figures divided the narrative tableaux, two biblical and three allegorical. They all bore legends exhorting the city fathers to public virtue. Christ commands, 'Do not do to others what you would not want them to do to you.' King David advises, 'Judge justly, O sons of men.' Wisdom asserts, 'The fear of the Lord is the beginning of wisdom.' Justice advocates, 'Forget private interests when pursuing the common good.' Moderation cautions, 'He who seeks more than his just reward will hasten his own destruction.'

As interesting as the decorations Holbein painted for the council chamber is the one he did not paint. Although his patrons were obviously very happy with all that he had done, they decided not to let him continue – for the time being at least. They preferred to be confronted by an expanse of empty wall space at one end of the room. The worsening atmosphere in the city may have been sufficient to cause this postponement of the work. But Holbein's proposed designs for the shorter, back wall of the chamber may well have alarmed them. It was 'Christ and the woman taken in adultery' and bore the legend warning against hypocrisy, 'Let him among you who is without sin cast the first stone.' The sentiment was unexceptional but there was something very uncomfortable about the sight of respectable Jews slinking away from the presence of Jesus. The implied criticism was certainly something the council members could do without at a time when their integrity was being frequently and loudly questioned.

The loss of this work was a blow to Holbein, as was the general contraction of the market. However, the positive aspect of the situation was that he had more freedom. Holbein's Basel years must have been far less static than the absence of records suggests. The quest for patrons, the desire to see and record new sights and general self-publicity all called for forays from home of greater or shorter length. As it is, we know of only one such journey. It took place in the spring of 1524 and friends and supporters helped him in various ways to defray the expenses of travel and lodging. In mid-April Jakob Meyer set out for Lyon with a force of 200 men to be put at the disposal of Francis I. The ex-burgomaster, undeterred by his humiliation and political opposition, was determined to maintain Basel's pro-French policy. A place was found in the entourage for his favourite artist. If we are to judge by the frequency with which Holbein painted and sketched them we must conclude that, like many artists, he was fascinated by men of action. He enjoyed drawing troops – their dress, their armour, their weapons. He depicted them in battle scenes, in Passion studies as rough and ready soldiers only doing their job; as supporters for heraldic devices and in various poses in house murals. Holbein found much to interest him as Meyer's party travelled by stages via Besançon, Dijon, Beaune and Mâcon to Lyon. From there Holbein made his way all the way down the Rhône valley to distant Montpellier. Here, he had been invited to spend some days with Amerbach, who was studying at the university. He bore a gift from Erasmus – nothing other than one of the portraits he had himself made of the scholar.

Soon after the return to Basel Holbein's father died. Old Hans maintained his faculties to the end of his days, as is proved by the few surviving paintings that we have. A late portrait of an unknown woman shows a mastery of structure and character delineation which enables the work to stand alongside several of his son's pictures (see plate section). But the fact that there are so few extant works indicates that the reversal of his fortunes had been permanent. The old man probably had to be supported, sporadically at least, by his son during his last years. His passing did at least relieve Hans and Elsbeth of that responsibility. However, the elder Holbein did bequeath another problem to Hans: for years the young man was involved in a struggle to extract his father's possessions from the Anthonite brothers at Issenheim. Their prior showed no inclination to relinquish the old man's painting materials and as late as July 1526 Hans had to prevail upon the Basel burgomaster, Heinrich Meltinger, to write to Issenheim on his behalf – whether successfully or not we do not know.

The passing of the painter's father left two members of the artistic Holbein family. Hans's Uncle Sigmund had settled in Berne. Still a bachelor, he had found there a profitable niche and was producing sufficient work to enable him to buy a comfortable house and meet his simple daily needs. The irascible old man who had once sued his own brother for debt and who did not care much for his sisters or their spouses, had a soft spot for his nephew. The two men rarely met but Sigmund followed Hans's career with interest and pride. It may be, as we have suggested, that the loss of close relatives turned Holbein's mind to thoughts of death. Between 1524 and 1526 he made the designs for forty-one woodcut engravings known – not wholly accurately – as the *Dance of Death*. They depicted Nemesis in the form of a skeleton claiming men and women of several stations in life from pope and emperor down to ploughman and pedlar.

The series[*] begins with the Creation and the temptation of Adam and Eve by the serpent. It is with the expulsion from Eden in the third woodcut that Death makes his appearance. Thereafter, he is to be the constant companion of Adam and all his race. Thirty-three drawings follow, in each of which the Last Enemy keeps his rendezvous with a different individual. The penultimate picture shows the final resurrection. It is usually described as the Last Judgement but this is – emphatically and significantly – what it is not. Christ sits on the rainbow over the earth surrounded by the hosts of heaven but no sword issues from his mouth. His scarred hands are held in what may be a gesture of acceptance. Beneath, the dead, now raised to new life, hold up imploring arms but no intimation is given of their ultimate fate. The series is not about heaven and hell or even moral and spiritual values. Good and bad alike keep their tryst with death. The earnest preacher, the avaricious merchant and the innocent child all tread the same road. But it does not end in the abyss. In Plate XL as in Plate I Death is absent: he who reigns supreme in the terrestrial sphere is of no account beyond it.

> One short sleep past we wake eternally,
> And death shall be no more; death thou shalt die.
> (John Donne, *Holy Sonnets*)

To emphasize the limited subject matter of the series Holbein's final drawing is the Escutcheon of Death: a well-dressed man and woman are the supporters for a shield the motif of which is a skull from whose grinning mouth a worm emerges. The crest on Death's helm is an hourglass surmounted by skeletal arms wielding a jagged rock. In this world death is ennobled, the supreme overlord – but only in this world.

If *Christ in his Tomb* provides a grille through which we can observe the intensity of Holbein's inner response to spiritual realities, the

---

[*] Here we consider the forty-one designs published in 1538. Seventeen further engravings appeared in later editions, some or all of which may not have been from Holbein's pen.

Dance of Death is a window through which we look out, with the artist, on his world. No grime or striations obscure the glass. We need make no allowances for the demands of a patron or the instructions of a publisher. These drawings, which were probably not commissioned, reveal Holbein's world as Holbein saw it. More than that, they proclaim him one of the greatest satirical artists of all time, a craftsman of the highest order combining observation, understanding and passion. The *Dance of Death* does not display the cold neutrality of the unengaged realist or the detachment of the cynic. It is a commentary on the vanity of human wishes delineated by a pen dipped in truth, indignation and wit. The beardless talent for serious humour which grinned sheepishly from the *Moria* marginalia now, a decade later, has matured and fixes the observed with an unwavering eye. Had Holbein lived in an age of press freedom, when cartoonists could make a living and irreverence was in fashion, he might have profitably concentrated on his gift for satire. The harsh authoritarianisms of the early sixteenth century allowed of no such possibility. The *Dance of Death* was his major contribution to the genre and even that found its way into the public domain only with difficulty and caution.

We owe the making and preserving of these great woodcuts to a series of happy chances. First there was the timing. The turbulence of the mid-1520s – the conflict of ideas and the bloody failures of the various peasant uprisings – made men think not only about death, rarely absent from the common consciousness, but about the reasons why people die and suffer pains, injustices, and indignities. Holbein no less than most of his contemporaries, and more than some, reflected on these things. Then there was the existence in the cemetery of the Dominican convent in Basel of a very famous *Totentanz* painting showing skeletal Death coming to claim men and women of every degree. This subject was far from being unique: for a hundred years or more Church authorities had had the *danse macabre* depicted on graveyard and charnel-house walls throughout Europe as a warning to the living to be prepared for their end. However, the Basel one was widely known and was a major tourist attraction. Holbein used several of the figures from this sequence in his treatment of the subject.

The next fortunate coincidence was the arrival towards the end of 1522 of Hans Lützelburger. This itinerant craftsman–entrepreneur was one of the finest blockmakers of the day. He originated in

Augsburg, and thus shared many friends and acquaintances with the
Holbeins, but he travelled widely and was well known in the printing
world. Blockmakers were the most highly regarded and best-paid
artisans in the printing industry. They were certainly better
remunerated than the mere artists who had only to *design* the plates
with which texts were adorned. The best ones earned their money in
two ways: they did straightforward commission work for publishers,
and they conceived their own speculative projects. Lützelburger and
Holbein worked together on various jobs between 1523 and 1526,
including Bible illustrations.

Exactly how they came to combine their talents on the *Dance of
Death* is not clear. The work may have been ordered by a radical Basel
printer, to illustrate a text dealing with the ills of the day. Alter-
natively, Lützelburger and Holbein may have hit upon the idea
themselves and produced the blocks for sale to one of Lützelburger's
many clients in the trade. On balance the latter seems more likely. In
this case, for an agreed fee, Holbein would have done the drawings
straight on to the blocks, which would then have become
Lützelburger's property. The artist was certainly glad of the work and
little interested in what happened to his designs after they had been
paid for.

If his bill was settled, Holbein must have counted himself fortunate,
for his colleague died in the summer of 1526. At this point the blocks
might well have disappeared without trace. The illustrations were
unpublishable, for reasons we shall consider shortly. What saved them
was the fact that Lützelburger died insolvent. His creditors battened
on the deceased's possessions and in the share-out a printer in Lyon
obtained the *Dance of Death* blocks. For more than a decade they sat
in his store room. Once again, they might have been lost to posterity
– forgotten, discarded or planed down for reuse. Then, in 1538, their
owners, the Trechsel brothers, found a way of publishing them and
were gratified to discover that they had a best-seller on their hands.
Holbein, of course, never received so much as a single sou out of the
Trechsels' profits. His name did not even appear in *Les Simulachres et
histoires faces de la mort,* the book containing his plates. But his
remarkable statements on contemporary life were preserved. As well
as being miniature masterpieces in themselves, they reveal Holbein's
responses to the turbulent events through which he was living.

The ubiquity of death is emphatically not the message of the drawings. At most the *memento mori* motif is a subterfuge, a loose camouflage thrown over the cannon of Holbein's militant wit. We understand the *Dance of Death* only if we set it against the background of 1520s socio-religious satirical debate. In the propaganda war that was being waged more fiercely year by year, no means of communication was ignored. The artillery of ridicule was loosed off on both sides in the form of pamphlets, plays, sermons and engravings. Catholic and Protestant protagonists all availed themselves of the armoury used by earlier elegant humanists, although none of them matched up to the sparkling originality of Brant and Erasmus. Most of them, indeed, aimed their salvoes at a less erudite audience. For that very reason they made more impact on their contemporaries. Their works may, by now, be lost or little known, but we should not underestimate their influence. It was these, not the *Praise of Folly,* that inspired peasants to rise in revolt and townsmen to tear down altars. It was gibes fired off by such as Gengenbach and Manuel that peppered the walls of the establishment and turned ordinary men and women into activists.

Holbein certainly knew both men by repute. He was familiar with his fellow citizen Gengenbach and may have met Manuel, who was well known throughout the cantons. Thomas Gengenbach was one of the more radical Basel publishers as well as an author in his own right. He concentrated on vernacular diatribes and satires. In 1521 he issued a poem, *Die Totenfresser* (*The Devourers of the Dead*), which exposed popes, bishops, priests, monks and all in the Church hierarchy who made money and exercised power by exploiting the fear of the living for the wellbeing of departed loved ones. Gengenbach produced a cast of souls who ridiculed requiem masses and prayers for the dead.

Niklaus Manuel (sometimes called Manuel-Deutsch) was much more widely known. By profession a painter, by temperament intense and turbulent, he has sometimes been compared with Grünewald. Manuel, too, created altarpieces and murals (most famously a *Dance of Death* for the Dominican convent of his native Berne) notable for the dramatic effects of colour, lighting and distorted figures. He was a prodigious producer of biblical and mythological engravings and also portraits. But art could not contain his talent, energy and enthusiasm. He served for many years on Berne council and was often involved in missions to other cantons. He saw service with his city's mercenary forces, though in the capacity of a secretary. He wrote pamphlets and plays. And he was early caught up in the movement for religious reform. In much of his art, both verbal and visual, Death features prominently; Manuel was an exponent of black humour.

Excited by Gengenbach's poem, Manuel immediately set about turning it into a stage play with the same name. It had its first performance during Lent in 1523 and its combination of low humour and earnest diatribe made a considerable impact on the population, particularly the illiterate. Manuel presented the leadership of the Church as members of a conspiracy against the laity, determined at all costs to keep ordinary people in a state of ignorance. Thus the pope exhorts his followers,

> Be quiet about the Gospel
> And preach only papal law.
> We will then be lords and the laity servants
> Who bear the burdens we lay upon them.
> All is lost, however,
> If the Gospel gets out
> And things are measured by it.
> For it teaches none to give and sacrifice to us –
> Only that we should live simple, impoverished lives.[2]

After the pope's self-condemnatory speech Manuel wheeled out bishops, priests, monks, nuns and friars and exposed them to biting and bawdy ridicule.

The similarity of *The Devourers of the Dead* to Holbein's the *Dance of Death* is much too close to be coincidental. As well as the mortality theme, Holbein also presents a series of tableaux, in which the failings and offences of the clergy and the religious are mercilessly paraded. In that he does not restrict himself to Church leaders his satirical ploughshare cuts even deeper into the tilth of contemporary society. The influence of Erasmus can be seen here. Where the humanist used Folly to deride the pomps and vanities of this wicked world, Holbein employed Death to emphasize their futility. Like his scholar friend, the artist exposed the sins and foibles of prominent men and women, hoping, as Erasmus hoped, that his universalist treatment of human weakness would deflect any criticism for those who considered some of his drawings subversive.

Yet they were indeed subversive and this, surely, explains why their publication was delayed and also why, when they were published, they were immensely popular. Every plate deserves minute exploration to see how Holbein wielded his pen so mercilessly, but we must be content with scrutinizing just a few.

Among the secular subjects in this cavalcade of human folly the exponents of the law come off badly. The Judge and the Advocate both condemn the corruptibility and partiality of the law. The judge is visited by death in the act of accepting a bribe from a wealthy litigant, while a poor suitor looks on helplessly. The lawyer, too, receives payment for his labours while a humbler, neglected client wrings his hands in dismay.

The Councillor: This engraving would not have pleased the rulers of Basel. One of their number is depicted, richly clad, in earnest conversation with an influential nobleman. His back is resolutely turned to a ragged suitor. A devil perched on his shoulder is the obvious inspiration of the councillor's attitude towards his responsibilities. The behaviour of the lawmen and the civic politician is precisely that which Holbein's council chamber paintings warned against.

The Count: In 1526, when Germany was still suffering the shock of the Peasants' War, this violent picture must have seemed particularly subversive. The representative of the wealthy landed class has cast aside his helmet and sheathed his sword. Beneath his feet he tramples a flail, an agricultural implement which would be immediately recognized as symbolizing the rural labouring class. Death here appears, clad in a peasant's simple tunic and turban and about to batter the count with his own body armour. What should have defended the feudal lord has become a weapon for his destruction. The symbolism would not have been lost on those who had been horrified by news of the massacres which had accompanied the defeat of several of the rebel hosts.

Holbein represented several other types in the *Dance of Death,* some poignantly and sympathetically. A child waves a cheerful goodbye to his grieving mother. A weary ploughman allows Death to divert his team towards a town suffused by a beautiful sunset which suggests Bunyan's Celestial City. An old man and woman are not altogether reluctant to walk with their sinister companion. However, it is the rich, the powerful and the pious who receive most attention and few of them come off well.

But it is the religious figures who are the most ruthlessly exposed. The Monk, who, of all men, should have been best prepared for Death, is horror-stricken by his appearance and tries frantically to escape, clutching his most precious possession, his money box. His exposed penis is a wry comment on the man's vow of chastity. The Nun is caught supposedly at her devotions. But though she kneels before the images of two saints she is willingly distracted by her lover, who sits suggestively on her bed strumming his lute and singing a wanton love song. Throughout Germany and elsewhere Luther's stinging criticisms were causing thousands to abandon the religious life and Holbein's pictures here translate his condemnation into visual imagery. The Preacher: Popular religious figures did not escape Holbein's satire. The orator leans forward with an eloquent gesture to hold a rapt congregation (except for one man who has fallen asleep). In the pulpit behind him Death mimics the speaker's sincerity with a leering grin and an expansive gesticulation.

However, there is no doubt about who emerges from this series as the real villain. The pope depicted here is almost certainly Leo X. Death brandishes a papal bull which probably represents *Exsurge Domine*, the excommunication of Martin Luther, condemned by humanists and religious radicals alike as a gross overreaction to the Wittenberg challenge. Christ's vicar is shown at the supreme moment of his temporal power – crowning an emperor, a reference to the long-running conflict between spiritual and temporal power in the Holy Roman Empire. But the most striking feature of the engraving is the inclusion of no less than three demons. In his entire *oeuvre* Holbein very rarely made allusions to hell (whose torments formed part of the stock in trade of medieval religious propaganda). Apart from 'the Councillor' no other picture in this series makes any allusion to the satanic underworld. Hell does not even feature in the Last Judgement, which concludes the cycle. Only the pope is depicted as sold body and soul to the Devil. He has become the Antichrist confidently identified by Luther.[*]

Holbein poured a great deal of his own indignation and resentment into this work. He shared the religious reformers' sense of outrage at

---

[*] These forty-one engravings do form a unit, in that all the subjects represent classes or occupations. The later editions introduced a moralizing element in the Drunkard, the Gambler, the Robber, or depicted social neutrals – the Bride and Groom. Their inclusion breaks up the cohesion of the collection.

the worldliness and corruption of Church leaders. As a member of a lesser craft guild he sympathized with those who felt themselves exploited and denied justice. As someone who had entrée to the establishment but did not belong to it he knew the weaknesses and failings of its members. As a companion of scholars but not one of the intellectual elite he found abstruse arguments on points of dogma irritating and irrelevant. What matters, he tells us through his drawings, is how men and women live; how they face the prospect of death, which puts all pomp and power and academic niceties into true perspective.

In the event all Holbein's and Lützelburger's publishing friends found the *Dance of Death* too hot to handle. The Little Council had begun to impose censorship. After long debate they had accepted Erasmus's recommendation that books and pamphlets that 'arouse turmoil rather than restore piety' should be suppressed. The Holbein–Lützelburger blocks came too close to that definition for anyone in Basel to risk buying them. Erasmus's erudite prose had set establishment rooks spiralling up in raucous protest, and popular diversions such as *Die Totenfresser* were even more disturbing. There can be little doubt that the more immediately accessible message of Holbein's pictures which could be passed from hand to hand and pinned up in people's homes would have loosed the hawks on both sides into aerial combat. What the impact might have been upon his career for good or ill of the *Dance of Death* being published in 1526 we can only conjecture. When they did appear in 1538, by which time Holbein was safely in England, they were immediately popular and ran to numerous editions published by the Treschels and by copyists. Several of the new versions were provided with Protestant texts. This led to them being placed on the Catholic Index of banned books, but by then the religious bushfire was unstoppable.

In 1526 the careless and deliberate sparks of Reformation were already igniting conflagrations in many parts of Switzerland and southern Germany. The peasant risings had failed. Once the territorial magnates had recovered from their initial shock and organized their resistance, their troops proved more than a match for countrymen armed with pitchforks, piety and political protest. Luther and other religious leaders had hastened to dissociate themselves from popular violence. The various movements lacked military and ideological cohesion and could not convincingly lay claim to high religious

resolve. Matters were very different in the towns. The concentration
of population, the availability of religious leadership, the presence of
scholars able to give protest an intellectual gloss, the persistent issuing
of propaganda and the complex of longstanding social grievances
ensured that disputes would run and run. Only in a few centres –
Zurich, Strasbourg, Berne, St Gallen – had corporations moved to full
acceptance of reformed worship, but there was no town or city of any
importance where change was not taking place.

A new *cause célèbre* was everywhere dominating the debate –
images. When preachers used magistrates to 'purify' churches; when
town councils ordered the removal of 'objects of superstition' from
places of worship; when iconoclastic mobs went on the rampage,
smashing windows and pulling down statues they were – or so they
claimed – only taking to their logical conclusions arguments urged by
moderate reformers, prominent among whom was Desiderius
Erasmus. In the *Moria* he ridiculed people who attributed quasi-
magical properties to pictures and statues, allowed themselves to be
gulled by grasping clergy into making votive offerings at shrines and
burned candles to the Virgin instead of emulating her virtues (and
Holbein had illustrated these superstitious follies). In 1526 he was still
concerned about the lavish attentions paid to religious objects: 'I
wonder what possible excuse there could be for those who spend so
much money on building, decorating and enriching churches . . .
when meanwhile our brothers and sisters, Christ's living temples,
waste away from hunger and thirst.'[3] From early on in the
Reformation epoch it seemed self-evident to many who had been
emancipated from doctrinal error that one way of eradicating
superstition was to remove the objects of superstition. Luther's more
radical followers took this line, though he himself rejected what he
realized would lead to conflict and disorder. Dürer, a convinced
Lutheran, had professional as well as theological reasons for resisting
the image-breakers:

> Although there are people here and now who despise the art of
> painting very much and say it is idolatrous, any Christian man is as
> little drawn to superstition by a painting or a portrait as a pious man
> is drawn to murder just because he carries a weapon by his side.
> Only a truly senseless man could worship a painting or an image
> made of wood or stone. . . .[4]

In reformed regimes to the south Zwingli's was now becoming the dominant voice and he adopted a more uncompromising stance on the images issue. Reformers in other centres looked to Zurich for a lead. When delegates were invited to a debate on superstitious abuses in October 1523, over 900 people from a wide area crammed into the hall. They heard Zwingli and his lieutenants argue that religious images were forbidden by the Mosaic law and that if Church leaders were not prepared to remove them that responsibility devolved upon temporal authorities. They also heard Zwingli warn against vandalism. The errors of centuries, he insisted, should be removed gradually so as to give no encouragement to civil unrest.

All responsible leaders – reformers and establishment men alike – abhorred social upheaval above all things. The Peasants' War had come as a terrible lesson to the exponents of change, who feared that all they were arguing for might be swept aside, not by the determination of their enemies, but by the seditious excesses of their supposed friends. 'Smite, slay, stab,' Luther had urged the German princes. The rebellious peasant was like a rabid dog, he said; 'if you don't strike him, he will strike you and the whole land with you'. It was the central tragedy of the Reformation that the confused but deeply felt social discontents and spiritual frustrations to which the ideologues gave coherent expression could not be contained by those same ideologues. Once simple men understood, or thought they understood, the reasons for the grievances they had hitherto but vaguely felt, there was little to stop them impatiently taking the law into their own hands. And there were, inevitably, hotheads – the 'little-talents' who are always thrown up by great movements – ready to encourage petty insurrection.

Several of these agitators were active in Basel in the 1520s. The most aggravating thorn in Luther's side was Andreas Bodenstein von Karlstadt. In 1522 he published a tract with the self-explanatory title *On the Abolition of Images,* and Petri hurried to rush out his own edition of the work. Soon afterwards, Karlstadt was thrown out of Saxony. He travelled widely, spitting out resentments against 'Dr Easychair' (Luther) and all who lacked the courage to pursue true reform. In November 1524 he appeared in Basel. His stay was brief and was shortened after a dinner party given by Oecolampadius ended with the guest leaving the house still ranting and raving. No sooner had he departed than even wilder spirits exploded into the city.

Thomas Müntzer and Balthassar Hubmaier were millenarian fanatics who wandered the land making converts, only to be expelled from town after town until they achieved the martyrdom they had unconsciously desired. Neither found free-thinking Basel fertile ground for their broadcast violence, but inevitably some seeds did germinate. From Zurich came a number of Zwingli's less restrained colleagues, hoping to make more impact in a city where they were not overshadowed by a masterly preacher and respected leader. They held earnest debates with Oecolampadius. They tried to get their militant tracts published, and met with partial success. But in tavern debates and meetings in private houses they attracted more than a few sympathizers.

The official line was set by Oecolampadius. He shared most of Zwingli's views, though he was not on a par with his Zurich counterpart either intellectually or as a forceful personality. He not only rejected the Catholic doctrine of the mass, but used a simplified form of liturgy at St Martin's and urged the council to oversee the removal of objects of superstition. But he did not force his opinions and in a city where the climate had long been one of sweet reasonableness the pace of change was very slow.

This very fact only added to the frustrations of the hotheads. In November 1525 a certain Hans Bertsaki was imprisoned for smashing windows in the cathedral. In July 1526 Fridlin Yberger was banished from the city for several months for pulling down a crucifix near St Alban's Gate and kicking it to bits. Hans Herbst, Holbein's old master, had to cool his heels in jail for a few days and was released only after apologizing to the clergy for publicly vilifying them for 'mass superstition'. These were only some of the citizens involved in minor acts of vandalism and breaches of the peace. Basel was not immune from one of the major developments of the time: religious protest by lay people. Everywhere artisans and semi-educated agitators were organizing demonstrations, writing pamphlets and igniting their fellows with inflammatory speeches. Ideas understood or half-understood from humanist lectures and reformist sermons were turned into simplistic demands for immediate action.

An increasingly worried Little Council monitored the situation and dealt, when necessary, with citizens who overstepped the bounds of peaceful protest. If they treated troublemakers leniently it was because they were constantly watching events in other towns and trying not to provoke the kinds of backlash happening elsewhere. To take just one example, Augsburg was in crisis in the summer of 1524 over the harsh treatment dealt out to a group of over-zealous artisans (including an unnamed painter) who had torn up a missal, polluted holy water and threatened to demolish the font. The ringleader, a Franciscan friar named Johannes Schilling, was exiled along with some of his friends and others were imprisoned. The next time the council met they were interrupted by a crowd of 1,800 people surging around the Rathaus and demanding Schilling's return. The councillors tried to take a tough line, summoned troops, made some arrests and executed two of the demonstrators. Inevitably, this only made matters worse. Jakob Fugger and other leading citizens fled for their safety. Disgruntled artisans rushed to join the peasant armies. The council had to bring Schilling back from exile but this did not, predictably, buy peace.

Art historians have often made an unwarranted assumption that has led them to misunderstand or be puzzled by the attitudes of Holbein and other contemporary members of his profession towards the Reformation. They have assumed that dedicated painters and sculptors could not make common cause with radical preachers who taught that religious art was idolatry and certainly not with fervent iconoclasts who tore down images of saints and burned altarpieces. Thus it has become customary to state that Holbein was scandalized by attacks on religious images and his departure from Basel for England in 1526 and, finally, in 1532 has been described as shaking the dust from his feet against a city which had fallen to the barbarians. Such a view must be now firmly rejected as anachronistic.

We now know that Hans was not in Basel when the worst iconoclastic outbreak occurred. Even if he had been, he could not have adopted a romanticized view of 'art' that would not become common currency until the Enlightenment. Most sixteenth-century patrons and artists north of the Alps regarded paintings and sculptures as utilitarian objects. They were bought and sold. They served a purpose, albeit in the case of religious paintings and sculptures an exalted purpose. When owners felt that that purpose could be better served by something else they had no compuction in removing the altarpiece, carved reredos or gilded effigy and selling it off, or even breaking it up. No one questioned their right to do so. No craftsman would have dreamed of protesting that his work should be preserved for posterity. On the contrary, the faster fashions changed the more work there was for them to do.

So far from being, as a body, opposed to the radical ideas that undermined their craft, artists in many parts of northern Europe were in the vanguard of protest against 'superstition' and 'vanities'. In 1524–5 several established and journeymen painters in Dürer's Nuremberg were examined by the authorities for a variety of very extreme religious views. Hans Greiffenberger was charged with painting vulgar satires of the pope and holding wrong opinions about the eucharist. In vigorous pamphlets he had attacked religious imagery and had also complained about colleagues who were devoting their talents to secular paintings and sculptures – they 'create whores and knaves for profit . . . because now the saints are out of fashion'.[5] Georg Penz and Barthel Beheim were among several of Greiffenberger's fellows to be exiled from Nuremberg for heterodox religious views and anti-authoritarianism. Many of their opinions about direct access to God without the need for priest, litany or richly decked altar came directly from the mystic Hans Denck, who was a local schoolmaster and a close friend of Oecolampadius.

We have already seen how Holbein's old master got into trouble. After his brush with authority Hans Herbst decided to abandon his craft because he had come to the conclusion that it tended to encourage idolatry. Grünewald, as passionate in his commitment to change as he was in his depiction of spiritual reality, was caught up in the Peasants' War. Although at the height of his powers and of his professional success, he was prepared to alienate his aristocratic and ecclesiastical patrons. He painted nothing during the last couple of years of his life and was earning his living in the saltworks at Halle, one of the first cities to embrace Lutheranism, at the time of his death. A fellow rebel, the carver Tilmann Riemenschneider, was not allowed the luxury of deciding whether he would continue with his craft; his hands and arms were broken by the public executioner. Jörg Ratgeb, a leading painter at Stuttgart, so far identified with the peasants that he eschewed courtly sophistication in his works and went for a folksy effect that would be understood by ordinary people. He led a rebel force in 1525 and, after defeat, was quartered alive by four horses. Several other artists suffered exile, imprisonment or death for their involvement with the Anabaptist wing of the Reformation which had declared itself quite emphatically against religious imagery.

Niklaus Manuel, as we might expect, was an eager iconoclast and, for his own part, refused, after about 1520, to provide any more 'idolatrous' paintings for churches.

It is difficult, from the viewpoint of a more secular age, to understand how artists could become philistines, particularly when that involved abandoning their means of livelihood. People will only make sacrifices for those things that are closest to their hearts. For very many sixteenth-century men and women it was their faith that came into that category. In an age when believers went to the battlefield or the stake for what they believed it should not surprise us that others turned their backs on their vocation. When Holbein and colleagues across Europe listened to scholars debating and attended sermons they were not indulging in mere intellectual exercise; they were forming their opinions about doctrines and religious practices that really mattered.

Although artists' guilds in many cities complained about lack of work they did not blame the drift of religious policy or demand its reversal. By and large the artisan class was in favour of change, either moderate or radical, and there are no records of craftsmen longing on artistic grounds for a return to the 'good old days'. The fact that the fall-off of ecclesiastical commissions created hardship for very many craftsmen tended to incline them towards, rather than away from, the new ideas. Despair breeds radicals and revolutionaries. Hungry artisans vented their anger, not against evangelical propagandists, but against religious and secular establishments. They found their solace in direct access to the Almighty instead of in the gilded shrines and carved saints to which their fathers had turned.

Naturally, not all had the capacity for the material sacrifice attendant upon forsaking their means of livelihood. Most members of artists' guilds, though temperamentally aligned with the advocates of a new order, were forced by economic necessity into compromise. Several, like Manuel, chose not to seek religious commissions (which had, in any case, radically dwindled in volume). An interesting example is Hans Weiditz of Strasbourg. He studied with Burgkmair before returning to the Rhineland, where he devoted himself almost exclusively to designs for engraving. He was a member of Brant's circle and restricted his output to illustrating classical and humanist texts. When radical reform reached Strasbourg, Weiditz actively encouraged the iconoclasts. What makes him particularly intriguing is the satirical element in his work, which aligns him closely in spirit with Holbein. His pictures often went beyond simple illumination of ancient texts to point up contemporary evils. His sympathies lay with peasants, artisans and poor scholars. He exposed with sardonic relish the failings of clergy, landowners, mercenaries and wealthy burghers.

Holbein, too, was reaching the point at which difficult choices would have to be made. The Janus-like stance of producing works of conventional piety while at the same time making satirical engravings designed to erode the medieval Church's basic suppositions was difficult to sustain. It was in 1526 that his output of traditional religious paintings came to an abrupt end. His last contribution to this genre was his finest yet it also reveals elements of disquiet. The *Darmstadt Madonna* was a *Schutzmantelbild* (a Virgin of Mercy) created for his old patron, Jakob Meyer. It was commissioned for the chapel of the Meyers' country estate at Gross-Gundeldingen and so would be exposed to very few eyes, a fact significant to both artist and patron in the current climate. The merchant had expiated his civic crimes but he still had his enemies, and their numbers were growing as religious opinion polarized. By the end of 1525 evangelical clergy had been appointed to five of Basel's six parishes. The major points of resistance were the cathedral, the university and the conservative faction on the council. Meyer led this last group and, though prepared to concede nothing on matters of faith, he was not so foolish as to parade his beliefs where they would invite opposition. However, in the seclusion of his rural retreat he was determined to affirm his family's devotion to the Virgin and his acknowledgement that, though men might be against him, he and his were under the protection of the Queen of Heaven.

In the *Darmstadt Madonna* Holbein gave a Renaissance treatment to a very old artistic convention (see plate section). The donor's family is grouped devoutly on either side of the Virgin and Child, set in a shell-shaped niche. Mary's mantle enfolds them and her infant son holds his hand over them in protective benediction. It is a stunning painting in every respect. Holbein has totally mastered the use of light and foreshortening to create spatial illusion. The architectural background, suggestive of statuary by Verrocchio and other Florentine masters, enhances without dominating the holy figures. The portraiture is superb, although, in the face of Jakob, Holbein did not quite manage to convey the mood of humble devotion which shines from his preparatory drawing for the painting. The arrangement of figures, particularly the pyramidal group on the left, is Raphaelesque. The colours vibrate; the soft tones of the Virgin's dress unite the whole composition and form a quiet backdrop for the gold of her sleeves and the daring scarlet of her girdle. Above all the picture abounds with 'homely' details which fix the scene very securely in this world and not some ethereal heaven: Jakob's younger son is gently restrained by his brother so that he does not fall down the step at his feet; the two boys do not share the devout poses of their elders. Holbein's sheer virtuosity in handling detail and varied textures is peerless.

Yet the *Darmstadt Madonna*, though at first glance a work of traditional Catholic piety, is not a conventional handling of a well-worn theme. Holbein's thinking had moved beyond the old forms. Even when working for a staunchly conservative patron he had to remain loyal to his own ideas of religious truth. Neither Mary nor Jesus is marked by a halo. Holbein seems to have been uncomfortable with this traditional device. His drawings for stained-glass windows showed him experimenting with various ways of depicting the nimbus. An unsuccessful drawing strikingly similar in general design to the *Darmstadt Madonna* depicts the Virgin conventionally haloed but also outlined in tongues of (presumably) flame. Yet the old devotion was struggling with Holbein's growing interest in the humanity of Christ and the terrestrial setting of saints and salvation acts. Thus he did not paint haloes into his more dramatic religious studies such as the Passion sequence and the *Christ in his Tomb*. In the *Darmstadt Madonna,* a highly conventionalized subject in which he might have been expected to provide for his Catholic patron a Virgin replete with the customary adjuncts of holiness, Holbein deliberately refrained from doing so. But the painting displays a more important departure from tradition. The usual way of presenting the Virgin of Mercy (as in Piero della Francesca's picture in Sansepulcro) showed her standing alone and holding her cloak open in an all-embracing gesture of acceptance. She represented the Church, within whose shelter sinful humanity could find favour and forgiveness. In Holbein's painting Mary's cloak is but lightly draped over Jakob's shoulder and does not appear to extend to the female family members on the right. More importantly, she cannot hold her arms out in universal welcome because they are occupied in carrying her infant son. All her attention is devoted to him and it is Jesus, not Mary, who blesses the family. Here we see the Reformation's Christocentric emphasis. The Son of God becomes the focus for the faith of the individual, rather than battalions of intercessor saints and the mediatory paraphernalia of the ecclesiastical establishment.

There is one more oddity about the *Darmstadt Madonna,* an enigma which, over the years, has attracted a remarkable collection of attempted explanations, some highly romanticized. The model Holbein used for the Virgin Mary was Magdalena Offenburg, a woman well known in Basel for her beauty and loose morals. Magdalena was the daughter of a wealthy citizen who had been married young to the son of former burgomaster Peter Offenburg and had borne him two daughters. When her husband died she preferred a succession of liaisons to remarriage. She derived some income from modelling for artists but she depended for life's necessities and little luxuries on providing more basic services. Her daughters, it seems, followed in her footsteps. Holbein employed her as a model on several occasions but notably for three paintings executed in 1526, the *Darmstadt Madonna* and a pair of remarkable portraits in the Lombard style.

One portrait depicts Magdalena as Venus. She looks out of the painted panel with a shy smile and an open-handed gesture. She is accompanied by Cupid, holding a couple of arrows. The second painting shows us Magdalena in a similar pose but now the expression on her face is wistful, her eyes do not establish frank contact with the viewer and her right hand is held out for payment, a point emphasized by the scattering of gold coins on the parapet. She wears the same dress as in the other picture but Holbein has made it more sumptuous by heightening the sheen of silks and velvets, by adorning Magdalena's hair with a gold band, placing a chain around her neck, adding sleeves to her dress and embellishing it with gold tags. The parapet carries the carved inscription 'Lais Corinthiaca' (see plate section). Laïs was a Greek courtesan and one-time mistress of Apelles, the greatest painter of antiquity.

Such are the facts. How are we to interpret them? There can be little doubt that Holbein painted the portraits for himself. They came, during his lifetime or immediately after his death, into the Amerbach collection. It is reasonable to assume that Magdalena was, for a time, Holbein's mistress. The chief clue lies in her depiction as Laïs. In the

Erasmian circle, whose members delighted to give each other classical names, Holbein was often dubbed 'Apelles', after the court painter to Philip of Macedon, who was particularly famed for his portraits. There is nothing unusual about a painter falling in love with a beautiful model and seeing her as his Venus, to whom he is devoted with an overmastering passion. Hans's marriage to Elsbeth was, as were most marriages at the time, an arranged union. If he had not indulged in adulterous affairs Holbein would have been the exception rather than the rule. But extramarital liaisons are expensive and it is unlikely that a struggling artist could keep his inamorata in the style to which she wished to become accustomed. The affair came to an end, perhaps because Magdalena found a wealthier lover, and Holbein relieved his anger and humiliation by painting a second version of the Venus portrait. This time his Laïs is shown in her 'true' colours as a grasping whore, interested only in money.

How does all this relate to the *Darmstadt Madonna?* Two puzzles are involved in any attempt to answer that question: why did Holbein portray as the ideal of pure womanhood the ex-mistress he had recently depicted with such sardonic bitterness and why did Meyer, who must have known the sitter's identity, raise no objection? When we scan the painting itself for clues we become aware that it contains layers of meaning. As Holbein's genius matured his pictures – or certainly the pictures which carried a special importance for the artist – became more complex. He included visual puns, private jokes and coded messages of the kind that delighted educated Renaissance patrons. Some of his portraits contain references to the subjects' identity and interests which, sadly, are wasted on modern observers. But other paintings make allusions to contemporary events or the artist's own opinions and these invite intelligent speculation.

We have already established that this Madonna is no conventional Virgin of Mercy. We can go further: Holbein deliberately introduces disturbing elements into what should be a wonderfully harmonious composition. The rucked carpet beneath Mary's feet suggests distortion, untidiness. There is a remarkable similarity between Magdalena and Jakob's elder son, which is emphasized by the clasp on her cloak and the medallions of his doublet. The boy's pose, protectively holding his brother, echoes that of the Virgin and Child and a still stronger link is established by the scarlet of the Virgin's sash taken up in the boy's hose. The loosely-knotted girdle itself is the most discordant note in the painting. Without that splash of vivid silk the altarpiece would be cool and reverential. Its prominent inclusion completely changes the mood. The ultimate impression left by the *Darmstadt Madonna* is that its central figure is not at all ethereal; she is 'of the earth, earthy'.

This painting was immensely important to both artist and patron. Because we do not know the background details our resolving of its enigmas can never be verified. Part of its significance for Meyer may lie in an earlier relationship with Magdalena. As for Holbein, his portrayal of his ex-mistress as the crowned Virgin seems to complete a trinity of studies of woman in the conventional roles of lover, whore and object of devotion.

Holbein was steeped in the Bible. Between 1524 and 1526 the greater part of his time was devoted to the design of ninety-one woodcuts for a version of the Old Testament which Petri was preparing and most of which Lützelburger cut. (For some reason these engravings, like the *Dance of Death* series, were not released for some years.) Each one penetrated unerringly to the dramatic heart of the incident it was portraying. Each was faithful to the details of the narrative. The artist used as models fairly crude pictures from the first illustrated Italian Bible – presumably provided for him to work from by Petri – but he brought to the task his own spiritual insight and understanding of the text. It could also only have been executed by someone in sympathy with the reformers' re-evaluation of the Hebrew Scriptures. Hitherto the Old Testament had been regarded only as a prelude to the New, its personalities and events prefiguring the fuller revelation in Christ. For Luther and his followers the whole Bible was the inspired word of God through which the reader might discern divine purposes and so redirect his life.

Holbein both expressed and catered for the New Learning and the New Devotion, which for several decades had been creating a fresh understanding of spiritual truth. In the late fifteenth century religious devotion had shown itself, among other ways, in a proliferation of votive art. That same devotion was now being channelled by mystics, humanists and reformist preachers into forms which were more interiorized, more personalized, less institutionalized. The new piety eschewed painted and carved images and embraced the word of God. Church art and book illustration were on a see-saw, the one falling as the other rose. Literate and semi-literate Christians wanted pictures that illustrated Bibles, devotional works and propaganda tracts. Just as they turned against a mediating priesthood, so they felt less need for paintings and sculptures which attempted to move their religious thinking in ecclesiastically approved ways. The decline of church art over a wide area of Europe was not the direct result of iconoclasm or violent preaching against images. Rather, all three phenomena grew from the same stock. If acts of vandalism were the thorns of a new-style religious life, vernacular Scriptures and the illustrations adorning them were the flowers. Pictures gave the illiterate and semi-literate access to the biblical text and to religious ideas.

Engraving was the principal contribution of German-speaking lands to the Renaissance. For a generation after 1520 the Reformation provided a continuous stimulus and gave work to many artists no longer required by ecclesiastical patrons. It is clear from the number of extant title-pages, illustrations and decorated capitals that Holbein was much in demand by the printers. His problem was not that he had no work but that the work he did was poorly paid and, he may have felt, not recognized for its true worth. With the benefit of hindsight we can see, what may not have been clear to con-temporaries, that Holbein was the major contributor to a revolution in book design. His inventiveness was prodigious and his innovations were copied all over Europe. In the borders for book titles he used humour, *trompe-l'oeil* conceits, architectural frames, landscapes, narrative sequences and vivid allegory. For a Greek–Latin lectionary in 1522 he depicted an array of scenes from human life and the qualities associated with them. In the following year for the title-page of Erasmus's *Paraphrases* he set the death of Cleopatra and other classical references in such a way that they appear to stand out from the page. Such examples do scant justice to the sheer range of Holbein's originality. By dint of advertising himself widely and turning down no commission, no matter how trivial or poorly paid, Holbein kept himself in work and managed to feed his family. As well as Elsbeth's son, she and Hans had their own infant, Philip, to feed and clothe. The income from Frau Holbein's tanning business was a help and Hans's reputation ensured that work was never entirely lacking. The Holbeins were not as badly off as the families of many of Hans's fellow guild members. But times were certainly hard. In 1526 Basel's painters, through their guildmaster, made an appeal to the council to provide municipal projects. 'Several painters have already abandoned their jobs,' they complained, 'and if the situation does not improve in this and other respects, one will have to reckon with more of them giving up.' At about the same time there were what we should now call demarcation disputes as woodcarvers trespassed on jobs that the carpenters considered to be their own preserve.[6] The story was the same in most cities. It is not unusual, of course, for trade and professional bodies to complain of hard times and to call for government aid, but clearly the decorative arts were in some disarray in the 1520s. Part of the problem was that the lean years came after years of plenty. For a generation or more popular and establishment piety had led to the adornment and embellishment of churches, chapels and cathedrals. Now there were different religious priorities and the overswelled ranks of the artists' guilds were feeling the pinch.

Hans Holbein was not the sort of man to sit back and wait for better times. He exploited whatever work opportunities presented themselves. As well as religious paintings, portraits, designs for windows and designs for printers, he painted coats of arms for the courthouse at Waldenburg and made fashion drawings for the wives of Basel's leading citizens. Such humdrum activities were little better than misuse of his talents. Holbein felt this. It was as much to find projects worthy of his artistic gifts as to seek new, wealthy clients that, in the middle of 1526, he made a fateful decision. He would go to England.

Chapter 6

LONDON–BASEL–LONDON

1526–1529

There was nothing at all remarkable about Holbein's choice of London. He had two very good reasons for visiting the capital of the Tudor realm. The first was that it was a powerful magnet attracting talented craftsmen of all trades, but especially those connected with the luxury end of the market. Agents were frequently despatched to the Low Countries, France, Germany and Italy to seek out the best carpenters, carvers, gilders, painters and workers in leather, iron and glass. Most of them were wanted for the royal court. *Folie de grandeur*, reasons of state and genuine cultural interest combined to produce in Henry VIII and his chief minister, Thomas Wolsey, a passion for ostentatious display. In the 1520s the Tudor dynasty was still a new and far from secure (Henry had no male heir) ruling family marginalized by geography from. artistic, intellectual and political movements on the continent. Henry's – or rather Wolsey's – answer was cultural and diplomatic exhibitionism. Treaty-making, alliance-brokering and energetic foreign ambassades, backed when necessary by shows of military force, were the means that Henry and his representatives used to achieve and maintain a place at the top table of international politics.

All this entailed lavish expenditure on the accoutrements of royalty. Europe still remembered the Field of Cloth of Gold where, in 1520, Henry and Francis I had met in the Val Doré, between Ardres and Guines, for two and a half weeks of unashamed showing off. The retinues of the rival monarchs jousted, feasted and danced amid richly hung pavilions, fresh-painted banners and gilded palaces of wood and canvas especially constructed for the occasion.

What can then be said of . . . the banquets and feasts lavish enough for the celestial court itself? What can be said of the pavilions, exceeding the miraculous pyramids of Egypt or the amphitheatres of Rome? . . . When one thinks of all this, one falls into the labyrinth of imagination, and submerges in the chaos of confusion, so that the feeble wit cannot undertake such grand themes.[1]

The exuberant prose of a contemporary French chronicler certainly caught the spirit of the occasion, although moralists complained about vanity and waste. Vanity was an essential attribute for those engaged in Renaissance statecraft, and especially for the rulers of a country which had some cultural 'catching up' to do. Visitors to England from the elegant courts of France and Italy found her people boorish, her dwellings insanitary and her customs archaic. Scholars, diplomats and merchants returning from the continent brought with them the latest fashions – sartorial, intellectual and artistic. Those who could afford to do so tried to recreate the splendours they had seen abroad. Henry VIII spent lavishly on the embellishment of his person and his setting. He refurbished royal residences and built new ones. His subjects and foreign representatives had to be constantly impressed by displays of visual splendour. That is why important events such as the visit of Charles V in 1522 called for unrestrained expenditure on pageants, decorations and special effects.

Where the king led, others followed. Courtiers, nobles and leading citizens were caught up in the necessity for profligate self-advertisement. Thomas Wolsey, Henry's number-one subject, set a standard that nobody could follow, but that did not stop them trying. Lesser men might ridicule the cardinal and complain, as did an English exile from the safety of Strasbourg,

> The bosses of his mules' bridles
> Might buy Christ and his disciples,

but old families and new envied his extravagantly furnished palaces at Hampton Court, York Place, Tyttenhanger and the More, and tried in smaller ways to emulate his magnificence. There were aspects of public display that prominent subjects had no choice about participating in. Part of the cost of royal progresses, national celebrations and diplomatic setpieces fell upon those charged with offering the court hospitality or demonstrating enthusiastic loyalty in other ways. When Henry conveyed Charles V through the streets of his capital in

June 1522 the City livery companies were ordered to provide a series of pageants and to see that the imperial route was suitably decorated. For this £900 was levied on the not altogether willing craft corporations. They even had to pay for printed pamphlets containing translations of the Latin inscriptions accompanying the tableaux, which otherwise meant nothing to most spectators.

Merchants and over-mortgaged courtiers might resent this enforced expenditure; preachers might denounce 'vainglorious' extravagance; but for craftsmen the pattern set by the king and the cardinal meant an abundance of well-paid work. England could not supply the numbers of top-quality artisans needed, hence the influx of foreigners who came on short- or long-term contracts. Account books of the period provide several names to whom substantial sums were paid. Among the painters and sculptors in royal service were Italians such as Vincente Vulpe, Antonio Tuto, 'Nicholas Florentine' and Ellis Carmian, and Netherlanders such as the several members of the Hornebolt family – Gerard, Lucas and Susanna – and Johannes Corvus. A large proportion of London's goldsmiths and clock-makers were of foreign extraction, and the printing industry depended heavily on a steady influx of setters, designers and blockcutters from across the Channel. The production of luxury silks and brocades was still a mystery little understood by native textile workers. As Holbein made his way to cosmopolitan London he was, therefore, just one member of a varied cavalcade of experts who sought their fortunes in the English capital and were not disappointed.

Holbein's second compelling reason for selecting London was the strong recommendation of Erasmus, who was a pronounced Anglophile. The scholar had made five visits to England between 1499 and 1517. The longest sojourn of his peripatetic life prior to his settling in Basel had been the five years 1509–14 spent in Henry VIII's realm, for half of which he had been a professor of theology at Cambridge.

These had been the heady days when the New Learning was first injected into the veins of English academic life. Scholars and men of culture thrilled to rediscover the classics, the New Testament and the Church fathers, now brought to life by the study of Greek. In those years Erasmus stimulated and was stimulated by academics, cultured courtiers and *hommes d'affaires,* even the youthful Henry VIII. He made friends and long continued in correspondence with some of

England's more advanced and innovative thinkers – John Colet, Thomas Linacre, William Grocyn, John Fisher, Cuthbert Tunstall, William Warham and Thomas More. These were the men – or so it seemed in the euphoric first decades of the century – who were going to be the standard-bearers of social, political and religious reform, the framers of a new commonwealth. In fact the quest for a better world would divide English humanists, just as it did their continental brethren. And there were those who would exchange the missionary zeal of youth for the reactionary dogmatism of middle age, particularly when promotion to high office inclined them to defend the establishment they had once ardently criticized.

However, in 1526 the fissures which would open up in the religious life of the Tudor state appeared as little more than cracks in hard-baked summer mud. When Erasmus peered across the choppy English Channel which he so much loathed he did so with rose-tinted spectacles firmly in place. He still adhered to the conviction stated three years earlier, that 'Britain is a far cry from Italy, but stands next to it in the value of its learned men'.[2] Some of them proved their superior judgement and commitment to learning in Erasmus's eyes by making occasional contributions to his funds. Albion might yet avoid the disasters which had elsewhere vitiated all his hopes.

In August 1526 Erasmus wrote letters of introduction to help Holbein on his journey and to assure him of a good reception in England. In Antwerp he commended the painter to one of his closest friends, the town clerk Peter Gilles (Petrus Aegidius):

> The bearer of this letter is the man who painted my portrait. I do not trouble you with any commendation of him, though he is an excellent artist. If he wants to call on Quentin, and you have not leisure to introduce him, you can send a servant with him to show him the house. The arts are freezing in this part of the world, and he is on his way to England to pick up some angels. . . .[3]

The Quentin referred to is Massys, the leading Flemish painter of the age who, in his sixties, was still producing excellent and innovative work. Holbein would certainly want to meet a master who shared his own ideas about honest, character-probing portraiture.

Yet sending his 'excellent artist' on a journey to London via Antwerp was for Erasmus vicarious indulgence in a nostalgia trip. A decade before, he, Gilles and More had been the closest of friends, meeting sometimes in England and sometimes in the Low Countries but always united in a common attitude towards Christendom and a common hope for its future. In 1517 Erasmus and Gilles had had their portraits done by Massys and presented as a diptych to More, 'so that, if fate should carry both of us off, we can in some form at least be with you'. The artist depicted his sitters surrounded by books and other reminders of scholarship and friendship. Gilles was actually holding a letter from More which made the Englishman marvel at Massys's skill in copying his handwriting.[4] Memories of happy times were very vivid in Erasmus's mind as he commended another portrait-painter to his old friends. Perhaps he was conscious that those golden days and gilded relationships were already slipping into an irrecoverable past.

Much has been written about the relationship between Erasmus and More and, though all the arguments cannot be rehearsed here, some points need to be made because they affect our understanding of Hans Holbein and his subsequent career. Within the international humanist fraternity Thomas More enjoyed a reputation which went beyond anything that scholarship or his written works merited (by 1526 his Latin works, known abroad, were *Utopia,* some translations of the Greek satirist Lucian and a collection of epigrams). Although he became a legend after his tragic and dramatic death, he was to some extent already a legend in his own lifetime. For this there were three reasons: his personality, his career and Erasmus.

Most people who came to know Thomas More fell under his spell. As a companion he was *simpatico* – profound and serious, yet always ready with a jest. He enjoyed erudite company and was the sort of man who easily attracts 'disciples'. At Oxford, at the inns of court and later in London as a successful lawyer and royal councillor he was frequently to be found at the centre of a group of admirers who listened delightedly to his *bons mots.* Not all who knew him were impressed. The chronicler Edward Hall recorded,

> I cannot tell whether I should call him a foolish wise man or a wise foolish man, for undoubtedly he beside his learning had a great wit, but it was so mingled with taunting and mocking that it seemed to them that best knew him, that he thought nothing to be well spoken except he had ministered some mock in the communication.[5]

Like many a man of solid conviction and fluid tongue, he could easily slip from the clever to the clever-clever, from the candid to the vicious, from the sardonic to the cruel, from the humorous to the vulgar. But for those who agreed with his opinions, were on the receiving end of his generosity or hospitality, or were flattered to be admitted to his friendship Thomas More was, in the original sense of the words, a scholar and a gentleman.

His career was a model for the Christian humanist. Champions of the New Learning looked to the international coterie of educated laymen to bring about reform. Scholars who married personal devotion with an appreciation of classical virtue would achieve high office, influence princes, change laws, initiate wise and humane policies and transform society permanently for the better. More had contemplated and rejected the vocations of priest, monk and reclusive academic in favour of the law and royal service. By 1526 talent and ambition had brought him the speakership of the House of Commons, participation in diplomatic missions abroad, a knight-hood, the chancellorship of the Duchy of Lancaster (among other court posts) and membership of the royal Council. He was intimate with Wolsey and a frequent companion of the king. Humanists in other lands watched his rise with admiration and approval and looked to the government of Henry VIII to produce enlightened policies of reform.

However, what counted more than anything else with the inter-national modernist elite, in the early days at least, was Erasmus's enthusiastic endorsement of Thomas More. He eulogized the Englishman in conversation and letters. Writing to the knight and littérateur Ulrich von Hutten in 1519, he praised More as 'the ideal of true friendship', a Christian given wholeheartedly to piety, an industrious lawyer with the common touch, a collector of curios with a lively interest in everything unusual, an eager and accomplished student of Greek classics and of the fathers. What he did not and could not in honesty commend was More's intellectual attainment. The rising star of English politics was not a master of independent thought, as were many of Erasmus's colleagues and correspondents. It was to More the advocate, not More the scholar, that he playfully dedicated the *Praise of Folly*. When he organized Froben's publication of *Utopia* and made a collection of More's epigrams, issued from the same press, he would not commit himself in writing to an author whose Latin style lacked elegance and whose arguments could not preserve the ivory-tower detachment he himself affected. There is no doubt that friendship was the main motivation for this sponsorship. Yet we cannot rule out an element of calculation – on both sides. The relationship which gave birth to More's national and international reputation was a symbiotic one. The Englishman gained recognition as a scholar throughout western Christendom. Erasmus, the wandering philosopher dependent on patronage, retained in his camp one of England's most influential figures.

By 1526 the accelerating current of the Reformation was already putting clear water between these old friends. More could not and would not avoid the religious controversy that Erasmus so much deplored. He felt passionately about the unity of Christendom and had no shred of doubt that the blame for fracturing it lay wholly and squarely with the 'Lutherans'. As the implications of the New Learning, biblical studies and demands for reform drove erstwhile humanist colleagues from the sunlit uplands of intellectual debate into the dark valleys of partisanship More did not simply find himself reluctantly in Catholic territory, sadly divided from old friends with whom he still felt some sympathy. He became a reactionary among reactionaries, a defender of the papacy against all comers, an enemy of the open Bible, an advocate of ruthless persecution. He explained to Erasmus that he found all heretics 'absolutely loathsome, so much so that, unless they regain their senses, I want to be as hateful to them as anyone can possibly be'. He was among those who urged Erasmus to come off the fence and declare himself unequivocally against Luther. And he explained to his old friend why he could no longer support the Erasmian attitude of independent-minded and reasoned debate:

> I am keenly aware of the risk involved in an open-door policy towards these newfangled erroneous sects. . . . some people like to give an approving eye to novel ideas, out of superficial curiosity, and to dangerous ideas, out of devilry. . . . All my efforts are directed towards the protection of those men who do not deliberately desert the truth, but are seduced by the enticements of clever fellows.[6]

By 1526 More had only partially come off the fence himself. Three years earlier his tortuously divided mind had resulted in the *Responsio ad Lutherum*. It was a diatribe so uncouth and splenetic, even by the standards of the day, that Erasmus complained that it could give Luther lessons in vehemence. A mild example of More's vituperation will give some indication of the incandescent fury locked behind the façade of scholarly benevolence seen by the world. Referring to the reformer's criticism of Henry VIII More thundered,

> Since he has written that he already has a prior right to bespatter and besmirch the royal crown with shit, will we not have the posterior right to proclaim the beshitted tongue of this practitioner of posterioristics most fit to lick with his anterior the very posterior of a pissing she-mule until he shall have learned more correctly to infer posterior conclusions from prior premises.[7]

Yet, even though More wanted his robust attack on heresy to be firmly in the public domain, he was not prepared to be recognized as the author of a work as vulgar as it was poorly reasoned. The *Responsio ad Lutherum* was published under a pseudonym.

In the closing weeks of 1526, the image of Sir Thomas More perceived by his wide circle of friends and admirers was that of the urbane, affable and witty companion that would continue to be projected in after years by simplistic hagiographers. This was how he wished the world to see him and he was only too willing to welcome his friend's portrait-painter, offer him hospitality and to render him whatever help he could. On 18 December More wrote to Erasmus to announce the safe arrival of his protégé: 'Your painter, dearest Erasmus, is a wonderful artist, but I fear he will not find England as fruitful as he had hoped. Yet I will do my best to see that he does not find it absolutely barren.'[8]

Holbein's affairs seemed to have taken a decided turn for the better. He had the patronage of one of the most powerful men in the realm whose support soon took very practical form, for More was as good as his word. London, too, would have fascinated him. Though crammed, cramped and crowded after salubrious Basel, it was an exciting place with many wealthy citizens as well as luxury-seeking courtiers and visitors from the country. It was a town full of promise for a multi-talented artisan. It must even have appeared, to a stranger not tuned to the vibrations of native discord, a much calmer place than the Swiss cities. There were no preachers thundering from rival pulpits; no partisan pamphlets fluttering from the presses; no scurrilous religious lampoons on sale in the markets. Yet the very year of Holbein's arrival was a turning point in the life of the capital and the nation. In the spring of 1526, Tyndale's English New Testament, published abroad and smuggled into the country, made its appearance and was eagerly snapped up by merchants, students and literate artisans. The authorities tried in vain to check the spread of books which, in the words of Bishop Tunstall of London, would otherwise 'contaminate and infect the flock committed unto us with most deadly poison and heresy'.[9] Holbein may not have arrived in time to witness the bonfire of confiscated volumes presided over by Wolsey in October at St Paul's Cross. This was one of many such demonstrations of official disfavour, which were as ineffective as they were dramatic. So great was the demand for vernacular Scriptures and so considerable the profit to be made from clandestine colportage that pirate editions had begun to circulate before the end of the year. Something else much more important occurred in 1526. Very few people knew about it and those who did could never have guessed at its significance. Henry VIII stopped sleeping with Catherine of Aragon, the Spanish-born wife to whom he had been married for seventeen years.

Over England the Reformation cloud may still have been no bigger than a man's hand but it rapidly filled the eastern skyline. That was the direction 'deadly poison and heresy' was coming from and the authorities, quite rightly, kept a close watch on merchants, mariners and coastal communities and anyone else having regular connection with the continent. Inevitably, that included German-speaking craftsmen. It was well for Holbein that the *Dance of Death* blocks were still languishing in a Basel or Lyon store room. Thomas More might not have welcomed so enthusiastically an artist who had so robustly expressed his criticism of Church leaders.

And this brings us to 'the curious incident of the dog in the night'. Like Sherlock Holmes's hound, Holbein – as far as we know – failed to do something during his first visit to England which certainly calls for explanation. Foreign residents in strange lands always congregate together to speak their own language, practise their own customs and sing the songs of home. They also need to offer one another mutual encouragement and protection, for racism and chauvinism exist even in the most liberal host communities.

London was a town of some 85,000 inhabitants. Some 6 per cent comprised families who had originated on the continent. Most of these were involved in crafts and trades. Through talent and industry they prospered. Naturally they formed communities within the community. Being different, being successful and being ghettoistic were reasons sufficient to make them unpopular among the coarser citizenry. There were occasional anti-foreign riots and the immigrant communities had long since learned to keep indoors on May Day when the City apprentices traditionally drank themselves into rowdiness in the taverns and wandered the streets in hooligan gangs. Foreigners were also discriminated against by the authorities. They paid higher taxes and many of them were not allowed to employ native-born apprentices. London's immigrant communities lived in their own quarters of the city. Most Germans lived in Dowgate Ward, near the bridge, where the merchants of the Hanseatic League had their factory, the Steelyard.

Holbein had come to England alone, without family or close companions. On his first arrival, when for some months at least he was struggling with the local language and customs, it would have been only natural for him to gravitate towards this neighbourhood. In later years he had many friends and patrons in the German community. He enjoyed their company and they appreciated his talent. Yet there is no evidence that he had close contact with the German residents in 1526–8.

The most obvious reason for this otherwise curious self-denial is that Holbein wanted to keep out of trouble. Suspicion of heresy and heresy-spreading focused, not without cause, on the Hanse merchants. Most of them came from or had close contact with the north-German towns and ports where Lutheranism was already established. Religious zeal and commercial opportunism alike encouraged the merchants to spread the new ideas and the books expounding them. The fact that *The Babylonian Captivity, The Liberty of a Christian Man* and other pieces of Wittenberg apologetic were banned in England only increased the curiosity of scholars and inquisitive free-thinkers. With a ready market and an assured profit it was worth the Hanse merchants' while to risk smuggling forbidden books and tracts into England in casks of wine and bales of cloth. In recent years heresy hunters had brought several of the Germans in for investigation. The pace hotted up in 1526. That was the year that the Steelyard council discontinued the celebration of their own regular mass at Allhallows the More, their parish church. This led immediately to an investigation by Wolsey's officers, as a result of which four members of the Steelyard were arrested and forced in February to make public abjuration. That was far from being the end of the matter. In an attempt to block this particular inlet the royal Council wrote to the burgomaster of Cologne, the Hanse town most favourably disposed to England, to demand that he prohibit the export of banned books. Meanwhile the authorities in London maintained their vigilance. During 1527 two surprise raids were launched in the Steelyard which led to further prosecutions. The organizer of these purges was Thomas More.

If More was no friend of the German merchants he had his reasons. In 1521, his favourite daughter Margaret had married William Roper, a young lawyer, and the couple lived in More's house. Either shortly before or soon after the wedding, Roper, like many members of the inns of court, became fascinated by Luther's teaching. He was encouraged in his studies – and may very well have been introduced to them – by members of the Steelyard, who sold him the reformer's books. At his father-in-law's table in Bucklersbury and Chelsea Roper urged the 'true faith' with all the zeal of a young convert. No amount of argument by Sir Thomas could sway him. It made for very strained relationships within the household. Eventually, Roper was fingered during one of the Steelyard raids (perhaps Wolsey's in January 1526, though no date is given by Nicholas Harpsfield, the narrator of these events). The merchants indicted with him had to make public recantations. Roper was spared this humiliation because of his family connections and was dismissed by the cardinal with a caution. The young rebel was eventually brought back to the Catholic faith, though how and when we do not know. What is clear is that at the time of Holbein's close connection with the More household, 1526–8, the words 'Steelyard' and 'Hanse' were not popular there.

The artist's new patron set him to work right away on precisely the project we would have expected him to initiate. He commissioned a portrait of himself (see plate section) and, in all likelihood a companion piece of his wife Alice (now lost). Thus began that revealing series of studies which have enabled later generations to 'see' several of the leading men and women of Henry VIII's court. This is the image by which we recognize Sir Thomas More. It is also the graphic representation we have to set alongside the eulogies of Erasmus and of the Catholic martyr's early biographers. This juxtaposition certainly reveals two sides of the lawyer–politician's character. Indeed, we would be hard put to it to recognize from the painting the jovial, witty, humble 'perfect model' of friendship whom Erasmus remembered with such affection.

The scholar described More as a lover of informality, a man who loathed ostentation and seldom wore rich clothes or gold chains. In the painting we are confronted by a sombre, dignified man conscious of his own importance. There is, to be sure, nothing ostentatious about the courtier's clothes, but the velvet, fur-trimmed gown with its crimson sleeves is expensive and the knight's chain and pendant Tudor rose are proudly worn. More's red-rimmed eyes and narrow mouth betoken the fanatical persecutor rather than the bonhominous companion and there is a suggestion of nervousness about the clasped hands. There is no religious symbol in this painting of a very religious man. The only suggestion of moralizing content is the slackly draped rope occupying the top right-hand corner. This esoteric reference to mortality (Latin *funis* = rope; *funus* = funereal, deathly) would have been appreciated by members of More's scholarly circle and was a sophisticated *memento mori* superior to the conventional skull, clock or hourglass.

Thomas More was a complex man to whom earlier hagiographies do no justice. Modern biographers have represented him as a bundle of contradictions: a retiring scholar with ambitions for high office; a would-be religious celibate who was a devoted family man; a gentle humanist and England's most fanatical reactionary; someone who shunned display but had more than one portrait painted. His willingness to commission Holbein to record his likeness is in fact less of a puzzle than might first appear. He shared with Erasmus and other humanists a delight in exchanging pictures with scholarly friends. He genuinely considered this to be no ostentation. In *Utopia* he actually advocated the public display of the portraits and statues of prominent citizens, 'for the perpetual memory of their good acts, and also that the glory and renown of ancestors may stir and provoke their posterity to virtue'.

Holbein evidently took great pains to get this particular physiognomy just right. As in most, probably all, of his later portraits, he made a drawing first, then 'pricked' it – that is, he made small holes along the main lines of the recorded features. By laying the drawing over the prepared surface for the painting and then smearing charcoal dust over it he had the outline for the final portrait. In the case of the More portrait reflectogram analysis has shown that the artist deviated at several points from his pattern, trusting eye and memory to achieve the required nuances of expression. Holbein was acutely aware of how important this commission was for the success of his visit to England. More was obviously pleased with the result. He sat for at least one other portrait study, of which only the preparatory drawing now exists and he commended his painter warmly to other members of his circle.

There is another painting which logically fits into this phase of Holbein's life. It was, as far as we know, his last small sacred painting designed as an aid to private devotion (see plate section). Art historians disagree on its precise place on a chronological list of the artist's works, current opinion seeming to favour the period 1524–6. However, the earliest records locate *Noli Me Tangere* securely in England: it was part of the royal collection as early as the 1540s. That implies that it was either painted for Henry VIII or acquired by him, through confiscation. Holbein was not in regular royal employ for another ten years so that we may reasonably assume the latter. That being the case, the arrows of possibility converge on Thomas More as the man most likely to have commissioned this work. As well as being Holbein's principal patron in 1526–8 and a Christian of famous piety, his property was forfeit to the Crown after his execution in 1535; moreover, in the mid-1520s, he had two chapels to furnish.

To mark his new dignity, in 1524, Thomas More like other leading courtiers acquired an out-of-town mansion. It was at Chelsea, three miles upriver from Westminster. The main house had its own chapel but the new owner constructed in the grounds a complex called the New Building, which was his own private retreat. It comprised his library, a gallery where he could walk and read at the same time, thus exercising body, mind and spirit, and a chapel for his private devotions. According to his son-in-law it was More's custom to immure himself here whenever possible, but especially on Fridays, 'spending his time only in devout prayers and spiritual exercises'. Here he emulated the eremitic life of those holy men he admired but could not wholly follow. Here he gave himself to prayer, fasting, study and self-flagellation, attuning himself to the business of heaven, raising his mind above worldly things, and bringing his body under subjection. For this agonizing discipline of self-denial he could have had no better model than the *Noli Me Tangere*.

The painting illustrates that strange, bitter-sweet moment in the Gospel story when Mary Magdalene recognizes the risen Christ, seeks to embrace him, only to be gently but firmly rebuffed. Here, as in all his religious narratives, Holbein is determined to capture the drama of the moment while being true to Scripture. All the essential elements of the story, as recorded in John's Gospel, are present. Dawn light streaks the sky, illuminating a distant Calvary. Several empty crosses are discernible instead of the conventional three – an indication that the Place of a Skull was a location much used for routine executions. Having witnessed the empty tomb, Peter and John are hurrying away and Peter is urging his more fleet-of-foot companion to slow down. Only the bewildered Mary has stayed behind, clutching her jar of embalming ointment. She has looked into the sepulchre and observed two angels seated at the head and foot of the burial slab. Turning from this vision she encounters a man whom, through her tears, she takes for the gardener. Holbein presents Christ fully clothed as a way of explaining this case of mistaken identity (though he does nod to convention by providing a faint halo). Jesus makes himself known. Mary ecstatically rushes towards him. But her master backs away with the words, 'Do not cling to me; I have not yet returned to the Father.'

This painting has often been contrasted with Titian's slightly earlier treatment of the same subject. The Venetian stripped away all 'unnecessary' biblical detail to present, more dramatically, a fluid composition in which a semi-naked Christ (who could scarcely have been mistaken for a gardener) fends off a devoted Magdalene who falls on her knees before him. The picture makes a religious statement but in a way that the truth-seeking Holbein could never have emulated. Holbein's *Noli Me Tangere*, judged purely in artistic terms, is not as accomplished a painting as the *Darmstadt Madonna* but, like the *Christ in his Tomb*, it takes us closer to his thinking on religious issues. There can be little doubt that he was as moved by the subject as John Evelyn was by the painting when he recorded, a century and a half later, 'I never saw so much reverence and kind of heavenly astonishment expressed in a picture.'[10]

However, its significance for More, if we correctly identify him as the commissioner, was more profound. For Sir Thomas, sexuality was an obsessing problem which distorted his self-perception and his view of the world. It was the impossibility of controlling his 'lower' nature which had kept him from the cloister and which caused him, after the death of his first wife, to rush into a second marriage with an older woman who did not raise his passions. The mixture of rigorous self-control and hair-shirt penitence he imposed on himself made him scream in tortured outrage against Luther and other ex-religious who lived 'under the name of wedlock in open, incestuous lechery without care or shame'.[11] To help him loosen the sin of sexual desire which manacled holy aspirations inside a susceptible body, More needed exemplars.

In traditional iconography Mary Magdalene was the model *par excellence* of the triumph of spirituality over carnality. She was the reformed prostitute of legend, from whom the demon of lust had been cast out and who was given a pure love of the Saviour. It was for this reason that she was granted the privilege of being the first witness of the Resurrection. Holbein's painting captures this ecstatic moment of recognition. But it also underscores the difference between the physical and the spiritual. Christ rejects the human embrace, the contact of bodies. The transit through death has changed him. His followers must now commune with him on the higher level of the spirit. More, who robustly defended the use of religious images, relied little on externals himself. But the *Noli Me Tangere* chimed precisely with his own devotional attitudes and needs, and it is easy to imagine him meditating on Holbein's painting in the privacy of his chapel.

There is no doubt about Sir Thomas's commissioning of Holbein's next important work. Before his own portrait was finished, he set his artist to producing what was to be a landmark in northern painting – a lifesize conversation piece to include several members of the family circle. It was to be painted in distemper on cloth and hung in one of the main rooms at Chelsea. Wealthy men customarily covered the walls of their damp and draughty houses with heavy drapes or tapestries. Such coverings usually depicted religious or mythical scenes. The commemoration of the patron and his family in such a way had, with one or two royal exceptions, never been seen outside Italy, certainly not in England.

The motive for this innovation was to record what was widely regarded as the perfect family. Part of the More legend concerned the happy domestic harmony at Chelsea, where the scholar–statesman lived with his second wife, his children and wards and their spouses. It was a family of the New Learning in which the girls studied alongside More's son and were famed for their facility in Latin and Greek. Erasmus, as ever, did much to perpetuate the legend. In 1519 he wrote,

> [More] rules his household . . . agreeably, no quarrels or disturbances arise there. If any quarrel does arise he at once heals or settles the difference; and he has never let anyone leave his house in anger. . . . Moreover, he is so disposed towards his parents and children as to be neither tiresomely affectionate nor ever failing in any family duty.[12]

Perhaps this seems too good to be true. One biographer says of More, 'the public spectacle he made of his real love for his family seems at times overmuch, part of the pageant he performed for an audience'.[13]

What More, Erasmus and other humanists such as the Spaniard Ludovicus Vives were advocating was an attitude towards the nurture of children which was much at odds with traditional received wisdom. This was an integral part of the New Learning crusade, and in England for a few years and within a very restricted circle it held sway. Gentle persuasion and reasoned argument replaced the regular use of the rod. Children – boys and girls – should be brought by patient and good-humoured teaching to love learning. Affection not fear should be the dominant emotions felt by children for their parents. We need not doubt that these principles applied in the More household. Sir Thomas was not being dishonest when he later reminded his son and daughters, 'I never could endure to hear you cry. You know, for example, how often I kissed you, how seldom I whipped you. . . . Brutal and unworthy to be called father is he who does not himself weep at the tears of his child.' And if his attitude towards women would not pass the test of modern political correctness, yet it was in advance of its time: 'If the female soil be in its nature stubborn, and more productive of weeds than fruit, it ought, in my opinion, to be more diligently cultivated with learning and good instruction.'[14] More's home at Chelsea had a warm and invigorating atmosphere but it was also a home on display to the world, and the group portrait commissioned from Holbein was a piece of humanist propaganda.

Hans welcomed this major commission not only for the financial reward it brought. It also gave him the opportunity to put into effect certain ideas that had been in his mind since his visit to Lombardy. Among the works of the mighty Mantegna that had impressed him were the frescos of the Gonzaga palace in Mantua. Perhaps artist and patron discussed some of the Italian masterpieces Holbein had observed and sketched during his travels. It may be that the new project grew out of the painter's enthusiasm for the magnificent Renaissance murals and More's desire to introduce such innovations into England. However the *Household of Sir Thomas More* came about, it clearly owed a great deal to the group portrait of Lodovico Gonzaga and his court in the Camera degli Sposi in Mantua (see plate section). The Chelsea group is more homely than that assembled in the ducal court and the composition of Holbein's picture is different from Mantegna's, but the back references are obvious. This we can see by comparing the fresco with Holbein's preparatory drawing (the original painting no longer exists). The poses of Thomas More and his daughter Margaret and their special relationship are similar to those of Lodovico and his wife. The figure on the left leaning forward to receive instructions from the duke is paralleled by Margaret Giggs, who is pointing something out to her grandfather. Perhaps most significant of all is the fact that in both works the only character who gazes straight out at the beholder and thus draws him into the picture is the fool. Henry Pattinson, More's simple-minded retainer, takes the place allotted by Mantegna to Lodovico's dwarf. Do we detect a humanist jest here? Are both painters wryly drawing attention to the folly of human pretensions?

The *Household of Sir Thomas More* was a more exacting project than any of Holbein's frescos to date. It involved accurate portraiture of ten sitters combined with various allusions to the liberal arts and scholarship which would create the desired impression of a cultured humanist environment. The artist made preparatory sketches for all the figures, and drawings to indicate the proposed composition. One of these ended up in Basel and provides our only indication of what the finished painting may have looked like. It also tells us about some of the alterations agreed between artist and client. It is clear that More wanted the emphasis to be on the cultural preoccupations of his family even if that meant under-emphasizing their piety. Alice, Lady More was originally depicted kneeling at a prayer desk, but

Holbein made a note in German, 'she will sit', and he sketched in a pet monkey playing around her skirts. More's daughter Cecily was shown with a rosary. By the time a later version of the painting was made this had disappeared. Another *aide-mémoire* in the artist's hand ordained 'clavichords and other musical instruments on the sideboard'.

However, it was another writer who added further notes in Latin, identifying each sitter with his or her age: Thomas More, and his wife, his father John More, his son, also called John, his three daughters, Margaret, Cecily and Elizabeth, his two wards Anne Cresacre and Margaret Giggs and his fool Henry Pattinson. These Latin labels were essential for Holbein since he had to include them in the finished painting. The man who provided them was another habitué of the Chelsea household and someone who became a close companion of the foreign visitor. Nicholas Kratzer was born in Munich and was the painter's exact contemporary. He studied at Cologne and Wittenberg before coming to Oxford to lecture in 1516 and later established a reputation as an astronomer–astrologer, mathematician and maker of mathematical instruments. He was employed by Wolsey and More and, in 1527, was a tutor to Sir Thomas's daughters. Powerful patronage had elevated him into royal service and Kratzer was now the king's astronomer. He was described as 'a man who is brimful of wit, jest and humorous fancies'[15] and he seems to have demonstrated his good humour by taking Holbein under his wing.

He and Holbein had much more than linguistic connections in common. Kratzer was a humanist with scholarly contacts throughout the continent. He was acquainted with leading artists, was a friend of Dürer and had spent several days with both Dürer and Erasmus in Antwerp in 1520. Kratzer was among the contacts to whom Erasmus commended Holbein by letters of recommendation. But by 1524 the astronomer's opinions had passed beyond those sanctioned by Erasmus and well beyond those espoused by More. In October of that year he commended himself warmly to Dürer: 'Now that you are all evangelical in Nuremberg I must write to you. God grant you grace to persevere; the adversaries indeed are strong, but God is stronger and is wont to help the sick who call upon him and acknowledge him.'[16] However tolerant More, the hammer of heretics, was of free-thinkers within his own household the two Germans will have been circumspect in what they proclaimed openly. There was, though, nothing to stop them sharing their opinions in private. Before he left England in mid-1528 Holbein made a portrait of his new friend which is as remarkable for its warmth of tone as for the exuberant delight the artist took in rendering the assorted instruments of Kratzer's craft (see plate section).

The astronomer was involved in the next major advance in Holbein's fortunes. In February 1527 the artist was offered the opportunity to work for the royal court. This exciting, rapid promotion must hitherto have been beyond his wildest dreams. The gamble of coming to England had paid off. At last, like his friend and mentor Hans Burgkmair, he was entering the service of one of Europe's leading rulers and one who, like the late Emperor Maximilian, prided himself on the splendour and cultivated taste of his court. For several weeks in the winter and spring of 1527 Hans had to abandon his work for the Mores and move downriver to Greenwich.

The occasion which provided Holbein's new employment was the arranging of a treaty between Henry VIII and Francis I. French ambassadors arrived at the end of February and the lengthy negotiations were concluded two months later. All that remained was the celebration of the renewed amity between the two nations with suitably lavish spectacle. On Friday 4 May the diplomats, their suites and their English counterparts repaired to Greenwich palace and the following day was given over to a tourney, banqueting and entertainments such as, according to the hyperbole of the Milanese ambassador, surpassed the magnificence of all princes ancient and modern.[17] A special building had been constructed at enormous expense for this single day's orgy of Tudor self-advertisement. Work had begun on 6 February on a structure comprising two great chambers: a banqueting hall and a 'disguising theatre' (that is, an arena for masques and pageants). Over the next three months a magnificent edifice of timber, gilded, painted and festooned with drapes, evolved under the watchful eyes of Sir Henry Guildford, controller of the household, and Sir Thomas Wyatt, who was probably standing in for his father, the treasurer of the household. Among the cohorts of carpenters, joiners, casters of lead, painters, gilders, ironworkers, carvers, leatherworkers, experts in lighting, cloth hanging, carpets and tapestries, to say nothing of their squads of apprentices and assistants, a place was found for the recently arrived Swiss painter.

Holbein's skill with lavish, large-scale decorative projects must have been well known to those in charge of the works, for he was entrusted with the two most spectacular paintings. One end of the banqueting hall was dominated by a triumphal arch over which was portrayed Henry VIII's siege of Thérouanne (1513) 'and the very manner of every man's camp, very cunningly wrought'.[18] The 'cunningly wrought' doubtless refers to Holbein's skill in using perspective and foreshortening to create illusions of depth which had so amazed the citizens of Lucerne and Basel. For this the artist received £4 10s. But the *pièce de résistance* of the whole ensemble was the ceiling of the disguising theatre.

> on the ground of the roof was made the whole earth, environed with the sea, like a very map or chart, and by a cunning making of another cloth, the zodiac with the twelve signs and the five circles or girdles and the two poles appeared on the earth and water compassing the same, and in the zodiac were the twelve signs curiously made, and above this were made the seven planets, as Mars, Jupiter, Sun, Mercury, Venus, Saturn and Moon, every one in their proper houses made according to their properties, that it was a cunning thing and a pleasant sight to behold.[19]

Holbein could not have achieved this complex celestial illusion without specialist help, and the records show that he and Nicholas Kratzer jointly received four shillings a day for work on the ceiling from 8 February to 3 March. So for these two projects the artist was paid between six and seven pounds. But we know that he also undertook other parts of the decorative schema, which would have made his total earnings appreciably greater. What that meant in real terms we can roughly calculate from a London municipal regulation of 1538 which fixed the wages of jobbing carpenters, masons, tilers, plasterers and bricklayers at eight pence a day. Holbein had every reason to be satisfied with his first experience of royal service.

It also gave him his first glimpse of the king. On 11 March Henry visited the site to inspect the work in progress. On that day some large painted cloths on which Holbein and his men had been labouring were temporarily hoisted into place for the royal approval. The artist gazed for the first time on the thickset frame, the face with its fringe of red beard and tiny, probing eyes that he was destined to delineate for posterity.

After the flurry of activity at Greenwich Holbein was able, in May 1527, to return to his group study of the More household. But he could not give it all his attention for, by now, other commissions were beginning to arrive. Despite the various likenesses he had painted in Basel, it was only in 1527 in England that his career as a portrait painter really took off. Two and a half centuries later, Hogarth wryly observed, 'In England vanity is united with [selfishness]. . . . Portrait painting therefore ever has and ever will succeed better in this country than in any other.'[20] There is more than a grain of truth in that apothegm. Portraiture was well established as an art form in Italy, France and the Netherlands in the late Renaissance. Yet, after Holbein had encouraged a taste for it among the Tudor elite, it became so much a part of the English social atmosphere that it never died away. Portrait painting is the only English art form that has an unbroken pedigree back to the early sixteenth century. So great was the demand that when native talent was lacking, as it often was, foreign artists skilled in limning could find ready employment. Holbein may have been the first portrait painter adopted by the English but he was followed by a noble line of great exponents of the genre – Eworth, Mytens, Van Dyck, Rubens, Kneller – the procession continues down to Sargent, László and others in our own century.

Several of the men and women whom the painter encountered through the More circle and through his court contacts at Greenwich wanted the remarkable Swiss visitor to capture their likenesses. Holbein became the latest fashion. One of the first to commission portraits of himself and his wife was Sir Henry Guildford. The artist could scarcely have secured a more important client. Guildford remained throughout his adult life a great favourite and companion of the king and the recipient of several court offices and land grants. As a past master of the revels he was adept at the organization of court entertainments and he oversaw the Greenwich festivities with an expert eye. In 1526 he had been awarded the Order of the Garter and Holbein depicted him with the Garter chain and his staff of office as controller of the household. His prominence, his wealth and his intimacy with the king made Guildford one of the arbiters of taste (even Erasmus from distant Basel curried favour with him). When the controller of the household took Holbein up others were eager to follow.

If we think of the English establishment in terms of overlapping circles, we can see Holbein, within only a few months, had begun to move in various of the groups that revolved around the king. He became known to several of More's friends. For Archbishop Warham he painted a portrait designed as a gift for Erasmus in response to the likeness the Dutch scholar had sent him. The ecclesiastic was among those who largely shared More's religious attitudes and who, like him, reacted with growing alarm to the changes of royal policy over the next few years. They and all English humanists revered the memory of John Colet, the founding father of the New Learning in England, whose New Testament lectures at Oxford, 1497–1503, had set a generation of scholars on the path of religious, educational and social reform. Colet had died in 1519, but one of his disciples, probably More, wanted a memento of him, so Holbein went to St Paul's cathedral and made a drawing from the bust on Colet's tomb made by the Italian sculptor Pietro Torrigiano. His likeness of Colet creates an uncanny effect of having been taken from life.

It is similar, in this respect, to two engaging studies he made in Bourges cathedral of the tomb figures of Duke Jean de Berry and his wife. Unfortunately, they do not relate to any of the artist's other work and it is impossible to decide at what stage of Holbein's journeying these drawings were made.

Holbein's work at Greenwich brought him into contact with various officers and officials of the royal household. The man jointly responsible with Guildford for the festivities was Sir Thomas Wyatt, the gifted young courtier and poet who was in his mid-twenties. He was one of the dashing young men the king liked to have about him. He excelled not only in the chamber, where his verses and satires, songs and lute tunes, his mastery of foreign languages and literature made him a cultured royal companion, but also in the tiltyard, where his athletic prowess thrilled especially the ladies of the court. Two drawings of Thomas Wyatt by Holbein survive but probably date from the artist's second English sojourn. However, the artist did paint the elder Wyatt, Sir Henry, the treasurer of the household. It was he who, through his underlings, actually paid the army of craftsmen working at Greenwich. Another official who was probably involved in the administration of court finance and who took over from Wyatt as treasurer in April 1528, while Holbein was still in England, was Sir Brian Tuke. His official correspondence reveals him to be a dyed-in-the-wool civil servant, a man of little imagination and a stickler for administrative detail. Holbein caught the mood of the man well in the portrait he painted, perhaps in celebration of Tuke's promotion. Yet there was another circle that Holbein entered via the Wyatts where, whether he knew it or not, events were moving which would affect the destiny of England and Europe — and his career.

In the spring of 1527 the possibility was first mooted, secretly at first, of the annulment of Henry VIII's marriage to Catherine of Aragon. The king was motivated by dynastic and personal considerations: his wife had failed to provide him with a much needed Tudor heir and he had fallen heavily for a nineteen-year-old girl, Anne Boleyn. Unlike her elder sister, Anne refused to become a royal plaything, the obsession of a season to be cast aside when the king's ardour had abated. Henry was not disposed to obtain a woman's favours by force; this was one of the few chinks in his indomitable will. In his determination to bring to a conclusion a courtship already two years old he obliged everything and everyone to serve his ends. His own conscience, his ministers, national policy, the Church — all were directed over the next few years to bringing about a satisfactory conclusion of the king's 'great matter'. Henry manoeuvred himself and his government into a position which made it impossible to back down. The proceedings and outcome of the 'divorce' issue constitute one of the biggest *causes célèbres* of English history and need no repetition here. What is of interest for the Holbein story is that there was emerging at court a new focus of power — the Boleyn circle. Early in 1528 Anne was installed in a suite close to the king's, and thither courtiers and the ambitious resorted in droves. The fashionable Swiss artist was taken up by several members of this set.

Anne's father, Thomas Boleyn, had been steadily advancing in royal service over many years but now favours fell thick and fast upon him and his family. In 1525 he was admitted to the peerage as Viscount Rochford. The flow of grants, monopolies, offices and sinecures continued over the following months and years. Every ambitious family that could find some connection with the new favourite clamoured to exploit it. There was no need for the Wyatts to drum up a spurious friendship with the Boleyns, for the two families had long been close. Both had their origins in Norfolk, and in 1511 Thomas Boleyn and Henry Wyatt had received jointly the constableship of Norwich castle. Thomas Wyatt was early captivated by Anne after her appearance at court and he wooed her with songs and verses:

> What word is that that changeth not
> Though it be turn'd and made in twain?
> It is mine Anna, God it wot,
> And eke the causes of my pain.

The courtier had to retire gracefully from the lists of love when the king entered the arena, but the mutual affection of the young people was another cord binding the Wyatts and Boleyns together.

In 1526–7 no one could have foreseen the religious and political turbulence that lay ahead and which would place Anne Boleyn on the throne as Henry's second queen. It must, therefore, have been sheer good fortune rather than calculation that, right at the beginning of Holbein's English career, he gained the patronage of the Boleyn circle. During his first stay the artist was commissioned to make portraits of men and women at court and in Norfolk connected to the Boleyns by ties of blood or amity. Anne, Lady Shelton was Thomas Boleyn's sister and Holbein made drawings of her and her husband, Sir John, for a glazier producing a stained-glasss window for the church at Shelton, ten miles south of Norwich. Not fourteen miles distant, as the crow flies, lies the village of East Harling, seat of Francis Lovell, esquire of the body to Henry VIII. Holbein was called upon for a portrait of Lovell's wife, Anne, and thus came into being *Portrait of a Lady with a Squirrel and a Starling* which, until recently, was a puzzle to art historians. The sitter has now been identified by means of establishing the significance of the animals. The squirrel was Lovell's heraldic badge and the starling is a pun on 'East Harling'.[21]

At about the same time Holbein painted another Norfolk worthy. Thomas Godsalve was registrar of Norwich and a man of substance in the country. He was eager to place his son, John, at court and energetically employed his social contacts to further his ambitions. Thomas commissioned from the newly-fashionable Swiss artist a double portrait of himself and his eighteen-year-old son. Out in the provinces a man might serve his king loyally and yet live his life in rural obscurity. Having a portrait done by an artist who was painting the highest in the land might persuade their social superiors that the Godsalves were a family of consequence and cultivated tastes.

In the complex machine with its connected regional mechanisms that was the Tudor court these and other circles revolved, overlapped and interacted like so many cogs. It was a frenetic, overburdened piece of engineering performing the functions of royal household and national government. It was in need of overhaul but it still creaked along with passable efficiency. It was into this lumbering clockwork that the sand of religious and dynastic controversy was about to be thrown. The royal court was England's principal gathering point of intellectuals, artists, diplomats, statesmen, ecclesiastics and place-seekers. Here all the newest ideas were discussed with a freedom denied to Henry VIII's lesser subjects. Tyndale's New Testament was read openly by many, including Anne Boleyn. Lutheran tracts were perused rather more circumspectly. Parents who were themselves content with traditional religious modes had their attitudes challenged by sons who came back from the universities and inns of court excited by new ideas. A growing corps of native pamphleteers was circulating demands for Church reform and deliberately playing on widespread anticlericalism. Bishops and advocates of reaction such as Thomas More might despatch their agents to ports, commercial warehouses and city taverns to sniff out banned books and propagators of heresy. The one place where their noses were tightly pegged was the royal court.

Their concern was not greatly excited as long as the orthodoxy of the man on the throne was beyond doubt. But what was happening even as Holbein packed his bags in preparation for his return to Basel was that Henry VIII was for the first time coming to share an experience common to many of his subjects. What galled ordinary people was the power exercised over their lives by a class of men for whom they had scant respect: the clergy. The king had never had a taste of ecclesiastical sanction – until he decided to change his matrimonial arrangements. It was as he found his will resisted by a papal establishment which – as everyone knew – was riddled with corruption that he came to understand the frustrations and irritations complained of by English men and women and exposed by radical pamphleteers. As soon as the king's 'great matter' dominated national and international policy and Henry began casting about for arguments and apologists to defend his cause, advocates of reform became bold; those close to the king began to take sides; old friendships and loyalties were put to the test; court factions acquired a religious hue; conservatives and radicals grabbed for the helm and sent domestic and foreign policy veering wildly from side to side.

In mid-1528 it is doubtful whether anyone, least of all a visiting foreign artist with an insecure grasp of English, could have accurately prophesied the troubles ahead. Holbein was probably aware only vaguely that the ideological conflicts upsetting Germany and Switzerland were now, tardily, being experienced in England. He had other things on his mind. He was going home to Basel, to his family, to his circle of intellectual and artistic friends. And he was going with a very satisfactory jangling in his purse as well as impressive stories to tell of his new-found success.

He reached Basel around the middle of August 1528 and there is no record of his movements for the next three and a half years. Earlier biographers assumed that he stayed in his home town until April 1532, at which time documentary evidence enables us to take up the chronicle of his life. The customary explanation for his movements is that he came back to his familiar haunts as a 'local boy made good' with the intention of settling down to enjoy his enhanced fame and that it was only the deteriorating situation in the city which finally forced him out. We have to discard this theory because it fails to fit with the few facts that we do know. In August 1529 Erasmus wrote to More acknowledging receipt of a version of the *Household of Thomas More* delivered by the artist. If Holbein brought the item in question back from London in 1528 it is inconceivable that he would not have handed it over immediately and that Erasmus would have waited a year before expressing his thanks. We also know that Holbein and Kratzer were working on a prestigious project for presentation to Henry VIII at the end of 1528 and that the artist must have been in London at that time. All these difficulties disappear if we make one simple change to the artist's previously accepted itinerary and assume that Holbein, after a flying visit to Switzerland in August 1528, returned for a further year to London.

He had very good reasons for going back to Basel and equally pressing ones for a swift return to England. Legal and emotional obligations were hauling him home. He had been granted two years' leave of absence by the Basel council. If he failed to comply with the items of his agreement he risked losing his and his family's citizenship rights and he would probably incur penalties from his guild. He wanted to get back to his wife and children. His son Philip was growing fast and he had not even seen his infant daughter, Catherine, born after his departure in August 1526. At the same time he had found a country where his genius was acclaimed and better rewarded. His circle of potential clients was widening all the time and he had a full order book. The obvious answer was to hurry back to Basel, fulfil his family obligations, present himself to the council and request an extension of his leave of absence.

Almost immediately after his arrival in Basel he did two significant things: he bought a house and he painted a portrait of his wife and children (see plate section). The dwelling was a fairly substantial building on two floors. It had views over the Rhine and was flanked on one side by Froben's book depository and on the other by a small cottage (which Holbein also acquired two and a half years later). He paid a hundred gulden in cash and took out a mortgage for the remaining two hundred. This was the action of a man of means whose first thought was for his family. Haunted, as he must have been, by the improvidence of his father and the insecurities of his own childhood, Holbein was determined that his own dependants should enjoy a permanent roof over their heads and the respect of their neighbours.

This is borne out by the portrait of Elsbeth, Philip and Catherine. It was the most emotionally revealing picture Holbein ever executed and the one above all others which disposes of any idea that he was a dispassionate observer of the human scene. We rightly read it for hints about the relationship between Hans, Elsbeth and their infant children. The initial impression is one of overwhelming sadness. This is partially the result of the drab background. Originally the figures were placed in a setting, probably of classical architecture, but at a later stage the paper on which the picture was painted was cut around the heads and shoulders of the sitters and laid down on panel in its present form. Yet, though the featureless backdrop focuses our attention on the three faces, it does not add to the stark, almost cruel honesty with which they are delineated. Holbein painted this picture quickly without the painstaking attention to textures and fine details that marked his portraits of the great and the good. This way of working must have been largely dictated by the fact that two of his models were restless children. But speed was also dictated by passion – the need to set down immediately what he felt for the only close family he had.

As always, Holbein, who was psychologically incapable of flattery, set down what he saw: a wife whose downcast, red-rimmed eyes proclaim mingled weariness and resignation; a son looking upward more in hope than in expectation; a baby daughter with no ready smile for this stranger who has suddenly come into her life. The emotional gap between this painting and the other family group Hans had been working on in Chelsea is vast. Analysts have found in the portrait of Elsbeth and the children evidence for all manner of domestic tragedies. The truth is, surely, less dramatic and more poignant. This is a picture of a marriage in which genuine affection has become strained by separation. Single-parenting was no less common in the sixteenth century than it is now and no less hard. For two years, throughout much of which she was pregnant, Elsbeth had coped single-handed. Her husband had returned full of honours, much needed cash and stories about the fine ladies and gentlemen of the English court, but he had also come to tell her that he was home only for a short visit. Soon she would be deserted again – and coping with another pregnancy.

It was a painting done for love. It may have been executed as a gift for Elsbeth or as a memento Hans could keep by him when he returned to England. Either way Holbein's motivation must have been partly to convince his wife that he did care about her and the children and that he did think about them when he was far from home.

As Holbein called on friends, bringing letters and messages from England, met up with Jakob Meyer and the other city leaders, and listened to the gossip in the taverns and printshops; as he sensed the atmosphere in the parish church and talked with other worshippers; and particularly as turbulent colleagues from his own guild plied him with their propaganda, he became painfully aware of the gathering low-pressure areas preparing to lash Basel with violent storms. By policies of moderation and tolerance this community on the Rhine had become over the years a refuge for radicals and free-thinkers and had avoided the conflicts which had caused other cities to lurch into reform or reaction. But the very programmes which had preserved Basel's peace were finally the ones that dragged her into war. It was here, in sweetly reasonable Basel, where the peace-loving Erasmus had made his home, that frustration and protest were soon to spill over into the worst iconoclastic violence yet seen in the Reformation.

Discontent was still double-headed: the lower orders in Basel society wanted both religious and political reform, but it was the guild leaders, aided and abetted by evangelical preachers, who were the agitators for radical change. The wealthier burghers and the senior clergy were united in desperate determination to preserve the status quo upon which their power and wealth and, they believed, the peace of the city largely depended. Anxious to avoid making any concessions at all, those in authority continued to prevaricate. They reacted with muddled severity and leniency to the growing acts of vandalism and public order offences. In the autumn of 1527 the Little Council made what was supposed to be a compromise settlement of the religious issue: they decreed that three churches might abolish the mass and hold reformed, vernacular services. The concession impressed no one. Six months later the council passed an edict of universal toleration, affirming that every citizen was free to believe whatever he considered necessary for his soul's salvation. This could not possibly satisfy either Catholic or Protestant extremists, convinced that truth could never be a matter of personal preference.

The first major confrontation had occurred during Easter 1528. Four artisans went into St Martin's, Oecolampadius's church, overthrew statues, pulled down the great crucifix and broke up altars. Seeing that this brought no immediate reprisals, a larger group descended on the Augustinian church a few days later and created similar havoc there. This time the Little Council had to act. They ordered the ringleaders to be rounded up and imprisoned. Guild leaders angrily demanded their members' release and when their protest failed they marched to the town hall at the head of a crowd several hundred strong. The council caved in, agreeing to discuss the guildsmen's demands with an elected delegation. As a result the culprits were released and the city's leaders agreed to five churches being purged of their decorations in an orderly fashion. All the other churches were to remain unmolested, on pain of dire penalties. Appeasement had its usual effect. The sight of the council falling back from redoubt to redoubt only emboldened the assault troops of reform. By the time Holbein returned in late summer it was obvious that the craft guilds were determined to keep up their pressure.

Everything we know about Holbein suggests that he was sympathetic towards the leaders of his own guild, who were clamouring for a more effective voice in city government as well as an end to clerical abuses and a purging of religion from superstitious excrescences. However, he did not involve himself in the conflict because he was anxious to get back to England. Thanks, perhaps, to Jakob Meyer and his other friends on the council Holbein obtained a further year's leave of absence. By early autumn he was in London once again.

One pressing matter which necessitated a speedy return was the project he had planned with Nicholas Kratzer. His friend had written a brief astronomical treatise, *Canones Horoptri,* which was for presentation to the king as a New Year's gift in 1529. As befitted its royal recipient it was magnificent though modest. A colleague of Kratzer's had written the manuscript on sixteen vellum pages and Holbein had provided elaborate capitals. The whole was encased in a green velvet binding. Since the object of New Year's gifts was to draw the king's attention to the sender and those associated with him, it is scarcely feasible that, having made his contribution to Kratzer's book, Holbein would have planned not to be in England when it was presented. The theory of a long sojourn in Basel (1528–32) would compel us to believe that Holbein did his work on the book early in 1528 and then deliberately left the country. The *Canones Horoptri* project strongly suggests that the artist intended his home visit to be a brief one and that he was still banking heavily on gaining royal patronage.

Life was certainly less frenzied in England's capital, but it was beginning to share features with events in several continental cities. Spontaneous iconoclasm was a growing problem. It is always easier to vent anger, indignation and frustration upon things than to challenge mistaken beliefs or confront the advocates of those beliefs. Heresy and anticlericalism spawned outrages in and around the capital and their perpetrators were encouraged by news of similar happenings abroad and by the circulation of pamphlets by Karlstadt and other extremists. In the mid-1520s a group of villagers in Rickmansworth, Hertfordshire, where Wolsey had one of his country retreats, went into the church, wrapped tarred rags around the rood and set fire to it. By 1529 minor acts of desecration had become so common and so uncontrollable as to make it necessary for parliament to issue a general pardon covering all offenders except those who pulled down highway crosses.

At the higher level of ideas, religious, political and social discontent focused on the ecclesiastical voluptuary Thomas Wolsey, who controlled most aspects of government. The Ipswich butcher's son who strutted in semi-royal magnificence was universally regarded as personifying all that was wrong in Church and state. When Londoners read in the discreet privacy of their chambers the latest anticlerical tract there was no doubt in their minds to whom it chiefly referred: '[priests] do nothing but translate all rule, power, lordship, authority, obedience and dignity from [the king] unto them'.[22] This virulent piece of radical propaganda was the *Supplication of the Beggars,* a diatribe written from the safety of the Low Countries by Simon Fish, one of Tyndale's confederates, which was circulating in the capital soon after Holbein's return. Fish was only expressing in tendentious tones for popular consumption ideas set forth in sophisticated argument by his more famous fellow exile, William Tyndale. Tyndale's *Obedience of a Christian Man* was available through the now well-established literary underground at the end of 1528. The book reproduced Luther's doctrine of the godly prince and gave theological gilding to absolutism. 'One king, one law is God's ordinance in every realm,' Tyndale asserted, and clergy, of whatsoever rank, have no business meddling in politics.

> Let kings . . . rule their realms themselves, with the help of laymen that are sage, wise, learned and expert. Is it not a shame above all shames, and a monstrous thing, that no man should be found able to govern a wordly kingdom, save bishops and prelates that have forsaken the world, and are taken out of the world, and appointed to preach the kingdom of God?[23]

The changes Tyndale advocated in the social and political balance were those being implemented in various principalities and free cities of German-speaking Europe where bishops were being deprived of temporal authority and civic leaders were issuing religious ordinances.

Some time in the early months of 1529 a quietly momentous event occurred in the inner recesses of the Tudor court which was to unleash revolution: Henry VIII read these banned publications and approved them. Whether he was convinced by the arguments of men he abhorred as heretics or came to the cynical realization that those arguments could be useful to him is a secret beyond our probing. The Erastian gospel was proclaimed to him at the right psychological moment. For personal and dynastic reasons Henry was determined to disembarrass himself of Catherine and marry Anne. The pope, supported by members of the English episcopate, was standing in the way of what should have been – for a king – a perfectly straight-forward annulment process. He had entrusted the 'great matter' to Wolsey, and Wolsey had failed him. The cardinal's heart was not in the business – or so Anne Boleyn claimed, for mistress and minister shared an intense mutual loathing. The king's treatment of Catherine of Aragon was widely unpopular, in the court, the capital and the country at large. Even Henry, secure within the ramparts of sycophancy, knew that. Public opinion was something he cared little about, but he could not afford to ignore it completely. The discovery that he had come to share with many of his subjects an indignation with the pretensions and arrogance of the ecclesiastical establishment suggested to him that curbing papal and clerical power would be popular.

The one person above all others who helped Henry to see the light was Anne Boleyn. She certainly had her own fish to fry but she was also inclined to religious reform. She had connections with London's contraband book trade and late in 1528 was bold enough to appeal to Wolsey on behalf of Robert Forman, a linchpin in this illicit commerce, when his activities were discovered. Anne and members of her circle read the *Supplication* and the *Obedience* and were not slow to see their implications for the immediate political situation. The headstrong girl who had stood up for known heretics was so secure within the protective walls of Henry's infatuation that she was not afraid to commend the forbidden books to her royal suitor. According to one story, Fish sent Anne a copy of his pamphlet and she showed it to the king, who was so impressed that he allowed the exile to return and extended royal protection to him. This account, set down by John Foxe a generation later, may be suspect, particularly so because the author also included another version of the same story which named two London merchants as the agents who brought the *Supplication* to the king's attention.

However, there is no doubt that Anne introduced Tyndale's latest work to Henry. The story goes that, having read the *Obedience of a Christian Man* herself, she lent it to one of her ladies-in-waiting, Anne Gainsford. This Anne 'lost' it to her lover, George Zouche, who playfully purloined it. The dean of the Chapel Royal discovered it and reported the find to Wolsey. Outraged, Anne Boleyn complained to the king, who obliged the cardinal to return the volume to its rightful owner. Naturally, Henry wanted to know what all the fuss was about and insisted on examining the *Obedience* for himself – or, at least, those passages Anne had underlined as particularly worthy of his attention. He was impressed. 'This book is for me and all kings to read,' he commented. He went further; he tried to induce England's most notorious heretic to enter his employ. Stephen Vaughan, a commercial agent in the Low Countries, was acting as a spy for More to gather information about English heretics 'skulking' abroad. However, Sir Thomas dropped Vaughan when the gamekeeper turned poacher and revealed alarming tendencies to religious radicalism. Almost immediately the agent received new instructions directly from the king. He was to locate Tyndale's hiding place and persuade him to come back to England, not to face trial but to wield his powerful pen in support of the annulment of Henry's marriage. The discovery that the reformer's conscience could not be bought put a speedy end to this flirtation.

It made no difference to government policy. By the autumn of 1529 Henry's mind was set decisively on new and vigorous courses. On 19 October he stripped Wolsey of political office and of most of his landed and portable wealth. Nine days later, at dinner with the emperor's ambassador, the king who had eight years earlier won from Pope Leo X the title 'Defender of the Faith' for his attack on Luther observed that much truth has come out of Wittenberg. The Church was in urgent need of reform and no section of it more so than the clergy. If popes, cardinals and bishops had heeded Luther's warnings and addressed their own vanity, greed and lust for power Europe would have been saved much bloodshed, division and heresy. He announced that he was determined to purge the English Church of abuses.

The various interest groups at court now solidified into factions

with distinct religious affiliations. The members of the Boleyn circle
were pro-reform. In the reactionary camp the leaders were Thomas
More, Stephen Gardiner (a noted heresy hunter) and the Duke of
Norfolk. As these caucuses jockeyed for power and as religious
conflict intensfied at all levels of society life became increasingly
uncomfortable even for such minor men-about-court as Hans
Holbein. But matters took a decided turn for the worse in October
1529 when Thomas More was appointed to succeed Wolsey as Lord
Chancellor.

> He was a very great tyrant against the gospel and shed much blood
> of the godly confessors of the gospel. He tortured them with
> strange instructions like a hangman. First he examined the
> confessors orally under a green tree. Then he stretched them on the
> rack in dungeons. Finally, when he had attained a place second to
> the king, he attacked the king himself . . .[24]

So Martin Luther recalled a few years later and this, only slightly
exaggerated, assessment of More's character was the one that reached
Germany along the Lutheran grapevine in the 1520s and 1930s. More
believed passionately that his principal task as Chancellor was the
extirpation of heresy. He confessed as much in a letter to Erasmus
immediately after his promotion and, on another occasion, he told his
old friend that it was his driving ambition to be 'as hateful as anyone
can possibly be' towards this 'absolutely loathsome breed of men'.[25]
During his period of office something of the rigour of the Spanish
Inquisition appeared on English soil. More issued royal proclamations
which proscribed certain books and required all holders of public
office to assist bishops in detecting and prosecuting suspected heretics.
An English diplomat was not alone in claiming that such measures
'threaten more hurt to the realm than the ministers who execute them
conjecture; for [the king's] subjects will be forced to leave the realm
in great numbers . . .'[26]

One man who had already left was Hans Holbein. There is no
proof that he was fleeing persecution and the Basel authorities were
certainly pressing him to return but he realized that he was a marked
man. More knew all about his connections with the German
community in London and with the Boleyn faction. And Holbein
knew that the persecutors were putting men to torture in order to

obtain information against prominent figures whose religious views were suspect. About the time of More's appointment, or possibly a few weeks before, he once again left England. He did not return until More had fallen from power.

Chapter 7

BASEL

1529–1532

In his absence Basel had passed through the most critical months of the Reformation. The settlement of Eastertide 1528 had resolved nothing. Religious truth admits of no compromise. 'Root and branch' was the motto of those clamouring for reform and they were emboldened by the successes of the new doctrines in other cities and states. Down the Rhine, Strasbourg had led the way with new liturgies and 'purified' churches in 1525. Within the Swiss Confederation Zwingli's Zurich had removed images and abolished the mass in the same year. Berne, Constance and St Gallen had followed in 1528. Basel's enthusiasts were only temporarily pacified by being permitted their own churches for evangelical worship. If religious images and the concept of mass sacrifice were abhorrent to the God of the Bible, they should be allowed no toeholds in the city and the canton. While guild leaders demanded action, and hotheads hurled abuse and more substantial objects at traditional objects of worship and their devotees, Oecolampadius held meetings with the Little Council in the hope of achieving total reformation peacefully.

The scholar–preacher had by now developed a complete reformed polity for the godly commonwealth of Basel. He had never been a firebrand and he deplored violence. Holbein would have listened often to Oecolampadius's biblical exposition at St Martin's, which was no more than a hundred paces from his own front door on St Johannes Vorstadt, and would have known him to be erudite and fair-minded when speaking on the great issues of the day. The reformer was no blinkered partisan. In his sermon illustrations he did not hesitate to point out the horrors all too easily perpetrated by over-zealous evangelicals in the name of religion. One cautionary tale he told was about the parish priest of Schlat who had been an early convert to the reform. Despite his radical convictions, his house was sacked by the rebelling peasants in 1525. In vain the old man reproved them, 'You pretend the gospel and have no peace of the gospel either in your mouths or in your hearts. . . . your gospel is rather the gospel of the devil than of God.' When the peasants' rising was suppressed someone informed against the priest as a stirrer of sedition. He was hauled off to Issenheim in chains and, although no incitement to revolt could be proved against him, he was tortured and drowned. The moral was that any man who resorts to violence in the name of religion, be he papist or supposedly true believer, is condemned by his own actions.[1]

The city fathers were still too cautious to be moved by reasoned argument. It took further demonstrations by the guildsmen to bring them back to the negotiating table. On 23 December a mass meeting at the gardeners' guild hall agreed a petition. Again the leading burghers procrastinated. They would negotiate. Then they offered a public debate – to be held on 30 May. Meanwhile the rival parties gathered together in their own quarters of the city. As the new year began civil war seemed imminent. And still the council failed to take firm control. On 8 February the frustrated radicals seized the initiative. An armed crowd some 800 strong filled the Marktplatz in front of the city hall. They chained off the adjoining streets, locked the city gates and commandeered cannon which they disposed strategically. Their demands now were extreme and specific: the council was to be purged of Catholics; all religious images and the mass were to go; the Little Council was to be elected annually by the Grand Council; all guild masters and aldermen were to be elected democratically. In brief, Basel was to become a Protestant democracy instead of a Catholic oligarchy.

The council was paralysed – or perhaps its members hoped that, as a frosty night drew on, the hostile crowd would disperse. What happened instead was that a mob made its way up to the cathedral, forced its way in past barricades hastily erected by the clergy and began a work of appalling devastation. Painted panels were hacked to pieces. The great alabaster retable was smashed. Statues were hauled from their niches. Their broken-off limbs were excellent ammunition for attacking the stained-glass windows. The large crucifix from the rood screen was dragged back to the market place by a cheering, jeering crowd. Other broken items were piled up in the cathedral square and, while poor people helped themselves to free firewood, a goldsmith and an artist were seen scrabbling around in the pile for any objects they could save. When Oecolampadius and the evangelical clergy tried to restrain the iconoclasts they were met with the response, 'In three years of deliberations you have effected nothing; in one hour we will complete everything.'[2] Their blood now thoroughly up, the angry citizens left the Münster and charged 'like bellowing lions' into those churches, cloisters and chapels where offending 'objects of superstition' still remained. When the vandals returned, sweating and exhilarated, to the Marktplatz and offered to turn their attention to the council chamber the civic leaders caved in and acceded to all the citizens' demands.

It was a ghastly orgy of destruction, frightening to any who witnessed it and were not a part of it. Erasmus reported to Willibald Pirckheimer:

> There was no one who did not fear for himself when those dregs of the people covered the whole market place with arms and cannons. Such a mockery was made of the images of the saints, and even of the crucifixion, that one would have thought that some miracle must have happened. Nothing was left of the sculptures, either in the churches or in the cloisters, in the portals or in the monasteries. Whatever painted pictures remained were daubed over with whitewash, whatever was inflammable was thrown upon the pile, whatever was not was broken to pieces.[3]

By contrast, Oecolampadius, when he gave an account of the events to a friend, expressed his relief that the inevitable outburst had spent itself within a few hours and without bloodshed. Dreadful though the Basel riots were, they were focused and, in their own bizarre way, principled. There was no looting, no arson, no violence to persons. No one was killed or injured, and when the vengeful marauders had done their work they stopped of their own accord. Basel's brief outbreak of iconoclasm was not a mindless, anti-authoritarian orgy of violence for its own sake. Worse things happened elsewhere. In Magdeburg, for example, urban riots claimed 500 lives. Even the destruction of works of art must be put in perspective. The sporadic medieval bonfires of the vanities had accounted for myriads of books, paintings, jewellery and 'sinful' luxuries. It is probably no coincidence that the day after the initial outburst, when supervised bonfires of confiscated objects were held, was Ash Wednesday, the fast day traditionally given over to the renunciation of 'vanities'. Certainly the doleful events in Basel were mild compared with the state-organized devastation that was to be visited upon England's abbeys and parish churches only a few years later. Many religious artefacts survived. In the cathedral these included doors Holbein had painted for the great organ, quantities of carved wood and stone and a series of Romanesque vault paintings in the crypt which are still among the Münster's prized possessions.

Over the next few weeks councillors, preachers and guild leaders worked on a complete reordering of the political and religious life of the city. In the *Reformationsordnung* which came into force on 1 April Church and state were completely integrated. There were now patterns of worship. Oecolampadius was installed as chief minister or 'antistes' at the cathedral with Myconius as his assistant. Parish boundaries were altered. All holders of public office had to declare for the reformed faith. Church attendance was compulsory, as it had been under the Catholic regime. Like most revolutions the 1529 upheaval changed much and changed little. While the citizens accustomed themselves to bare churches and vernacular services, the Catholic establishment was replaced by a Protestant establishment just as much buttressed by privilege and walled by expected deference. The vision of democracy rapidly dissolved. The electoral reforms never materialized. City government remained in the hands of a mercantile oligarchy.

In the churches, what the mobs had begun groups of workmen more systematically finished off. All over the city combustible materials were heaped in piles for burning and it is said that the conflagrations continued for two days and two nights. Long before Holbein returned in August every church in the city had a plain, whitewashed interior. Several of his own religious works had been destroyed or damaged – how many we shall never know. Part of the 1520 *Last Supper* is missing and the Amerbach inventory described it in the late sixteenth century as having been broken and stuck together. Traditionally the 1529 rioters are blamed for this. The Oberried Altarpiece, now in Freiburg, lacks its central panel, and legend insists that Hans Oberried, the Catholic Basel councillor who had commissioned the work in 1520, rescued the wings when he left Basel after the 1529 upheaval. Other paintings from Holbein's brush were probably in the cathedral and other churches on that violent February day when so many sacred medieval artefacts perished. If even some of the scores of designs for stained-glass windows, statues and wall paintings preserved in Basel's Kunstmuseum represent finished works then the loss is considerable. However, we should not automatically assume that these pieces perished in the 1529 holocaust. Of the hundreds of Holbein's finished works that have disappeared over the centuries only a tiny fraction have been the victims of religious bigotry or mindless vandalism. To take an obvious example, the Windsor collection of portrait sketches suggests that there once existed dozens of finished paintings which have long since vanished – victims of time, neglect and changing fashion.

Nor should we assume that the artist himself reacted against 'the full fury of the Reformation'[4] and angrily quit Basel to turn to 'happier fields for his genius'.[5] Holbein must have known full well from the letters of family and friends the dramatic events which had overwhelmed the city in the early months of 1529, yet he returned in August and stayed there for two and a half years, during which time Basel recovered some of its poise and settled to life under the new order. It was not disapproval of the pace of reform that drove Holbein away again in 1532. He would not have been human if he had not visited with a heavy heart the 'bare, ruined choirs' where his workmanship had once been displayed. But his own mind had already turned against traditional Catholic iconography and, like many of his guild brothers, he knew why the old images had had to go. The craft fraternities had fully supported the demands made on the council in January and February, and the mobs which rampaged through the churches with ropes and crowbars may even have included some of Holbein's friends and colleagues.

Not all Hans's acquaintances were in favour of the changes, however. Jakob Meyer and Hans Oberried were among those whose political careers came to an end because of their adherence to the old faith. The latter was one of several prominent citizens and clergy who moved to Freiburg-im-Breisgau, the nearest Catholic centre. Bonifacius Amerbach spent some months out of the city and did not fully accept the reform for several years. But the most notable emigrant was Erasmus. On 13 April 1529, watched by a considerable crowd and attended by members of the council, Basel's most famous resident went down to the landing stage and boarded a Rhine transport for the first part of his short journey to Freiburg. It was not the new services or even the Zwinglian doctrine of the mass that drove Erasmus from his favourite city. The violence of the mob had upset him, but that soon passed. The new ruling elite were certainly not hostile to him. Oecolampadius and his colleagues urged the great scholar to stay. What Erasmus really feared was the loss of his impartiality. Basel had ceased to be a place for the free exchange of ideas. All heads of households were required to subscribe to the reformed doctrines. The university was closed in the early days of the conflict and only gradually reopened. Printers were placed under a more stringent censorship. Erasmus knew that if he remained in a city committed wholeheartedly to the reformed faith (which was first dubbed 'Protestantism' in 1529) he would lose the independence he had jealously preserved all his life. On a practical level, the donations he received from wealthy Catholic patrons might well have dried up had he remained in Basel. So, just as he had left Catholic Louvain in 1521, now he wearily took his departure from another city that had become doctrinally committed.

In Freiburg, at the comfortable house eagerly placed at his disposal by the city fathers, Erasmus received a welcome guest in the last days of August. Holbein arrived conveying news from England and a picture of Thomas More's family which brought happy memories flooding back. A few days later the scholar wrote letters of thanks to Sir Thomas and to Margaret Roper. (If we assume that Holbein returned home bearing the picture in August 1528, we are hard put to explain why it took Erasmus a whole year to respond.) He marvelled, as Holbein's patrons often did, at the likenesses achieved by the artist and assured More that he gazed 'with the utmost joy imaginable' on the faces of his dear friends captured in the picture. And to Margaret he wrote, 'I can scarcely express in words . . . what hearty delight I experienced when the painter Holbein presented to my view your whole family in such a successful delineation, that I could scarcely have seen you better had I been myself near you.' His greatest desire, he told her, was to be reunited once more with his friend and his children. 'A fair portion of this wish has now been fulfilled by the gifted hand of the painter. I recognize all [he had last seen them twelve years previously], yet none more than you and from the beautiful vestment of your form I feel as if I could see your still more beautiful mind beaming forth.'[6]

This exuberantly expressed gratitude raises the question of exactly what gift More sent his friend. It has always been assumed that it was the sketch Holbein made for the Chelsea painting which later came into Amerbach's possession (Bonifacius was the principal beneficiary under Erasmus's will) and is now preserved in Basel. But there are several problems with this. Splendid though the drawing is, does it really merit the lavish praise of the alleged receiver? Could Erasmus credibly claim to recognize in it the twenty-year-old Margaret who had been a little girl of eight when he had last seen her? Was not a working sketch covered with the artist's scribbled notes a rather niggardly gift? Could this scrap of paper be regarded by the prestigious and prestige-conscious More as a suitable return gift for the finished portraits Erasmus had commissioned for despatch to his friends? And, anyway, Holbein's working drawing was scarcely More's to give. Finally there is the fact that in Erasmus's letter and in Margaret's reply the word used to refer to Holbein is *pictor* (painter) and not the more general *artifex,* and the gift is a *pictura,* a rather grand word for a sketch. What Holbein brought with him from London was more likely a small but much more finished work executed in oils, chalks or watercolour. It would be considerably more in keeping with what we know of the customs of the Erasmus–More circle for the Englishman to have ordered copies of the great Chelsea painting as presents for friends abroad and as a means of propagating the cultured image he wished to project. Several of Holbein's works at this time were painted in oil on paper. They could be easily transported and, if later laid down on wooden panels, achieve a state of permanence. However, in their original condition they were fragile. They could be damaged accidentally, lost or discarded like old photographs. Miniature copies of large-scale works exist in many collections. The Victoria and Albert Museum actually possesses a small version of the *Household of Thomas More.* Though it was painted late in the sixteenth century by Rowland Lockey and not at the same time as the original, it provides a clear example of what was a common practice. Holbein was a skilled miniaturist and perfectly capable of reproducing the Chelsea group painting in such a condensed way as would amaze beholders with its accuracy of detail and rendering of facial expression. Such an object would have made a worthy gift for Erasmus.

Holbein had now been away from home for the greater part of

three years and he would spend the next two and a half in Basel. How enthusiastic he was about the prospect is difficult to assess. His city had changed a great deal. The religious reform was something he basically approved of, although, as we shall see, he did not give the new faith unthinking support. Eventually, the relaxed, free-thinking character of Basel reasserted itself but in the immediate aftermath of the 1529 revolution the religious leaders, with the partial support of the council, tried to enforce a strict regimen of belief and practice. Everyone was to listen to Protestant sermons. Children were to be catechized. The authorities were to watch zealously over public morality. The university was not fully reopened until 1532. The ethos of the city became one of earnest, pious endeavour. Vanity and ostentation were discouraged, and that certainly inhibited rich and self-important burghers from commissioning portraits. Yet Basel in the 1530s was never the monochrome theocracy that Calvin's Geneva became a decade later. With the exception of those families wedded to the old faith, civic power remained in the hands of the established ruling clans. Their old-boy network did not always support Oecolampadius and the evangelical synod. Amerbach, for example, was permitted to absent himself, for four years, from the new communion service without prejudicing his position as professor of jurisprudence and legal adviser to the Little Council. Across the river in Kleinbasel some Catholic congregations were allowed to meet together unmolested.

Change had overtaken Holbein's own circle of friends. Johannes Froben had died in 1527 as the result of a painful illness brought on by a fall. Erasmus had departed, and with him the soul had gone out of the Basel humanist group. Most of its members were still around but the swing to the religious left had put distance between scholars who had once enjoyed the fellowship of radicalism. Men who had blithely sat around the tavern and the printshop planning a better world found coping with the politics of change a very different proposition. Within the painters' guild the events of the previous winter must also have created tensions. How, one wonders, did some of Holbein's economically hard-pressed colleagues feel about a member who had been chasing fame and fortune in a foreign land while they had been fighting for truth and extended privileges? There can be no doubt that the homecomer had a great deal of adjusting to do. The very contrast between life in the glittering, amoral court of a

Renaissance prince and that in the solid, industrious, bourgeois Swiss municipality will have been borne in upon him every day.

The leaders of that municipality were determined that now that Holbein was home he should stay there. He was something of an international celebrity – not in the same league as Erasmus, but definitely an adornment. There was to be no question, as far as they were concerned, of any more leave of absence – for the time being at least. However, it seems that more than half a year elapsed before the council was actually prepared to put any paid employment Holbein's way. It was in the summer of 1530 that he began work on the wall of the council chamber which had remained blank since he had been obliged to abandon the project in 1523.

Holbein went back to the practice of taking on whatever commissions were available, a step that must have been galling to someone whose skills were so much in demand in England. If the pickings were meagre he could at least draw on the capital brought back from London. But this would not last for ever. He called on old friends in the printshops and obtained orders for title-pages and illustrations. The finest designs made at this time were those for the publisher Heinrich Petri and the author Sebastian Münster. Münster, an ex-Franciscan turned Lutheran, had arrived in Basel in 1527 to take the Hebrew chair at the university. There he worked for several years editing a Hebrew Bible, a new Latin version and a trilingual dictionary. But this considerable humanist scholar is better remembered by posterity as a mathematician and cartographer of prodigious industry who published books of astronomical tables, maps, geographical treatises, an edition of Ptolemy's *Geographia Universalis* and (his crowning glory) the *Cosmographia,* the first description of the world in German. Münster must have heard from Erasmus, Petri and, probably, from Kratzer in England that Holbein was without peer as a draughtsman of great precision and was delighted to have him on hand. Holbein produced a series of magnificent drawings which appeared in Münster's various publications over the ensuing years.

Jakob Meyer had a commission that only Holbein could fulfil. The ex-burgomaster, now living in semi-retirement, wanted changes made to the *Schutzmantelbild* Hans had painted for him back in 1526. The intervening years had been sad and troubled ones for the merchant. He had found himself increasingly at odds with his colleagues on the council and the target of partisan gibes from sections of the populace. What was harder to bear, however, was the loss of his two young sons, who had died of some unspecified disease. This bitter blow drove him, as an anguished, faithful Catholic, to offer earnest prayers for the repose of his departed loved ones. When he had commissioned the original painting, Jakob had ordered Holbein to represent the living members of his family. Now he needed a reminder that all his nearest and dearest, in this world and the next, were under the Virgin's protection. He asked Holbein to paint his first wife into the picture, thus completing Jakob's family circle. With subtle skill the artist added the profile of Magdalena Baer in the background without upsetting the composition. The problem that he did not know what the first Frau Meyer looked like he solved partially by swathing most of her face in cloth. It was probably during this retouching that Holbein added young Anna's elaborate, flower-decked headband – a symbol of her recent engagement. Jakob had little time left in which to contemplate his altered painting: within months he had joined Magdalena and the boys. For Holbein another link with the Basel of yesteryear had snapped.

He returned to his work in the council chamber in May or June. It may be that the delay in taking up his brush was caused in part by Holbein holding out for a larger fee than his patrons wanted to pay. He could certainly claim that he was worth more than he had been when he had covered the room's three walls back in 1522–3. He was now internationally famous and could command generous payments from men who knew the value of genius. His original contract for the entire room had entailed a payment of 120 gulden, which he had received when the work was broken off. A fresh bout of haggling resulted in an extra seventy florins – not princely remuneration by any means.

What is fascinating about the new paintings in view of the changed political circumstances is their subject matter. The existing murals exhorted council members to honest and just dealings and were inspired by incidents from classical history. The new paintings were different in highly significant ways. In keeping with the Protestant state Basel had now become, the narratives illustrated came from the Bible. And their messages went beyond vague exhortations to virtue in public life. They told of two rejected Old Testament kings. In 1 Samuel 15 the prophet castigated Saul on his victorious return from battle with the Amalekites, because he had not carried out to the

letter the military instructions of Yahweh. The bottom line was 'the
Lord has rejected you as king' and Saul's specific sin was that, instead
of exercising holy ruthlessness by wiping God's enemies from the face
of the earth and leaving no trace, he had brought back booty in the
form of sheep and cattle. Now, in places where the reformed faith was
established, hostility was rapidly deflected from Rome to those left-
wing extremists commonly but incorrectly called 'Anabaptists'. The
new laws of Basel decreed that such radical heretics were after
conviction to be ducked in the Rhine and then expelled. If they
returned they were to be put to death. Hans Ludin von Bubendorf
was the first to suffer the extreme penalty on 12 January 1530. His
courageous end attracted much popular sympathy and may have
sowed doubts in the minds of council members. Was not the story of
Saul depicted in order to remind them of the need for uncompromising zeal in dealing with God's enemies?

By contrast the other painting admonished them never to disregard
vox populi. In 1 Kings 12 there is related a story from later in Israel's
history: the break-up of the Davidic kingdom. When Rehoboam,
Solomon's son, succeeded to the throne the people begged him to
instigate a less oppressive regime. Rehoboam's reply was, 'If my
father whipped you, I will flog you with horsewhips.' As a result the
people of the northern kingdom rebelled and Rehoboam was left
with only Judaea to rule over. Moral: a wise ruler will not antagonize
his subjects. Obey God; listen to the people: the councillors of Basel
had learned these lessons the hard way in recent months. They were
not to be allowed to forget them. It is highly likely that the details of
Holbein's new commission originated in the evangelical synod. The
vigorous and dramatic treatment the artist gave to these frescos
indicates his wholehearted approval of their message. They survive
only in preparatory drawings, but later copies indicate that Holbein
made significant changes to the finished works to strengthen their
impact. They also reveal his habitual practice of illustrating a precise
moment. Thus Rehoboam raises his little finger as he thunders to the
dismayed elders, 'My little finger is thicker than my father's waist!'

These summer weeks when he was back working for the Basel
municipality provide us with the only direct, documentary evidence
about Holbein's religious views. All prominent citizens were required
to ascribe to the officially approved doctrines and have their names
recorded on the 'Christian Recruitment' register. Holbein's turn

came on 18 June. The record states, 'Master Hans Holbein, the painter, says that we must be better informed about the [holy] table before approaching it.' Earnest conversations with reformed ministers and evangelically minded friends must have ensued, for shortly afterwards Holbein's name is found on a list of those 'who have no serious objections and wish to go along with other Christians'. Strawless bricks of various shapes have been made from this watery clay. Holbein has been nominated as a reluctant convert to Protestantism, as a latitudinarian and as a sceptic with no religious convictions. Since none of these descriptions fits the man whose character emerges from the records and from his works, a better explanation for these tantalizing archival titbits must be found.

Among the various doctrines to which citizens were asked to assent was the Zwinglian understanding of Holy Communion. (Oecolampadius's teaching was not totally in line with Zwingli's, but the difference between them revolved around intricate semantics into which it would not be appropriate to probe here.) Apparently it was on this point and this alone that the painter sought elucidation. Well might he be confused by the service he had returned to find being held in his parish church. There were no bells or candles; no elevation of the host; no adoration of any kind offered to the elements; the laity received both bread and wine standing and not kneeling; and reception was just one part of an act of worship in which preaching and the reading of vernacular Scriptures were equally prominent. Everything about the service was new and unfamiliar. It is possible that Holbein absented himself for a while from a ceremony he did not understand and that this had come to the attention of the authorities. But if the liturgy was hard to comprehend the theological reasoning behind it was much more so. Differences over the Lord's Supper divided not only Protestant from Catholic, but Lutheran from Zwinglian, Zwinglian from Anabaptist and radicals of all parties and none from each other. The Swiss reformers regarded the sacrament as a simple memorial of the sacrifice of Calvary and not a re-enactment. Bread and wine were symbols and were not transmuted into Christ's flesh and blood. The act of consecration thereby lost most of its significance. Luther threw up his hands in horror at such irreverence. Christ himself had declared, 'This is my body' as he broke the bread. It was, therefore, not far short of blasphemy to decline to take him at his word.

Such abstractions may have made sense to trained theologians and framers of reformed liturgies: to a practical craftsman not schooled in philosophical subtleties they can have meant little. Most of Holbein's neighbours who, to a greater or lesser extent, supported religious innovation no doubt shrugged their shoulders and signed their names where their ministers indicated. For Holbein, with his keen mind and passion for truth, it could not be so simple. For him it was axiomatic that a man should know what he was doing before he approached the Lord's Table. The fact that, after a period of reflection, Holbein was among those who had no serious objection to the new teaching and was prepared to accept it in the name of Christian unity, unfortunately tells us nothing about his degree of commitment. Those thus categorized may have ranged widely between the extremes of happy enlightenment and unhappy acquiescence. But Holbein would have given the matter careful consideration and have put his name on the list of dutiful citizens only when his reservations had ceased to be serious.

If he still felt the need to discuss such matters in depth he soon had the opportunity. In the autumn of 1530 he made the short journey to Freiburg. Erasmus had decided to have more portraits done for distribution to friends and supporters. His reason for commissioning a second batch of paintings may well have sprung from a brief interval of hope which presented itself in the middle of 1530. Peace and concord were in the air. Men of goodwill from all parties were appalled at the splintering of Christendom taking place before their eyes. While the champions of papalism and reform roared their defiance, theological diplomats, no less bravely, were seeking discussion and compromise to bring about peace in the Church. At the end of 1529 a colloquy at Marburg attempted, unsuccessfully, to unite the Swiss and German elements of the reform. But something much more ambitious was attempted in Augsburg during the very weeks that Holbein was working in the Basel council chamber. At the imperial diet held there from June to September Lutheran and Catholic representatives strained their intellectual muscles to achieve a rapprochement. Erasmus wrote in eirenical vein to some of the participants. His correspondent in the Lutheran camp – the only one of Dr Martin's followers for whom he had any respect – was Philip Melanchthon. This moderate strove manfully with the assembled princes and scholars to heal the breach which was proving so costly.

He spent the night before his scheduled presentation to the diet praying tearfully over the division of the Church. His labours came to naught but he did help to establish dialogue, and as long as people were talking there was at least hope for a settlement. From his Freiburg retreat the elderly Erasmus, complaining more frequently than ever of ill-health, lent the influence of his reputation to the campaign. And this included sending gift portraits to friends and potential allies.

Erasmus gave his painter at least two sittings, probably more. The portraits in this second batch all show the scholar in the same pose – three-quarter face, looking to the left. Holbein could have made several versions from the same template. Many copies exist and experts still debate which ones came from Holbein's own brush. What is significant is not who actually executed each picture but how widespread was their distribution. Friends and admirers all over Europe wanted likenesses of the ageing scholar, whose very preservation seemed something of a miracle and carried with it hope that moderate solutions might yet be found to dire predicaments. From Freiburg paintings were despatched to the Elector of Saxony (Luther's prince), the English courtier John Norris, Professor Conrad Goelenius at Louvain, Hieronymus Froben in Basel and several others. A correspondence between Goelenius and his friend the Bishop of Julm indicates just how much these pictures were prized. The bishop wrote to ask for a copy. Goelenius generously sent an earlier Holbein original. 'Thank you very much,' his friend replied, returning the painting, 'but I was hoping for something more up to date.' Goelenius replied that he would commission a new portrait from Holbein himself. This exchange also shows us that Erasmus did not originate – and pay for – all this painterly activity. Friends and admirers had written asking him for mementoes. Holbein's return to Basel provided the opportunity for the scholar to oblige them. As soon as the artist was free he invited him to Freiburg. Nor did his favourite painter disappoint him. The Erasmus who appears in the 1530 paintings is more frail and sunken-cheeked. His fur-trimmed gown is hugged around him to keep the cold from his thin frame. But the eyes are as keen as ever and reveal a mind yielding nothing to advancing age.

Even more magnificent in its way is the drawing Holbein made at this time for an engraving of the scholar. Erasmus is shown full length, one hand resting on a bust of Terminus, the mythical god he had taken for his emblem. He is set in a niche whose arch and flanking pillars display Holbein's total mastery of Renaissance forms. The woodcut was designed as the title-page for a book and appeared for the first time in a collection of Erasmus's works put out by the Froben press in 1540. And now the scholar bestowed on his artist friend a remarkable accolade. For this, the last representation Holbein made of the age's leading intellect, Erasmus composed a Latin inscription which generously linked their two names. Erasmus no longer regarded the artist as merely a good craftsman: Holbein, he considered, was worthy to stand at his side before the tribunal of the muses. The inscription read:

> When Pallas marvelled at a painting by Apelles he said
> 'Let it forever have an honoured place in the library'
> In this [engraving] Holbein demonstrates his skill to the muses
> Just as Erasmus's works demonstrate his supreme intellect.

It was about the same time that Holbein painted another European celebrity. There is no record of Philip Melanchthon visiting Erasmus but after the Augsburg diet he did travel to Bretten, his home town in Baden, which is only some 130 kilometres from Freiburg as the crow flies. It would certainly have been very natural for Melanchthon to report personally on the diet to Erasmus and other humanist friends in southern Germany. Apart from this there is no known link between Holbein and the Lutheran scholar and the likelihood is that Erasmus brought them together. Thus Holbein met another of the architects of the Reformation. For Melanchthon he painted a little keepsake, perhaps a present for Katharine, Melanchthon's wife. The sitter's face was depicted on the bottom of a circular box, and the lid carried, amid floral swags, the legend (in Latin), 'You will not perceive in the living Melanchthon as much as Holbein's uncommon skill bestows.'

Back in Basel the painter attracted few, if any, prestigious commissions. He was engaged on a number of small jobs, ranging from block-engraving and jewellery designs to the refurbishing of the clock on the gateway overlooking the river bridge. This was the elaborate mechanism (now in the Historisches Museum) with the grotesque figure of the *Lallenkönig* ('Babbling king') which with every tick stuck out its tongue at Kleinbasel. For the man who could stand proud before the muses as the interpreter in paint of great scholars this must have seemed demeaning work. However, it helped to pay the bills and there is no evidence that the Holbein family suffered financial hardship. Quite the reverse; the following March Hans increased their living and working accommodation when he bought the cottage next door to his house.

Such an act might suggest that he had no thought of leaving Basel and had finally put down roots, determining that the restless years were behind him. Yet within twelve months he had left and would, thereafter, make only brief visits to his home town and his family. What might have been the reasons for this comparatively sudden decision?

The years 1529 and 1530 yielded poor harvests throughout most of the region to the immediate north of the Alps. That meant high prices. Religious conflict in the cities inevitably brought economic dislocation in its wake. In Switzerland the failure of the reformed cantons to make common cause with the Lutherans left them exposed to Catholic counter-attack. By 1529 it had become clear that some cities were not going to accept reform. Old rivalries turned into new hostilities and there was a brief clash of arms followed by a precarious peace. The air was heady with the atmosphere of possible further conflict. Catholic municipalities looked to the emperor for support. Their Protestant counterparts hoped that France would declare for the reform. This uncertainty only added to the difficulties of everyday life and of any constructive future planning as the new decade opened.

In fact, in Basel there were signs of hope for those able to discern them. The printing industry had kept going and was gradually reasserting its old independence. The morale of the university was reviving and, in 1532, it was once again fully open. Within a few years the city's old reputation as a centre of liberal studies and free debate had been re-established. Scholars of international repute such as Calvin and John Foxe would come to study, teach and publish. Basel achieved renown as a major centre of late Renaissance learning.

However, these hints of future recovery were hard to see. 1531 brought a tragic event that impacted heavily on morale in the reformed cities. In October war broke out again between Catholic and Protestant alliances. The Battle of Kappel (11 October) was little more than a skirmish but it resulted in the deaths of Zwingli and several other evangelical clergy and effectively put a stop to the spread of reform in Switzerland. When Erasmus received the news he remarked sourly to Amerbach, 'Zwingli has his judgement among men: would that he might meet with a kinder from God.'[7] In Basel, Oecolampadius was devastated. Already ill, he took to his bed and died, three weeks after the demise of his Zurich friend and fellow campaigner. Myconius took over as antistes but he was nowhere near the intellectual equal of his predecessor. It was the end of an era.

Dramatic changes had also taken place in England. The man who had stepped into Wolsey's shoes as Henry VIII's 'first minister' was not Lord Chancellor More but Thomas Cromwell, a ruthless lateral thinker and a friend to the reform movement. Henry had put away his queen and it was common gossip throughout Europe that he meant to marry Anne Boleyn. The stumbling block was the pope's refusal to grant the necessary annulment of Henry's marriage to Catherine of Aragon. Wolsey's efforts to remove this obstacle had failed but Cromwell had convinced the king that he would apply whatever draconian measures were necessary to achieve the desired objective and it was this that elevated him suddenly to a position of supreme power under the Crown. Already the process had begun of engineering attacks in parliament to soften up the Church. One result of all this was that Thomas More, who could not support the annulment, was increasingly sidelined and a brake applied to his heresy-hunting activities.

News of these stirring events in London reached Basel through someone well known to Holbein. Simon Grynaeus was a reformed scholar and Oecolampadius's right-hand-man. He had been very close to Erasmus but the great scholar now shunned a friend who had gone 'too far' theologically. In 1531 Grynaeus spent four months at the English court. King Heny, guided by Archbishop Cranmer and the Boleyn faction, was looking to foreign evangelical leaders for support and Grynaeus acted as a go-between in this process. He returned to Basel in July excited and over-optimistic about the success of the Reformation movement in England.

Holbein quizzed his friend closely on the events and personalities at the royal court and he liked what he heard. Not only might it be safe for him to return but the absolute ascendancy of the Boleyn patrons and their friends promised a very attractive flow of commissions. This was an opportunity that could not be missed. Once again Elsbeth had to walk down to the landing stage and watch her husband board the boat that would take him away from the uncertainties and insecurities of Basel to a London which seemed full of promise.

Chapter 8

LONDON

1532–1533

There were shocks in store for Holbein after his journey down the Rhine and his early spring crossing of the Channel. Whatever news may have reached him in Basel cannot have prepared him for the fevers that had broken out in the English body politic in a mere two and a half years and were about to reach pandemic proportions. The infection that had raged on the continent for a decade had now reached England and any hope that the island might be visited by a weaker strain of the virus or that preventive medicine might lessen its impact proved vain. Holbein will very readily have recognized the symptoms of impatience for religious change that he had seen in Basel and other Swiss cities.

As soon as it was known that anticlerical grievances were being seriously considered in parliament, demands for widespread social and religious reform had become more strident. Tension, riot, vandalism, abuse hurled from rival pulpits – all had become commonplace. Prosecutions for heresy alone had risen tenfold since 1529. The forces of law and order were losing ground. The government's increasingly draconian measures quite failed to stop the outrages committed by Catholic and Protestant mobs. Royal, episcopal and city officers made increasing use of the prison, the stake and the gallows. Citizens were aware of the growing number of men and women brought under guard by land or water to the Tower. Never before nor since in the fortress's history were as many prisoners lodged within it. Men spoke bitterly of the new lieutenant the king had put in charge – a monster named Leonard Skeffington who took pleasure in interrogating prisoners with the 'scavenger's daughter', a device that doubled an unfortunate's body till his bones smashed, his chest crumpled and blood gushed from every orifice. But activists saw repression as a sign of government weakness, not strength. Public protest continued and demands became more pressing. The question was no longer whether the conflict between reform and reaction would reach England, but what shape it would take.

Spontaneous acts of iconoclasm were now frequent. Scarcely a week passed without news of some fresh outrage setting tongues wagging and heads shaking in the capital. Travellers coming in from Essex told of the fate of four zealots who had put an end to the supposed miracle-working of the Rood of Dovercourt, near Harwich. The men, generally assumed by historians to have been members of a gang who had indulged in a recent orgy of vandalism throughout Dedham Vale, walked ten miles on a frosty night to attack the most famous shrine in the region. Their task was made easier by the local superstition which maintained that the celebrated crucifix exerted a power which prevented the church door from being closed.

they found the idol, which had as much power to keep the door shut as to keep it open; and for proof thereof they took the idol from his shrine, and carried him a quarter of a mile from the place where he stood, without any resistance of the said idol. Whereupon they struck fire with a flint-stone and suddenly set him on fire, who burned out so brim, that he lighted them homeward one good mile of the ten.[1]

Three of the Essex hooligans or fanatics were hanged, but the iconoclasm continued. Long pent-up hostility towards catchpenny religious wonders and the priests who exploited them now burst forth and could not be restrained. Some clergy took the lead in emptying their churches of statues while their parishioners mocked those age-hallowed objects of veneration and stuck pins in them to see if they would bleed.[2] One offender was known to Holbein. He was an old man named Cliffe, a simpleton who enjoyed More's protection at Chelsea and had lived there for many years. Hearing that some zealots had pulled down a statue of Thomas à Becket on London Bridge, Cliffe decided to imitate them. He went to the bridge, railed obscenely at an image of the Virgin, grabbed the child from its arms and broke its head off.[3] After the recent events in Basel Holbein knew exactly what these outbreaks of violence presaged.

Old friends were not slow to regale the returned traveller with the latest news. Prominent in the talk of the town in 1532 were current legal actions between no less than five city clergymen and their parishioners. A recalcitrant clique at St Andrew Hubbard who were cited to the bishop's jurisdiction for non-payment of tithes reacted by hauling the rector before the sheriffs court and won an action for malicious behaviour. In a similar dispute the people of All Hallows Honey Lane made common cause with members of the rich Bridge Ward merchant community residing in the parishes of St Benet Gracechurch, St Leonard Milkchurch and St Magnus. They appealed their case to Star Chamber, claiming that the exactions of their clergy lacked royal warrant.[4]

One of the stories going around the taverns when Hans reached London concerned a fellow artist. Edward Freese was born in York and apprenticed to a painter there. While he and his master were doing some work at Bardsey Abbey, the abbot paid the craftsman to release his boy into his charge so as to have permanent control over Freese's talent. The young man had no taste for the religious life and, after a while, made his escape. Eventually, he fetched up in Colchester, settled there as a journeyman painter, got married and put his troubled past behind him.

He was commissioned to paint some wall coverings for the town's new inn and chanced to include some vernacular sentences of Scripture in the borders of the cloth panels. This was enough for some of the townsfolk to suspect him of heresy. He was carried to the Bishop of London's palace at Fulham and kept under lock and key. When his pregnant wife tried to see him, the porter kicked her violently, killing both her and the child.

Freese was chained in his cell and when, to preserve his sanity, he took up lumps of stone or coal to draw on the wall, his wrists were manacled so tight that he could not raise his hands to his face and his swollen flesh bulged above the level of the iron. When, after months, possibly years, he was at last released he was nothing but a haggard, frail, lank-bearded idiot, 'what by the long imprisonment and much evil handling, and for lack of sustenance, the man was in that case, that he could say nothing, but look and gaze upon the people like a wild man; and if they asked him a question, he could say nothing but, "My Lord is a good man." '[5]

The guiding hand in much of this religious oppression had been Thomas More's but his influence was waning rapidly and, on 16 May, which was about the time that Holbein arrived on English soil, he resigned as Lord Chancellor, after only two and a half years in office. He had clung to power as long as he could but his was, essentially, a backward-looking attitude to Church–state affairs: crown and mitre should combine to maintain the unity of the Catholic faith and all perceived enemies of that faith should be coerced into belief. He was quite clear in his mind about what should happen to those who failed to recant: 'the clergy doth denounce them . . . the temporalty doth burn them. And after the fire of Smithfield, hell doth receive them where the wretches burn forever.'[6] During his brief tenure of office six men were burned at the stake compared with none during the previous eight years – testimony to entrenched conviction on both sides.

As late as the winter of 1531–2 More had been able to pursue his inquisitorial way and it was one notorious sequence of events that was reported by Lutheran correspondents to their friends in Germany and which, as we have already seen, permanently blackened More's name in the Protestant world. James Bainham, a gentleman of the Middle Temple and of good Shropshire family, had been denounced to More as a heretic. The chancellor decided to deal personally with this fellow lawyer and immediately had him conveyed upriver to Chelsea. Failing to talk him out of his error or induce him to betray his friends, More – so rumour insisted – had Bainham tied to a tree in the garden and flogged. After this he sent the prisoner to the Tower, where he personally supervised his racking. He also ordered Bainham's wife to be taken to the Fleet and confiscated the couple's goods. After several weeks of imprisonment and repeated examinations, the lawyer cracked. He abjured his error, did public penance at St Paul's Cross and, on 17 February, was released. But he was tormented with remorse, and, days later, before his fellow Protestants, meeting in secret at a warehouse in Hosier Lane, he confessed his apostasy. Buoyed up by the prayers of the brethren he went, the following Sunday, to St Augustine's church, hard by St Paul's Yard, and there recanted his recantation before the whole congregation. As a relapsed heretic only one fate awaited him. After several weeks of further indignities – including, so men said, being chained to a post for two days and nights in More's house – he was burned at Newgate on May Day. According to the Venetian ambassador, most of the city turned out to watch his courageous end.

But More's freedom of manoeuvre was already being restricted. In

November 1531, he had been obliged to improvise a cover-up to protect his agents in the case of Thomas Bilney. This celebrated preacher of 'novelties' had been recently burned in Norwich in circumstances which troubled some of the local officials. When they determined to raise the matter in Council and parliament More launched his own inquiry, which of course exonerated the persecutors.[7]

At the centre of power the Lord Chancellor's advice now counted for little. Henry still enjoyed More's company but the man he listened to, the man who told him what he wanted to hear, was the son of a Putney brewer-cum-blacksmith-cum-cloth-shearer of modest means. When they looked back two or three years later, courtiers and court-watchers could not grasp clearly just how Thomas Cromwell had worked his way into the king's trust, although everyone acknowledged that, as well as being a workaholic, he was an amiable fellow with a talent for friendship. He had reached royal service via Wolsey's entourage. By early 1531 he was a minor member of the Council. Yet within a year he had taken command of policy-framing. The Duke of Norfolk, who, as leader of the Council and premier peer assumed that the position vacated by the cardinal was his by right, was taken aback by the sudden rise of the 'upstart' and remained his implacable foe. Eustace Chapuys, the imperial ambassador, in an undated letter but one which probably belongs to 1533, expressed his bewilderment at Cromwell's rise to power:

> The king appointed him to the Council although his promotion was for several months kept a secret from the rest. . . . he has risen above every one, except it be the lady [Anne Boleyn], and the world says he has more credit with his master than ever the cardinal had. . . . Now there is not a person who does anything except Cromwell. . . . For the rest he is a person of good cheer, gracious in words and generous in actions.[8]

Through the accumulation of various household offices, through his adroit management of parliament and through feeding the king with adventurous, appealing and feasible ideas about royal supremacy, Cromwell steadily gathered into his hands the reins of power.

It was More's attempt to unseat this *arriviste* that precipitated his own downfall. The chancellor recognized in Cromwell everything he most abhorred. Not only was he the king's chosen champion in his tourney with the pope, he was also a friend and patron of radical thinkers. Above all he was a creative and talented administrator who might just be able to turn dangerous, advanced ideas into political reality. In the autumn of 1531 More's pursuit of heretics in high places had brought one George Constantine within his clutches. Under interrogation at Chelsea, Constantine had produced a list of names. One of them, Stephen Vaughan, provided More with the lead he needed to strike at the most dangerous man in England. Vaughan was a long-time friend of Cromwell and had risen with him through the ranks in Wolsey's service. An important member of the English mercantile community, he was Henry VIII's principal agent in the Netherlands and, as such, was entrusted with several delicate financial negotiations. He had recently been given the task of silencing England's most troublesome exile. Tyndale's books continued to penetrate the east coast ports, stirring up conflict as unwelcome to the patient advocates of reform as it was to Catholic stalwarts. Vaughan was ordered to talk the translator out of his erroneous opinions and persuade him to return home. But Vaughan was himself heavily tarred with the Lutheran brush and was not at all happy with his role as bounty-hunter. He came to a secret understanding with Cromwell not to be successful in his royal mission. It was this duplicity More hoped to expose and thus to drive a wedge between the minister and a king who, in the midst of his quarrel with the pope, prided himself on his religious orthodoxy.

More's plan very nearly worked. For a time he made his enemies extremely insecure. Anxious letters passed to and fro across the North Sea. Cromwell urged his friend to distance himself from Tyndale and his sect. Vaughan fervently disavowed heretical opinions and denounced More's practice of extracting information under torture. He implored his patron to tell him if More had turned him against him. The closing weeks of 1531 were uneasy ones for Cromwell and his circle. But the crisis passed. Constantine escaped to the Low Countries, where he insisted that he had informed on his friends only under the most appalling torture. Henry found other work for Vaughan to do and decided that Cromwell was too valuable a servant to lose. The king may even have come to agree with Vaughan's analysis of the efficacy of persecution: so far from ridding the realm of heresy, the agent suggested, 'it will cause the sect in the end to wax greater, and these errors to be more plenteously sowed in [the] realm'.[9] Henry was far from squeamish about torture and execution, but for him they were calculated instruments of policy, not expressions of principle.

After this failure More knew that if he maintained his position on the Council the rivalry with Cromwell would intensify and that he would come off second best. He could not travel in the direction royal policy was going with ever increasing momentum. Even if he survived a personal confrontation with Cromwell it was only a matter of time before he was manoeuvred into denying either his faith or his king. He concluded that he could serve 'the interests of Christendom' better in a private capacity. He asked Henry to release him from public office, but the king was in no mood to sanction what would widely be seen as a vote of no confidence in his policies.

Cromwell certainly wanted the chancellor to stay in place until he had brought off the coup he was planning during the weeks of winter. He was masterminding a coherent attack on the Church hierarchy which would appear to proceed, not from the court or the Council, but from his majesty's loyal Commons.

Clergy, bishops' officers, common lawyers and students at the inns of court were always squabbling over the limits of temporal and spiritual jurisdiction. The king's dispute with Rome over the annulment of his marriage greatly emboldened the protagonists in this ancient conflict. Those who represented the interests of lawyers, merchants and landowners in parliament often complained about the misuse of spiritual power. Cromwell's agents fanned the dissent. At the end of February, the Duke of Norfolk reported to the king an unprecedented and 'infinite clamour of the temporality here in Parliament against the misusing of the spiritual jurisdiction'.[10] Cromwell gathered together into a tidy and coherent bundle the grumbles and grudges of the Commons and the result, a few weeks later, was the so-called Supplication against the Ordinaries. This appeal to the sovereign alleged nine specific abuses of ecclesiastical authority ranging from over-zealous heresy prosecutions to the independence of Church courts.

Over the next few weeks the clergy meeting in Convocation made a trenchant defence of their ancient rights and privileges. Henry, ostensibly, weighed carefully the charges and counter-charges and, on

11 May, delivered his considered opinion to a group summoned from the Commons to his presence:

> Well beloved subjects, we thought that the clergy of our realm had been our subjects wholly, but now we have well perceived that they be but half our subjects, yea, and scarce our subjects: for all the prelates at their consecration make an oath to the pope, clean contrary to the oath they make to us, so that they seem to be his subjects, and not ours.[11]

The king sent an ultimatum to Convocation ordering them to renounce any pretence to juridical independence. After much huffing and puffing and taking of votes, the clergy yielded to royal pressure. They made their submission on 15 May. When the news reached the city, law students threw their caps in the air, guildsmen celebrated and ballad-sellers composed new pieces of ribaldry to sell on street corners. As a reward for bringing the clergy to heel Cromwell was appointed master of the king's jewels and keeper of the hanaper of chancery (he still had no major state or household office). The day after the submission of the churchmen More resigned.

Everyone close to More received the news with shock, anger and anxiety. Tremors of dismay and alarm radiated the network of foreign scholars and diplomats who had enjoyed Sir Thomas's friendship and honoured his reputation. At the centre of that network Erasmus found himself receiving worried reports and providing information to alarmed enquirers:

> With what speed the rumor has flown all the way to your country that the distinguished Sir Thomas More has been removed from the office of chancellor and succeeded by another nobleman, who immediately released those who had been imprisoned by More for their contentious teachings. . . . any speed possessed by a winged creature seems to be slow and sluggish compared with the swiftness with which this rumor has quickly spread over all the world. It was almost like the speed of lightning when it flashes into every quarter of the globe. . . .
>
> And I have no doubt that More had very solid reasons for pleading with the king to grant him that release. Otherwise, he would never have been so presumptuous as to ask for a discharge

so soon, nor would the king have been so compliant as to grant his request for any excuse whatsoever. . . . . He entered upon his office with the warmest congratulations of all the realm, such as no man had ever received before him; and when he resigned, it was with the deep sorrow of all wise and good men. For he resigned after earning the most wonderful praise: that no predecessor had administered that office with more skill or with greater justice. And you know how hypercritical the people usually are of the conduct of the top civil officials, especially during their first years. However, I could easily convince you of what I am saying by producing letters from the most eminent men who extended their congratulations with unbounded enthusiasm to the king, to the realm, to More himself, and even to me when More accepted that high office; and then I could show you letters written later by those same men deploring the fact that the state had lost such a justice and, to use the Homeric word, such a counsellor.[12]

What Erasmus did not say but what soon became perfectly clear to all the ex-chancellor's friends was that More was in disgrace. Sir Thomas may have hoped that he could go into voluntary exile from public life and enjoy years of pious reflection at Chelsea. Such a plan was never feasible. For a prominent and respected figure, a man known to have been the king's friend, to distance himself from royal policy was a public slight that Henry would not tolerate. More's days were numbered.

Erstwhile colleagues, friends and hangers-on assiduously distanced themselves from the fallen minister and Holbein was no exception. No longer did he visit the Chelsea household. His hopes for advancement now lay with the Boleyns and their close ally, Thomas Cromwell. It was this calculated transfer of allegiance and the religious motivation which, in part, prompted it that annoyed Erasmus when he heard about it. Writing to Bonifacius Amerbach about people who came to him for letters of recommendation, he observed,

They seek your patronage because they know you are the one man to whom I cannot refuse anything. In this way Holbein extorted through you letters to England. But he lingered in Antwerp for over a month and would have stayed longer had he found someone stupid enough [to succour him]. In England he deceived those to whom he was recommended.[13]

Erasmus's indignation presumably arose from the fact that he had taken the trouble to recommend the painter to More and other humanist friends, only to discover that he had gone over to 'the enemy'. Antwerp was the refuge from which William Tyndale was engaged in a bitter pamphlet war with More. Holbein's change of allegiance was an astute move. It gained him access to Cromwell, the man of the hour (he painted the minister's portrait within months of his arrival back in London) and that led, as we shall see, to royal patronage. But without the restriction of More's support he was able to associate more freely with and work for patrons, like the Steelyard merchants, who favoured reform.

Having said that, it is clear that Holbein did not restrict himself to working for men and women on the religious left. As a mere artist he could pass without too much attention between the households of ideological and political rivals, but the deep animosities between More's friends and those of the Boleyns must have produced many uncomfortable encounters. We only have to consider some of the men and women who called upon Holbein's services in 1532–3 to realize the tensions, fears and anxieties to which he must have been party. One old friend Holbein contacted was Sir Thomas Elyot, scholar and reluctant diplomat. In the summer of 1532 he had just returned from the imperial court in the Low Countries where he had had the virtually impossible task of trying to reconcile Charles V to King Henry's treatment of his aunt. As if that were not difficult enough, he had then been assigned to help Vaughan in the tracking down of the elusive Tyndale. His recall was a relief but Elyot was still not a happy man. Anxiety is often a distinguishing mark of the ambitious, but in the snakes and ladders of the Henrician court, where it was almost as easy to lose a head as gain a manor, anxiety all too readily shaded into paranoia. Elyot was worried that he did not have the king's confidence. He was known to be a friend of Thomas More and he was suspected of being secretly in sympathy with Queen Catherine. Such suspicion was well founded. His heart had not been in his mission to the emperor and his royal paymaster reposed little confidence in him. Elyot received scant support from London. His letters and reports went unanswered. His pay was heavily in arrears.

In a letter to a friend in the Netherlands, which he probably expected would be reported back to Cromwell, Elyot protested his loyalty and his orthodoxy, and revealed his unease:

I wish I had some comfortable news to send you, but we have hanging over us a great cloud, which is like to be a storm. The King is in good health. I beseech God to continue it and send his comfort of spirit unto him, and that truth may be freely and thankfully heard. I am determined to live and die therein. Neither mine importable expenses, unrecompensed, shall so much fear me, nor the advancement of my successor, the bishop of Canterbury,* so much allure me, that I shall ever decline from truth, or abuse my sovereign lord to whom I am sworn. You shall hear before long some strange things of the spiritualty. They are not agreed among themselves. Some say they digged the ditch into which they are now fallen. . . .[14]

Elyot and his wife Margaret sat for a pair of portraits during this time of impending storm and if we knew little about the troubled courtier we would be able to deduce much from Holbein's preparatory drawing. The picture of Sir Thomas is a masterpiece of character delineation. At first glance we see a mask, expressionless and cautious – an essential piece of equipment for the diplomat and for the habitué of the household of a capricious monarch. Then we notice the sadness in the almost imperceptibly downturned mouth-line. It is when we look at the blue eyes surveying the world from behind the assumed impassivity that we become aware of an expression rarely depicted in Holbein's portraits. It is a look of weariness and profound apprehension. It is a look shared by Elyot's wife in the companion piece and one which reappears, even more pronounced, in the contemporary drawing of Sir John Gage. A rare feature of Sir Thomas's portrait is that he wears a crucifix on a thin chain. Here is a man whose Catholic faith is important to him and who fears that it is under threat. The storm clouds he discerns are those bringing a Protestant deluge.

John Gage was a no-nonsense soldier in his mid-fifties. He had

---

* Thomas Cranmer had been despatched as ambassador to the imperial court shortly before this letter was written.

proved his loyalty to the Tudors many times over and now was vice chamberlain and captain of the royal guard, a member of parliament for Sussex and a Knight of the Garter. Yet this self-assured commander of men wears a haunted, troubled look in Holbein's sketch. Gage was another courtier whose conscience was increasingly troubled by the political and religious changes being instituted by the new regime. In April of the following year he frankly expressed his misgivings to the king. Henry angrily dismissed him from court and, not content with that, sent interrogators to Firle, Gage's home, to question the royal servant about his attitude towards Catherine of Aragon. He left his examiners in no doubt about his chosen loyalties. He was, he said, 'more ready to serve God than the world'. Gage was the brother-in-law of Henry Guildford, Holbein's earlier patron, who had distanced himself from court the year before.

Gage and Elyot were very different men, united by a traditional religion which placed limits on their support for the king. Elyot, the scholar, spoke of retiring to the country to write books. He had already, in 1531, produced a treatise on the education of a ruling elite (*The Boke named The Governour*) and in later years he explored in print the practical application of many aspects of classical and Renaissance philosophy. Gage, the soldier, announced his intention of renouncing both court and married life in order to enter a monastery. When it came to the crunch, neither followed his stated inclination. Gage and Elyot returned to court, acquiesced (openly, at least) in Henry's continued onslaught on the Church and were among the many members of the establishment who shared the proceeds. But not before Holbein had captured for all time the apprehension and disquiet they felt at the changes being forced upon the country and upon their consciences.

John Godsalve was a friend at court who was not troubled by religious scruples. This ambitious son of an ambitious father had come up in the world since Holbein had last met him. As soon as Cromwell was appointed to the Council, Thomas Godsalve had cultivated him assiduously. On at least two occasions he sent the minister six swans 'of my wife's feeding' and once a basket of pears 'of my own grafting'.[15] At last his persistence paid off. Cromwell took John under his wing, employing him first as a messenger and gradually advancing him to more responsible posts. In 1531 John was given his first salaried post as a clerk in the signet office, and a year later the first significant perks began to come his way. Jointly with William Blakenhall he was advanced to the office of 'common meter of all cloths of gold and silver tissue, tynsett (gold and silver thread), satin, damask and other cloths and canvas of aliens and others called "foreyns", alias the Steelyard in the city of London'.[16] This lucrative post brought Godsalve a share of the fees paid by the Hanse importers and their customers on textile goods passing through the London customs house. It also provided an excellent opportunity for corruption. Godsalve and his officers took bribes as a matter of course, and Holbein's Steelyard friends complained that English officials systematically robbed them:

> we require that the weighers, whose naughtiness without exception is to be rejected . . . may weigh with true balances and weights, neither unto the favour of Englishmen, nor unto the prejudice of us, weighing otherwise than may seem to stand with reason, equity and justice.[17]

As the *arriviste* prospered, he lost no time in setting up himself and his wife in some style. He embellished his London house with fine furnishings and decorative items including certain royal cast-offs obtained for him by the clerk of the works at Hampton Court – 'golden balls', 'vanes', 'the head under the stair' and 'an antique I left in the spicery',[18] and he hired Holbein for a pair of portraits to grace his home. As was his custom, Hans made preliminary drawings. But, unusually, he worked up the sketch for John's picture in considerable detail (see plate section). He applied not only pen and ink to his prepared pink paper, but coloured chalks and watercolour. He drew the hands as well as the face in detail and provided colour for the sitter's clothes and the background. He even added the *trompe-l'oeil* effect of the hand resting on a ledge. He certainly worked hard to persuade this potential customer to order a painting. No painted version of this drawing, if ever made, survives, but a couple of years later Holbein did execute a pair of Godsalve portraits in which he showed John in an almost identical pose.

As we look at the drawing we may wonder whether Holbein was *too* successful. The up-and-coming courtier looks at us out of the corners of his eyes, warily, almost shiftily. This treatment of the eyes, which seem to indicate a lack of candour, is rare among the artist's surviving drawings. Other sitters either look straight from the paper or direct their gaze elsewhere. Holbein also enhanced his desired effect by slightly distorting the left side of Godsalve's face, which he drew in a different plane from the other features. The contrast with the later version, where Godsalve wears a much more bland expression, is very marked. Holbein, fresh from his encounters with the Elyots and others clinging painfully to principle, could not prevent himself depicting the parvenu Godsalve in a less than sympathetic manner. Godsalve, perhaps, sensed the artist's feelings.

Yet Holbein did share one trait with the ambitious courtier. Godsalve would doubtless have called himself a realist, a man who accepted the world as it was and made his way in it without allowing religious or intellectual conviction to manacle his striding feet. Holbein, too, was aware that he was set in the rocky terrain of court patronage that somehow he must traverse. If he was to pursue his career in England he would have to choose his friends and patrons circumspectly. He could not afford the wilderness experience which seemed so attractive to More and Elyot. As he was weighing his options he discovered a highly profitable source of employment which was not complicated by political rivalries. He rented a house in Maiden Lane, close by Cordwainers Hall. This was an area of the city popular with immigrants. In fact over 10 per cent of the population were of European origins. Also, his dwelling was only a ten-minute walk to the Steelyard in Dowgate Ward where his fellow countrymen of the Hanse merchant community lived in opulence behind high walls. Hans was now under no inhibitions about making friends and seeking patronage there. Soon commissions began to come in.

Over the next few months Holbein produced some of his finest portraits. The representation of Georg Gisze of Danzig may have been the first in the series, designed as an elaborate *tour de force* to display Holbein's skill in depicting a variety of shapes and textures (see plate section). The merchant is shown at a table covered with a Turkey carpet (a standard element the artist included when he was keen to impress) and strewn with the symbols of his trade – money, pen, seal, inkpots, a ring and scissors. On the shelves around him are books, letters, a balance and other paraphernalia. Beside him stands a delicate glass vase holding carnations. In contemporary iconography the carnations stood for true love and indicated a wedding or an engagement. To the sitter and his friends many of the other objects would have possessed intriguing significance and would have provided pleasant talking points. The passage of time prevents us reading them as the artist intended. The positions of Gisze's head and eyes are almost identical with those in the contemporary drawing of Godsalve, yet the merchant does not look shifty.

When we contrast Gisze's portrait with that of his colleague Derich Berck of Cologne we can appreciate Holbein's astonishing mastery of different styles. In the latter painting the artist has opted for classical simplicity. The striking similarity with Titian's *Gentleman in Blue* (1511) has often been commented on and Holbein must have based his composition on that of the Venetian master. The patrician bearing of the sitter and the carved inscription on the stone parapet ('Add but the voice and you have his whole self, so that you may question whether it was his father, or the painter who has made him') are images carried on winds blowing from beyond the Alps.

Berck, like other Hanseatic merchants who sat for Holbein, was a Lutheran and may well have been involved in the importation and dissemination of reformed books and ideas. John of Antwerp certainly was. He was one of Cromwell's key contacts with and messengers to the Lutheran princes and theologians of Germany. He was an intimate of the minister; as an advanced thinker and also a practical man of affairs, he was precisely the sort of man Cromwell liked to have around him. He was a goldsmith who executed work for the king and for Cromwell and who sometimes worked from Holbein's designs. 'John of Antwerp' was the name by which he was commonly known and which appears in all contemporary documents, but it seems that his family name was van der Goes. There has, however, always been something of an enigma about his precise identity and no one of his name is recorded as a member of the Steelyard. It is unlikely that this problem will ever be fully resolved. His importance in the present context is that he became a very significant figure in the artist's life. In 1532–3 Holbein made at least three portraits of John of Antwerp. Like Bonifacius Amerbach, John recognized Holbein's talent and became both a patron and a friend. That friendship was to last until the very end of the artist's life.

The numerous Hanse portraits that Holbein painted during these months suggest eager competition for his services among the Steelyard community. They also betoken an active social life. The artist was a habitué of these men's homes as well as their business premises. He enjoyed with them a camaraderie that exists only among strangers in a foreign land who share a common language and culture. The merchants were happy to put work Holbein's way and were happy with the results. Well-travelled and well-connected men that they were, they knew of Holbein's wider reputation and realized, perhaps more readily than Tudor courtiers, the talent they had in their midst.

Their confidence resulted in the largest commission Holbein ever received in England. The corporation of the Steelyard set the artist to work on two monumental paintings to decorate their long, timbered banqueting hall. They asked for something grandiose which would illustrate the motto over their main gateway: 'Gold is the father of deception and the son of sorrow; he who lacks it is sad; he who has it is uneasy.' Holbein responded with designs for two life-size processions whose ultimate inspiration came from Mantegna. They were moralizing allegories like those in the council chamber at Basel but much more splendid. Two cavalcades of men, women, horses and chariots, executed as *trompe-l'oeil* reliefs, represented the *Triumph of Riches* (see plate section) and the *Triumph of Poverty*. Wealth's heavily laden car was drawn by fractious horses representing the human vices while a blindfolded Fortune flung coins in the path of rich attendants. In the pendant painting, Penia (Poverty) was hauled on a simple wagon by oxen and asses (sloth and stupidity), but Hope led them and Industry distributed the tools of honest labour to Penia's ragged attendants. If the moral needed to be pointed out to the feasting Hanse brethren it was so in Latin verses:

> The desire of mortals is fleeting and wavering; they are moved and driven as a whirlpool in the storm. Thus we cannot trust in glory. He who is rich fears ignominious poverty. He fears hourly that the inconstant wheel of fate may turn, and so his life becomes a disappointment. He who is poor fears nothing; no less threatens him, but joyful hope fills him. He thinks to acquire, and he learns from virtue to serve God.

Holbein can scarcely have painted those lines without reflecting on the illusory permanence of fame and wealth as it applied to his English patrons. The see-saw of fortune had now cast down Thomas More and allowed Anne Boleyn to kick her heels in the air, but was there any reason to suppose that it had come to rest? For the moment there seemed no sign of any reversal. In March 1533, following Warham's death, the pliant Thomas Cranmer was duly installed as archbishop and lost no time in cutting the last strands of the Gordian knot of Henry's marriage to Catherine of Aragon. Henry had anticipated the event. In January he and Anne had been secretly married. By Easter it was widely known that the new queen was pregnant. Her coronation was fixed for the weekend of 31 May–1 June and Henry was determined to make it an occasion of unrivalled splendour. Defiant of critics and secure in the rightness of his actions, he ordered the most spectacular demonstrations of loyalty to be staged in London throughout the entire reign. On the Saturday Anne was borne from the Tower to Westminster on a litter beneath a canopy of cloth of gold and the streets were adorned with bunting and punctuated with stages for the performance of elaborate pageants and triumphal arches provided by the city corporation and the worshipful companies.

The Hanse merchants were required to bear their share of the burden of public rejoicing and, without great enthusiasm, undertook to provide the decoration for the corner of Gracechurch Street. Having agreed, it then became a matter of prestige to put on a good show. They called upon Holbein to design their tableau and he did not disappoint them (see plate section). The Easterling contribution to the festivities certainly made an impression. Once again, artist and patrons chose a classical theme:

> therein was the Mount Paranassus, with the fountain of Helicon, which was of white marble, and four streams without pipe did rise an ell high, and met together in a little cup above the fountain, which fountain ran abundantly with Rhenish wine till night. On the mountain sat Apollo and at his feet sat Calliope; and on every side of the mountain sat four muses, playing on several sweet instruments, and all their jests, epigrams and poesies were written in golden letters, in the which every muse according to her property praised the queen.[19]

Holbein supervised the construction of this splendid edifice and was doubtless on hand close by to throw his cap in the air when the royal procession passed by. Someone who was not present was Sir Thomas More.

Anne's public triumph was bitter indeed to the retired minister and he refused to celebrate it. When anxious friends begged him not to offer such a slight to Henry and his new queen he pleaded that he could not afford a new gown for the occasion. They sent him the necessary money. Still he would not go. Yet he was very far from sulking in his Chelsea retreat. If he had maintained a completely low profile and allowed men to forget him it is just possible he might have saved his head. This he disdained to do. He was determined to keep up the struggle against the rampant evil of heresy and he was anxious that everyone should know that he was doing so. Soon after resigning the great seal, he had written an explanatory letter to Erasmus in the hope that Erasmus would circulate it among their scholarly col-leagues. But, secure in his sanctuary at Freiburg, the great humanist was determined to distance himself from all controversy (especially as he wanted to remain on good terms with Cranmer, Gardiner and other correspondents still enjoying royal favour). He had only just published a little treatise on the Apostles' Creed, dedicated to Anne Boleyn's father. In the spring of 1533 More wrote to his friend again:

> You need not be afraid of publishing my letter. Gossip gives out that, whatever I may pretend, I left my post unwillingly. So long as God approves of my doing, I do not care about what men say; but as I have put out several treatises in English against the heretics, I thought it my duty to defend my integrity. I have not had any proceedings taken against me; and beyond what my modesty will allow me to say, the King ordered the duke of Norfolk to speak in honorable terms of me at the appointment of my successor; and in Parliament in his customary address my successor was directed to commend me. I have purposely stated in my epitaph that I molested the heretics, for I so hate that folk that, unless they repent, I would rather incur their animosity, so mischievous are they to the world.[20]

At Chelsea More received a string of visitors, such as the Basel reformer Simon Grynaeus, whom Erasmus commended to him in 1533. He kept abreast of all the news at home and abroad. He advised Erasmus to ignore rumours that Melanchthon was coming to London but then passed on another tale about Luther's colleague being involved in secret negotiations in Paris.[21] Above all, he wielded his pen daily in his one-man crusade against English heretics. The greater part of 1532 had been spent completing half a million words of vitriolic argument entitled the *Confutation of Tyndale's Answer*. More was on safe ground in attacking the Lutheran Bible translator, for whom King Henry entertained a cordial dislike. But on 5 April 1533 he moved into the tangled thickets where religion and politics intertwined. A few months earlier, Christopher St German, an elderly and highly respected common lawyer, had published *A Treatise Concerning the Division Between the Spirituality and the Temporality*. It was not a piece of official government propaganda but it neatly made many of the points Cromwell's supporters were urging in parliament. It condemned the clergy for idleness, avarice, pride, litigiousness and over-zealous prosecution of heresy. It called for drastic Church reform by the civil power and, particularly, the curbing of ecclesiastical courts.

Because St German wrote as a private individual, More felt safe in rushing into print against him. *The Apology of Sir Thomas More Knight,* which reached the booksellers' stands on 5 April, was in part a justification of his own theological viewpoint and in part an answer to St German's charges. The hermit of Chelsea chose his words very carefully but the *Apology* was seen as an attack on the philosophical basis of the government's reform programme and irritated many in Cromwell's circle. More continued for several months to write in defence of traditional Catholic faith and practice, but before the end of the year he was ordered to stop.

Thomas More was a symbol of something that was deeply troubling Europe's intellectuals – the conflict between tyranny and learning. As in Basel, so all over the continent as governments took sides in the religious debate, enlightened tolerance of new ideas, and freedom of academic argument were giving way to suppression – by the secular state, by Catholic reactionaries, by new Protestant regimes. It is against this background that we must see one of Holbein's greatest – and more enigmatic – paintings.

The Ambassadors originated from the hectic diplomatic activity of 1532–3 (see plate section). In October 1532, Henry VIII crossed the Channel for a summit meeting with his 'brother' Francis I. This tête-à-tête, surrounded by all the customary pomp and ceremony, had been carefully prepared over several months of diplomacy. The new entente had temporary mutual advantages for the two monarchs, both of whom were adept in the scene changes of European power politics. What Henry needed above all was an ally in his conflict with the pope. Francis agreed to bring pressure to bear on Clement VII and to further Henry's cause at a personal meeting with his holiness. To facilitate the increased diplomatic activity between London and Paris he selected one of his most trusted servants to take up residence at Henry's court.

The new ambassador, who arrived the following February, was the twenty-nine-year-old Jean de Dinteville, Sieur de Polisy Bailly of Troyes and Maître d'Hôtel of the French court. The de Dintevilles were a well-established family, riding high in royal favour. Jean's brother Francis was Bishop of Auxerre. What is more significant is that both brothers belonged to the reforming humanist section of the French intelligentsia. They were intimate with leading free-thinkers such as Jacques Lefèvre d'Etaples and Gérard Roussel. Lefèvre, second only to Erasmus as an internationally famed scholar, translated the Bible into French in 1530 and, in several of his works, asserted the supremacy of Scripture over tradition. He was for many years the doyen of the reformist coterie at Meaux, east of Paris, although by 1533 he had already been twice forced to flee when persecuted by the conservative hierarchy. What saved many unorthodox thinkers like Lefèvre was the patronage of Marguérite of Navarre, King Francis's sister. She gathered around her many men of holy life and independent thought and exerted her influence to defend them from persecution. It was certainly Marguérite who saved Gérard Roussel, Bishop of Oloron, in the spring of 1533. Another member of the Meaux clique, Roussel was more extreme than several of his colleagues and sympathized readily with the reformed churches that were being formed on the other side of Francis's Swiss and German borders. At Easter 1533, he preached before Marguérite in the Louvre. Whatever he said was enough to bring a deluge of condemnation down upon his head from the leaders of the Church and the Sorbonne. Responding to the entreaties of his sister, Francis extended his protection to Roussel. Like Henry, he considered himself an orthodox Catholic and he was not averse to burning heretics. But, also like Henry, he was not prepared to allow scholarship and intellectual enquiry to be stifled by witch-hunting clerics who saw Lutherans under every bed and lurking behind every bush. Even so, royal protection (and, in the provinces, noble

protection) covered only a few favoured intellectuals. Throughout
France religious dissent was vigorously hunted down among
academics as well as among semi-literate artisans.

De Dinteville was no doubt chosen for the English embassy
because he was a moderate, a man sympathetic to the New Learning
which lay behind many of the changes being introduced by
Cromwell and his circle. We know that, a few years later, he proved
to be too unorthodox for Catholic zealots in France. In 1537 Jean and
his brother came under suspicion of heresy. They forfeited royal
favour and were restored only on the intercession of the dauphin. It
was about this time that they had a family portrait painted by an
anonymous artist. The picture was laden with biblical imagery. Jean
and Francis were depicted in the guise of Moses and Aaron standing
before Pharaoh (if the Egyptian tyrant was meant to represent the
French king, the imagery was decidedly unflattering). The portrait
carried a text from the epistle to the Romans: 'Abraham believed God
and it was reckoned to him as righteousness.' This was a quotation
Luther made much use of in his *Commentary on Romans* and *Bondage
of the Will,* where he developed his key doctrine *of sola fidei.* So, like
many others in the Renaissance courts of Europe, Jean de Dinteville
was a member of the international humanist community wrestling
with the doctrinal and philosophical issues of the day.

However well chosen the French ambassador was, his position was
impossible. He was a go-between trying to maintain good relations
between two sovereigns who were devious, unpredictable and
hypersensitive. Even before he arrived in England the pointer on the
political pressure gauge had moved well into the red, thanks to the
king's remarriage and his open defiance of Rome. In April,
parliament had passed the Act in Restraint of Appeals which
prevented Catherine referring the decision to Rome and also put an
end to the judicial power of the pope in 'this realm of England'.

Despite all this, Henry still hoped for an accommodation with
Clement and he expected Francis I to play his part in securing it. The
French king sent frequent assurances to his 'brother', and the official
goodwill was reciprocated through diplomatic channels. However,
relations were cooling rapidly as ambassadorial reports make clear.
Francis is alarmed by Henry's religious 'innovations'. Henry hears that
the French clergy are urging their king to side with the pope. Francis
'marvels' at a report that his 'brother of England' is in negotiation

with German Lutheran princes. Henry retorts that Francis's declared fervour against heretics is not helpful at that time.

The English king was, indeed, making overtures to Protestant and humanist rulers in the empire. He expected his rejection of all papal authority to make an impression in these quarters and boasted that, with German support, 'we shall be able to give such a buffet to the Pope as he never had before'.[22] Henry's agents were, as Erasmus had heard, trying to induce the eirenic Philip Melanchthon to come over. Cromwell and Cranmer wanted to establish good relations and theological accord with those states where reformed Catholicism had been established by law. This was so much talked about that the imperial ambassador told his master that the German reformer was rumoured to be already arrived and secretly housed in one of the king's lodgings in London.[23]

Henry Tudor was keeping all his options open and that made life very difficult for those responsible for the maintenance of friendly international relations. By the spring de Dinteville was finding the English king very heavy going. The ambassador withdrew, trembling, from one interview vowing that he had never seen Henry so angry[24] – and Henry VIII in wrath was a terrifying spectacle indeed. Small wonder that, within months, the ambassador was begging for a recall and insisting that in England he had never been well for more than a week.[25]

It was probably to help de Dinteville in his difficult work that his friend Georges de Selve was sent over from Paris in May. Though younger, de Selve was an experienced diplomat and came from a family of diplomats. His father was first president of the Paris parliament and had rendered the king notable service. Georges, appointed Bishop of Lavaur by a grateful monarch, had spent some time on the French diplomatic staff at the imperial court. He had been present at the Diet of Speyer in 1529 – the occasion when the term 'Protestant' was coined – and had been among those urging moderation and tolerance in relations between orthodox and reformist rulers. De Selve's mission was enwrapped in secrecy. Francis was adamant that it should be kept from the leaders of the French Church, who would have regarded it as an encouragement to the heretical King of England and a snub to Rome. Were it not for Holbein's painting, therefore, de Selve's brief visit would, very likely, have escaped notice.

The secrecy provides a clue to the reason for the commissioning of *The Ambassadors*. De Dinteville, who took the painting back to France with him, wanted an impressive record of his mission and of what it represented in terms of the leading concerns and crises of the time. The involvement of himself and his friend in the tumultuous events of 1533 in England and Europe was so important that de Dinteville was prepared to pay for an elaborate and costly painting covering ten oak panels and measuring 207 by 209.5 centimetres. Holbein was given the commission because he was the only painter in London who could carry it off, but also because he was well known in Erasmian circles to be sympathetic to those principles dear to the sitters.

Holbein threw himself with great enthusiasm into his painting of *The Ambassadors,* which is still regarded as a showpiece of technical brilliance, displaying the artist's facility in reproducing a variety of objects and textures. The human elements in the composition are relegated to the sides, rather like the supporters of a coat of arms. Our eyes rove over the Turkey carpet, the books, the musical instruments, the globes, the astrolabe, the sundial and the other pieces of cultural paraphernalia. Then they fall to the grotesque anamorphosis, the distorted skull dominating the bottom centre of the painting. Only when we have registered these puzzling details do we transfer our gaze to the figures. Even then it is the clothes of the two men that strike us more than their faces. By 1533 Holbein had reached the summit of his skill as a portrayer of fabrics. We gain an almost tactile pleasure from the velvet, satin and ermine of de Dinteville's highly fashionable attire and the silken tassel of his dagger. We marvel at the sheen and the soft folds of de Selve's luxurious brocade over-gown with its sable lining.

The Ambassadors, as has often been pointed out, is a celebration of Renaissance scholarship and culture. The objects on display represent the quadrivium of higher learning, the mathematical arts of harmony and precision: astronomy, geometry, arithmetic and music. Holbein probably borrowed some of these props from his friend Nicholas Kratzer. Certainly, the astrolabe in the centre of the upper shelf and the white decagonal sundial close to de Selve's elbow also appear in Hans's portrait of the astronomer. *The Ambassadors* captures the self-conscious excitement of the New Learning. Holbein presents his sitters as they saw themselves and wished to be seen: men of culture, taste and intelligence; supporters of intellectual enquiry; patrons of the arts; men caught up in the exhilarating pursuit of knowledge.

Yet there is more to the painting than this. It is a testament by Holbein and his patron to their shared concerns in the uncertain England of 1533. The picture coruscates with inconsistencies and enigmas. The death's-head in the foreground is not only distorted, its shadow is cast in a direction at variance with those belonging to the other objects. The lute has a broken string. The crucifix in the top left-hand corner is almost obscured by the curtain. On the celestial globe a hen attacks a bird of prey. There is something disconcerting about the human figures too. If we ask ourselves, 'Who is the more important of these two men?' our first answer is, 'The man on the left.' De Dinteville, with his sumptuous clothes, his pose of relaxed self-assurance, his medallion of the Order of St Michael and his trappings of wordly power, seems to 'outweigh' his companion. He completely occupies one half of the painting, whereas de Selve is fitted into little more than a quarter of the surface area. Yet we immediately have to revise this estimate. In Holbein's composition the younger man literally upstages his friend. Set slightly further back, he appears introverted, nervously clutching the folds of his gown and tightly grasping his gloves. Yet Holbein makes us fix our attention on him. He does this by the solid mass of de Selve's robe and by the strong diagonals which lead our eyes inevitably to him – or, as we shall see, to his clothing.

It would be a mistake to look for a single didactic objective. The virtue of a painting is that it can say several things at the same time. In *The Ambassadors* certain allusions are straightforward and unsubtle. The terrestrial globe on the lower shelf is placed so as to reveal France. On it, among such obvious place names as Paris and Lyon we can discern Polisy, de Dinteville's home village. The gloves clasped in de Selve's right hand are a conventional symbol of gentility. The ages of the two sitters are recorded on de Selve's Bible and de Dinteville's dagger, indicating that one is a man of the cloth and the other a prominent layman.

Other meanings have to be teased out from Holbein's iconography. The artist chose to set this portrait (if we can call it a portrait) on an elaborate marble floor. In this regard *The Ambassadors* is unique among all his extant works. There seems to be no artistic reason for this – unless it provides a further opportunity for the display of painterly virtuosity and elegance. Hans went to Westminster Abbey to make his notes and sketches for this floor, which was (and is) in the sanctuary adjacent to the shrine of Edward the Confessor. It was a well-known piece of Italian craftsmanship and was unique in England at that time. Its inclusion here, as earlier writers have pointed out, makes a direct reference to the religious life of England.

The open book on the lower shelf of the cupboard continues the theme. It is a hymn book by Johannes Walther published in Wittenberg in 1524, containing devotional lyrics by Martin Luther. Two of these songs are clearly visible in the painting. One is the ancient hymn 'Veni Creator Spiritus', translated into German. The other is Luther's exaltation of the Ten Commandments, beginning, 'The man who would live in joyful communion with God must keep the laws which he has given.' Both texts indicate the reformer's adherence to basic Christian belief and his dependence upon the one God to whom all Christians have always given allegiance. Some scholars have read this element of the picture as a plea for tolerance of the Protestants. There may well be an element of this present but if we see – as we are surely meant to – the hymn book as part of a little still-life group within the painting, we can find more meaning. The book is 'enclosed' on three sides by a lute with a broken string and a nest of flutes in a box which is open but which still has its ribboned key in the lock. The music Luther would have us make is all very well, but it has its limitations.

And then there is the crucifix. Relegated to the extreme corner of the picture and almost enveloped in the folds of the curtain, it suggests that the ancient and orthodox faith, the faith of Christ crucified, is under threat. This reflects the alarm felt by all Christian humanists that religious conflict obscures the truth.

So we return to the elongated skull which has perplexed generations of Holbein lovers. It is an anamorphosis, a distorted image which can only be seen properly from a special angle (in this case from the extreme left of the picture) or with the aid of a lens. This kind of artistic parlour trick was quite popular in the early sixteenth century. In the National Portrait Gallery in London, a distorted image of Edward VI is on display. The original frame has an eyehole cut into it, through which the king's head can be seen in true perspective. Erhard Schön of Nuremberg, a pupil of Dürer, produced a series of engravings of European monarchs using the same technique. Such objects were toys, fashionable gimmicks designed to amuse. They were not incorporated into major works of art. There is certainly nothing whimsical in Holbein's sinister grotesque. The artist put it there and the patron accepted it because it made an important point – a point which they and others in the know clearly understood. Those not in on the secret (and that includes almost everyone who has ever looked at the picture) found the enigma impenetrable. Some suggested that the skull was a de Dinteville emblem. The ambassador wears a skull badge in his cap. Others looked for punning references: *crâne mère* = 'empty skull' = Cranmer; *hohl bein* = 'hollow bone' = Holbein. A less obscure interpretation takes us much closer to the spirit of the age. It suggests that the anamorphosis is simply a *memento mori*. What Holbein is telling us, according to this view, is that all human pomp and dignity and all intellectual attainment are transitory. Death makes mock of them all. In other words, it is a return to the theme of the *Dance of Death* engravings.

This idea cannot be discarded, but it does not exhaust the significance of this unique feature. When we remind ourselves that *The Ambassadors* is a painting of the moment, springing from and commenting on a particular set of circumstances, we are ready to make some startling discoveries.

Let us consider, first, what technical function the extended skull performs within the painting. It provides a diagonal line. That line intersects with three others: the bottom shelf of the buffet, the extension of de Dinteville's dagger which he is holding almost as a pointer, and de Dinteville's left shoulder and arm. It is these diagonals Holbein uses to direct our eyes to the man on the right. They are the main pieces of scaffolding in the painting's framework. They intersect precisely in the lower part of de Selve's gown. Can there possibly be anything about this garment to which Holbein wishes to draw attention? Its most unusual feature is, surely, its colour. Certainly, it is not a shade common to Holbein's palette. The name for this purple-red hue is murrey, mulberry-colour. The French for 'mulberry' is *mûre* and the Latin is *morus*. (It may also be that the pattern in the lower part of de Selve's gown is intended to represent mulberry fruit.) Holbein is, indeed, making a visual pun – on the name of his old friend and generous patron. And he reinforces it with another. The anamorphosis is indeed a *memento mori*. It exhorts the beholder to keep his mortality ever before his eyes. But it also exhorts him 'Remember More'. Holbein, the humanist artist, emulates Erasmus, the humanist writer, who used the same kind of play on words in the title of his *Encomium Moriae, In Praise of Folly*.

If we can pinpoint a specific event which prompted the commissioning of *The Ambassadors* we should look to Anne Boleyn's crowning and More's ostentatious absence from it. De Selve was in England for only a few weeks during the spring of 1533. One of his functions was to augment the French suite at the coronation of Anne Boleyn. He was, therefore, vividly aware that More had shunned the event and that his behaviour had been noted. He had talked with those worried friends who had gone to remonstrate with More and urge him to accept the *fait accompli*. From them he heard what Sir Thomas's response had been. He had reminded them of a tale told by Tacitus about Tiberius Caesar. The emperor wished to execute a woman convicted of a certain crime but was inhibited by a law which declared that virgins could not suffer the death penalty. His advisers pointed out that the solution was simple: 'deflower her first and destroy her afterwards'. More intimated that his friends had lost their honour and must now look to their heads. For himself, even if his life were forfeit, he would preserve his purity to the end. De Selve knew also from keeping his ear to the ground at Westminster that 'the king's good servant' was in real danger. He knew that the government kept careful watch on More's movements and his visitors. Cromwell's agents read More's books and intercepted his correspondence. When Chapuys wanted to send More a personal commendation from the emperor Sir Thomas besought him to do no such thing, since news of it would undoubtedly get back to Cromwell. De Selve was extremely concerned for Thomas More's welfare and even more concerned about the implications of his fate for the wider world of Christian thought and piety. These were feelings which, as we have seen, were shared by humanists everywhere. De Selve thought it well worth putting them on permanent record.

The layers of meaning in *The Ambassadors* directly express the patron's thoughts about Church and state in England. A society which should have been incomparably enriched by the New Learning was being disrupted by religious and political discord. The hen and the hawk were symbols of a world turned topsy-turvy. But *gallina* (hen) and *vultus* (bird of prey) were also gaming terms. Dire misfortune had befallen England, and the fate of Thomas More blazoned the fact to the world.

This brings us to another large-scale painting which has, for centuries, been the subject of argument and conjecture. Like *The Ambassadors* it is heavily coded and has reference to contemporary events, most of which we can only guess at. But it poses other questions of a more fundamental nature: who painted it? When? And why? The work referred to is the version of *The Household of Sir Thomas More*, now hanging at Nostell Priory in West Yorkshire. The beginning and end of the story of this painting are quite clear. In 1527–8 Holbein made a group portrait for his patron which was passed down in the family until it was destroyed by fire in the eighteenth century. We now only have the sketch preserved in Basel (see above, p. 131) to tell us what the original *probably* looked like. Over the years various versions of the group portrait were made for Sir Thomas's descendants and it is one of these which can now be seen at Nostell Priory. It bears the signature 'Rowland Lockey' and the date '1530'. Since the only Rowland Lockey known to art history was working around the end of the sixteenth century the inscription cannot be correct as it stands. But Lockey did make other versions of the Holbein original and the weight of current opinion is that, despite the wrong date, which scientific examination shows to have been added later, the Nostell Priory painting was done by Lockey towards the end of the reign of the first Elizabeth. So far, so good. The problems begin when we compare the existing painting with the earlier sketch. It immediately becomes clear that the Nostell Priory picture is *not* a straight copy of the original. In fact, there are over eighty differences between the two versions. So, what came in between? What was Lockey copying and was it painted by Holbein? We cannot answer those questions with absolute conviction but there are several clues in the Elizabethan painting which enable us to place its execution close to that of *The Ambassadors*.

Let us start by listing some of the changes from the Chelsea original. The more obvious ones are: the centrally placed clock with its open door; the incorrectly painted chain worn by Thomas More; the extra figure in the doorway; the transposition of the two ladies on the left; the inversion of a handle on the vase in the window; the Turkey carpet on the *dressoir* littered with objects (very similar to *The Ambassadors* and to the portrait of Georg Gisze); the roses in Henry

Pattinson's cap; the books; and the busy hands. This painting might almost be called 'a study of hands'. The artist draws our attention to seven people in this room, not by their faces but by their fingers.

The focal point of the painting is not Thomas More, the head of the household, although he occupies the central position in the picture. It is the pointing left hand of Margaret Roper and the book in her lap that Holbein forces us to look at by making them the hub of all the picture's strong diagonals. (The main structural lines run from the viol, through the right arms of Sir Thomas and of Cecily Heron, down to the monkey's tail; through the left arms of Alice and Margaret across to the hem of Margaret Giggs's gown; along the scroll held by the man in the doorway and down Margaret's left shoulder.) But, whereas in *The Ambassadors* this technique was used to draw attention to an apparently unimportant item of clothing, here it directs us to printed words in the book More's favourite daughter is reading. It is Seneca's *Oedipus* and her awkwardly arranged fingers form an arrowhead pointing to the title at the top of the right-hand page. The exposed lines on the left page are those spoken by Chorus in Act IV of the tragedy. In translation they read: 'If I were allowed to change fate according to my will, I would move my sails with a gentle zephyr, so that the spars would not be strained to breaking point by strong winds. A calm breeze would ripple softly along the sides of my rocking ship.' The facing page has lines from the story of Icarus: 'Madly he makes for the stars and, relying on his new limbs, tries to outdo the real birds. Thus, the boy trusts too much to his false wings.'

Beside Margaret, her sister Cecily Heron counts on her fingers – 'one, two'. Thomas More, whose hands in the drawing were wrapped in his black muff, now exposes three fingers. Elizabeth Dauncey is drawing on her right glove. But she will never succeed until she moves her oddly crooked little finger. Margaret Giggs ostentatiously holds open a book whose pages are blank. In the earlier version, which showed her leaning forward to discuss her reading matter with More's father, Holbein clearly indicated lines of print in her book, so the absence of text on the painting is quite deliberate. The servants, relegated to the back row, are also doing interesting things with their hands. Henry Pattinson, More's fool, firmly clenches the hilt of a sword. 'Johanes heresius', Sir Thomas's secretary, clasps a sword, a buckler and a sealed scroll.

The clock has been moved to the top centre of the picture. Its door is open, as though it has just been wound or adjusted and its single hand tells us that the time is a little before midday. The pendant rose on More's chain no longer hangs straight, as in the drawing, and the *S* links running over his right shoulder have been reversed. In the portrait in the Frick collection which shows Sir Thomas in a similar pose the links are correctly depicted. In the drawing, all the *S*s are reversed and it may be that the chain was double-sided and so could be worn either way (some of the many later miniatures of More also have the links back to front). What is impossible is the 'half and half' treatment in the Nostell Priory painting. The titles of two other books are shown. Boethius's *Consolations of Philosophy* is on the cupboard and Seneca's *Epistulae Morales* is under Elizabeth Dauncey's arm.

There seem to be three types of message in this picture. The first consists of affectionate in-jokes and observations about individuals which would be appreciated by intimates of the More household and would be enjoyed all the more because outsiders could not share them. Presumably these amendments were made for the original painting at Chelsea. The clearest personal joke in the picture is at the expense of Thomas More's son. In the sketch three members of the family are not actually reading the books they are holding. In the painting it is only young John More who gazes at the pages before him. He does so with an expression which could hardly be called intelligent concentration. As a classical scholar John was not up to the standard of his sisters. The critical father had his painter emphasize the point in the inscription above John's head. The correct Latin would read 'Joannes Morus Thomae Filius'. It actually reads 'Joannes Morus Thomae Filuis'.

In the original sketch Holbein placed Elizabeth Dauncey on the edge of the family group and had Margaret Giggs engaging Judge More in conversation. Here their positions have been reversed. Subsequent history revealed the Daunceys to have been the least committed members of the family group. Margaret Giggs openly attended More's beheading, and she and her spouse fled into exile afterwards. Cecily's husband Giles was executed in the aftermath of Sir Thomas's death. The Ropers – Margaret and her husband William – suffered much and William later wrote an adoring biography of his father-in-law. Only the Daunceys seem to have been less affected by the crisis and to have come through it unscathed, despite the fact that William Dauncey was Giles Heron's colleague as MP for Thetford (More secured their election).

In the second strand of comment the artist makes observations about Thomas More and his situation. The open door of the clock suggests that the time has been changed. This coupled with the fact that the clock is now placed centrally with its lower weight directly above the number '50' depicting More's age implies that the scene depicted is not contemporary. We are looking at the household as it was a few years ago (some time before noon, 'noon' being the present). Since 1527, when the original drawing was made, the situation has changed drastically. The back-to-front Ss must refer to a reversal of fortune and the displaced Tudor rose emphasizes that the wearer is no longer in royal service.

The books depicted are much less enigmatic comments on Sir Thomas's changed fortune. Humanist friends would readily have picked up the parallels between More and the two classical authors referred to in the picture. Seneca and Boethius were both scholar–statesmen who were ultimately disgraced and who devoted their enforced retirement to writing. Seneca reached the height of his political influence during the reign of Nero. While the emperor amused himself with dilettante pursuits Seneca organized the work of government for five years. When the tyrant eventually forced him out of public life, his disgraced minister devoted himself to philosophy and satire, his most important work being the collection of *Epistulae Morales* in which he exposed public vices and advocated Stoic resignation. But he was an embarrassment to the libertine emperor and, in AD 65, Nero accused him of treason and ordered his suicide. Boethius, four and a half centuries later, served with equal faithfulness and distinction the King of Italy, Theodoric, before being accused of necromancy and subversion. In his *Consolations of Philosophy,* written in prison while awaiting execution, Boethius ranged over the major themes of good and evil, fame and fortune, suffering and injustice, and concluded that happiness lay only in the serene contemplation of God. These parallels relate closely to More's position after May 1532.

The painting clearly states Thomas More's proclaimed desire to spend his remaining days in quiet reflection and writing. In his letters and books More had always insisted, rather ingenuously, that public office had been forced on him and that his own inclination was towards a secluded life, given to spiritual and intellectual pursuits. The ex-chancellor is identified with the words from *Oedipus:* 'If I were allowed to change fate according to my will, I would move my sails with a gentle zephyr.' But More knows that this is impossible. He already senses the violent storms that lie ahead. The quotation about Icarus is a rueful, self-deprecatory comment on his own career: if he had not flown so high he would have avoided disaster. As to the *Epistulae Morales*, is it not significant that the book about public virtue is firmly closed under Elizabeth's arm?

There remain a group of unexplained allusions which do not fit in with what we have discussed so far. If the interpretation we place on them here is correct they take us into very dangerous political waters indeed. At the painting's focal point the hands of Margaret and Cecily address the viewer in expressive dumbshow. Moving along the diagonal of these hands our eyes meet the three exposed fingers of Sir Thomas and his sleeve of rich red velvet.

As with *The Ambassadors,* Holbein, the master of painted textures, makes an item of clothing significant. All More's friends knew that the disgraced minister was in reduced circumstances. There may even be a reference here to Sir Thomas's wry jest that he had nothing to wear for the coronation. In the magnificent 1527 portrait (and, almost certainly, in the lost group portrait) Holbein had shown More sumptuously dressed in a fur-lined velvet gown. Here the artist depicts him again in almost identical pose and dress. But the alterations are significant. Luxurious sleeves and collar remain but the body of the garment is now incongruously made of woollen cloth. In the sixteenth century, when clothes were much more pronounced symbols of status, oddities of dress had great significance. It would seem to a friend, looking at this picture, that an impoverished More was desperately trying to keep up appearances.

We now move to what may be a third, deeper and more dangerous level of allusion. For it is possible that we can discern here a stratum of political comment. Whoever commissioned this version of the family group may have wanted to go beyond reference to Sir Thomas's reduced circumstances and to tie the fallen minister's fate in with that of the realm. We come back to those disturbing hands – fidgeting hands making enigmatic gestures. Margaret Giggs holds a volume of blank pages. An empty book was a common metaphor for a barren womb, which may, in this case, have either personal or symbolic reference. Elizabeth Dauncey has only one glove and she cannot draw it on. She is doomed to failure. The hands of the standing women counterbalance and point to those of the women squatting on the floor. Margaret indicates quite unmistakably the word *Oedipus*. The ancient myth tells the story of a man who achieved the crown of Thebes by, unwittingly, murdering his own father, and thereby unleashing an appalling succession of tragedies. It is the tale of a murderous usurper. But Cecily's counting fingers suggest that the viewer should think, not of one violent king, but of two.

More came to realise in his last years that Henry VII and Henry VIII had gained and held a crown through usurpation and tyranny. Yet, despite all the angst and suffering they had imposed – suffering which had engulfed himself – the Tudor dynasty was doomed to extinction. Henry VIII has put away one wife who could not produce a male heir only to take another who suffered an identical misfortune. The nation seems locked in disillusion, frustration and bitterness.

Henry VIII *is* depicted in the painting – or rather a Henry VIII look-alike is shown. In all probability, Henry Pattinson, More's fool, had, as part of his stock in trade an imitation of the king but this is now visually amplified and there can be no doubt about the *alter ego* of the servant. Not only does he have the self-assertive stance and full-face presence that Holbein used in his depictions of royalty, his cap displays the red and white roses of Lancaster and York and his left hand grasps the hilt of a sword.

We come, finally, to the wholly new character introduced into the composition, the strange man leaning in at the doorway. He is labelled 'Johanes heresius' – 'John Harris', More's secretary. He carries a scroll which would certainly be in keeping with his avocation. But, like Pattinson, he is also provided with a sword *and* a buckler (a small shield). He seems to be looking in wistfully on the family scene and to be emerging from a darkened room. Or is he? The space behind this figure is actualy an optical illusion. It can be read as an open doorway or the edge of a door. Other characteristics distinguish him from all the other subjects in the painting. The man's dress is antiquated and his features are pallid. Is he a *revenant*, a figure from the world of shades who can only watch with melancholy what has become of More's family and their England? Some students of the Lockey version have identified the mysterious figure as Richard III and inferred that the painting is evidence of Yorkist sympathies among the sitters.[26] It seems to me extremely unlikely that Sir Thomas, who had written so scathingly about 'Crookback Dick', would have done a complete U-turn. He loathed tyranny and the fact that the Tudors were as bad as their predecessors would not have made him nostalgic for the 'good old days' of the last Plantagenet. Perhaps we can go no further than this: if there is a political message in this picture it is a philosophical reflection on the sad times through which the Mores were living. Kings may come and kings may go but absolute power will always work to undermine impartial justice and honest royal servants are often faced with the choice of compromising their beliefs or being ruined. This pessimistic view is in tune with what More had suggested in *Utopia*: the perfect society is a dream which can never become reality; philosophers who seek high office are riding for a fall.

Are we now any closer to identifying the circumstances under which the forerunner of the Nostell Priory group portrait was executed? There can be little doubt that this version was created after Thomas More's fall from favour. It may even postdate his execution. If we have read the coded messages aright it was also painted when the Tudor line had failed for want of a male heir. Now, in 1537, Henry's long-awaited son, Edward, was born and within ten years he inherited the crown. He died in 1553. That gives us two possible time frames for the portrait: 1532–7 and 1553–90. The absence of any allusions to Mary Tudor or Elizabeth I suggests that we can rule out the later dating. The painting is a commentary on recent or current events, albeit its secrets could only be unravelled by the Mores and their more intimate friends. There is no suggestion of Catholic triumphalism, such as we might expect from a painting made during Mary's reign and had it been made for a recusant family suffering under the Elizabethan regime we might have expected some reference to Mary Queen of Scots, the claimant to the throne in whom Catholic hopes were vested. The 'second-stage' *Household of Sir Thomas More* relates to a very immediate situation and the further we move away from the latter years of More's life the less relevant it seems.

In the early 1530s the issues of a tyrannical, usurping dynasty doomed to extinction was *very* relevant. Courts all over the realm were kept busy hearing indictments against disgruntled subjects charged with spreading malicious rumour or speaking 'treasonous words'. The government was on the defensive because the probable failure of the male Tudor line was acting like a lens to focus the assorted discontents of the people. The king's inability to sire an heir was, for many, proof of God's disfavour.

Preachers and fanatical 'prophets' gave divine sanction to the dark murmurings of malcontents. One such religious celebrity was a frequent visitor to London. Elizabeth Barton, the 'Nun of Kent', was an ecstatic and visionary whose prophecies had for some years impressed not only simple folk, but senior ecclesiastics such as Archbishop Warham, Bishop Fisher (who was moved to tears by her holy demeanour and divine revelations) and the superiors of several religious houses. Some ladies of the court even became Elizabeth's patrons and her ardent devotees. By 1532 she was making frenzied attacks on the royal divorce and prophesying that, if Henry did put away his lawful wife, he would, within a month, die a villain's death. The demented creature thrust herself into the king's presence and said as much to his face when he passed through Canterbury towards the end of the year. But Henry did put Catherine aside and sanguinary divine retribution did not fall upon him. Elizabeth and her entourage had to suffer the fate of failed apocalyptists. Cromwell made sure that their trial and execution at Tyburn achieved maximum publicity. The fear of rebellion was never far from the minds of the king and his ministers. There were certainly those in the country and skulking abroad capable of raising a rival standard if they calculated that the time was right. Chapuys, the imperial ambassador, openly warned the Council about a recrudescence of the Lancaster–York conflict, 'heretofore the Roses had troubled the kingdom, but now it seemed they desired to sharpen the thorns of the Roses'.[27] The Yorkist cause was by no means dead. Several princes of the blood, descended via the female line from Edward II or Edward IV, had survived earlier Tudor purges. Most of them had been rendered safe in one way or another. Some had taken holy orders, some were at court where Henry could keep an eye on them. One was in the Tower. Others had found refuge on the continent. Yet, in the common culture of myth, rumour and magical prophecy, stories of rival claimants to the crown abounded. The belief persisted in some quarters that the 'princes in the Tower' had not perished but had escaped and sired sons of their own, and that somewhere a rightful heir was waiting to claim his crown. In the last days of 1532 a dabbler in alchemy and necromancy was clapped into the Tower to be examined by Cromwell for spreading seditious prophecies. The king, according to this Richard Jones, would not live beyond 1533. His throne would be taken by a descendant of Edward V, currently waiting in Saxony.[28] Particularly in the north and the south-west an underground 'white rose party' led by the Courtenays and Poles could count on widespread support.

The Nostell Priory painting is not a Yorkist tract but it is certainly one from which enemies of the regime could take comfort. It records how the intimates of the fallen chancellor regarded his fate and the fate of the realm. It is a painting redolent with tragedy. The artist illustrated the foreboding that More felt, both for himself and for the nation – a foreboding shared, in the 1530s, by an increasing number of his fellow countrymen. The future was bleak for Sir Thomas and for England, and the destinies of both were intertwined. Two royal lines had come to an end, a fact emphasized in September 1533 when the son Henry had confidently and excitedly expected turned out to be another daughter, Elizabeth. More, who had written the history of one tyrant and served another, had fallen victim to Henry's desperate and doomed attempts to perpetuate the dynasty. These were the sad observations that whoever commissioned this painting wished to make.

So, who did commission it, and when? More resigned in May 1532. He was sent to the Tower in April 1534. The circumstances alluded to in the painting only existed between those dates. The dynastic message would have had greater point after the birth of Henry's second daughter in September 1533. Yorkists and Catholics alike were exultant at the arrival of Elizabeth: it was, surely, yet one more sign of God's rejection of a usurping and heretical king. The autumn and winter of 1533–4 thus seems the most likely period for the painting's execution. It is possible that More himself, sensing his impending fate, may have wished to record through the enigmatic medium of a painting what he could not express in writing about his own situation and that of the nation. It is more likely, however, that William and Margaret Roper, bitter at More's fate and wanting a copy of the Chelsea group portrait for their home at Well Hall, Esher commissioned a politically contentious painting. Certainly the picture belonged to their descendants later in the century.

Did Holbein make this second version of the *Household of Sir*

Thomas More? Like *The Ambassadors,* to which in some ways it now appears as a companion piece, it was a commentary on current events. These two large paintings stand alone in the Holbein canon. They are intense and intricate political pieces and they focus attention on the downfall of Thomas More as a symbol, in humanist eyes, of the ills that had befallen England and Europe. There are technical similarities between both paintings and the portrait of Georg Gisze, also produced in 1533. All three pictures are impregnated with meaning. All three are more riotously crammed than any of his other works with those allusions and illusions that Holbein loved and that so intrigued the Renaissance mind. Since we know of no contemporary artist working in England capable of making this extraordinary version of the 1527–8 original, there seems no reason to deny it to Holbein.

In conclusion, can we deduce anything from these remarkable works which will illuminate for us Holbein's state of mind as a sensitive man close to the centres of power during one of the most tumultuous decades in English history? Were the ideas he translated into paint solely those of his patrons? The question is no sooner asked than it receives a negative answer. The artist could not be unaffected by the uncertainty and instability of the times. *The Ambassadors* and the *Household of Sir Thomas More* were major commissions that he would have been foolish to turn down but he was not only interested in the money. These large canvases, representing several months' work, show us the artist at an intellectual and spiritual turning point. They are the result of working through turbulent thoughts and emotions. Holbein, no less than his sitters, is trying to make sense of a world going mad. He had accepted the Lutheran reform but that did not mean that he was unassailed by doubt. Radical reform had given licence to iconoclastic Swiss mobs. Now its espousal by the new English regime was creating the same violent partisan confrontations. *The Ambassadors* is an anguished cry against theologians and politicians who are obscuring true religion behind a curtain of arcane disputes and national rivalries. The reworked *Household of Thomas More* becomes a piece of bitter self-satire; an angry-sad expression of disillusionment. The family's change of fortune mocks the serene humanistic harmony that had seemed, a few short years before, to offer solutions and hope. These two extraordinary paintings illustrate a crisis within humanism and within Hans Holbein.

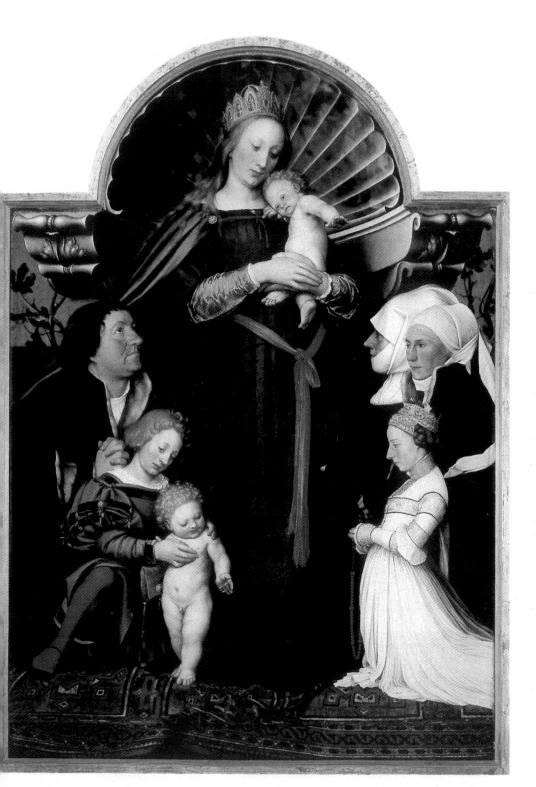

Madonna of the Burgermeister Meyer, c.1526 (Schlossmuseum, Darmstadt)

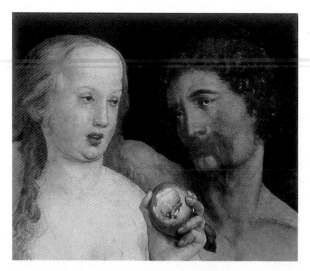

(*above*) *Adam and Eve*, 1517 (Offentliche Kunstammlung, Basel)
(*below*) *Noli Me Tangere*, c.1522 (The Royal Collection © H.M. the Queen)

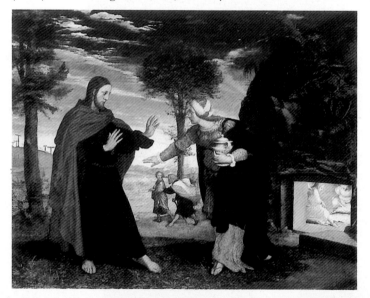

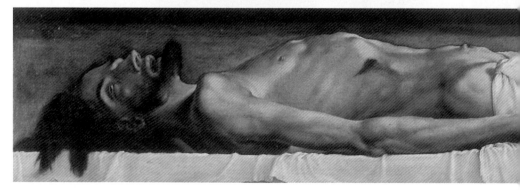

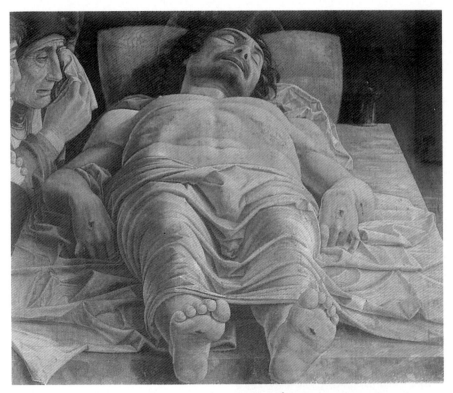

(*top*) *The Dead Christ*, Andrea Mantegna, *c*.1500 (Pinacoteca di Brera, Milan)
(*below*) *The Deposition*, Issenheim Altarpiece, detail, Matthias Grünewald, *c*.1515
(Musée d'Unterlinden, Colmar)
(*bottom*) *Christ in his Tomb*, 1521 (Öffentliche Kunstammlung, Basel)

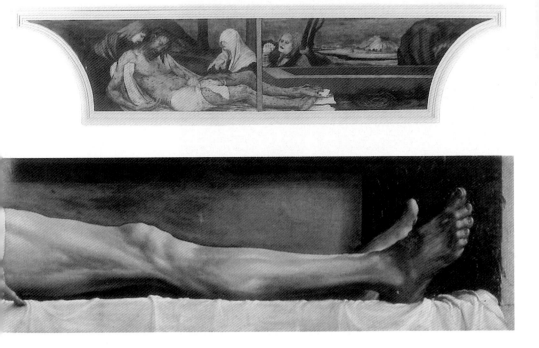

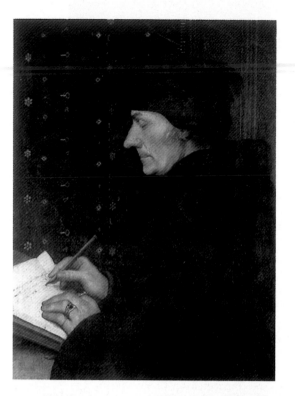

(*left*) Erasmus, *c.*1523 (Louvre, Paris)

(*below*) Georg Gisze, 1532
(Staatliche Museen, Berlin)

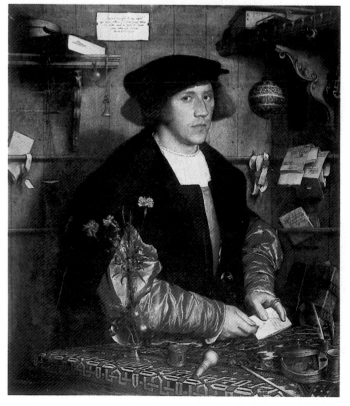

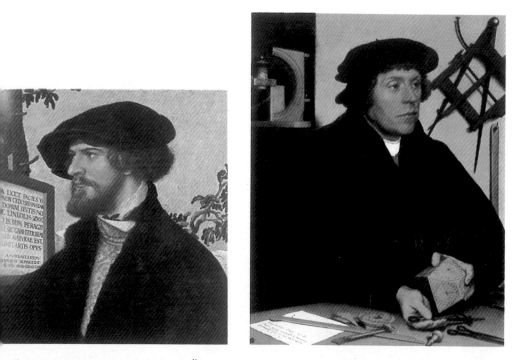

(*left*) Bonifacius Amerbach, 1519 (Öffentliche Kunstammlung, Basel)
(*right*) Nicholas Kratzer, 1528 (Louvre, Paris)

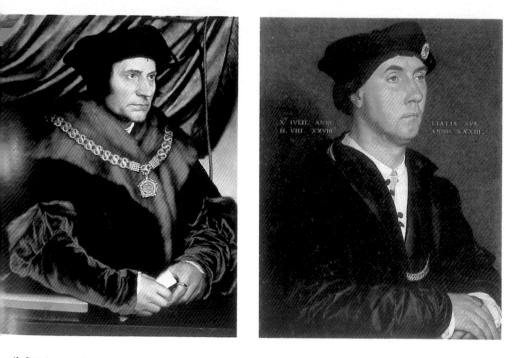

(*left*) Thomas More, 1527 (National Portrait Gallery, London)
(*right*) Richard Southwell, 1536 (Galleria degli Uffizi, Florence)

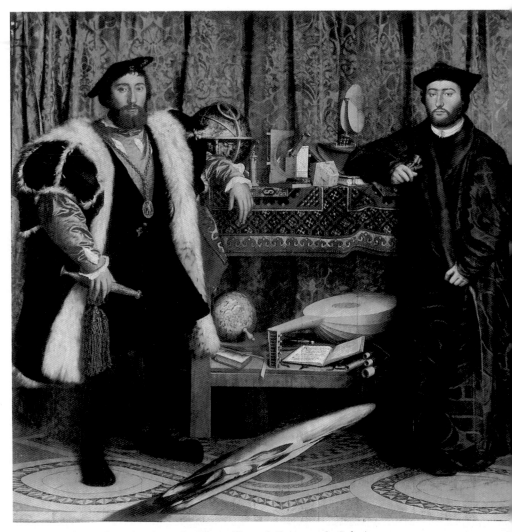

The Ambassadors (Jean de Dinteville and Georges de Selve), 1533 (National Gallery, London)

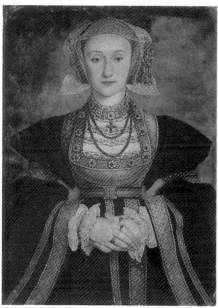

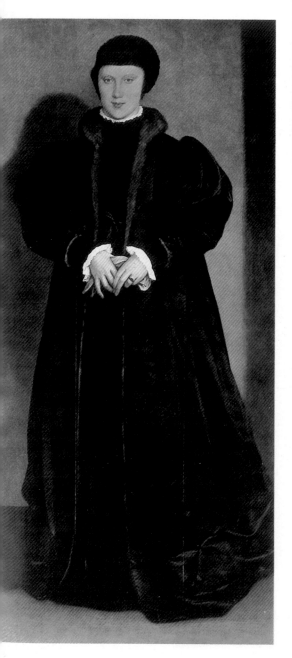

(*above*) Anne of Cleves, 1539
(Louvre, Paris)

(*left*) Christina of Denmark, 1538
(National Gallery, London)

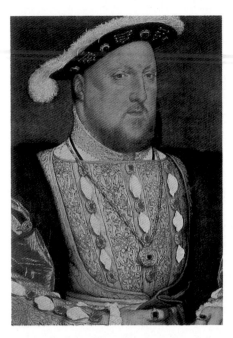

(*left*) Henry VIII, *c.*1536
(Thyssen-Bornemisza Collection,
Madrid)

(*below*) Edward VI as a child, 1539
(National Gallery of Art, Washington DC)

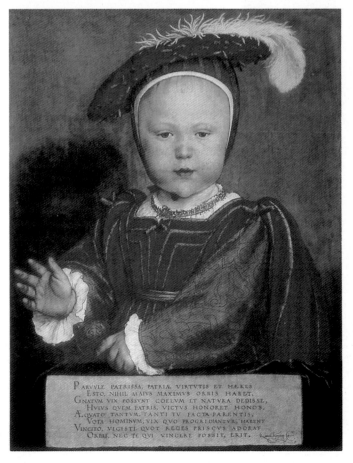

PARVVLE PATRISSA, PATRIA. VIRTVTIS ET HÆRES
ESTO, NIHIL MAIVS MAXIMVS ORBIS HABET,
GNATVM VIX POSSVNT COELVM ET NATVRA DEDISSE,
HVIVS QVEM PATRIS, VICTVS HONORET HONOS,
ÆQVATO TANTVM, TANTI TV FACTA PARENTIS,
VOTA HOMINVM, VIX QVO PROGREDIANTVR, HABENT
VINCITO, VICISTI, QVOT REGES PRISCVS ADORAT
ORBIS, NEC TE QVI VINCERE POSSIT, ERIT.

The painful moment passed. Over the following months and years the artist found that he could identify with a spiritual and intellectual movement which had moved beyond the polite humanism of Erasmus's circle. The evangelical programme sponsored by the emerging leaders of Tudor England might be the manifesto of Thomas More's enemies but it was based on an ideology Holbein accepted while at the same time sympathizing with the grief of his old patron's family and friends.

Chapter 9

LONDON

1534–1536

There is a story that on the day of Thomas More's execution in July 1535 Anne Boleyn came upon one of Holbein's portraits of the ex-minister in the royal palace. Seized with anger or remorse, she snatched it from the wall crying, 'Oh me, the man seems to be still alive!', opened a window and flung it out. The tale may be apocryphal but it expresses the queen's resentment against the one who had been the main focus of opposition to her marriage. It also indicates the course upon which Holbein had to set his career if he wished to remain in favour at court. He might feel deeply about More's fate but his old patron represented the past and Holbein now had to ally himself with those who were taking policy in a very different direction.

Calculated self-seeking undoubtedly played its part in the artist's plans but involvement with the Boleyn circle had very real attractions for a man who had always enjoyed the stimulating company of scholars. It was around the queen that English reformists gathered. Anne attracted and encouraged radical academics, churchmen and preachers. Members of her entourage read and discussed books which challenged orthodox teaching and proposed changes in society that Erasmus and his friends had long advocated. Moreover, thanks to England's strong centralized government there seemed a real possibility of putting many of the desired reforms into practice.

Recent discoveries and researches have proved that, between 1532 and 1534, Holbein built upon his former connections with the Boleyn faction and gained the patronage of the queen herself. There is a drawing in the Basel collection of a standing cup and cover topped by a crown and engraved with Anne's device, a falcon standing on roses (see plate section). This piece was ordered either by Anne herself or for her.[1] The library of Alnwick Castle possesses a beautiful manuscript translation into English of the book of *Ecclesiastes* which was made for Anne. Holbein designed the metalwork scutcheons applied to the leather binding and may have drawn the intricate illuminated capitals which are reminiscent of those he produced for Kratzer in the *Canones Horoptri*. There are other designs for jewellery in Holbein's sketchbooks which combine the symbols and initials of Anne and Henry, pieces probably made up, on royal command, by Cornelius Heyss, the king's goldsmith.

Further proof of Holbein's involvement with the queen's entourage comes from the Windsor drawings. The collection contains sketches of several younger women. Of those who can be positively identified, all belonged to Anne's private suite. Seven of them are of particular interest because they appear to form a 'set'. All are drawn in exactly the same way – half length and full face. Two of the sitters are unknown, but the others are identified as Grace Parker, Mary Zouch, Frances de Vere, Mary Howard and Lady Ratcliffe (see plate section). Grace Parker was the queen's sister-in-law. Her husband, Sir Henry Parker (knighted at Anne's coronation), was the brother of George Boleyn's wife. Mary Zouch (née Gainsford) we have already met as a lady-in-waiting and confidante of the queen, and one of her relatives was the principal financial officer of Anne's household. Frances de Vere married, in 1532, Anne Boleyn's cousin the Earl of Surrey, the poet and friend of Sir Thomas Wyatt. Mary Howard, daughter of the Duke of Norfolk, was a first cousin to the queen and is named as attending her on ceremonial occasions. The identity of 'Lady Ratcliffe' is problematical. The best fit seems to be another Mary Howard, the queen's aunt, who, in 1524, married Henry Ratcliffe, heir to the earldom of Sussex and a committed Boleyn supporter.

The question that now arises is whether Holbein ever painted Anne Boleyn. Only one disputed drawing survives and, even if we make allowance for Henry's palaces being purged of all trace of Anne after her fall, it seems strange that, if Holbein recorded her image in paint, neither an original nor a copy has been preserved. The controversial drawing from the royal collection bears the legend 'Anna Bollein Queen'. The inscription has traditionally been discounted, but in recent years some experts have argued the case for Anne Boleyn as the sitter. The original attribution was made by Sir John Cheke, and though he did not arrive in the Tudor court till 1542 he had contact with the Boleyns via William Butts and had benefited from their patronage while at Cambridge. It is difficult to see how he could have made a mistake. Contemporary descriptions agree that Anne was not beautiful in any conventional way. One witness referred to her coronation appearance: 'She wore a violet, velvet mantle, with a high ruff of gold thread and pearls, which conceals a swelling she has resembling a goitre.' We know that she habitually wore her hair shoulder length, perhaps to conceal this defect. The subject of Holbein's drawing is certainly not prepossessing, and she does have a swelling beneath her chin. However, the writer of the above description was certainly hostile to the queen and may not be reliable. In Holbein's drawing the sitter is dressed very simply, which suggests that, if this is Anne, the sketch must have been made before she became queen. This is reinforced by the fact that the paper Holbein used for this drawing came from the same batch as that employed for his sketch of John Colet.[2]

After 1533 Anne Boleyn was, next to the king, the main fount of court patronage. She used her authority not only to encourage artists and writers who took her fancy, but to ensure the growing influence of avant-garde thinkers at court. At the same time, Cromwell (with Henry's backing) was prosecuting reform in the country at large.

If the revolutionary events of the previous couple of years had been merely side-effects of the political physic applied to bring about a replacement royal wife, the pace of change would have slowed noticeably after that objective had been achieved. In point of fact, the English Reformation had built up a momentum which had to increase. To have stopped the policy machine would have left several vital issues unresolved. To have put it into reverse (for example, by submitting to Paul III, who became pope in 1534) would have displayed indecision and weakness and lent credence to Catholic propaganda that the sole driving force behind the breach with Rome had been Henry's lust. For several interconnected reasons the reform programme had to be continued. Throughout the country there were pockets of discontent and incipient rebellion. Those who sym-pathized with Yorkist pretensions or who wanted the full restoration of the old religion or who were uneasy about the growth of centralized royal power had to be shown that government decisions were unassailable and irreversible. Among the populace there was a core conservatism which had to be addressed by a programme of education and propaganda. Religious fluidity had diplomatic advantages: England was courted by Catholic and Lutheran princes and by Francis I, who was at this time ambiguous about religious reform. Above all in Henry's mind there were the implications of the royal supremacy. Having staked his claim to headship of the Church, the king would not abandon it. Equally, the pope and bold supporters of the papacy like More and Fisher could not concede it. Moreover, having assumed full responsibility for the state of the English Church, Henry had to instigate those reforms which most of his informed subjects regarded as long overdue.

Revolutions can only be carried out by convinced radicals. In Henry's name, control of policy in Church and state was taken over by earnest reformers, most of whom were committed to going much further than the king had foreseen or intended. The reforms already instigated in parliament had been based on nationalism, administrative tidiness and financial acquisitiveness. Those of the next few years were driven by ministers, bishops, preachers, parliamentarians and courtiers (encouraged by visiting theologians from Germany and Switzerland) who wanted England to ally herself with the forces of the Gospel. 'So long as Queen Anne, Thomas Cromwell, Archbishop Cranmer, Master Denny,* Doctor Butts,† with such like were about him, and could prevail with him, what organ of Christ's glory did more good in the church than [Henry VIII]?'[3] So wrote John Foxe, the Elizabethan martyrologist, who had good reasons for looking back nostalgically to the early 1530s as a golden age for the evangelical cause. Those were the years when, as a student at Oxford, he became devoted to the new religion. When, later, he began writing evangelical tracts his patroness was Anne Boleyn's relative and close friend Mary, Duchess of Richmond.

Another Protestant scholar who warmly recalled the dawn light of evangelical truth was John Cheke. His career closely paralleled that of his friend and contemporary John Foxe. While the latter was guzzling on the milk of the New Learning at Oxford, Cheke was doing the same thing at Cambridge. In 1542 Henry VIII commanded the Greek lecturer to come to court as tutor to Prince Edward, and there can be

---

* Anthony Denny, scholar and courtier; groom of the stole and close friend of the king. He and his wife were bold in their defence of persecuted Protestants.
† The King's physician. See below p.231.

little doubt that he knew Holbein during the last year of the artist's life. He remained high in the favour of the new king but fled into exile during the reign of Catholic Mary, as did Foxe. It is to Cheke that we are indebted for the preservation of the collection of eighty-five Holbein portrait drawings now in the royal collection. These connections place Holbein firmly among the reforming party at court, but there are other even clearer indications that the painter was to be found in the company of progressive thinkers and activists.

Among the French reformists centred at Meaux and enjoying the protection of Marguérite of Navarre was an eccentric Latin poet in his early thirties named Nicholas Bourbon. In 1533 he was foolhardy enough to publish a vitriolic attack on reactionary thinkers in Paris and ended up in jail, stripped of all his possessions – even, he dolefully claimed, his pet nightingale. Knowing of Anne Boleyn's close connections with the French court, Jean de Dinteville appealed to her on the young man's behalf, using as intermediary William Butts, who, as the king's doctor and trusted friend, was one of the most influential Protestants at court and one who survived all the cuts and thrusts of faction fighting. The queen secured Bourbon's release and he came to England in 1534 to render personal thanks. He lodged first with Butts and later with the king's jeweller, Cornelius Heyss, and Anne found employment for him as tutor to the children of some of the leading courtiers, including Henry Norris. During his stay he made several firm friends, including Hans Holbein, all of whom became the subject of lavish praise in his verses. Of Anne he wrote, 'the Spirit of Jesus enflames you wholly with his fire'. Cromwell he apostrophized as 'aflame with the love of Christ', while Cranmer was 'a gift from God'. Butts was 'my Maecenas and my father'. Hugh Latimer he dubbed 'the best of preachers'. And Holbein was 'the incomparable painter'. In praise of a miniature of Holbein's he composed the following eyebrow-raising encomium: 'My Hans has painted on an ivory panel a slumbering boy, looking like a reposing Cupid. I see him; I am astonished; I regard him as Charintus whom my heart loves most warmly. I approach burning with passion; yet, as I kiss him, it is only a semblance.'[4] During his stay Bourbon sat for his portrait to Holbein, and on his return to France he wrote a thank-you letter to Thomas Soulemont, Cromwell's secretary, in which he asked to be remembered to his special friends: 'I . . . beg you to greet in my name as heartily as you can all with whom you know me connected by intercourse and friendship.' His list included Thomas Cranmer, Mr Secretary Cromwell, Mr Cornelius Heyss, 'my host, the king's goldsmith', Sir William Butts, Mr Nicholas Kratzer, 'the king's astronomer, a man who is brimful of wit, jest and humorous fancies'; and 'Mr Hans, the royal painter, the Appelles [*sic*] of our time'.[5] Holbein's connection with Bourbon did not end with the latter's return to France. He provided a woodcut engraving for the 1538 edition of the *Nugae,* a collection of Bourbon's poems in which still more laudatory verses extolled Holbein and his art. Bourbon's linking of Holbein's name with illustrious representatives of the reform movement in the Church, at court and in the City places the painter at the very centre of the radical movement in England.

With all these varied contacts, not to mention Holbein's ambition and opportunism, there is no mystery about how he came to join the clientage of the man of the hour, Thomas Cromwell. The minister was still, as Chapuys reported, second to the queen in influence upon Henry and was careful to maintain a firm alliance with Anne and her circle, but by 1534 he was recognized, under Henry, as one of the twin founts of patronage and policy. It was at this time that Holbein was drawn into the magnetic field of the one man who, above all others, stood for those beliefs and courses of action that his old patron Thomas More most abhorred.

In April 1534 Thomas Cromwell was finally successful in shunting aside the Bishop of Winchester to become the king's secretary. He rapidly expanded the scope of this office to cover all parts of the executive and legislative machine. He possessed a clarity of vision, an eye for detail and a seemingly inexhaustible capacity for hard work which have seldom if ever been combined in a British chief minister. He was the mastermind which carried through the most far-reaching transformation of English society this millennium. But he could not do it single-handed.

This valiant soldier and captain of Christ . . . as he was most studious of himself in a flagrant zeal to set forward the truth of the Gospel, seeking all ways and means to beat down false religion and to advance the true, so he always retained unto him and had about him such as could be found helpers and furtherers of the same; in the number of whom were sundry and divers fresh and quick wits, pertaining to his family; by whose industry and ingenious labours,

divers excellent ballads and books were contrived and set abroad,
concerning the suppression of the pope and all popish idolatry.[6]

Cromwell assiduously encouraged and employed playwrights, poets,
pamphleteers, social commentators, theologians, preachers and artists
in setting forth the royal supremacy, denouncing the papacy and
advancing the evangelical cause.

The first definite contact between Holbein and the minister
probably occurred some time in 1533. In April the previous year
Cromwell had added to his other household offices the mastership of
the king's jewels and it was in that capacity that he commissioned the
best limner in London to paint his portrait (see plate section). It exists
now only in contemporary copies which the sitter had made for
friends and clients. It is hard, at first sight, to find much of interest in
the heavy features, small, alert eyes and unyielding, pursed lips. Even
if we make allowances for the flat technique of the copyist, we still
perceive little behind those placid features of one of the most creative
minds of his generation. Intelligence does not blaze forth from the
partially narrowed eyes as it does from the gaze of More or Erasmus.
But perhaps that is the point. The king's secretary was not university-
trained. He was the epitome of the New Learning: a man of native
wit and keen mind who could, through study, natural talent and the
company of scholars, break into those privileged enclosures largely
peopled by men of noble birth or ecclesiastical qualification.
Cromwell was a man of action for whom speculation was not an end
in itself and had no value if it did not lead to policy; a man who drew
his exemplars from the book of experience rather than the volumes
of the sages. A late-sixteenth-century commentator bracketed him
with John Dudley, Duke of Northumberland, Francis Drake and the
swashbuckling mercenary and renegade Thomas Stuckey, and went
on to categorize him as a man of 'small learning but nobly-minded
and industrious, with sufficiency of common wit, utterance and
experience'.[7] This is the no-nonsense politician to whom Holbein
introduces us. There are no Italianate fancies in this portrait, no
scholarly paraphernalia. The beautifully bound book (perhaps a gift
from a would-be protégé) lies before Cromwell, closed and clasped,
next to a scattering of correspondence (a mere fraction of the volume
of letters he dealt with every day). The top sheet, addressed to 'our
trusty and right well beloved councillor, Thomas Cromwell, master

of our jewel house', indicates the sitter's importance. Purse, pen and scissors lie at his elbow, where they have been hurriedly dropped. He grasps and almost crushes another note while giving rather sceptical attention to some unseen speaker. Just so must Mr Secretary have appeared to the many suitors who daily sought audience with the king's right-hand man.

Tudor patronage and clientage was a two-way system. A prominent figure acted as 'good lord' to a petitioner whose career he decided to advance and in return the suitor served in any capacity the patron required. For example, Richard Taverner, a destitute, young Oxford scholar, drew himself to Cromwell's attention in 1532. In return for financial support and, later, the clerkship of the privy seal, he devoted himself to the study of the law. But his subsequent career was very varied. He was sent to Germany to report on the Diet of Augsburg and write an English version of the Lutheran Augsburg Confession (which had a considerable influence on faith statements produced by Tudor theologians). Taverner produced Scripture translations and commentaries reflecting the mild form of Lutheranism that Cromwell favoured and, as well as these literary activities, he seems to have been something of an impromptu preacher and apologist for the new religious ideas.

Cromwell assiduously advanced Holbein's career and ultimately secured for him the position of king's painter. Mr Secretary's support, added to that of the queen, ensured that the Swiss painter remained in fashion. Most of Holbein's known sitters in the 1530s who were not members of the Steelyard or the Boleyn entourage were clients or relatives of Thomas Cromwell. A particularly fine painting once rather optimistically labelled 'Catherine Howard' is now considered on grounds of provenance to feature a member of Cromwell's family. Her elaborate gown and splendid jewels might suggest royalty, and there was one lady 'Aetatis Suae 21', as the picture's inscription describes her, in the mid-1530s who fits the bill. In August 1537 Cromwell succeeded in marrying his son Gregory to Elizabeth Seymour, the then queen's younger sister. He thus became related by marriage to the king, an event well worth recording for posterity by a portrait of his daughter-in-law.[8]

Wyatt became a close friend of Mr Secretary and was a useful contact in the Boleyn camp. So were his brother-in-law George Brooke, Lord Cobham, and Charles Wingfield, both of whom were closely related to ladies in the queen's entourage. Holbein's drawings of Brooke and Wingfield pose an unusual problem in that both gentlemen are depicted in a state of undress. It has been suggested that they were busy men and that the artist had to capture them when they were rising from their beds or taking exercise. This is not a convincing explanation. Most of the men and women about the court whom Holbein painted were very busy or liked to think themselves so. For most of his preliminary drawings Holbein was interested only in faces. Clothes could be depicted from memory with the aid of jotted notes when necessary. The two friends must have requested the artist to paint them bare-chested or with open shirts for a particular reason, now obscure. Since both were firm adherents of the reformed religion it may be that they had wished to eschew the vanity of costly attire and marks of rank.

Holbein's portraits introduce us to some of Cromwell's lieutenants who were at the centre of national affairs or who controlled areas distant from the capital where the monitoring of disaffection was just as important. John Godsalve commissioned another portrait and also one of his wife in 1536. Two inquisitors who played major roles in the trial of More – Richard Southwell (see plate section) and Richard Rich – were depicted by Holbein. Among those who came to court for briefings from Cromwell and were then despatched to the shires to supervise the enforcement of policy and report on possible troublemakers were the Welshman Thomas Parry and Nicholas Poyntz (cousin of John Poyntz), who was Sheriff of Gloucestershire in 1536. In Norfolk Sir Thomas Strange of Hunstanton, sheriff in 1532, was a vital agent in bringing the religious orders to heel. A prominent member of Middlesex society was Robert Cheseman and, in 1533, Holbein painted him with his falcon, a symbol of his status. The West Country was a notoriously conservative area of the country. In Devon and Cornwall men paid more heed to the Courtenays, the Marquises of Exeter, than to the distant king. These remote counties needed careful surveillance, and among Cromwell's men there Holbein met and drew Sir George Carew, Sheriff of Devon, in 1536. William Reskimer of Merthen, whose brother was a page of the chamber, and Simon George of 'Quotoule' (Cotehele?).

Holbein thus gained a rapidly growing clientele and other perks followed as he drew closer to the man who was in an excellent position to reward faithful service. On the other side of the bargain there were several ways the artist could be useful to the minister. Cromwell recognized Holbein's skill and knew of his religious sympathies. The more men of like mind Mr Secretary could place in positions of trust around Henry (even men of modest station) the better. Holbein was already a familiar and accepted figure round the court and someone much in demand as a portraitist by Mr Secretary's friends and foes alike. He was a habitué of the queen's circle, and Anne's influence with the king was vital. Yet what may have been of even greater interest to Cromwell was the free access Holbein enjoyed to Thomas More's household and his acquaintance with the ex-minister's servants, family and friends. More in exile was becoming an aggravating focus of opposition to the new policies, and some of his more hotheaded sympathizers were hatching plots. Cromwell needed all the information about them that he could lay hands on. There was one other important sphere in which Holbein moved and that was London's immigrant Protestant community. The artist could be a valuable contact between Westminster and the German Steelyard. The Hanse merchants were the most reliable and usually the first recipients of news from Protestant Europe. As the decade wore on Mr Secretary looked increasingly to the princes of the Lutheran Schmalkaldic League to buttress England's negotiating position with Catholic Spain and France. Once Holbein had gained Cromwell's complete trust he was employed in very delicate foreign missions.

Holbein therefore had much to offer but what first attracted the minister's attention was his potential as a propagandist. Central to the revolution Cromwell was intent on carrying out was nothing less than the creation of a new public persona for the monarch. Henry might claim to be supreme head of the Church in England, ruler of the nation in its spiritual as well as its temporal identity, but this concept had to be presented to his subjects in terms they could understand and consent to. Cromwell recognized in the Swiss artist a man who could give the lead to a new trend in royal propaganda. He knew the intricate, detailed drawings Holbein prepared for engravers and saw that he had a grasp of the biblical canon which would be essential in representing Henry as a spiritually enlightened sovereign. And he identified in Holbein a quick wit capable of grasping an idea and realizing it graphically.

The first example of this new style of royal adulation (or, at least, the earliest extant example of it) is the delicate miniature drawing *Solomon and the Queen of Sheba* (see frontispiece). In the guise of showing the wise Old Testament monarch receiving the homage of his rich visitor, it presents Henry VIII accepting the submission of the Church. The Reformation Parliament, which met for seven sessions between 1529 and 1536, trundled out statute after statute giving legislative form to the revolutionary changes demanded by the government. In November 1534 it produced the coping stone, the 'special statute', among the 'many and sundry good, wholesome and godly statutes [which] authorised the king's highness to be supreme head of the Church of England, by the which the pope and all his college of cardinals with all their pardons and indulgences, were utterly abolished out of this realm, God be everlastingly praised therefore'.[9] This Act of Supremacy, like the Act of Succession of the previous March, was to be rigidly enforced and all Englishmen were obliged to swear an oath to signify their acceptance. All those who supported progressive, nationalistic religious policies were triumphant. None more so than Cromwell. He had taken a huge gamble. Surveying the piecemeal, strife-torn progress of reform in various parts of the continent and knowing that England could not avoid religious conflict, he had resolved to force *apolitical* reformation, using parliament to outmanoeuvre the convocations and conservative factions among the ruling classes. There had been nerve-racking moments, but he had remained cool and he had won. The appropriate way to celebrate was to assure the king that the victory was his.

There is no date on *Solomon and the Queen of Sheba* and no indication of the circumstances in which it was produced. However, it can scarcely have been drawn before November 1534 and is unlikely to have been produced much later. Its elegance and high quality suggest that it was made for presentation to the king. Any of the leading court evangelicals might have devised this timely gift (perhaps for New Year 1535), but the person most likely to have commissioned it for this purpose is Cromwell. The miniature is Holbein's first representation of Henry VIII, though the throned figure is an icon, not a portrait. Solomon towers over his court in an aggressively triumphalist pose. The queen proffers an array of costly offerings, and her words, as recorded in 2 Chronicles 9, are printed (in Latin) in letters of gold in the upper part of the picture. Above the king's head we read 'Praised be the Lord your God. He has shown his pleasure in you by making you king to rule in his name.' On either side of the throne above Solomon's admiring courtiers (and this surely indicates the purpose and origin of the work) is written, 'How fortunate are the men who serve you, who are always in your presence and are privileged to hear your wise sayings.'

This was a private celebration of the new-style monarchy. Holbein's next contribution was very public. Yet, once again, the circumstances of its production are partially obscured by wisps of enigma. The one major reform looked for from the depapalized regime by evangelical humanists was the one that had been achieved by religious radicals in Germany, France, Switzerland, Italy and the Low Countries: a vernacular Bible. Prompted by Cranmer and Cromwell, convocation besought the king to sanction an acceptable translation. There was no question of putting the royal seal of approval on Tyndale's work; after a brief period in Henry's favour the exile was once more officially regarded as a damnable heretic. The king referred the matter back to an episcopal committee. But while they were hastening slowly a zealous scholar and keen-witted entrepreneur in Antwerp and London grasped the initiative. Miles Coverdale, a Cambridge-trained evangelical and sometime assistant of Tyndale, worked with feverish haste from the autumn of 1534 to the summer of 1535 to make an English translation using a combination of Latin, Dutch and German texts and Tyndale's New Testament. His mentor was Jakob van Meteren, an Antwerp merchant long experienced in smuggling banned books into England. By August 1535 enough pages had been printed for James Nicolson, a Southwark merchant at the English end of the chain, to approach Cromwell:

> As your goodness ever and only hath put forth your foot for the preferment of God's word: even so that your mastership will now set to your helping hands that the whole Bible may come forth, whereof as much as is yet come into England I have sent unto you by this bringer, George Constantine, a copy which I beseech your discretion for the zeal you bear unto the truth so to promote, that the pure word of God may once go forth under the king's privilege. . . .[10]

With the pages came a dedication to Henry.

Despite the tone of the letter it is difficult to believe that Cromwell had heard nothing of this bold project before he received the parcel from Nicolson (see below). However, it was certainly a matter in which he had to tread warily. He had no idea how the king would react to Coverdale's offering and he had no wish to be seen as a patron of the black market in heretical books. Since January, when Cromwell had been appointed vicegerent in spirituals (commonly referred to as 'vicar general'), Henry had delegated to his minister the conduct of ecclesiastical affairs, but that did not mean that he had abandoned all interest in religious matters or that he might not, on a sudden whim, or at the suggestion of the Catholic clique, reverse the whole drift of policy. Here Anne Boleyn came to Cromwell's aid. She lent her support to the Coverdale Bible. The George Constantine referred to by Nicolson was a zealot we have already met who had long been involved in book smuggling, had fallen foul of More in 1531 and had escaped to the continent. He returned now under the protection of none other than Henry Norris. Anne was, therefore, fully aware of Constantine's mission. Coverdale's work was shown to the king soon afterwards and he passed it to some of the bishops for comment. The instigators and backers of the project waited nervously for the verdict. When it came it was one of moderate approval: the Bible might be sold in England but not under royal licence. By the first weeks of the new year stock was moving rapidly through the bookshops.

It carried a magnificent title-page by Hans Holbein (see plate section) which pictorially expounded the doctrine of the royal supremacy and showed Henry VIII, the beneficent monarch, distributing the word of God to his grateful subjects. In this one woodcut the artist summarized all the positive aspects of the Henrician Reformation. At the bottom centre the king, flanked by his lords spiritual and temporal, grasps the Sword and the Book. In his preface Coverdale explained the iconography for any who might miss its full significance:

> the office, authority and power given of God unto kings is in earth above all other powers; let them call themselves popes, cardinals, or whatsoever they will. The word of God declareth them (yea and commandeth them under pain of damnation) to be obedient unto the temporal sword, as in the Old Testament all the prophets, priests and Levites were.

The figures of David and Paul on either side of the king illustrate both the spiritual authority by which he reigns and the scriptural (as opposed to papal) sanction for that authority. The apostle's presence is doubly significant. It is Paul the evangelist not Peter the papal prototype who buttresses the new order. And he carries a sword which henceforth in Protestant lands would symbolize the Bible and not, as traditionally, the apostle's martyrdom. The rest of the border is given over to the Lutheran theme of law and grace. From the divine name, fount of all power and authority, the genesis of the Torah (to the left) is balanced by the setting forth and proclamation of the Gospel (to the right).

There was nothing novel in any of the images Holbein delineated so skilfully. Since 1520 Luther had urged princes to rule and reform their Churches. In *The Obedience of a Christian Man* Tyndale had advised kings to take Moses as their example, as one who 'in exercising the law was merciless; otherwise more than a mother unto them'.[11] Around the same time Joos van Cleve had portrayed Henry with a scroll bearing the text, 'Go ye into all the world and preach the Gospel to every creature,' a quotation from Mark 16 that Holbein used on the title-page. Furthermore, Holbein's title-page has similarities to Jacques Lefèvre d'Etaples's French Bible (Antwerp 1530) and the Lübeck edition of Luther's Bible (1533). What *was* new was the juxtaposition of images to illustrate a Protestant theology of Christian kingship.

The question that cried out for answer is 'Who was responsible for this striking and powerful iconography?' That leads on to a consideration of who commissioned Holbein's drawing and discussed with him the general layout. The design and perhaps the block were ready before Coverdale wrote his preface. The title-page was printed with the rest of the Bible in Cologne, where van Meteren had fled from persecution in Antwerp. It was in place in the first finished copies which reached London in October 1534. We know that van Meteren was in London earlier in the year and it is likely that he would have been discussing his great project with sympathizers at that time. Thus Holbein's involvement probably dates from the spring or early summer of 1535. He would certainly not have become associated with the publication without the knowledge of a powerful patron. The man in whose mind the title-page originated must have been familiar with contemporary Protestant (especially Lutheran) imagery and must have known what elements of it would appeal to Henry VIII. The most obvious contender is Cromwell. That means that, months before he was prepared to come out into the open as an advocate of Coverdale's work and while he was still consulting with the bishops about an official English Bible, he was covertly in league with members of the underground press. And Holbein was at the heart of the secret.

There was, inevitably, another aspect, a negative and at times sinister aspect, of government policy. In this, also, Holbein was involved. While Cromwell and his team encouraged acceptance of the revolution they also had to stamp out defiance and stifle discontent. Since there was scarcely a community in which the sweeping changes (and they were but the first of many) did not stir up controversy, the regime had to be ruthless and efficient if it was to survive. In the wake of the propagandists came commissioners, spies and informers. Government agents in the shires called townsmen and villagers together to swear their allegiance to the supreme head of the English Church and his heirs born of Queen Anne. They were quick to notice when subjects showed reluctance. Reports and letters tumbled on to Cromwell's desk from paid activists, amateur inquisitors who wanted to ingratiate themselves with the government, zealots for the new order and men with personal axes to grind. They told of those who grumbled about the new statutes, confronted evangelical preachers, sang ribald songs about the king. In part of Nottinghamshire, to take just one county, Cromwell's man on the spot was Sir John Markham. In the spring of 1534 he arrested the prior of the Observant friars in Newark for preaching a seditious sermon. A few months later he reported the wife of a certain Alan Hey for making insulting comments about Anne Boleyn. The following April he examined the proctor of Beauvale priory on suspicion of being a stubborn papist. Most cases were dealt with locally but a cavalcade of obdurate troublemakers was sent up to London to be examined by the Council.

Cromwell, of course, was particularly interested in prominent malcontents. These consisted of three groups. There were ecclesiastics, particularly in the monasteries, who could not be weaned away from papal allegiance. Another potential threat was the Catholic nobility; Courtenays, Poles and other leaders of local society who made common cause with them and who were encouraged by the imperial ambassador's network of agents. Thirdly there were those men at the centre of power who disliked the drift of policy and who vied with Cromwell for influence at court – councillors such as Norfolk and Bishop Gardiner. Such people had to be watched and their activities carefully monitored. The king's secretary therefore had to maintain a large and vigilant intelligence-gathering service.

The assertion that Holbein was a 'spy' must be accompanied by a very careful definition of what that word means in a sixteenth-century context. Professor Elton has demonstrated that Cromwell did not develop 'a system of espionage, the most effective that England had ever seen', as one historian had claimed.[12] The minister did place his own agents in monastic houses and he probably kept a planted informer in the household of the suspect Earl of Derby. Beyond this there is little evidence of any army of paid infiltrators whose sole task was to pry into other men's secrets. Such paucity of documentary material actually reinforces our belief in Cromwell's efficient intelligence-gathering system rather than otherwise. The minister did not keep dozens of paid spies on his payroll because he had no need to. He already possessed a sophisticated and extensive information service, one that was vital to the success of his politico-religious programme. It was one aspect of his widespread patronage system. His protégés at court, in government employment, or travelling abroad as merchants or students were expected to report back any information that might be valuable to their 'good lord'. As we have already seen, hundreds of people relayed snippets of news or gossip to Cromwell's office in the hope of ingratiating themselves with him. The king's secretary was not unique in this regard. Foreign diplomats, leading courtiers and royal councillors all relied on their servants, correspondents, clients and well-wishers to keep them informed about what potential and real enemies were saying about them and plotting against them. It was part of the patronage deal and it would not have occurred to those who had attached themselves to Cromwell that passing information was not a part of their responsibility.

When Holbein entered Mr Secretary's environment it was to further his own career but it was also because he identified with what Cromwell stood for. He cannot have failed to be impressed by the striking contrast between England's centrally organized Reformation and the new regime which had been forced on Basel's dithering authorities by a determined populace. He deliberately associated himself with it and he brought with him his talent, his international contacts and his knowledge of members of the More circle. All were at the disposal of his new patron. He also had the potential to be a very useful intelligence-gatherer. As a painter he had access to the households of leading figures in whom Mr Secretary had an interest. Just as Cromwell placed agents in abbeys where there might be resistance to his policies, so he encouraged Holbein to acquire as clients men on whom he wanted information.

At the top of the government's hit list were the names of Sir Thomas More and Bishop John Fisher. In April 1534 they were both immured in the Tower for declining to swear the oath attached to the Act of Succession because it carried with it rejection of papal authority in legal matters. For over a year the two friends languished in their separate cells, frequently visited by Cromwell or his representatives. The king's secretary was not a brutal man. He had a genuine respect for the prisoners and for More he felt a real affection. Moreover, as a political realist he understood that it was not in his interest to create popular martyrs. He, therefore, used every stratagem to break their resolve. He sent politiques like Richard Southwell to threaten and cajole and he also despatched friends of More and Fisher who had been able to square their consciences with the new legislation to persuade the two men to join the consenting majority. Only when royal vindictiveness demanded blood did Cromwell change his tactics. The king felt More's obduracy as a personal betrayal. He was less interested in the bishop but when he heard that Paul III had created Fisher a cardinal he flew into one of his terrifying rages and the doom of the men in the Tower was sealed. Cromwell's sole objective now was to prove treason against More and Fisher. He despatched agents to grill servants and close friends and turn up damning evidence. Those he sent to visit the prisoners now concentrated on tricking them into unguarded words.

One of them was Hans Holbein. Among the artist's most haunting drawings is a sketch of John Fisher (see plate section). It depicts the drawn, anxious features of a man in his mid- to late-sixties. The paper and the technique employed place the portrait in the period 1532–5 and it is distinct from Holbein's other drawings in that it carries a scrawled inscription in a later hand. The legend, in poor Italian, is unclear and seems to have been written over earlier lines, perhaps set down by Holbein. All that can be ascertained with certainty is the name 'the bishop of Rochester' and the date '1535'. The suggestion has been made that the missing and defaced words refer to Fisher's execution, but this can only be guesswork. No painted portrait based on the sketch exists and the drawing itself bears no hints which would suggest that it was made in preparation for a painted version. Fisher was an ascetic with a traditionalist cast of mind – not the sort of man likely to indulge the vanity of having his likeness taken. If we assume the date on the drawing to be accurate, the circumstances under which it was made become clear. Holbein drew Fisher in the Tower. He can only have been sent there by Cromwell and only as part of the vicegerent's strategy of breaking the prisoner. Perhaps he was a member of a 'friendly' delegation of agents talking about old times, common friends and flattering the bishop with their solicitous attentions.

Another man with the ability to cause problems was George Neville, Lord Bergavenny. This sexagenarian head of an ancient family was linked with the Courtenays, Staffords and Poles in a faction never fully at ease with the drift of Tudor policy. He was imprisoned in 1521–2 for suspected complicity with his father-in-law, the Duke of Buckingham (executed for treason in May 1521). Bergavenny and his kin reinstated themselves in royal favour, but the government was always, and with reason, nervous of feudal lords who continued to enjoy near-royal power on their distant estates and who resented the increasing centralization of government. Chapuys, the imperial ambassador, played on their deep-seated jealousies, traditionalist tendencies and dislike of new men such as Wolsey and Cromwell. He did his utmost to foster disaffection and was liberal with his master's gold in his attempts to organize a faction of powerful men opposed to the Cromwellian regime. In September 1533 he reported that Bergavenny was one of those who could be counted on to support the imperial–Catholic cause. Among those known to be close to the baron was Bishop Fisher. In July 1534 one of Bergavenny's friends, William, Lord Dacre of the North, was called to account for certain alleged treasons on the Scottish border and Bergavenny himself was among those peers detailed to try him in the House of Lords (Dacre achieved an almost unique triumph at a state trial by successfully defending himself – in a seven-hour speech). The old nobleman died in 1535 and thus avoided being caught up in the tumult which broke over England in the autumn of the following year. Of that event his son-in-law Henry Pole, Lord Montague, observed, 'If my lord Abergavenny were alive he were able to make a great number of men in Kent and Sussex.' We now know that, in 1533, Cromwell was deliberately courting Bergavenny's company, concerned no doubt to keep an eye on this disaffected nobleman. At the same time Holbein made a portrait of Bergavenny, of which two copies remain, one dated 1533 and the other 1534.

Sir Nicholas Carew was younger than Neville by twenty years, and of him too Chapuys expressed high hopes. As master of the horse and a seasoned courtier and diplomat Carew was high in Henry VIII's favour but not so high that he was above suspicion. He supported the possibility of an imperial alliance and had close contacts with the Poles and Courtenays. But what turned him from a grumbling though faithful royal servant into a scheming activist who ended his life on the scaffold was his intense dislike of Anne Boleyn and his continued adherence to her predecessor. Carew organized the whispering campaign which brought Anne down, and he went on from that to more disastrous and ultimately fatal intrigues. He was certainly a candidate for close observation by Cromwell. Holbein had drawn Carew during his first visit to London and had carried the sketch with him to Basel, where it remained. Whether or not this resulted in a commission we do not know but Carew sat to Holbein again in the early 1530s at a time when he was known to be working against the interests of the queen.

Sir John Russell was another courtier whose loyalties and sympathies needed close monitoring. Long a favourite of the king, he was a seasoned diplomat and soldier (he had lost the sight of one eye in an engagement in 1522) with extensive foreign connections. When he was not abroad on royal business he attended on the king as one of the gentlemen of the privy chamber. He came from a Devon family and had close relations with the Courtenays and their ilk. All this made Russell a man worth cultivating and watching. But what rendered him particularly interesting was his antipathy towards the queen. Their mutual hostility dated from the early days of Anne's influence when she had intervened in a personal dispute in favour of Russell's adversary. Russell found it hard to stomach that he, who had enjoyed Henry's favour and support for several years, had had to give place to a chit of a girl who now ruled the royal roost. Since that early clash queen and courtier had found themselves on opposite sides over several issues. Sir John was far too practised a royal servant to make his true feelings felt. He was a born survivor who would come unscathed through the political ebbs and flows of the reigns of Henry VIII, Edward VI and Mary. Because of the man's reticence Cromwell would value any insights into Russell's thoughts that Holbein might be able to gain during the portrait sitting Sir John gave him in 1534 or 1535.

Conceivably, we should include Thomas, Lord Vaux of Harrowden, among those with whom Holbein's relationship was not solely professional. Hans drew the young man twice in the 1530s and probably worked up one of the sketches into a painting (now lost). He certainly made a finished portrait of Elizabeth, his wife. Vaux was an up-and-coming courtier who began his rise in Wolsey's household. He was knighted in 1533 and appointed captain of the Isle of Jersey. But, in 1536, he suddenly gave up his court prospects. Disliking the government's religious policies and unhappy at being obliged to swear acceptance of the new statutes, he withdrew to his estates. Vaux was something of a poet and was a member of the Wyatt–Surrey circle, and it may be that we should seek no more convoluted reason for his connection with Holbein than his involvement with the more cultural aspects of court life. However, we should never lose sight of the fact that no one in the Tudor solar system – from the major planets of the Council to the hopeful, remote satellites – could avoid a political role. In the intense 1530s a man could not escape suspicion simply by removing himself from the centre. Cromwell kept a close watch on all those whose loyalty was dubious and Holbein was one of his more important pairs of eyes.

Dissembling and flattery were essential skills for all trying to survive or advance themselves in the Henrician court. This raises the question of Holbein's sincerity and his degree of commitment to his patrons and what they stood for. If Holbein's involvement in the Cromwellian reform programme was purely pragmatic we would be forced to impute to him a massive cynicism. This goes against everything else we know about the artist. In 1532, an opportunist would have turned his back on Thomas More without a second thought. Holbein detached himself with difficulty, his emotional and intellectual turmoil producing two remarkable, intricate paintings. If he had serious reservations about the situation in England he could have left at any time. His earlier career had been one of frequent relocations but, after 1532, he resisted all blandishments to return permanently to Basel. When he was in his home town he spoke warmly of the English regime and bragged about his intimacy with its leaders.

If a man is to be judged by the company he keeps, then there can be no doubt of his adherence, by 1534, to a brand of evangelical Christianity close to Lutheranism. Nicholas Kratzer and Jan van der Goes (John of Antwerp) were among his closest friends and were committed to reform. His habitual companions were the Steelyard merchants, most of whom were adherents of the Wittenberg religion. He worked closely and, as far as we know, amicably with several of Cromwell's agents. All those people in England with whom Holbein's name is linked after 1532 were supporters of religious change.

More fundamental is what we know to be Holbein's commitment to truth. This was his guiding principle whether representing biblical scenes or probing the human psyche. Certainly it governed his own quest for faith, as is indicated by his response to the new doctrines in Basel.

Like all intelligent men living through the crisis years of the Reformation, Holbein travelled on his own spiritual pilgrimage. His works provide glimpses of that journey. Fortunately, he executed one painting which gives us a close insight into the stage his own religious beliefs had reached by the mid-1530s.

Holbein produced, for an as yet unidentified patron, a version of what was the most powerful and pervasive graphic representation of Lutheran theology. This was *Law and Grace* or the *Old and New Law*. Zwingli and the Swiss reformers had rejected all devotional religious imagery. Luther emphatically had not. He wanted people to use paintings and engravings as a means of meditating on religious truth, especially the key doctrine of justification by faith. In 1529 Lucas Cranach the Elder, Luther's friend and chief political propagandist, originated or developed a doctrinal icon that was rapidly copied and adapted in various media all over Protestant Europe. This was a painting in two halves. On the left-hand side, surmounted by Christ in judgement, the prophet Isaiah told the story of man's fall, his judgement under the Mosaic law and his consignment to hell. The right-hand section, divided from the other by the tree of life, showed

John the Baptist pointing to the Lamb of God, whose crucifixion and resurrection overcame death and Satan. A written commentary along the bottom of the panel explained the salient details. Within a few years engravings and, perhaps, paintings after the Cranach original had reached England, and would certainly have been familiar to the Hanse merchants. It may have been one of them or a friend at court who asked Holbein to make a new version *of Law and Grace*. In doing so the painter transformed a somewhat crude visual treatise into a painting no less didactic but possessed of much greater artistic merit (see plate section).

The image had made an enormous impact in several countries and had influenced Protestant iconography in many ways. The French artist Geoffrey Tory had made a woodcut version. Erhard Altdorfer (died 1533) had drawn on it for the title-page of the Lübeck Bible (1532), and the Antwerp publisher Martin Lempereur had commissioned a title-page alluding to it for Jacques Lefèvre's French Bible (1530). We have already noted the similarities of these printed works to Holbein's woodcut for the Coverdale Bible. The latter is similar to Holbein's allegorical painting, in its general layout and particularly in the figure of Moses receiving the tablets of the law. The exact sequence of all these treatments is a matter of debate among scholars, but their overall ideological relationship is obvious. What is of particular interest to us is the content of Holbein's painting.

It seems to be closest to a workshop version of Cranach's painting now in Prague, and Holbein must have taken this sub-species as his starting point. It is an altogether more sophisticated and moving treatment than Cranach's original. The naked figure of Homo is placed centrally, asking of Isaiah and John the Baptist the question from Romans 7, 'Wretched man that I am, who shall deliver me from this body of death?' Both prophets point him to Agnus Dei and the principal events of the New Testament: the Annunciation, Crucifixion and Resurrection. 'Behold,' they both explain, 'a virgin shall conceive a child' who shall be 'the lamb of God who takes away the sin of the world'. As in all versions of the painting there are allusions to the sin of Adam and Eve, the giving of the law, the brazen serpent, seen as a prefiguration of Christ, and man's inheritance of death from his first parents. What is significantly lacking in this strand of evangelical thinking is the theme of judgement. The medieval image still present in the Cranach original of Christ upon the rainbow with the sword and the lily, representing the damned and the blessed, has disappeared, as has the naked figure of the condemned being prodded towards hell by demons. For Holbein, death rather than eternal torture is the final enemy which Christ, Victoria Nostra, treads beneath his feet.

What we have in this strain of the *Law and Grace* motif is a more refined, almost a more humanistic, Lutheranism. It is not that the German reformer did not believe in everlasting punishment and reward; he did. But the significance of his theologial revolution was that he had shifted the emphasis from the next world to this. The penitential system of the medieval Church insisted that men perform certain acts on behalf of their own and their loved ones' eternal well-being. The indulgences racket rested upon the concept of purgatory and the concern of the devout or panic-stricken to shorten their sojourn there. For Luther – and here most humanists were at one with him – what needed stressing was the necessity of personal faith here and now. This entailed a different way of thinking about heaven and hell: 'We cannot reach heaven until we first descend into hell. We cannot be God's children unless first we are the devil's children. Before the world can be seen to be a lie it must first appear to be the truth.'[13] So wrote Luther in his commentary on Romans. These were insights that Holbein shared. His *oeuvre* is almost devoid of demono-logical references: only in some satirical engravings do the imps of hell appear. But death had held a fascination for him ever since he had portrayed Christ as a rotting cadaver, and probably before. This was the 'last enemy' from which he sought deliverance. Holbein shows no sign of being caught up in preoccupation with and speculation about matters apocalyptic, a subject of fascination to many contemporary preachers, both Catholic and radical. Like Luther, and even more like Zwingli and Oecolampadius, he espoused a version of Christianity which represented the drama of salvation as being played on a terrestrial stage.

Among most of his friends and acquaintances he was able to live and express his ideals with little restraint. Despite the tumult of religious ideas and the disquiet caused by government policy, daily religious life in London was comparable to that which the artist had known in Basel in the 1520s. Rival sermons were being preached from pulpits. Occasional acts of iconoclasm occurred. Anti-papal tracts were openly on sale. Protestant treatises were easily available.

But the Reformation had yet to change the pattern of worship in the churches. There was no consistent and integrated policy for rooting out heresy. The government was interested only in eradicating support for the papacy. In comparison with several continental cities, London was more tolerant of religious radicals. In March 1535 all Anabaptist sectaries were ordered to leave the realm, but this was not followed up by an organized witch-hunt. More people arrived in London seeking refuge than fled from it to avoid persecution. When Professor Gaulter Delanus quit Amsterdam on suspicion of Anabaptism he found employment with Henry VIII. Foreign communities like the Steelyard merchants were largely left to their own devices. Beneath the waves and ripples on the surface there were calmer deeps, and once Holbein had settled into a pattern of social life and religious observance he found his situation tolerably comfortable.

Even in the more *mouvementé* atmosphere of the court Holbein's opinions broadly chimed with those prevailing in the queen's apartments. The brand of evangelicalism espoused by Anne has been described as 'real spiritual experience, yes; the priority of faith, yes; access to the Bible, yes; reform of abuses and superstition, yes; but heretical views on the miracle of the altar, no'.[14] Holbein could go along with that. He had acquiesced in the reformed doctrine of the mass in Basel but only after careful thought. In England he moved back from that teaching to a point of view closer to the less extreme Lutheran position. But it is unlikely that the more abstruse points of theology disturbed him greatly. At court he doubtless enjoyed the 'practical Christianity' of people like Sir William and Lady Butts. The royal physician won the approval of most of those with whom he came into contact, from the king downwards. Though committed to the reform, he was kind and generous to all. He moved freely between the queen's chambers and the quarters allocated to Princess Mary, who loathed her mother's usurper. He used his patronage to advance men like John Cheke and Hugh Latimer to court favour and supported foreign evangelicals, such as Nicholas Bourbon. It was Butts who was the link between Cambridge university and the royal household and he was always on the lookout for young men of talent and Protestant faith.

Recent reassessment of Anne Boleyn has emphasized the depth and sincerity of her religious commitment. She read evangelical treatises and works of devotion, with a preference for those written in French, and circulated them among her entourage. The radical chaplains with whom she surrounded herself were enjoined to encourage her attendants 'above all things to embrace the wholesome doctrine and infallible knowledge of Christ's gospel'.[15] She advanced several reform-minded clergy to bishoprics and was a generous patroness of writers and students. As we have seen, she was assiduous in interceding on behalf of men who found themselves in difficulties over their religious opinions. Anne did not dabble in government business but she certainly used the institutional changes of the 1530s to advance the cause of reform. Chapuys called her 'the principal cause of the spread of Lutheranism [that is, of all Protestant heresy] in this country'.[16] If Cromwell was the brain of the Reformation Anne Boleyn was its heart. The minister worked closely in harmony with the queen. He acted as her steward. Stephen Vaughan, one of his trusted agents, was married to one of Anne's silk women. Holbein certainly had cause to be grateful to Anne for introducing him to a wide circle of potential clients and for bringing him more firmly to the king's attention.

At the end of 1535 all must have seemed *couleur de rose* for Holbein. At least one visitor (Nicholas Bourbon) referred to him as the 'royal painter', and though he was not yet on the Tudor payroll he was certainly well placed to reach the summit of his ambition; to become, like his uncle, court painter to one of the leaders of the Renaissance world. But within a few weeks all his hopes and plans were thrown into chaos.

Three events in January 1536 changed drastically the course of English history. On the 7th Catherine of Aragon died of cancer. Catholics at home and abroad no longer had a figurehead to rally round. But Anne Boleyn no longer had an insurance policy. As long as Henry's first wife lived Henry could not contemplate getting rid of his second. On the 24th the king had a bad fall from his horse in the tiltyard. He was in pain and some incapacity for several weeks and it may well be that his health and mental equilibrium suffered in the long term from this accident. On the 29th Anne Boleyn miscarried of a deformed, male foetus. It was her second such misfortune. The shock to Henry was intense. In earlier years he had convinced himself that Catherine's childbed calamities were signs of divine disapproval. How, then, could he doubt that God was still displeased with him? He had set aside the opinion of the pope, the goodwill of the emperor and the support of thousands of his subjects to marry the woman who would give him an heir. He had further sought divine approval by reforming the Church. Now, it would appear, he had been mistaken. Henry Tudor had the knack of being able to drive his conscience and his will in double harness. The storm of his passion for Anne had spent itself and he was already looking elsewhere. The queen, as determined as ever not to share her husband with another woman, had made no secret of her annoyance. Henry, more irascible after his fall, reacted angrily. Enemies of the Boleyns sniffed the change in the wind and hastened to take advantage of it. When the king realized that disembarrassing himself of Anne would be popular as well as desirable he instructed Cromwell to take care of the details. On 19 May the queen of a thousand days was dead. Her brother George, Henry Norris and others also went to the scaffold. Thomas Wyatt was sent to the Tower. Anne's evangelical friends feared that all the religious gains of the last few years might be set aside. Others, including Hans Holbein, worried about their own positions.

Chapter 10

LONDON–BRUSSELS–DÜREN–BASEL

1536–1540

On 19 May 1536 Anne Boleyn's head was struck from her body within the precincts of the Tower of London. She was the second of Holbein's major English patrons to meet this fate in or close to the Tower. She would not be the last.

Anne's death was the prelude to four years of political and social turmoil. These were the *années crises* of the Tudor dynasty and of the English Reformation. From them the monarchy emerged strong enough to survive the succession of a minor and two women. Thereafter the process of religious change would be irreversible; not even that sad fanatic Mary Tudor would be able to recapture for papal Catholicism the hearts and minds of the people who really mattered. Yet the outcome of the period 1536–40 could so easily have been very different. Thousands of English men and women, from the highest to the lowest, were caught up in a conflict based on self-interest, power and greed but also on profound social and religious principles. No one close to the centre of public life could be unaffected by the clash of personalities and ideals. Certainly not Hans Holbein.

The king's determination to be rid of his second queen stirred up and confused the already agitated ants' nest of the royal court. *Sauve qui peut* was the watchword of the Boleyn's kith and kin. Anne's Howard relatives and her evangelical protégés alike deserted her. Household servants such as George Brooke's wife and Charles Wingfield's mother hastened to give evidence at her trial. Cromwell wielded espionage, torture and bribery to effect the queen's condemnation by due judicial process.

Anne's enemies and those who blamed her for encouraging heretics were cock-a-hoop. They looked for a swift reversal of the policies of the last few years. They expected revenge for the blood of

More and Fisher and vindication of the beliefs for which they had died. Contrasting Anne Boleyn and her successor Jane Seymour, Russell observed, 'the king hath come out of hell into heaven for the gentleness in this and the cursedness and the unhappiness in the other'.[1] Princess Mary expected to be recalled to her rightful place in the court and to the succession to the crown. 'Nobody dared speak for me,' she grumbled, 'as long as that woman lived, which is now gone.'[2] Now things would be different. Supporters of reform feared precisely what Mary's adherents hoped for. Bishop Shaxton of Salisbury urged Cromwell to continue upholding the Gospel as the late queen had so often urged him.

Paradoxically, Cromwell was able to hasten on the reform programme by applying himself to the destruction of the one who had been its most exalted champion. His survival and therefore the prosecution of the policies he believed in depended on his ruthless faithfulness to the king's wishes. Henry was a coldblooded tyrant who became more viciously unpredictable as age and illness eroded the bonhomie which originally lent his personality a certain cheerful grace. By studied subservience to the will of his master combined with a scalpel-sharp perception of the drastic surgery England still required Cromwell was able to dominate the remainder of the decade. There would be no about-turn. Despairing opponents of government policy would be forced into plots and rebellions – and would pay a terrible price.

The king married his third queen, Jane Seymour, and a new brood of royal relatives took their place at court. As the realm moved out of a damp spring into a wet summer the centre of national life was a confusion of shifting alliances and clashing expectations. But there was no haziness or competition of principles in Henry's mind. Both Catherine and Anne were out of the way; a new Succession Act bastardized Mary and Elizabeth and proclaimed as rightful heirs the issue of his new union; legislation had been passed in March for the suppression of lesser monasteries, and this, as well as underlining Henry's supremacy over the English Church, would bring much needed loot into his coffers. In Henry's mind there now existed no cause of conflict between him and the emperor. None of his subjects therefore had any excuse for plots at home or treasonous dealing with foreign powers. In July Lady Hussey, wife of a courtier with extensive Midlands estates, was sent to the Tower for several weeks when she was overheard referring to Mary as 'Princess' ('the Lady Mary' was her only official title). Henry was always ready to back government pronouncement with acts of petty vindictiveness. Then, in July, he sent a clear signal to all potential malcontents: he raised Cromwell to the peerage and conferred upon him Thomas Boleyn's old office of lord privy seal.

This only reinforced the hostility of many who, for sundry reasons, opposed the regime. In May Reginald Pole, humanist scholar and white hope of Catholic and Yorkist activists, had sent Henry (at the king's request) a treatise, *De Unitate Ecclesiastica,* setting out his views on Anglo-papal relations and current religious policy in England. It cogently attacked Henry's dealings of recent years and urged him to slide no further down the slippery slope to perdition. *De Unitate* was not published in Henry's realm but the ideas it expressed provided a cloak of theological respectability for naked aggression in support of traditional religion.

By mid-July a sad piece of news was speeding along the trade routes of Europe which suggested to many that the age of moderate and reasoned reform had passed: Erasmus was dead. The aged scholar had returned to Basel, determined to lay his bones in the city rendered once more acceptable now that the cloud of religious fanaticism had passed over. There, in the house of his godson Hieronymus Froben, amid a new generation of admirers (most of his close contemporaries had predeceased him), he died on 12 July. He was laid to rest in the cathedral, and Myconius – a man for whose intellectual qualities Erasmus had never had much respect – gave the funeral oration.

Back in England it was not only the leaders of ancient nobility and traditional religion who believed that the realm was on the edge of a snakepit in which heresy, tyranny and barbarism coiled and hissed. In different localities clergy, landowners, townsmen and villagers were being driven close to open revolt by the activities of Cromwell's agents. Bands of commissioners, supported by centrally appointed preachers, were examining smaller abbeys and nunneries, valuing the assets of parish churches, enquiring into the moral and intellectual standing of the clergy, requiring them to read out royal injunctions to their congregations and collecting taxes. If the government had set out to engender widespread disaffection it could hardly have achieved its purpose more successfully.

The Council was far from being oblivious to the mounting anxiety and anger felt by many and expressed by some. Cromwell and his colleagues received reports almost daily from official and unofficial sources. Their response was to press ahead with determination and vigilance. For the king's chief minister that meant increasing the propaganda campaign at all levels and maintaining a still closer watch over individuals and localities from which trouble might come. Cromwell was always on the lookout for new talent and always ready to promote protégés who had proved their worth. In 1536, from among the throng of pamphleteers who either had been or hoped to be employed in the cause of the regime he chose Thomas Starkey and Richard Morison to be his principal exponents of government policy. And from the corps of English and foreign artists available to him he selected Hans Holbein to be advanced to the position of king's painter.

This was not a position that Holbein achieved easily. Despite his popularity with Anne Boleyn and several of her circle and his work as a propagandist it had been several years before he gained the king's favour. In fact, Holbein reached the peak of his career not so much because of his obvious talent, or the satisfaction previous royal commissions had given, or his popularity at court as because of his backing by an immensely powerful patron who knew that he could project the image of the Tudor regime which the king required. Holbein was totally dependent on Cromwell. He achieved ultimate fame and fortune in 1536, the year Cromwell gained complete mastery. He fell from royal favour in 1540, the year of Cromwell's death. It may even be that the minister had some proselytizing to do on Holbein's behalf because of the artist's close connection with the Boleyn set. When Bourbon wrote from France on 5 September 1536 he referred to Kratzer as the 'king's astronomer' and Cornelius Heyss as the 'king's goldsmith' but to Holbein as the 'royal painter'. This suggests that according to the Frenchman's last news about the artist he was still occupied on commissions for the king but had yet to find a place on Henry's payroll. That situation had changed by early the following year when Holbein was recorded in the accounts as receiving £30 per annum. The accolade of king's painter thus seems to have been bestowed towards the end of 1536.

It is hard to resist the conclusion that what clinched his appointment was the masterpiece in miniature that Holbein painted in the last months of 1536. Henry was prevailed upon to sit for his portrait.

Holbein, always adept at grasping his opportunities, pulled out all the stops. He created a small, very personal representation which was to become the prototype of his own perception of the king and of the image which the name 'Henry VIII' inevitably conjures up in our minds four and a half centuries later (see plate section). Within the confines of a panel only 24 centimetres by 19 Holbein presented an image of power, splendour and egocentricity. Even in such a vitally important test piece the artist would not abandon his commitment to truth. He showed a hard face with flat cheeks, unsmiling lips and shrewd eyes. If there was any flattery here it was only in the accentuation of the impression Henry deliberately strove to convey – total authority and an indomitable will. Holbein accentuated the jewels and the embroidered collar by using real gold. The *H*s on the chain reinforced the assertiveness of the king's personality. The pudgy hands, though only partially shown, yet managed to enhance the impression of dominance. It has sometimes been thought that this painting may have been one half of a diptych which also depicted Jane Seymour (perhaps the painting of similar dimension now in the Mauritshuis at The Hague), but it is hard to imagine the picture of a demure wife being set alongside this truculent icon.

What is not immediately apparent from Holbein's image of Henry VIII is that it was a concept for a time of crisis. The king's bulk and assertion of unquestioned autocracy appears utterly secure and we take it at face value. Here is a personification of *potestas,* of inflexible will and might that none dare challenge. Yet the painting dates very precisely from the time when the crown *was* being challenged; when Henry was confronting the worst rebellion ever to threaten the Tudor dynasty. In October the storm which had rumbled around the periphery of English society broke overhead. First Lincolnshire, then a large swathe of the North thundered into open, if confused revolt. Local magnates failed to establish control of scythe-wielding peasant hosts and some of them were in league with the rebels anyway. The Dukes of Suffolk and Norfolk marched to the disaffected areas with hastily gathered troops. The six months of crisis fused a variety of resentments and anxieties: abbots fought for the survival of their houses, gentlemen protested against changes in the laws of inheritance, townsmen feared government-backed desecration of their churches. But the 'Pilgrimage of Grace' was given a religious gloss, a political purpose and a degree of cohesion by a desperate faction who decided 'to take the battle out of the court into the nation, to raise the standard of loyal rebellion as the only way left to them if they were to succeed in reversing the defeats suffered at court and in Parliament, and in forcing the King to change his policies'.[3]

Henry's gut reaction was demonstrated clearly in his reply to the demands of the Lincolnshire rebels. He asserted his determination to continue with necessary reforms in Church and state and defended Cromwell and others who had been specifically named in the insurgents' complaints. Above all he attempted to put his subjects firmly in their place:

How presumptuous . . . are ye the rude commons of one shire, and that one of the most brute and beastly of the whole realm, and of least experience, to find fault with your prince . . . and to take upon you contrary to God's law, and man's law, to rule your prince, whom ye are bound by all laws to obey, and serve with . . . your lives, lands and goods. . . . think ye that we be so faint hearted that, perforce, ye of one shire (were ye a great many more) could compel us with your insurrections and such rebellious demeanour . . .? We pray Almighty God to give you grace to do your duties and to use yourselves towards us like true and faithful subjects . . . rather than by your obstinacy and wilfulness to put yourselves, lives, wives, children, lands, goods and chattels, besides the indignation of God, in the utter adventure of total destruction and utter ruin by force and violence of the sword.[4]

The royal bluster covered a very real awareness of danger. The dynasty was vulnerable. It had no male heir. Mary still had her supporters, who would rally to her standard on Henry's death in defiance of statute law. Her accession would transform England, by inevitable royal marriage, into the satellite of a foreign power. If the rebellion had been handled more efficiently the Courtenays, Montagues and Poles would have raised the South-west, thus turning the Pilgrimage of Grace into a civil war and plunging the nation back into the chaos from which Henry's father had delivered it. For all these reasons the government was circumspect in its exaction of vengeance. Of the 40,000 or so insurgents only 200 paid with their lives and most of them were men of low rank and only local significance. Cromwell and the king refrained from reprisals which would encourage their most influential opponents to continue with their plots. For the time being they would lull committed Yorkists and papalists into illusions of security. They would watch and await the best opportunity to strike.

At the same time they would assert the permanence and stability of the dynasty and the determination to continue with its religious policy. In April 1537 Lord Cromwell of Wimbledon was instituted to that stall of the Order of the Garter vacated by the execution of one of the northern traitors, Thomas Darcy. A few months later Richard Morison published (through the royal printer, Thomas Berthelet) *Apomaxis,* an extensive defence of government activity since 1533 designed to be read both at home and abroad. Thomas Starkey's *An Exhortation to the people instructing them to Unity and Obedience* was already in print.

For another work, supporting the dissolution of the monasteries and now unfortunately lost, Holbein produced satirical illustrations. The execution of his designs leaves much to be desired but the connection with his earlier partisan engravings is obvious. Holbein illustrates a variety of Gospel texts and in each depicts monks as the villains: Christ casts out a demon while cowled Pharisees protest; a humble publican dares not approach the altar where a religious kneels, thanking God that he is not as other men; a habited hireling shepherd flees while wolves devour the flock. Did the artist, one wonders, as he drew these simple indictments recall conversations with his recently departed friend? Erasmus had been a resolute enemy of the enclosed religious life. These pictures were intended for popular consumption and to illustrate the claim made in the Act for the Dissolution of Lesser Monasteries (1536) that within such institutions 'manifest sin, vicious, carnal and abominable living [are] daily used and committed'.[5] They also signalled the government's intention to put an end to conventual religion.

But more important than applying his art to the minutiae of reform policy was Holbein's continuing image-building on behalf of the Tudor Crown and dynasty. Henry obviously approved the small portrait made at the end of 1536 for he sat for another a few months later. This was designed to be the basis for the sixteenth-century equivalent of an advertising campaign. The full-length portrait carried the assertion of regal power still further. Henry stands square on to the viewer in a pose that goes beyond what contemporaries like Cranach and Seisenegger, the imperial painter, had ventured for their patrons. Henry's wide-splayed legs were, it seems, a breach of contemporary etiquette,[6] but the stance is magisterially effective. It may be that Seisenegger's portrait of Charles V (1532) was known, in copy, at Henry's court and that Holbein was under pressure to outdo it. He certainly succeeded. The clothing of the two monarchs is not dissimilar but Henry's tunic, falling as it does to the knees, emphasizes his girth, already exaggerated by the puffed sleeves. The English king gazes defiantly out at the viewer and the protruding codpiece proclaims his virility (by the early spring of 1537 Queen Jane was known to be pregnant). The emperor's portraitist was intent on showing his master's refined and regal bearing. Holbein was interested only in naked power. His painting was designed to be copied by loyal and wealthy servants for display in their houses, where it would have a salutary effect on such of Henry's subjects as saw it.

Yet even this impressive painting was less overwhelming than the grand design which was Holbein's principal project for 1537. Indeed, the full-length portrait of Henry VIII was a corollary of this design. The king commissioned his painter to produce a wall painting which would stand at the very centre of the Tudor state and would be the apotheosis of the Tudor dynasty (see plate section). When Wolsey fell from favour Henry appropriated his splendid town house of York Place and set an army of builders and craftsmen to work to transform it into Whitehall palace, his principal residence and a magnificent setting for his court. At the heart of the complex of state rooms, corridors and galleries was the privy chamber, the royal holy-of-holies. Here stood the canopied chair of state upon which the monarch sat to receive ambassadors and dignitaries. Admittance to the privy chamber was a mark of special favour, most business being conducted in the outer or presence chamber. This inner sanctum was lavishly decorated with hangings, carvings and furniture. It was here Holbein was invited to exhibit his skill at *trompe-l'oeil* fresco by painting the king, his parents and his wife.

The Whitehall group was not as complex as the Steelyard paintings or the narrative subjects depicted in the Basel council chamber, but it was still a masterpiece of spatial illusion. Niches, pillars and carved friezes placed in the background had the effect of thrusting forward the four figures, standing on a Turkey carpet loosely draped over marble steps. The Tudors were arranged around a stone pillar bearing a Latin inscription which left no doubt about the purpose of the painting: it was to record for posterity the achievements of the founder of the dynasty.

> If it rejoice thee to behold the glorious likeness of heroes, look on these, for greater no tablet ever bore. Great the contest [and] the rivalry, great the debate whether the father or the son were the victor. Each was the victor, the father over his foes, for he quenched the fires of civil strife and to his people granted lasting peace.
>   The son, born to yet greater destiny, from the altars banished the undeserving and in their place set men of worth. To his outstanding virtue the presumption of popes yielded, and when Henry VIII in his hand wielded the sceptre [true] religion was restored, and in his reign the precepts of God began to be held in their due honour.[7]

This is pure Polydore Vergil, Tudorized history. It is precisely that understanding of past and present which was called in question in the 1533 version of the *Household of Thomas More*. The two family groups stand in antithesis to each other. Separated by a mere four years they make mutually exclusive statements. One laments the woes brought upon the nation by the Tudor regime; the other exalts its stability and glory. Should we, therefore, conclude that, after all, Holbein was merely a 'hired brush', doing the bidding of patrons, irrespective of his own convictions? Certainly it was the job of a court painter to praise his master. Holbein had left home and settled in a foreign land in order to achieve the goal of royal employment and his major concern now was to give satisfaction. But in pursuit of his ambition he had not only travelled geographically. In the Cromwellian entourage he was rubbing shoulders daily with *practical* Christian humanists: men who were not content to talk about reform but were actually reordering Church and society along broadly Erasmian lines. It was exciting to be part of a regime that was instituting Reformation firmly on the basis of clearly constructed policy. Without falling into extremist heresy or requiring subscription to complex doctrines Cromwell and his cohorts were re-educating the English people. They were eradicating abuses. Their motives, as proclaimed in their propaganda, were in line with the ideals of the New Learning – to create a Christian commonwealth. According to the theorists of the movement, the confiscation of Church lands hitherto used for the benefit of idle monks and clergy, and the stripping of jewels and plate from superstition-shrouded shrines were freeing resources for the care of the poor and the provision of schools. Superstition was being expunged and the population offered enlightenment through the pages of vernacular Scripture. And all this was taking place under the auspices of a king who, despite his bullying, his ruthlessness and his unpredictability, ruled without employing bands of *Landsknechte* (mercenaries) against his own subjects. His realm enjoyed comparative peace. Even the recent revolt and its suppression could not be compared with the peasant uprisings and the massacres that had pockmarked the face of Germany a decade before.

For Holbein, who had seen weak municipal government manoeuvred into radicalism by shouting mobs and wild-eyed preachers, this must have seemed a highly satisfactory method of social engineering. As for More, he who had once advocated reform had finally set his face against it, at least in the shape in which the government proposed it. When Cromwell and others of the political avant-garde spoke the ex-chancellor's name it was still with sadness. The prevailing opinion was that More had been an obscurantist out of his depth in theological argument. This was the view Richard Morison argued in *Apomaxis*. In intellectual stature, he asserted, More was dwarfed by several English bishops and scholars who supported the king. Had not the lawyer tacitly acknowledged his limitations when he had issued his *Responsio ad Lutherum* pseudonymously? This was the considered evaluation of many of the humanist circuit. Erasmus himself wrote, when lamenting More's fate, 'Would that he had never embroiled himself in this perilous business and had left the theological cause to theologians.'[8] We need not charge Holbein with hypocrisy or with cynical detachment because he came round to supporting the party line on his old patron and applied his talents to eulogizing a regime More had found abhorrent.

Throughout 1537 Holbein was kept busy with royal commissions, to the extent that he had little time for private work. Unfortunately, little has survived from the summit years of his career. On the night of 4–5 January 1698, a fire raged through the palace of Whitehall. By morning there were 'nothing but the walls and ruins left'.[9] The conflagration deprived us not only of the privy chamber painting but also of other works commissioned for the king. No non-royal portrait exists which can be dated to 1537 and probably very few were executed. At the beginning of the next century the Dutch biographer Karel van Mander recounted a story which, if not apocryphal, probably dates from this busy period of the artist's life. An unnamed nobleman wanted his picture painted by Holbein and became so importunate that eventually Holbein lost this temper and threw the potential patron downstairs.

It may be that this is not just a colourful story. There is other evidence to suggest that success may have gone to Holbein's head. When he visited Basel the following year, he behaved with what seems to have been insufferable braggadocio. He was now a man of substance. His basic salary of £30 a year provided him with a lifestyle equivalent to that of a moderately successful merchant. To this he could add income from private commissions when the king's service allowed, and his position also carried various perks. He had board and lodging in Whitehall and in other palaces if his talents were required when the court was on progress. One of the monumental entrances to Henry VIII's new palace was known as the Holbein Gate and it was commonly but erroneously believed that the king's painter had designed it. If Holbein had any connection at all with this part of the building it is more likely that he lodged there. The early-nineteenth-century topographer and antiquarian James Dallaway identified a chamber called the New Library as the one 'in which Holbein was accustomed to employ himself in his art, and the courtiers to sit for their portraits'.[10] The artist could expect spontaneous tokens of Henry's approval for work done. Holbein, like all ambitious denizens of the court, was in a position to sue for special favours from time to time. Thus, in May 1538, he obtained licence to buy and export 600 tuns of beer and he presumably contracted with Steelyard friends to ship and sell the barrels for him. With a host of royal duties to perform and profitable commercial sidelines to be attended to it should not surprise us that he could afford to turn away unwanted clients – and even turn them away with displays of arrogant violence.

Of course, his new-found eminence involved Holbein in additional expense. When attending the king or visiting the royal apartments he had to be appropriately dressed. He had a love of expensive clothes. For years he had painted rich men and women clad in gorgeous brocades, silks and velvets while he himself had had to make do with coarse, hard-wearing, practical garments. Now, at last, he could indulge his taste for grander attire. Mixing with courtiers and wealthy merchants meant assuming many of their social habits. He wined and dined his friends and doubtless played cards and shuffleboard with them. He had a mistress and in the later 1530s he sired at least two children. By the time of his death these children were put to a nurse, which suggests either that their mother was dead or that she came from a social class which was accustomed to farming out its infants so that they would not be socially inconvenient. Holbein kept a horse – essential for someone who had to move with the court on summer progress. He also had assistants – apprentices who worked with him on larger projects and did some of the routine work in his studio. On top of his new responsibilities and expenditure on luxuries he maintained a lodging in Aldgate. The house he occupied certainly from 1541 and, in all likelihood, from 1532 was in the parish of St Andrew Undershaft. Like his earlier dwelling this was in an area of the city popular with foreign residents. The picture one perceives is of a successful man of middle age (by the life-expectancy norms of the mid-sixteenth century) and some celebrity who, if not living beyond his means, was certainly living well up to them.

He was working for a monarch whose love of profligate expenditure abated nothing with the passing of the years. It is a commonplace of Tudor historiography that the massive inflow of funds from the confiscation of Church property which might have put royal finance on a sound footing for the rest of the century was largely squandered by Henry during the last decade of his life. Most of the waste was on futile wars, but the king's personal expenditure swallowed up substantial sums. As well as adorning himself sumptuously, surrounding himself with beautiful things and making magnanimous gifts to other monarchs and to court favourites, he embarked in 1538 on the monumental white elephant of Nonsuch palace, Surrey. It was designed to be an exuberant architectural extravaganza which should outdo Francis I's Fontainebleau, and Henry employed some of the craftsmen who had worked for the French monarch. Everything created for the king, from architectural features, wall decorations and tapestries to clocks, ornamental silver, dagger sheaths and jewelled pendants had to begin on the drawing board. His painter was kept busy.

Once again we have to remind ourselves that the portrait drawings and paintings of Tudor court personalities which come most readily to mind when the name of Hans Holbein is mentioned constituted only a small part of his artistic output, particularly after he became king's painter. Hundreds, perhaps thousands of designs for artefacts went out from his studio, of which several have survived in collections in Basel and London. In no case are we able to link a drawing provided for architect or jeweller with the finished object. The closest we can get is the Jane Seymour cup and cover, given by Henry to his wife, probably as a New Year's gift, in 1537. In 1626 Charles I sold this item of royal treasure and the description given then still survives:

> a fair standing cup of gold, garnished about the cover with eleven diamonds and two pointed diamonds about the cup, seventeen table diamonds and one pearl pendant upon the cup, with these words BOUND TO OBEY AND SERVE, and H and J knit together; in the top of the cover the queen's arms . . . Queen Jane's arms holden by two boys under a crown imperial, weighing threescore and five ounces and a half.[11]

When we consider this in conjunction with Holbein's exquisite drawing we can imagine something of the splendour of this gift. A glance at the pages of designs for chimney-pieces, book-covers, sundials, buckles, brooches, pendants and so on in the Basel Kunstmuseum or the British Museum (some of which were executed at other times and for other clients) shows that Holbein's studio must have been a conveyor-belt of magnificent and intricate concepts. At one end there flowed in an unceasing stream of royal orders which had to be met without delay. Somehow, miraculously it seems, there poured forth at the other a cascade of original ideas, realized in sufficient detail for the craftsmen to begin work on them. There can be no doubt that Hans Holbein earned his salary.

In October 1537 Jane Seymour did something which none of Henry's other wives ever managed to achieve; she presented him with a son. Sadly, and ironically, it cost her her life, for she died a few days after the birth. Her death was destined to have as profound an effect as the survival of baby Edward on the rest of Henry's reign and on Holbein's life and career. The woman he had depicted a few months earlier in a pose of hand-clasped humility befitting her family's motto 'to obey and serve' was sharp-featured and old-maidish. It may be that, for once, the professional sourpuss Eustace Chapuys got it about right: 'She is . . . no great beauty, so fair that we would call her rather pale than otherwise. . . . not a woman of great wit, but she may have good understanding. It is said she inclines to be proud and haughty.'[12] One feels that by concentrating on the varied textures and intricate patterns of her dress in the two extant versions of Jane's portrait Holbein presented her to best advantage. Had the king tired of this vapid creature, as it is quite certain he would have done, he would have found it no easy matter to disembarrass himself of the mother of his heir and the saviour of the dynasty. In fact, he was spared the problem.

Henry did not allow grief to sully his own and his nation's rejoicing. Bells were rung and fires were lit throughout the land. Not for a moment did the king allow a miasma of doubt to obscure his conviction that he enjoyed God's favour and approval. He had overcome his enemies; he had a healthy male heir; even Jane's death could be seen as providential, for now he was free to marry again. Now he could make a dynastic match with some young foreign princess, who, as well as promising more sons, would bring England the security of a powerful alliance. Before Jane was twenty-four hours dead Cromwell had been instructed to draw up a shortlist of candidates for royal bride number four. Thus began the course of events that would bring about the minister's downfall.

Cromwell had been playing the marriage-alliance game in his own interests. He had, with the king's approval, effected the union of his son and Jane's sister. Since the Boleyn clan had been replaced as trump suit by the Seymours on the green baize of Whitehall he wanted to make sure that they were well represented in his own hand. Never for a moment did Cromwell underestimate the animosity of his enemies or his need of powerful friends. However, with Jane dead, the Seymours never achieved the prominence that Anne's relatives had attained. Her brother Edward was designated Earl of Hertford and received other marks of royal favour, but he was a lightweight on the Council. Court politics now became far more fluid, and therefore more hazardous. But what really struck at the root of Cromwell's security was that he was dabbling, at the king's insistence, in matters about which Henry was extremely touchy. He was being asked to make decisions about whom the king got into bed with – literally and diplomatically.

He carried out his master's will with diligence and tact, and at the same time he watched his back. The complex manoeuvres of the next few months put to the test all his political skills. The diplomatic activity he and his agents engaged in was intense and sometimes bizarre. Henry was convinced that Europe's most eligible royal ladies were queuing up to marry him. Coarse jokes about him went the rounds of foreign courts. Francis I let it be known that he was not a horse trader prepared to line up his female relatives for the King of England's inspection. But, of course, behind the ribaldry there were important issues of national interest at stake, and Cromwell took his task very seriously.

That was why, in all the more delicate negotiations, he used only those men he could trust implicitly, men who would report only to him and would not leak information to other interested parties. Thomas Wyatt, a key figure, was ambassador to the court of Charles V. Christopher Mont was Cromwell's representative to the Lutheran princes of northern Germany. Early in 1538 the minister despatched an unusual envoy to Mont. This was Jan van der Goes, 'John of Antwerp', who was charged with conveying 'with all diligence' certain of 'the king's letters of importance' at the lord privy seal's insistence. In the Low Countries, Cromwell had various contacts through his mercantile connections, such as John Hutton in Brussels, and now John Mason joined him there. Mason, a promising young man of humble origins, like Lord Cromwell himself, had been groomed for a diplomatic career and, until recently, had been Wyatt's secretary in Spain.

It was Hutton who provided the first positive lead for the wife-seekers. In December 1537 he drew his master's attention to a young lady who had recently arrived at the court of Mary of Hungary, the Regent of the Netherlands, and had captivated many men, including, obviously, Hutton:

> The Duchess of Milan . . . is of the age of 16 years, very high of stature for that age . . . a goodly personage of body, and competent of beauty, of favour excellent, soft of speech, and very gentle in countenance. . . . She resembleth much one Mistress Shelton, that sometime waited in the court upon Queen Anne. She useth most

to speak French, albeit that it is reported she knows Italian and High German.

In another letter addressed to Cromwell's secretary Thomas Wriothesley, Hutton went further:

> There is no one in these parts of personage, beauty and birth like unto the Duchess of Milan. She is not so pure white as was the late queen . . . but she hath a singular good countenance and when she chanceth to smile there appeareth two pits in her cheeks and one in her chin, the which becometh her right exceeding well.[13]

This paragon who resembled Anne Boleyn's cousin was the daughter of Christian II, the exiled King of Denmark, whose country had just emerged from a civil war which had, among other results, established Lutheranism as the state religion. Young Christina, however, was not tainted with heresy. She was a niece of Charles V on her mother's side, had been married briefly to Francesco Sforza, Duke of Milan, and had been a widow since the age of twelve. She seemed suitable in every way, and Wyatt and Hutton were instructed to make the necessary overtures. Hutton was also asked to obtain a portrait of Christina.

Cromwell, however, decided that he wanted a second opinion and also a likeness painted by a man he could trust not to create a deceptively flattering image. In March 1538 he sent Philip Hoby and Hans Holbein across the Narrow Seas. Hoby was another of the young protégés Cromwell was grooming for the diplomatic corps. He had seen some service in Spain and Portugal and had recently been elevated to a place in the privy chamber. He was, by all accounts, a cultured man, fluent in several foreign languages. Later in life he was a friend of Titian and Aretino. He was one of the next generation of radicals who would have to be in place if the Reformation were to be consolidated and further developed. Holbein's sketch of him shows a thoughtful, perhaps anxious man with a wispy moustache and beard. However, there was nothing hesitant about his commitment to the causes he believed in. He would later endure several days in the Fleet for supporting Lutheran preachers and he was prominent in urging further reforms during the reign of Edward VI.

After a few days spent in the necessary court formalities, Holbein was granted a three-hour sitting with the duchess on 12 March. He and Hoby left for London that same evening and were back in Henry's court a mere six days later. One reason for the haste was that Hutton was in a dither. He had, as instructed, organized another portrait of the potential bride but as soon as he saw Holbein's drawing he realized the contrast in quality between the two likenesses. 'Mr Hans . . . having but three hours' space hath showed himself to be a master of that science, for it is very perfect. The other is but slobbered in comparison to it.'[14] Hutton was desperate to have Holbein get back to court, if possible before the other picture could be shown to the king.

Hoby, perhaps with Holbein, obtained an audience with Henry within hours of his return and presented the portrait. The king was bowled over by it, so much so that 'since he saw it he has been in much better humour than he ever was, making musicians play on their instruments all day long'. He took his music-makers with him on a visit to survey the progress at Nonsuch, 'and ever since cannot be one single moment without masques, which is a sign he purposes to marry again'.[15] It is scarcely any wonder that his painter's handiwork set Henry's middle-aged heart dancing. What Henry saw was probably a coloured, finished drawing. Even Holbein could not have made a painting in the post-houses and lodgings between Brussels and London. We have the advantage of being able to gaze on the finished portrait he created later (see plate section). It is the loveliest painting of a woman that he ever executed, which is to say that it is one of the finest female portraits ever painted.

To have captured in a mere three hours the complex personality of a girl emerging into womanhood was sheer alchemy. There can be little doubt that Holbein was yet another man to fall under Christina's spell. As he worked, he was able to converse with his sitter in the language she had spoken since childhood. This permitted that closer communication which often imparted a greater warmth to his images of German subjects. He would have learned at first hand that this lively princess was something of a tomboy who loved, above all things, riding and hunting. The full-length portrait is an exposition of deceptive simplicity. Holbein juxtaposes blocks of colour – green, yellow, the black of the duchess's mourning dress (obligatory for widows in Italian court circles) and the mysterious strip of shadow down the right-hand side. The fall of the overgown accentuates Christina's height and bearing. The relaxed, elegant hands are exquisitely painted and suggest refinement (there is a remarkable similarity between the crook of the princess's right little finger and that of Elizabeth Dauncey in the *Household of Thomas More,* though what it signifies, if anything, is obscure). In the girl's frank full-face gaze we see poise with just a suggestion of youthful uncertainty, openness, and the slight smile and the dimples which so entranced John Hutton.

Unfortunately for Henry and very fortunately for Christina various political and diplomatic obstacles strewed the path of this marriage project and prevented it taking place. The duchess herself was far too intelligent ever to have been willingly conveyed to Henry's bed. As she wittily put it, 'If I had two heads I would happily place one at the disposal of the King of England.' However, the negotiations went on for months before being finally aborted. But this was far from being the only matrimonial hook dangling in the water. Some at court favoured a French marriage alliance, and the charms of various of Francis I's relatives were canvassed. Cromwell did not share the enthusiasm of the francophiles, but when Henry evinced real interest in Louise de Guise he once again despatched Hoby and Holbein, in early June, to bring back verbal and graphic accounts of the princess. They found their quarry at Le Havre and again the artist worked rapidly to achieve a true likeness. It was not long before Henry was intrigued by the charms of Louise's younger sister, Renée, and the diplomatic duo were once more on the road, this time headed for the high country of Lorraine.

This journey took place in August but was first mooted in mid-June. As soon as he heard that he might be required to travel to the French border country Holbein seems to have applied for leave of absence. It must have looked like a good moment. He was riding high in the king's favour and the proposed journey would take him most of the way to Basel (and would therefore be paid for out of the royal purse). On Midsummer's Day he received a generous nine months' advance on his salary and this was obviously to cover a visit home which might last well into the autumn, and perhaps the winter too.

The Hoby–Holbein summer mission became complicated by the manoeuvrings of the Guises and Henry VIII's changes of mind. The emissaries reached Joinville only to find that Renée was not there.

The girl was destined for a religious life and had no interest in talking with marriage-brokers. Messages from Henry now caught up with his representatives. Other exciting possibilities had been mooted and the envoys were to go on to Nancy to interview Francis I's cousin, Anne of Lorraine. This they did, and Holbein drew a likeness of the princess to be added to Henry's growing gallery of royal female portraits.* Hoby hurried back to London with it while his colleague visited his home for the first time in six and a half years.

In that time, municipality and artist had both changed, and one wonders what they made of each other. The old spirit of Basel had reasserted itself. Once it had been a broad-minded Catholic city. Now it was a broad-minded Protestant city. The ghost of Erasmus still walked its streets and its civil leaders claimed the scholar almost as a patron saint. At the Froben print house a panel of editors were working on the first collection of Erasmus's writings (published in 1540). But in Basel, too, Jean Calvin had published the first edition of his *Institution of the Christian Religion* two years earlier. As principality after principality and city after city took sides on the Reformation issue, creating for the first time in Europe a religious refugee problem, Basel accepted more than its fair share of strangers. Officially, radical extremists were not tolerated, but, as one resident observed, 'if a man keeps quiet, refrains from spreading false doctrines, and behaves like any other Christian in worship and everyday life, he has nothing to fear'.[16]

Holbein certainly gave the impression that he was glad to be back and that he still regarded Basel as his home town. He made a tour of inspection of the internal and external frescos he had painted in earlier years and declared his intention of coming back soon to touch them up at his own expense. This may, of course, have been a pose. He enjoyed playing the benevolent *grand seigneur* and swaggering across the Marktplatz resplendent in silks and velvets. Holbein made no secret of his new affluence when talking with old friends and still-struggling fellow guild members. And he enthused about his chosen place of domicile. 'He gives such a glowing account of the happy condition of that kingdom,' wrote someone who met Holbein in September, 'that after a few weeks' stay he means to go back again.'[17]

The city certainly gave him a hero's welcome. On 10 September

---

* None of the drawings Holbein made in France has survived.

the council held a banquet in his honour and all the leading citizenry turned out to rejoice with Holbein at his good fortune. The exile had consistently ignored summonses from the council and from his guild to return to fulfil various duties and obligations. By accepting paid employment from a foreign prince he had actually breached the citizenship rules, but celebrities are easily forgiven and Holbein was met with no reproaches. Quite the reverse: the council agreed to allow him to remain in England a further two years 'in order to merit a gracious discharge and to receive salary', and they offered their city's famous son a pension:

> From the special and favourable will which we bear to the honourable Hans Holbein, the painter, our dear citizen, since he is famous beyond other painters on account of the wealth of his art; weighing further that in matters belonging to our city respecting building affairs and other things which he understands, he can aid us with his counsel, and that in case we had to execute painting work on any occasion, he should undertake the same, for suitable reward, we have therefore consented, arranged, and pledged to give and to present to the above-named Hans Holbein a free and right pension from our treasury of fifty gulden. . . .[18]

During Holbein's absence his wife was to receive forty gulden.

That brings us to the artist's family. What kind of homecoming did the long-absent husband and father receive when his door on St Johannes Vorstadt was closed to back-slapping friends? Elsbeth had accepted that economic necessity had taken Hans away and must have been proud to see him fêted by his fellow citizens. His obvious success enhanced her own social position. She can have had little to reproach him with as far as care for the family was concerned. What little we know of Holbein's personal relationships suggests that he took his domestic responsibilities seriously and that he will have made provision for his dependants during his absence. He would scarcely have received such a warm welcome from his peers had he been guilty of leaving his wife and children destitute. Yet long absences imposed strains on the closest of relationships and Hans must have been considerably changed by all that had happened to him in the last six and a half years. By this time, Franz Schmid, Elsbeth's son by her first marriage, had reached manhood and had assumed the role of

head of the household. The fact that after all that time away Holbein
was proposing to spend less than a month with his family might not
have been well received by a wife who was living as a widow.

There are two facts which may suggest a damaged or broken
relationship. The first is that Hans either never returned to Basel again
or appeared there only for one short visit. He was due to resettle in
the city in October 1540. He did not do so. That meant that he broke
his agreement with the municipal leaders and, technically at least,
released them from their obligation to pay Elsbeth her forty gulden
per year. Holbein had some very good reasons for quitting England
in 1540, but he chose not to. The second fact is that at some time
before 1542, that is within the lifetime of her husband, Elsbeth sold
the portrait Hans had painted of her, Philip and Catherine. The buyer
was Hans Alper, another artist and possibly one-time pupil of
Holbein. Its new owner prized it so highly that he refused all offers
for it and it did not find its way into the Amerbach collection until
after Alper's death. For reasons considered below it seems unlikely
that Frau Holbein was in such straitened circumstances that she was
obliged to sell some of her most treasured possessions. Perhaps she had
ceased to regard the highly personal painting as a treasured possession.

Holbein left Basel before the end of October. At about this time his
son Philip was apprenticed to Jakob David, another exile from Basel,
who was living and working in Paris as a goldsmith. Perhaps Holbein
himself made this arrangement with an old friend and took Philip to
Paris to sign the necessary indentures and to see him settled.

Holbein returned to England to find the marriage crisis still
unresolved and the international situation worsening. While Henry
wavered between French and imperial alliances, Charles and Francis
drew closer together, and in January 1539 they signed a pact at
Toledo. England was isolated. The worsening foreign situation and
the activities of Reginald Pole, who was now touring Europe with
the pope's blessing trying to organize a crusade against heretical King
Harry, precipitated the government into making an end of the White
Rose and all its hybrids. While Holbein was out of the country a spate
of arrests, imprisonments and interrogations had begun. The Poles,
Courtenays and Nevilles were ruthlessly purged. Between 1538 and
1541 five prominent members of the Yorkist faction went to the
block or entered the Tower never to emerge. Henry VIII, as

proactive in vengeance as in matters matrimonial, was determined to make the throne as secure as possible for his heir. Meanwhile in the microcosm of the court Holbein was still riding high. Cromwell commissioned a new portrait from him, for which in January he paid forty shillings. And at the year's end the painter received an unexpected bonus of ten pounds from the king for his to-ings and fro-ings along the matrimonial highways and byways of Europe.

'If God be for us who can be against us' – so ran, in Latin, the inscription on one of the few private portraits Holbein found time to execute during hectic 1538. The quotation from the Epistle to the Romans appeared on the painting of a young man holding a dormouse. If, as we may reasonably assume, the sitter was a member of Cromwell's entourage, the chosen text illustrates the mood which pervaded his camp. What England's reformers – preachers, pamphleteers, legislators and diplomats alike – were engaged on was, they believed, a divinely inspired crusade. Nothing else could explain the striking successes achieved in so few years, and, with God on their side, nothing could stop the process of social and religious metamorphosis. Holbein shared this excitement, as he made plain to his old friends in Basel, and it was the sense of being part of something important – even holy – that was one reason for his speedy return to London.

However, if we read St Paul's stirring battlecry not as a rhetorical question but as an earnest one, then in the England of 1539 it had one very straightforward answer: 'the king can be against us'. This was a truth for which, fatally, Cromwell failed to make sufficient allowance. He was both pragmatist and idealist. In the decade of his political dominance he had severed the nation's Catholic mooring ropes and steered it towards a new berth, as yet not fully visible, and he had done all this in the name and with the blessing of Henry Tudor. Every move had involved careful calculation to ensure that the king supported it and that powerful enemies could not thwart it. But now, perhaps blinded by his vision of a Protestant commonwealth, the king's chief minister failed to discern clearly the direction in which his master's mind was moving. Though he prudently told enquirers that 'as the world stood [he] would believe even as his master the king believed',[19] Cromwell was tending increasingly towards Lutheranism.

He was particularly impressed by the writings of Georg Spalatin, an influential disciple and political supporter of Luther. In 1530 Spalatin worked with Melanchthon to draft the Augsburg Confession, which legally established the Reformation in Germany and in 1531 he helped set up the Schmalkaldic League of Protestant princes (see below). More than once Nicholas Kratzer obtained Spalatin's books for Cromwell. In a letter whose dating is not certain, the astronomer reported the receipt of the German's latest offerings by sea from Antwerp and explained, 'These I gave to Hans Holbein in order that he might give them to you.'[20] This is one of those apparently insignificant passing references which yet throw light on the close relationship between Holbein and Cromwell. Clearly the artist had an ease of access to the chief minister which was denied to most other people in and around the court.

In 1539 Cromwell pressed on with the Reformation. He completed the destruction of monastic life by putting through parliament an Act for the suppression of the larger houses and he carried an innovation particularly close to his heart, the setting forth of a new English Bible with the instruction that a copy should be placed in every church. The Great Bible carried a splendid frontispiece by one of Holbein's pupils. The explanation why Holbein himself was not appointed to carry out this important project is that the work was done during 1538 when he was otherwise engaged on royal commissions abroad. The book ran into considerable production problems and it was not until late in the following year that it actually became available. In September 1538 the vicegerent in spirituals had issued an injunction to parish clergy:

> That such feigned images as you know of in any of your cures to be so abused with pilgrimages or offerings of anything made thereunto, ye shall, for avoiding that most detestable sin of idolatry, forthwith take down and delay, and shall suffer from henceforth no candles, tapers, or images of wax to be set before any image or picture.[21]

Without actually instituting an official campaign of image-breaking the injunction gave a nod and a wink to all radicals with iconoclastic tendencies. The pace of reform was accelerating and it was not unknown for the government to support local zealots reported by their neighbours for removing traditional objects of devotion.

The propaganda campaign was also stepped up. John Bale, the caucus's dramatist, wrote several nationalistic and anti-papal plays which were performed in towns and villages anywhere in the realm where a bishop or local magnate could be found ready to finance a show. The most spectacular propaganda display was given for the benefit of London's citizens. In June 1539 Cromwell's masters of ceremonies organized a riverain pageant. A royal barge and a papal barge 'rowed up and down the Thames from Westminster bridge to the king's bridge; and the pope [and his cardinals] made their defiance against England and shot their ordnance one at another . . . but at last the pope and his cardinals were overcome and all his men cast overboard into the Thames'.[22] The provision of bread and circuses was designed to win over all classes. The confiscation of ecclesiastical property was calculated to secure the support of landowners who would ultimately benefit from grants and purchases. The 'goodly pastimes' were attempts to hijack patriotism for party advantage and gain the support of the common man.

Where Cromwell came unstuck was in his efforts to shift the logjam of the royal marriage alliance. The third option, besides France and the empire, and the one that he favoured, was a union with the Protestant principalities and cities of Germany, banded together since 1531 in the League of Schmalkalden. Following negotiations carried out through Christopher Mont, envoys arrived in London in May 1538 and stayed for five months. The protracted talks at various levels came to nothing because Henry considered himself totally orthodox in matters of Christian doctrine and refused to make the concessions the Lutherans wanted. The visit coincided with (and perhaps to some extent encouraged) another outbreak of radical heresy in the capital. In November four sacramentaries were burned and, ominously, the king personally took part in the examination of one of them. He began to listen to those men of high and low estate who were pointing to Cromwell as a disseminator of heresy. In the Council the vicegerent now had to contend with opponents who were bolder in opposing his religious programme. But as long as he had the ear of the king he believed he could overcome minor setbacks, derail his enemies and keep Henry on board the Reformation train. In February 1539 we find him passing to the king for his edification a copy of Spalatin's *The Solace and Consolation of Princes*.

Mont was already working on another possible solution to the marriage-alliance problem. The dukedom of Cleves-Mark-Jülich-Berg lay north of Bonn and straddled the Rhine. It was a small but rich territory and was strategically placed athwart Europe's main transport artery. Duke William V, a serious-minded twenty-two-year-old, had just inherited from his father. Because of a territorial dispute with Charles V he needed allies. By inclination and education William was an Erasmian. His father had put the church in his territory under state control and instituted a reform programme. William was happy to allow Lutheran preachers to operate but declined to join the Schmalkaldic League, although one of his sisters was married to its leader, John Frederick of Saxony. He thus had a great deal in common with Henry VIII. And he had two more, unmarried, sisters.

To Cromwell it seemed the ideal solution. Influence in the Rhineland would give England a powerful bargaining position and a Cleves match would signal clearly her religious position. It would also get the troublesome marriage issue out of the way. Once his hard-to-please master had settled down with a new wife, home and foreign policy would become less complicated. It was an outcome so desirable that the minister allowed it to cloud his judgement. For six months messengers went back and forth between London and Düren, Duke William's capital. Varied reports of the attractions of William's sisters reached the English court, and once again there was much talk of obtaining a reliable portrait of the young women on offer. In July, the decision was made to send Holbein, the only artist Henry trusted.

He arrived in Düren accompanied by Richard Beard, one of the grooms of the privy chamber, in the early days of August. By the 11th of the month he had completed his studies of Anne and Amelia of Cleves, whereupon he hastened back to London once again, to present the impatient king with the results of his genius.

So much has been written about Holbein's portrait of Anne of Cleves, its impact on Henry and its contribution to the downfall of Cromwell and, indeed, of Holbein himself that we need to re-examine the evidence very carefully. Those responsible for the negotiations were in a tough spot. They knew that Cromwell was determined to further the match and they strongly suspected that neither of the Cleves girls would please the king. The head of the English delegation was the cleric and seasoned diplomat Nicholas Wotton. This was his sober assessment of the elder sister, Anne:

All report her to be of very lowly and gentle conditions, by the which she hath so much won her mother's favour that she is very loth to suffer her to depart. . . . She occupieth her time most with the needle. . . . She can read and write [her own language but of] French, Latin or other language she [hath none], nor yet she cannot sing, nor play any instrument, for they take it here in Germany for a rebuke and an occasion of lightness that great ladies should be learned or have any knowledge of music. . . . I could never hear that she is inclined to the good cheer of this country and marvel it were if she should, seeing that her brother . . . doth so well abstain from it.[23]

So Wotton wrote to the king in order to counter some of the more glowing reports sent by flattering courtiers who believed they were saying what the king and his minister wanted to hear. About Anne's physical appearance Wotton was carefully non-committal. That was Holbein's problem.

The artist discussed both women at some length with Wotton and Beard and their colleagues before he presented himself at the palace for the sittings. The reality, when he eventually encountered it, matched the diplomats' descriptions: Anne and Amelia were pleasant, talentless, naive, lumpy girls in their mid-twenties, homely perhaps, but certainly not pretty. As they talked in their common language Holbein had plenty of opportunity to verify Wotton's opinion. How was he to represent this truth in paint? Simplicity had been the appropriate technique with the Duchess of Milan. Holbein had deliberately concentrated attention on the face and hands; had let the girl's beauty speak for itself. With the Cleves women exactly the opposite was called for. Holbein would not, dared not, improve on nature. All he could do was attract attention away from the features by making the most of jewellery, elaborate court dress and gem-studded hair-covering. In order to present as sumptuous a picture as possible Holbein worked this painting up into a finished or near-finished form before leaving Düren. The portrait of Christina had been executed in oil on panel in the leisured atmosphere of the painter's studio. For Anne of Cleves Holbein employed tempera on parchment, which he glued on to canvas when he reached London. (Although Holbein painted both sisters, all trace of the portrait of Amelia has disappeared. There seems never to have been any serious suggestion of the younger woman as a bride for Henry. Perhaps she was even less prepossessing than Anne. Certainly, she never married.)

If ever the artist was nervous about the reception of a portrait he must have been particularly anxious about this one. Like Wotton he had serious misgivings about the Cleves match. He had to do what he could to sound a note of caution. That meant that he was obliged to express his doubts in the painting. If we study the portrait of Anne of Cleves we are struck by an oddity of composition (see plate section). This is the most 'square-on' portrait Holbein ever painted. Everything in it is perfectly balanced: it might almost be a study in symmetry − except for the jewelled bands on Anne's skirt. The one on her left is not complemented by another on the right. Furthermore, her right hand and the fall of her left under-sleeve draw attention to the discrepancy. This sends a signal to the viewer that, despite the elaborateness of the costume, there is something amiss, a certain clumsiness. We can, however, go further. Here we have another example of Holbein's love of visual puns. It was a device he used when he had something important to say, as with *The Ambassadors* and the *Household of Thomas More*. He does it again here and he uses a homophone based on court French. Thus 'trait (à) gauche, pas à droit' ('band on the left, not on the right') sounds like 'très gauche, pas adroit' ('very awkward, not skilful'), which puts in a nutshell what Wotton had expressed at greater length. For whom was this coded message intended? Certainly for Cromwell. Although Holbein would have been able to report orally to him, if for any reason the minister was not immediately available he would certainly soon see the painting. Beyond the minister Holbein intended giving the broadest hint he dared to the king. Henry would not ask his opinion about his intended bride, and the painter certainly could not venture it. Therefore he communicated unpalatable truth through his art. He could do no more. The king either did not grasp or chose to ignore the allusion with dire consequences.[24]

The suggestion still to be found in some books that Holbein fell from royal favour because of this painting is nonsense. The story of Henry's shock at coming face-to-face with the 'Flanders Mare' and his inability to consummate the marriage is well known. In his anger the king blamed those who had deceived him about Anne's appearance and personality. Yet this censure was directed, not against his painter, but against courtiers who had written flattering reports about Anne. The whole episode set a black mark against Cromwell's name, but there is no evidence that Holbein's reputation suffered. Later in the year he painted a charming portrait of Prince Edward and presented it to Henry as a New Year's gift in 1540 (see plate section). Not only was this a remarkable painting combining superb observation of infancy (note the loosely clenched hand holding the rattle) with iconic treatment of a royal subject; it was also a work of collaboration with another leading member of Cromwell's entourage. Richard Morison wrote the Latin eulogy, which reads, in translation:

> Little one, imitate your father and be the heir of his virtue. The world contains nothing greater; heaven and nature could scarcely give a son whose glory should surpass that of such a father. Only equal the acts of your parent; the wishes of men cannot go beyond this. Surpass him, and you have surpassed all the kings the world ever worshipped, and none will ever surpass you.[25]

In the exchange of New Year gifts Holbein received from Henry a silver-gilt cup and cover from the workshop of Cornelius Heyss.

The year 1540 thus started auspiciously. It did not continue so. Henry bitterly resented his marriage and the deteriorating relations with Charles V which resulted from it. He wanted out of his union with Anne and looked to Cromwell to arrange it, but Cromwell could not see an easy way to pull his master clear of the matrimonial swamp. Meanwhile some of the vicegerent's known protégés went to the stake for heresy. In the Council the Duke of Norfolk and Stephen Gardiner headed an effective opposition which nourished itself and grew stronger on the chief minister's embarrassments. The politiques of the Tudor court had learned well one very obvious lesson: the best way to Henry VIII's head was through his heart. Ministers, queens, favoured courtiers and others who had seemed unassailable in their closeness to the throne had been brought down, not by policy blunders nor by inability to perform conscientiously their assigned roles, but by becoming vulnerable in matters of royal love and marriage. From the beginning of 1540 Norfolk began dangling before the king another of his nieces, Catherine Howard, a twenty-year-old beauty with the grace of a Siamese and the morals of an alley cat. The ageing Henry was captivated and increasingly out of sorts with what stood between him and the object of his desire – his unwanted wife and the men who had shackled him to her.

If there is a painting of Holbein's which stands close to the events which brought about Cromwell's fall it is not the portrait of Anne of Cleves but that of Norfolk, which he executed during these months of subtle intrigue. There was nothing coincidental about the timing of this commission. Holbein had painted other members of the Howard family over the years, including, on more than one occasion, Norfolk's son and heir, the Earl of Surrey. Yet never before had the head of the clan, Thomas Howard, third Duke of Norfolk, deigned to sit for a portrait. Proud, traditionalist and conservative in every aspect of his life, he wanted nothing to do with someone so completely involved with the reforming party. Now, he changed his mind. It may have been a matter of prestige. The king's painter had recently made a new portrait of the upstart Cromwell; very well, he should create an even more impressive icon of the king's longest-serving, truly noble councillor, Thomas Howard. However, once again we must not divorce the artefact from its immediate *Sitz im Leben*. In the crucial winter and spring months of 1540 the rival court factions were like wrestlers, circling the ring, eyeing each other keenly, watching for any opportunity to obtain a hold. We may doubt that during his sitting to Holbein the duke maintained an aloof silence. He had two or three hours alone with one of Cromwell's intimates. He would have been a fool not to have used that time to probe, cajole, even browbeat the artist into revealing useful information about his archenemy. Thomas Howard was no fool.

'His only known principle was self-advantage ensured by spaniel-like sycophancy to the king,'[26] so a modern historian summarizes the character of the third Duke of Norfolk. Howard is the *éminence grise* of Henry's household, the whisperer behind the arras, the back-room intriguer, the proud courtier disdaining the rough-and-tumble of open politics but relishing the prominence of staged events, particularly if they involved the downfall of others who enjoyed more power than himself. He engineered Wolsey's downfall and was on the commissions that condemned Thomas More and Anne Boleyn. After the Pilgrimage of Grace he hanged seventy-four rebels at Carlisle, the one act of gratuitous, spontaneous vengeance carried out in the aftermath of the rising. His only strong conviction was that by nobility of breeding he deserved that place in the king's counsels which lack of ability denied him. It was frustration that drove him to vent his spleen on 'lesser' men. All this can be read in Holbein's portrait. Behind the technically brilliant re-creation of rich silk, fur and Garter chain and the staves of earl marshal and treasurer depicting Norfolk's pride of office, we can see haughtiness and cruelty. One might place the portraits of Norfolk and Henry side-by-side and reflect that these two men deserved each other.

Despite the machinations of such determined opponents Cromwell appeared to ride the storm. In April he became Earl of Essex and felt strong enough to go on the offensive against his enemies. It was a serious miscalculation and it was his last. The conservative councillors turned the tables on him. On 10 June he was arrested and sent to the Tower. There followed the usual trumped-up charge of treason – this time with heresy thrown in for good measure.

On 28 July 1540 Hans Holbein's third great patron was beheaded.

Chapter 11

LONDON–BASEL–LONDON

1540–1543

Henry VIII himself provided Cromwell's epitaph when, some eight months after the minister's death, he rounded on the opposition faction and accused them of depriving him of 'the most faithful servant he had ever had'.[1] It was true – if an understatement. Thomas Cromwell was not only loyal; he was industrious, clear-headed and idealistic. In the annals of England he stands alongside only three or four 'greats' who, single-handedly, changed the character and destiny of a nation. To be part of Mr Secretary's entourage was to be caught up in something radical, innovative and exciting. Cromwell's friends were shattered by his fall and the suddenness of it, but circumspect silence could be their only reaction – for the time being. Two days after the Earl of Essex's head fell on Tower Green, Robert Barnes, one of his emissaries and closest associates, was burned as an Anabaptist (which he most certainly was not) at Smithfield along with two other prominent supporters of the new policies – warning indeed to anyone rash enough to challenge the new-found power of the reactionaries. Only Archbishop Cranmer, who had stood up for Anne Boleyn, dared to remonstrate with the king over Cromwell's incarceration. The minister's departure left the political stage in the possession of little men – Norfolk, Gardiner, Seymour, Dudley and the like – who could not distinguish the kingdom's wellbeing from their own petty rivalries, ambitions and vendettas. At times the great religious and political issues of the day became sub-plots in a drama which was little better than bedroom farce. Before Cromwell's remains had been a year buried, the new queen's sexual activities were being gleefully exposed by one of his supporters at court, John Lascelles, gentleman of the privy chamber. Catherine Howard perished and, along with her, Lady Rochford, who had played a prominent part in the fall of Anne Boleyn her own sister-in-law. The

Howard faction was spun out of favour and the 'Protestant' group was in. Now it was the turn of Catherine Parr to assume the role of wife–nurse to the ageing king. At the next turn of the wheel Norfolk and Gardiner came within a whisker of crushing her. They had to be content with seeing John Lascelles burn for heresy. To such a level had the government of England sunk in six brief years. This is the court background against which the last years of Holbein's life must be seen.

Hans Holbein's career did not survive the fall of Cromwell. Of the artist's three great English patrons, only Cromwell appreciated his true worth. It was he who had seen Holbein's propaganda potential, his talent for the grandiose image, his commitment to truth in portraiture; he who had entrusted Holbein with the sensitive task of limning potential queens, had drawn him into the fellowship of reform, and had promoted him to the position of king's painter. After 28 July 1540 there was no patron capable of filling the hole which had opened up in the artist's fortunes.

Holbein remained king's painter until the end of his life, and in his will he would describe himself as 'servant to the king's majesty'. But, for two years after Cromwell's death, he was entrusted with no major royal works and only in the last months of his life was he regaining Henry's favour. Having no one of consequence to intercede for him, he was simply ignored. He became just one of a number of foreign painters working in London. In the 1540s Hans Eworth, Guillim Scrots, Gerhardt Flicke and Cornelius Massys were only some of the artists whose talents were attracting attention and who were being patronized by members of the court. The society figures who did not wish to be associated with the tainted artist had others they could turn to when they wanted their portraits painted. The younger men represented new ideas and brought new styles with them. It has been suggested that changing fashion is sufficient to account for Holbein's comparative neglect in these years. When we compare, for example, the Mannerist exuberance of Scrots's portrait of the Earl of Surrey with Holbein's revealing and realistic studies of the same sitter we can see the direction in which sophisticated taste was moving. Yet those who did resort to the studio of the official king's painter found his talent as fresh as ever. He was forty-three in 1540 and at the height of his powers. None of the extant works datable to his last years suggests that either eye or hand had lost its cunning. He may not have been an excited convert to Mannerism but there were still those who appreciated his style. We must look to circumstances beyond Holbein's control to explain his sudden and temporary eclipse.

In Tudor high society patronage was all. Not only did the ambitious courtier, scholar or artist seek to attach himself to an established or up-and-coming favourite, he also understood that he would be adversely affected by the decline of his 'good lord'. If such an event could be foreseen, that was the time to switch horses. When Holbein transferred his allegiance from More to the Boleyns in 1533 he was simply playing Tudor court snakes and ladders by the accepted rules. In 1540 Cromwell's downfall had been so swift and unexpected that none of his associates had been able to make contingency plans. Morison wrote no more Protestant and nationalistic diatribes. Hugh Latimer stopped preaching. Archbishop Cranmer remained the leading ecclesiastic in name only. John Bale fled the country, as did others. Like these men, Holbein had given a very public face to Reformation ideas that were anathema to the Howard–Gardiner faction. Whatever Norfolk thought of his new portrait, he had no interest in advancing the career of its creator. As for Bishop Gardiner, he had all the antipathy of a reactionary churchman towards Cromwell's religious changes and could display it in quite petty ways. In Mary Tudor's reign he once hauled a painter over the coals for depicting Henry VIII holding a Bible. As long as these men and their cronies were cocks of the walk Holbein's reputation at court was in shadow.

In the autumn of 1540 the artist was due to go back, finally, to Basel. He had obligations to the Little Council, not to mention his family. His reversal of fortune in London might have suggested that this was the appropriate time for his thrice-deferred return, and it is likely that he did, in fact, travel back to Switzerland in October. At Michaelmas he once again received six months' salary advance and this may have been to cover the expenses of a journey (although this was not the only occasion on which he asked for his emoluments to be paid up front). There is no documentary record for such a visit, but by the same token there is no evidence for his remaining in London during the dying months of 1540 and no datable works of pen or brush which would fix him there. On balance we may conclude that, since he never sought naturalization in England (unlike many other foreign workers) and described himself officially as *Joannes Holpenius*

Basileensis', he intended to remain on good terms with the Basel authorities, and that he went home to seek yet a further leave of absence.

There is no record of his receiving a warm civic welcome on this occasion. Although he was still a celebrity, the leaders of Basel society were, perhaps, tiring of his determination to remain abroad. Certainly Myconius and the religious leaders would have quizzed him anxiously about affairs in England. All reform leaders were concerned about the progress of 'true' faith in other lands. They would want to know the sordid details of Cromwell's overthrow and its implication for the Reformation.

Another event occurred in that autumn of 1540 which had an obvious effect upon Holbein's plans for his own and his family's future. On 18 November the town clerk of Berne wrote to inform all interested parties of the death of Hans's uncle, Sigmund Holbein. The old man left a long will, accompanied by a detailed list of his effects, setting out in meticulous detail who was to get what. As we read it we can only regret that history has assigned to almost total obscurity an artist who was painstaking in all his affairs, straightforward to the point of brusqueness in his dealings with others and, apparently, not a little eccentric. In this document, dated 6 September 1540, Sigmund explained that he was setting his affairs in order prior to paying his Augsburg relatives a final visit, a journey before the conclusion of which 'death in some manner may have befallen me'. Sigmund seems to have had little regard for his sisters in Augsburg: one reason for his itemized testament was to ensure that they would be satisfied with his bequests to them 'and not enquire after the rest, nor annoy my nephew Hans in any way'. For Hans was to be the principal beneficiary:

. . . I will and bequeath to my dear nephew, Hans Holbein, the painter, citizen at Basel, both as my blood relation and my own race and name, as well as from the especial love I bear him and from the affinity in which he stands to me, the free gift of all my goods and property which I have and leave in the city of Berne, namely my house and courtyard and the garden behind, standing in the Brunnengasse, on the sunny side, above by the Trom wall, near George Zimmerman, the tailor's house. The said property is free from taxes. . . . Item, my silver utensils, household furniture, colours, painter's gold and silver, implements for painting and other things, nothing excepted, that he shall appropriate the same as my appointed heir, have it in his possession, do with it and live as with his own possessions and property unmolested by my sisters and by anyone.[2]

Sigmund, it seems, though he describes his legacy as 'the small property I leave behind', had done reasonably well for himself. He proudly pointed out that he died unencumbered by debt and that his possessions had been 'hoarded entirely by my works'. The man who could take his brother to court over an unpaid loan and who made clear in his will that his sister Ursula owed him fifty gulden in outstanding interest on a loan must have been something of a skinflint, prompting the family to await with eager expectation the death of the miserly old bachelor.

Coming into such a handsome inheritance enabled Holbein to provide permanently for Elsbeth and the younger children. In the following January his stepson, Franz Schmid, made the journey to Berne armed with letters from his mother and the Burgomaster of Basel to claim the house on Brunnengasse and its contents. The proceeds from the sale of Uncle Sigmund's property and the income from the tanning business (run latterly by Franz) must have left Elsbeth with no financial worries. When she died, in 1549, an inventory of her goods included silver and silver-gilt plate as well as an ample supply of furniture and household goods. It also included a chest of her husband's better clothes, including a velvet-trimmed cape and doublets of silk, damask and satin, further evidence of Hans's exotic taste in personal apparel.

This raises the recurring question of where Holbein's heart really lay. In 1538 he had assured the Little Council that he needed a couple more years in England in order to complete commissions for Henry VIII and bring his employment at the Tudor court to an amicable end. Yet clearly he made no attempt to relinquish his post as king's painter. If he did return to Basel in the autumn of 1540 he was gone again before the year's end, leaving Franz to tie up the details of the Berne inheritance. Had he really wanted to spend his remaining years in Switzerland, Sigmund's bequest would have provided the ideal opportunity for him to settle down with some capital behind him. He did not grasp it. It seems that, whatever he told Elsbeth and the council, perhaps whatever he told himself, his life in England had an irresistible hold on the reins of his will.

Did that other family, about which we know nothing, have first claim on his loyalty and affection? The domestic side of Holbein's life in England is a closed book. His will reveals the meagre fact that he was survived by two infant children who were in the care of a nurse. In the British Museum there is a charming sketch of a woman and four small children on a wooden bench (possibly a church pew). The two boys wear the feathered caps and puffed sleeves then sported by fashionable fathers and their sons. The woman is dressed altogether more modestly and may be a nurse. Can it be that we have here Holbein's four English offspring, destined to be reduced to two by the rampant infant mortality of the age? A later inscription reads, '*exaltate cedrus H. Holbein*', which is a reference to Ecclesiasticus 24. There Wisdom observes,

> I have taken root in a privileged people; in the Lord's property, his inheritance.
> I have grown tall as a cedar on Lebanon . . .
> I am like a vine putting out graceful shoots, my blossoms bear the fruit of glory and wealth . . .

How appropriately these words might be applied to the foreign artist who had not only prospered in England but 'taken root' and 'put out shoots' in the form of children. Holbein's reluctance to drag himself away from London suggests the existence of strong emotional ties.

Professionally this was not a good time. Recent changes and chances had affected him grievously. There was no call for religious paintings and the overturning of Cromwell's policy had led to a clampdown on anti-papal books and pamphlets. New censorship laws inhibited printers from producing religious satires and diatribes and some of Cromwell's writers had left the country. Holbein was still in demand for decorative work, but during the 1540s an ageing king kept his goldsmiths, tailors and architects less fully occupied and, as we have seen, Henry was employing other immigrant artists on designs for Nonsuch. It can only have been upon his skill as a limner that Holbein pinned any hopes for employment and a return to full royal favour.

The painter was also tied to his adopted country by idealism. The

English Reformation was unfinished business and Holbein was among those who wished to see it brought to a conclusion. The campaign had lost its general. Some of the officer corps had resigned their commissions. But the army had not disbanded. Vast tracts of territory had been gained during the 1530s and were not to be given up. More than monastic property had been converted. Hearts and minds had been won. When Norfolk complained that England was no more merry since the vernacular Bible had been circulated he was inadvertently complimenting the success of a movement that was in the process of changing the national consciousness. Censorship and sporadic outbursts of persecution could not fix the Reformation at the point that Henry VIII thought appropriate and certainly could not force it back to a state of affairs with which Bishop Gardiner might feel comfortable. Merchant and yeoman households gathered around the Scriptures. 'Gospellers' read the word of God to the illiterate. Students debated how to bring about a truly Christian common-wealth. Tutors fed their charges with Erasmian and radical ideals. Holbein took his place alongside those who were conscious of a job still to be done. He was a man who set truth above all things, who had worked out his own faith in discussions with others of the Erasmian circle and with the great man himself and had debated the social aspects of reform with fellow guild members and Cromwellian propagandists. He not only enjoyed the friendship of men who risked their lives smuggling banned books, but had been able to make first-hand judgements of Erasmus, Melanchthon, Zwingli, Oecolampadius and More as well as disputants of lower intellectual rank. What was more, he had been thrilled to be part of a superbly organized reform programme, and genuinely mourned the loss of a friend and patron hacked down by lesser mortals. Such a man would continue to do all in his power to further the causes he believed in.

For this he needed patrons. He still had his Steelyard friends and he painted several of them during the months after his arrival back in London (see plate section). When he designed for his old friend John of Antwerp a magnificent standing cup and cover, perhaps for presentation to the Goldsmiths Company, its central feature was, significantly, the figure of Truth. Holbein returned to court and cautiously sought out those who could help him. Not surprisingly, they were men and women who not only were close to the king but also favoured reform – the Butts, the Brandons, the Dennys, the

Seymours and the Parrs. Despite the 1540 coup there were, thanks partly to Cromwell's patronage of recent years, several people in positions of trust and confidence about the monarch who, in varying degrees, favoured continuing change in the religious and social life of the nation. They had no love for the Catholic reactionaries and awaited only an opportunity to hit back at the Howard faction. That opportunity was handed to them on a plate by a stupid, over-sexed young woman. When the extent of Catherine Howard's deliberately concealed pre-marital relationships was revealed in the autumn of 1541 Henry was so possessed by self-pitying fury that the French ambassador thought he had gone mad and Norfolk wisely absented himself from court. The duke's enemies immediately gathered round to console the stricken king. It would be a few years yet before kinship and patronage groups coalesced into 'Catholic' and 'Protestant' factions. For the time being, in the absence of a queen or a powerful minister around whom a party could cohere, influence remained on a personal basis.

Through all the chances and changes of more than two decades Sir William Butts, the royal physician and advocate of reform, remained close to the king. Henry relied on him increasingly as his health deteriorated, and only Thomas Cranmer was as well trusted, both men being made privy to Henry's most secret thoughts. Butts now helped Holbein re-establish himself at court. The doctor was instrumental in obtaining for the king's painter the commission for his last large-scale work, the *Presentation of the Barber–Surgeons' Charter* (see below). In preparation for that, Holbein made Butt's portrait and, at the same time, painted his wife and his son.

The artist had other well-connected customers. Charles Brandon, Duke of Suffolk, was one of the king's oldest and closest friends. No one but he could have got away with secretly marrying Henry's younger sister in 1515. Brandon was no advanced thinker in religion, but that was certainly not true of his second wife, Catherine Willoughby. She was a spirited woman, who perhaps inherited her fire from her Spanish mother, and early espoused radical Protestantism. She sat to Holbein in 1541 and had him do exquisite miniatures of her two little boys. After Suffolk's death four years later, her spirit undiminished, she acquired the services as tutor to her sons of no less a person than Martin Bucer, the reform leader in Strasbourg. At one time she was suspected of harbouring heretics and when Catholic

Mary came to the throne she decamped to the continent with her entire entourage.

Through William Parr, an up-and-coming courtier (he was twenty-eight in 1541) who had entered the royal court under Cromwell's wing and had formed a close alliance with the Seymours, Holbein edged a little closer to the throne. Parr's rise had been meteoric: knighted after the birth of Prince Edward he was raised to the peerage in 1539. One of Cromwell's household reforms had been the reorganization of the king's bodyguard. In 1541 Parr was appointed the captain of this band, the Gentleman Pensioners. It was around this time that Holbein made a sketch of him, presumably followed by a painting. Little was then heard about William's sister Catherine, the wife of John, Lord Latimer, but those who knew her spoke of her piety, her learning and her patronage of reformist scholars and clergy, including Miles Coverdale and Hugh Latimer.

More intimate was Holbein's relationship with another courtier. In January 1547, when a small group of the king's men were gathered around the bed of their dying master, the only one who had the courage to advise him to prepare for his end was Sir Anthony Denny. Denny was another of the younger men about the court who had risen under Cromwell's aegis. He was a Cambridge-trained humanist and a friend of scholars like John Cheke and Roger Ascham. Sir Anthony's growing intimacy with the king and his Protestant sympathies were bitterly resented by the conservatives. In 1546 they tried to implicate Denny and his wife during one of their periodic purges of court 'heretics'. Holbein painted Denny in 1541 and, two years later, accomplished for him a superb clock design which was to be among the last projects he undertook. In 1543 Anthony Denny (he was not knighted until the following year), now elevated to the position of lord chamberlain, gave much thought to the provision of a suitable New Year's gift for his sovereign. As others had done before, he involved Holbein in the design of his offering. It was to be an astronomical clock. Holbein's conception had lost none of its mastery. The standing structure, decorated with satyrs, comprised an hourglass and was topped with two naked boys supporting the clock face. Denny's gift may, in part, have been intended to remind Henry of his painter's versatility. The courtier was certainly more than an enthusiastic patron. As a man of cultured taste and religious conviction he was drawn to Holbein, and their friendship was firm enough for the artist to borrow not inconsiderable sums of money from 'Mr Anthony'. And there may be yet another connection. According to the chronicler John Stowe, the Denny family owned property in Aldgate. We may have here no more than a coincidence of name but it is certainly possible that Holbein and Denny were neighbours.

Such were the men and women of rank whom Holbein courted in the years 1541–3. He busied himself with private commissions and the routine work associated with his office as king's painter. His income seldom matched his expenditure, or so we may assume from his borrowings from friends and requests for salary advances. He desperately needed the large commissions which paid well and which enhanced his prestige. The king was not disposed to initiate such projects. He had other matters on his mind. When he was not confined to his chambers nursing his ulcerated leg he was devising grandiose plans for those military adventures which would gobble up all the money Cromwell had carefully garnered, and more.

On 29 August 1668 Samuel Pepys recorded in his diary, 'At noon comes by appointment Harris to dine with me; and after dinner he and I to Chirurgeon's Hall . . . and there to see . . . which was our business, their great picture of Holbein's, thinking to have bought it, by the help of Mr Pierce, for a little money. I did think to give £200 for it, it being said to be worth £1000; but it is so spoiled that I have no mind to it, and is not a pleasant though a good picture.' By the time Pepys saw the *Presentation of the Barber–Surgeons' Charter* it had been hideously spoiled by seventeenth-century additions to the original and then smoke-damaged in the Great Fire. Yet it is doubtful whether even if the diarist had seen the painting in its original state he would have been prepared to part with hard cash to acquire it. In 1541 the Guild of Surgeons and the Barbers' Company were brought together by Act of parliament and the new body commissioned a large painting to grace their hall. The result was a disaster – so much so that experts have long debated how much hand Holbein had in it. It is obvious that the painting was finished by an inferior hand (or hands). But that does not help us to solve the problem, for it is not detail alone that is poor; it is the whole conception. A lifeless, oversized king dangles the charter from a limp hand while a row (the second rank was added later) of comparatively diminutive recipients kneel in relevant homage. The treatment is archaic and atypical. Hans

Holbein was the man who created the public image of Tudor kingship. In *Solomon and the Queen of Sheba,* the Coverdale Bible title-page and the Whitehall fresco he had presented a dynamic vision of power and authority which bore no resemblance to the watered-down medievalism of the Barber–Surgeons' picture. And another question poses itself: *why* did Holbein leave the painting unfinished? If we assume he began work soon after the granting of the charter, he had two years left during which he could certainly have brought the painting to completion or near completion. The most obvious answer to both questions is that there was disagreement between artist and patron, a situation which has recurred over and over again in the history of art. Holbein had worked for corporations before – happily as far as we know. The Basel town council and the leaders of the Steelyard had probably left him much to his own devices once they had accepted his draft designs and reached agreement over his fee. If the London doctors disputed Holbein's original concept, argued over it in committee, sent him back to the drawing board time and again, the artist would certainly have lost his enthusiasm for the work and plied his brush in a desultory fashion.

Much of his preliminary work involved making detailed studies of the men to be featured in the composition. Some of his sketches, including those of Drs Butts and Chambers (another royal physician), were worked up into full portraits and sold as separate commissions. He was also granted a sitting by the king. When we compare the 1542 portrait of Henry VIII with those made five and six years before it is hard to believe we are looking at the same man. At about the same time that Holbein was working on the later version the French ambassador reported that Henry was 'very stout and daily growing heavier . . . He seems very old and grey since the mishap of this last queen.'[3] Illness and enforced lethargy had quite obviously taken their toll. In his painting Holbein presents the king half-length and wearing a velvet surcoat, thus minimizing Henry's corpulence. The full-face pose and the tight grip on his staff depict an authority that is in theory not diminished, but Holbein's undeceived eye and hand reveal a power no longer bolstered by unquestioned certainties. If the brief sitting Henry gave to his painter reminded him of Holbein's existence it did not lead to further work of any significance.

It may have been because he had time on his hands or because he needed publicity that he made a number of self-portraits. In 1542 and

1543 he painted several miniatures to be given to friends and potential customers. He also created the compelling drawing now in the Uffizi. This unadorned, no-nonsense portrait bears the legend 'Johannes Holpenius Basileensis ipsius effigiator Ae XLV' and was obviously designed for some member of the educated elite whom the painter wanted to inform or remind of his existence. The face that confronts us is intelligent and unsmiling. There are no wrinkles to signify anxiety or ageing. Holbein appears sternly self-assured, a man in full command of his faculties, the king's painter and an artist worthy of patronage.

His confidence was well-founded and was soon rewarded. Once again he gained the attention of the highest person in the land, next to the king. In the ongoing game of court poker the Protestant faction won the latest hand in the summer of 1543. Lord Latimer had just died, which meant that his thirty-one-year-old widow, the former Catherine Parr, was back on the marriage market. She was being wooed by Thomas Seymour, Jane's younger brother, a notorious gallant and ladies' man. His interest was, perhaps, all that Henry needed to quicken his own passion. Just as he had snatched Anne Boleyn away from Wyatt, so now he proved that he could still steal a march over younger lovers. The marriage was celebrated at Hampton Court on 12 July and was followed by a royal progress through the southern shires. Once again the reformed cause had a figurehead, a source of patronage and a person able to incline the king towards those beliefs and principles Anne Boleyn had championed. There was little outward similarity between the two women but, like Henry's second queen, Catherine maintained a humanist salon, eagerly discussed religious ideas with her chaplains and attendants and encouraged her ladies in the study of Scripture. Holbein's friends were soon receiving marks of royal favour. Foremost among them was William Parr, the queen's brother. He was admitted to the Order of the Garter, received Cromwell's old earldom of Essex and joined the Council.

The artist's supporters did not fail him and Holbein was presented to the queen. She realised that he was just the person to help her with a project close to her heart. From the early days of her marriage Catherine set herself to bring together Henry and his three children. The girls were almost permanent exiles from court and their brother fared little better, though for different reasons. The precious heir was cosseted within his own strictly regulated entourage well away from the capital and any other potential centres of contagion. Catherine resolved to end the isolation of Mary, Elizabeth and Edward. As a first step she commissioned Holbein to make small portraits of the king's children. This can only have been with Henry's permission, but he was disposed to grant his new bride anything, and thus in the late summer or early autumn Holbein travelled to Ashridge, near Berkhamsted, to take the prince's likeness and joined the court on progress to paint Mary. Probably he also did a companion portrait of Elizabeth but it has not survived. The matching roundels which show the prince and princess in profile reveal that Holbein's delicate touch was as sure as ever.

As the first leaves of autumn began to fall it was clear that a new season was beginning at court. An element of gaiety had returned to the royal household. There was talk of lavish festivities for Christmas and other celebrations to follow. A real prospect existed of the royal court of England becoming known, once again, for its culture, piety and intellectual pursuits. After a brief interlude the work of reform might be taken up again. Any return to the atmosphere of the 1530s could only be welcome to Holbein and encourage him to face the future with optimism.

It was at this positive turning point in his affairs that disaster struck. Holbein became a victim to some sudden disease or injury. On 7 October, in his Aldgate house, he made a hurried will, in the presence of his old friend John of Antwerp and a few neighbours from the German-speaking community. It was a simple document:

> In the name of God the father, Son and Holy Ghost, I, John Holbein, servant to the king's majesty, make this my testament and last will, to wit that all my goods shall be sold and also my horse, and I will that my debts be paid, to wit, first to Mr Anthony, the king's servant of Greenwich the sum of ten pounds, thirteen shillings and seven pence sterling. And moreover I will that he shall be contented for all other things between him and me. [This is almost certainly Anthony Denny, the court being then at Greenwich to avoid the plague in London. 'All other things between him and me' must refer to work outstanding for his client.] Item, I do owe unto Mr John of Antwerp, goldsmith, six pounds sterling, which I will also shall be paid unto him with the first. Item, I bequeath for the keeping of my two children which

be at nurse, for every month seven shillings and sixpence sterling. In witness I have sealed this my testament the 7th day of October in the year of our Lord God, 1543. Witness Anthony Snecker, armourer, Mr John of Antwerp, goldsmith before said, Ulrich Obinger, merchant, and Harry Maynert, painter.

Karel van Mander wrote in the early seventeenth century that Hans Holbein died of the plague. He was doubtless restating an older story, and it has been repeated ever since, though whether it has any basis in fact is debatable. The reasoning behind it seems to be that because the plague was bad in London in the autumn of 1543 and Hans Holbein died in the autumn of 1543 he must have died of the plague. However, there were many ways a man could meet his end in Tudor London's cramped streets. Reasons certainly exist for treating the traditional story with caution. We may question whether the most loyal of friends would have ventured to the bedside of a man smitten with the feared disease. During the 1543 outbreak the aldermen of the city issued strict quarantine instructions. Infected houses were to be marked with a cross and kept locked. Those afflicted were to remain indoors and were only allowed to be moved if they were conveyed swiftly to another secure lodging. Bedding and straw was to be burned, dogs destroyed and beggars to be kept off the streets. Plague had already visited John of Antwerp's house, so he should not have been out and about.

Whether or not it was the contagion that killed him, Hans Holbein the Younger died, some time in October 1543, in a foreign city eerily quiet because most of its inhabitants had either fled or were shut within doors. There is something almost unbearably bathetic about the ending of this brilliant life. Holbein was forty-five, a man in his prime. The 'Apelles of our time' deserved better than to die abruptly, obscurely and, perhaps, alone. Even the site of his grave is unknown. Legend asserts that he was buried in the precincts of St Catherine Cree. If the spot was marked with any kind of memorial it must soon have been obliterated, for when in later years his admirers wished to mark the place where the master was interred it could not be located. Yet in all probability no stone ever did indicate Holbein's final resting place. He was, as far as the city authorities were concerned, just another foreigner who had no family to take care of the last formalities or to interest themselves in the whereabouts of his tomb.

On 29 November John of Antwerp took out letters of administration so that he could attend to his friend's last wishes. Technically, Holbein had died intestate. The will had been drawn up without benefit of lawyer and as a result John of Antwerp had not been formally nominated as executor. To John fell the task of selling up Holbein's possessions, settling his debts and taking care of his English-born children. Who these children were, whether they survived to have sons and daughters of their own, whether the artist was succeeded by generations of descendants some of whom may have inherited a portion of his talent are questions which will never be answered because, in the sixteenth century, they were questions no one thought it important to ask.

Swiss and German records are more helpful about Holbein's Basel family. Elsbeth survived her husband by six years and her will indicates that she was relatively well off at the time of her death. Four children matured into adulthood. Some of the father's skill passed down the line of his elder son. After completing his apprenticeship in Paris, Philip prospered as a goldsmith and eventually settled in Augsburg where, early in the seventeenth century, his son was referred to as imperial court jeweller. Jakob, Philip's younger brother, was also a goldsmith. He followed his father to London and died there in 1552. Two daughters of Hans and Elsbeth made good marriages in the Basel mercantile community.

Although no interest was shown in Holbein's mortal remains, the same was not true of his works. When John of Antwerp attended to the dispersal of his friend's effects he discovered several sketchbooks containing designs for jewellery, tableware and architectural features. Van der Goes found customers for all these among Holbein's friends and admirers, and some still survive in private and national collections. There were also many of the artist's preliminary portrait studies. John Cheke showed an interest in these. The scholar had been appointed tutor to Prince Edward a year earlier and may well have met Holbein around the court or in the city. Cheke, one of the leading intellects of the age, was both highly cultured and zealous for reform. He recognized in the portrait sketches a gallery of heroic men and women who, over the previous decade, had been involved in the struggle for religious truth. He was able to identify many of the sitters, although he got some names wrong (Margaret Giggs, whom Cheke had not met, became 'Mother Jak', Prince Edward's sometime nurse), and others were the product of wishful thinking (an unknown, middle-aged gentleman was captioned as 'Philip Melanchthon'). Cheke saw the collection as an invaluable aid in his tutelage of Edward. He was determined that the future king should grow up a convinced Protestant. In this he was completely successful. During the reign of the boy monarch his ministers, with his approval, carried the Reformation on from the point at which Cromwell had left it. Holbein's drawings played their part in convincing Edward of his pious responsibility to continue the work to which Anne Boleyn, Colet, Dr Butts and courtiers faithful to reform had been pledged. Holbein's contribution to the Reformation did not end with his death.

'It is the privilege of fools that they alone may speak the truth without offence' – Desiderius Erasmus, *In Praise of Folly*.

Erasmus's reason for putting his sharp satires into the mouth of Folly was so that he might merge into the background while she cavorted outrageously in her pied costume, cap and bells, and feign astonishment when anyone charged him with holding hallowed institutions and long-revered practices up to ridicule. He knew only too well that speaking the truth does give offence. Yet he had to do it and much of his life was, consequently, spent in fending off outrage, shielding himself from those who did not understand what he said or understood it too well. What is important for us is that he was able to go on writing, year after year, pouring out ideas that stimulated, challenged and stirred readers across Europe. It was only after his death that his books were placed on the *Index Librorum Prohibitorum*.

That was because, by the middle of the sixteenth century, iron-hard orthodoxy was reasserting itself. In both Catholic and Protestant Europe truth had been recaptured by the establishment. Experimentation and speculation were discouraged. 'It is the part of a good mind to accept the truth as revealed by God and to acquiesce in it,' Melanchthon observed. In 1573 Veronese was examined by the Inquisition for introducing blackamoors, buffoons and animals into a painting of the Last Supper. 'Dangerous' knowledge was to be shunned. When the Arabic Koran was published in Venice the pope ordered all copies to be burned and when Oporinus produced a Latin version in Basel the Little Council had him arrested. Satire and unrestrained humour were also frowned on. In the year that Holbein died the Sorbonne condemned Rabelais's *Gargantua* and *Pantagruel*.

The world had changed. For the few decades of Holbein's life there existed a glorious confusion and profusion of ideas. Thinking men refused to give automatic veneration to old dogma. Artists and scientists trained themselves to see what was before their eyes rather than peer through the dimmed spectacles of tradition. Rival preachers pointed their hearers along paths that led in different directions to, ostensibly, the same God. There was a passion for truth. No thinking person doubted that it had an objective existence and that, even if it could not be finally found in this life, it could be sought – and should be.

Hans Holbein was caught up in this quest. He drew and painted what he saw. To that extent he was a realist. His draughtsmanship, whether in intricate jewellery designs or large allegorical frescos, was near miraculous. But he was much more than a mere recorder of the passing scene. He sought the meaning within and beyond. To his Passion drawings and biblical engravings he brought intellectual intensity and soaring imagination. His determination to 'tell the truth' resulted in the simple yet profound *Christ in his Tomb*. As he matured he mastered the technique of conveying intuitive understanding on to paper, panel or canvas with astonishing facility, so that even a quick sketch of a face, such as Bishop Fisher's, captured the sitter's character. Like Erasmus, Holbein wielded satire as a tool for delineating truth by exposing error. His genius was not all of the mind. Anyone who describes Holbein as a 'cool appraiser' of the human scene has never studied properly the peasants cavorting on the *Haus zum Tanz,* the emotional range of the *Dance of Death* engravings or the tenderness of the artist's painting of his wife and children.

Seeking and trying to express the truth is a personal and at times a lonely business. Holbein was a self-contained man, too enthralled with the vision within to make many deep and lasting friendships. The people he admired were those who thought deeply and acted boldly. That was why he could enjoy the company of men as diverse as Amerbach, Erasmus, Kratzer, More, Cromwell and John of Antwerp. He belonged to no artistic school and founded none. As far as we know, he trained no apprentices. From time to time he used assistants when he was engaged on large projects. They and other painters made copies of his work. Yet, much as later sixteenth-century artists revered him, none of them sought assiduously to follow him or continue developing his techniques. Holbein remains among the great 'one-offs' of art history.

Yet Hans Holbein the Younger does not belong solely to art history. When we have explored his work to discover its relationship to the output of earlier and contemporary masters and assessed his dependence on 'Gothic' and 'Renaissance' influences we have not said all that needs to be said. When we have exhaustively studied the development of his painting and drawing techniques we have not probed the essence of the man. Holbein was more than an artist. He believed passionately in things that were higher and more important than art. Those things he directed his talent to serve. A. B. Chamberlain wrote of him:

> Philosophical thought or theological subtleties left him untroubled. That he was on the side of the Reformation is made clear by more than one of his woodcut designs, but his share in the controversy was after all a minor one, and marked by little or none of that passion which swayed the more eager partisans on either side.[4]

This opinion has largely prevailed so that, for example, G. H. Villiers could bluntly assert that Holbein completely lacked a spiritual outlook: 'a typical product of the full Renaissance, [he] was entirely objective'.[5]

It is no longer possible to hold this view, which gets to the heart of neither the man nor the age. Religion was at the epicentre of the intellectual and spiritual earthquake whose repeated shocks rocked Christendom. Thinking and feeling men could not ignore them and Holbein was a thinking, feeling man. He was also a creative genius. He did his theology with brush and pencil. In his paintings and drawings he worked out a very terrestrial soteriology. As his own faith took shape he abandoned the realm of haloed saints and gruesome demons. He discovered a religion anchored both to this world and to the Bible, as we have seen in *Noli Me Tangere* and *The Old and the New Law*. In his propaganda pieces, his mature religious works and in the spiritual and moral content of his portraits, Holbein, and only Holbein, gave visual expression to Protestant humanism.

It was not a speculative religion, a philosophy to be talked about and graphically illustrated. It was a faith to be lived and advocated to others. That was why Holbein found his fulfilment in the entourage of Thomas Cromwell. The English reformer embodied many of the qualities he admired. He espoused the principles of Erasmus. He had More's clear-headedness. And he bound both together with a determination to carry forward a well-formulated policy of reform.

This was refreshing and exciting to a man who subscribed to religious radicalism but had witnessed the blundering and bloody tragedies its implementation had brought to Germany and Switzerland. For eight years he placed all his talents at the service of the Henrician Reformation and drew no distinctions between artistic, propagandist, diplomatic and intelligence-gathering activities.

Art is not what a man does; it is what he is. The same may be said of religion. Both truths point us to a better understanding of Hans Holbein and reveal for us a portrait of one who is no longer an unknown man.

NOTES

INTRODUCTION

1. P. Ganz, *The Paintings of Hans Holbein*, 1950, p.3

CHAPTER 1: AUGSBURG 1497–1515

1. R. Marius, *Thomas More*, 1984, p.65
2. P.A. Russell, *Lay Theology in the Reformation*, 1986, p.51
3. P. Villari, *Life and Times of Girolamo Savonarola*, 1888, p.499
4. Shakespeare, *Macbeth*, I, iv
5. *Memoirs of Benvenuto Cellini, a Florentine Artist, written by himself*, Everyman edition, 1907, p.1
6. Thomas à Kempis, *The Imitation of Christ*, Collins Library of Classics edition, n.d., pp.245–6
7. L. Campbell, *Renaissance Portraits*, 1990, p.150
8. E. Newton and W. Neil, *The Christian Faith in Art*, 1966, p.148

CHAPTER 2: BASEL 1515–1517

1. Erasmus to Capito, 26 February 1517. Cf. J. Huizinga, *Erasmus of Rotterdam*, 1952, p.218
2. Erasmus, *Collected Works*, 1976, III, p.244
3. H.J. Hillerbrand (ed.), *Erasmus and His Age, Selected Letters of Desiderius Erasmus*, 1970, p.84

CHAPTER 3: LUCERNE AND NORTH ITALY 1517–1519

1. Cf. J. Courvoisier, *Zwingli, A Reformed Theologian*, 1964, p.18
2. R. Bainton, *Here I Stand: Martin Luther*, 1987 edition, p.87

CHAPTER 4: BASEL 1519–1523

1. J.C. Olin, *The Catholic Reformation: Savonarola to Ignatius Loyola: Reform in the Church 1495–1540*, 1971, p.55
2. Ulrich von Hugwald to Vadianus. Cf. *F. Saxl Lectures*, 'Holbein and the Reformation' in *A Heritage of Images*, 1970
3. Cf. H.J. Hillerbrand (ed.), op. cit., p.141
4. Cf. O. Bätschmann and P. Griener, *Hans Holbein*, 1997, pp.116–8
5. Cf. A.G. Dickens and W.R.D. Jones, *Erasmus the Reformer*, 1994, pp.156–7
6. H.J. Hillerbrand (ed.), op. cit., p.169
7. Cf. Bätschmann and Griener, op.cit., pp.116–8
8. Cf. R.L. De Molen (ed.), *Leaders of the Reformation*, 1984, p.25

CHAPTER 5: BASEL 1524–1526

1. A.G. Dickens and W.R.D. Jones, op.cit., p.131
2. Cf. S.E. Ozment, *The Reformation in the Cities*, 1975, pp.111
3. Cf. C.M.N. Eire, *War Against the Idols: The Reformation of Worship from Erasmus to Calvin*, 1986, p.44
4. Cf. F. Anzelewsky, *Dürer: His Art and Life* (trs. H. Grieve), 1980, pp.225–7
5. Cf. P.A. Russell, op.cit., p.160

6. Cf. C.C. Christensen, *Art and the Reformation in Germany*, 1979, p.166

CHAPTER 6: LONDON–BASEL–LONDON 1526–1529

1. C. Marot, *Oeuvres diverses* (ed. C.A. Mayer), 1966, pp.100–101
2. Cf. A.G. Dickens and W.R.D. Jones, op.cit., p.194
3. Cf. A.B. Chamberlain, *Hans Holbein the Younger*, 1913, I, p.225
4. Cf. L. Campbell, op.cit., p.165
5. Cf. R. Marius, op.cit., p.518
6. Letter to Erasmus, 14 June 1532, cf. D. Wilson, *England in the Age of Thomas More*, 1978, pp.191–2
7. Cf. R. Marius, op.cit., p.281
8. A.B. Chamberlain, op.cit., I, pp.290–1
9. Cf. C. Sturge, *Cuthbert Tunstall*, 1938, p.132
10. *The Diary of John Evelyn*, 2 September 1680, 1959 edition, p.692
11. R. Marius, op.cit., p.519
12. J. Huizinga, op.cit., p.236
13. R. Marius, op.cit., p.519
14. L. Stone, *The Family, Sex and Marriage in England, 1500–1800*, 1979 edition, pp.119–20, 142
15. A. Woltman, *Holbein and His Time* (trs. F.E. Bunnett, 1872), p.369
16. W.M. Conway (ed.), *The Writings of Albrecht Dürer*, 1958, p.28
17. G. Hinds, (ed.), *Calendar of State Papers, Milan (1385–1618)*, 1912, i, 804
18. E. Hall, *The Union of the two noble and illustre Famelies of Lancastre and Yorke*, 1809 edition, p.722
19. Ibid., p.723 (spelling modernized). Cf. also, S. Anglo, *Spectacle, Pageantry and Early Tudor Policy*, 1969, p.217
20. Cf. R. and S. Redgrave, *A Century of Painters of the English School*, 1866, i, p.5
21. D. J. King, *Apollo*, May 2004
22. S. Fish, *Supplication of Beggars*, cf. J. Foxe, *Actes and Monuments* (S.R. Cattley, 1837 edition), IV, p.660
23. William Tyndale, *Works*, (ed. H. Walter, Parker Society, 1848–50), I, pp.206–7
24. Luther's Works, Philadelphia, 1955, vol. 54, p.288
25. P.S. and H.M. Allen (eds), *Opus Epistolarum Des. Erasmi Roterodami*, vol. VIII, 2228 and X, 2831
26. Stephen Vaughan and Thomas Cromwell, 9 December, 1953, L.P. V, 574

CHAPTER 7: BASEL 1529–1532

1. J. Foxe, op.cit., IV, pp.367–9
2. C.C. Christensen, op.cit., p.101
3. A.B. Chamberlain, op.cit., I, pp.340–1
4. H. Langdon, *Holbein*, 1994, p.17
5. A.B. Chamberlain, op.cit., I, p.352
6. Ibid, I, p.342
7. A.G. Dickens and W.R.D. Jones, op.cit., p.159

CHAPTER 8: LONDON 1532–1533

1. J. Foxe, op.cit., IV, pp.706–7
2. J.S. Brewer, et al, *Letters and Papers Foreign and Domestic of the Reign of Henry VIII, 1860–1910*, (hereafter L.P.) vi, 1311, 1381
3. Cf. M. Aston, *England's Iconoclasts: Laws against Images*, 1988, p.214
4. S. Bridgen, *London and the Reformation*, 1989, pp.201–3
5. J. Foxe, op.cit., IV, pp.693–4
6. R. Marius, op.cit., p.406
7. J.A. Guy, *The Public Career of Sir Thomas More*, 1980, pp.167–71
8. Chapuys to Charles V, n.d. 1535(?), L.P. IX, 862
9. Vaughan to Cromwell, 9 December 1531, L.P. V, 574
10. Cf. S.E. Lehmberg, *The Reformation Parliament, 1529–1536*, 1970, p.138
11. E. Hall, op.cit., 1809, p.788
12. Erasmus to John Faber, n.d. 1532, in J.H. Hillerbrand, op.cit., pp.270–2
13. P.S. and H.M. Allen, op.cit., X, 2788

14. Elyot to Sir John Hackett, president of the English factory at Antwerp, 6 April 1533, L.P. VI, 313

15. L.P. V, 514; VII, 1189

16. Grant, 23 November 1532, L.P. V, 1598

17. Complaint of the Hanseatic merchants, 1540; R.H. Tawney and E. Power (eds), *Tudor Economic Documents*, 1951, II, p.34

18. John Godsalve to Eustace, Clerk of the Works at Hampton Court, n.d. 1533, L.P. VI, 492

19. E. Hall, op.cit., p.801

20. More to Erasmus, n.d. 1533, L.P. VI, 303

21. Ibid.

22. Henry VIII to Sir John Wallop, ambassador in France, n.d. 1533, L.P. VI, 1491

23. Chapuys to Charles V, 23 February 1533, L.P. VI, 180

24. De Dinteville to Jean du Bellay, 9 June 1533, L.P. VI, 614

25. Ibid.

26. Cf. J. Leslau, *The Ricardian Bulletin*, September 1978 and June 1981.

27. L.P. VI, 465, Chapuys to Charles V, 10 May 1533

28. G.R. Elton, *Policy and Police: The Enforcement of the Reformation in the Age of Thomas Cromwell*, 1972, pp.50ff

CHAPTER 9: LONDON 1534–1536

1. E.W. Ives, *Anne Boleyn*, 1986, p.287

2. Cf. J. Rowlands and D. Starkey, 'An old tradition reasserted: Holbein's portrait of Queen Anne Boleyn', *Burlington Magazine*, cxxv, February 1983, pp.88–92

3. J. Foxe, op.cit., V, p.602

4. E.W. Ives, op.cit., pp.319–21; A. Woltmann, op.cit., p.369

5. Ibid.

6. J. Foxe, op.cit., V, p.403

7. *Gabriel Harvey's Marginalia*, quoted in G.R. Elton, *Reform and Renewal: Thomas Cromwell and the Common Weal*, 1973, p.11

8. Cf. R. Strong, 'Holbein in England I', *Burlington Magazine*, cix, May 1967, pp.276–81

9. E. Hall, op.cit., 1809 edition, p.816

10. L.P. IX, 226

11. William Tyndale (ed. H. Walter), op.cit., I, p.203

12. G.R. Elton, *Policy and Police*, pp.327ff

13. R. Bainton, op.cit., p.218

14. E.W. Ives, op.cit., p.326

15. W. Latimer, *A Brief Treatise or Chronicle . . . of Anne Boleyn*, quoted in M. Dowling, 'Anne Boleyn and Reform', *Journal of Ecclesiastical History*, 35 (1984), pp.39–40

16. L.P. V, ii, 85

CHAPTER 10:

LONDON–BRUSSELS–DÜREN–BASEL 1536–1540

1. E.W. Ives, op.cit., p.413

2. Ibid. p.414

3. G.R. Elton, *Reform and Reformation*, 1977, p.267

4. *State Papers of Henry VIII*, 1830–52, i, 463–70

5. S.E. Lehmberg, *The Reformation Parliament 1529–1536*, 1970, p.225

6. L. Campbell, op.cit., p.95

7. Translation given in R. Strong, *Holbein and Henry VIII*, 1967, p.57. Strong believed the inscription dated from 1667 but this opinion has been challenged, cf. J. Rowlands in *Burlington Magazine*, cxxi, 1979, p.53

8. J. Huizinga, op.cit., p.252

9. J. Evelyn, *Diary*, E.S. de Beer edition, 1959, p.1022

10. J. Dallaway (ed.), *Walpole's Anecdotes of Painting*, 1826–8, I, p.133

11. A.B. Chamberlain, op.cit., II, pp.274–5

12. L.P. X, 901

13. L.P. XII, ii, 1187, 1188

14. L.P. XIII, i, 507

15. Chapuys to the Queen Regent, 23 March 1538, L. P. XIII, i, 583
16. H.R. Guggisberg, *Basel in the Sixteenth Century*, 1982, p.39
17. A.B. Chamberlain, op.cit., II, p.156
18. Ibid., II, p.159
19. R.B. Merriman, *Life and Letters of Thomas Cromwell*, 1902, i, p.279
20. L.P. XIII, i, 179. On the dating problem see A.B. Chamberlain, op.cit., II, p.152
21. M. Aston, op.cit., p.227
22. S. Anglo, *Spectacle, Pageantry and Early Tudor Policy*, 1969, pp.269–70
23. L.P. XIV, ii, 33
24. Cf. J. Leslau, op.cit.
25. A.B. Chamberlain, op.cit., II, p.165
26. E.W. Ives, op.cit., p.253

CHAPTER 11: LONDON–BASEL–LONDON 1540–1543
1. L.P. XVI, 589–90
2. Cf. A. Woltmann, op.cit., pp.106–7
3. L.P. XVII, 178
4. A.B. Chamberlain, op.cit., II, p.319
5. G.H. Villiers, Hans Holbein, *The Ambassadors*, n.d., p.4

SELECT BIBLIOGRAPHY

Unless otherwise indicated place of publication
is London, Great Britain.

BOOKS

Abray, L.J., *The People's Reformation, Magistrates, Clergy and Commons in Strasbourg, 1500–1598*, Oxford, 1985

Anglo, S., *Spectacle, Pageantry and Early Tudor Policy*, Oxford, 1967

Anzelewsky, F., *Dürer: His Art and Life* (trs. H. Grieve), 1980

Aston, M., *England's Iconoclasts: Laws against Images*, Oxford, 1988

Averbach, E., *Nicholas Hilliard*, 1961

Bainton, R., *Here I Stand: Martin Luther*, 1987 edition

Bätschmann, O., and Griener, P., *Hans Holbein*, 1997

Benesch, O., *German Painting from Dürer to Holbein,* Geneva and Cleveland, 1966

Beutler, C.B. and Thiess, M., *Hans Holbein der Ältere, Die spätgotisch Altar und Glasmalerei*, Augsburg, 1960

Brewer, J.S., Gairdner, J. and Brodie, H.R. (eds), *Letters and Papers Foreign and Domestic of the Reign of Henry VIII, 1860–1910*

Brockwell, M.W., *Catalogue of the Pictures at Nostell Priory*, 1913

Bruce, A.K., *Erasmus and Holbein*, 1936

Bushart, B., Reinking, K.F. and Reinhardt, H., *Hans Holbein der Ältere*, Augsburg, 1966

Cameron, E., *The European Reformation*, Oxford, 1991

Campbell, L., *Renaissance Portraits: European Portrait Painting in the 14th, 15th and 16th Centuries*, Yale, 1990

Chamberlain, A.B., *Hans Holbein the Younger*, 2 vols, 1913

Christensen, C.C., *Art and the Reformation in Germany*, Ohio, 1979

Clerk, J.M., *The Dance of Death by Hans Holbein*, 1947

Conway, W.M. (ed.), *The Writings of Albrecht Dürer*, New York, 1958

Courvoisier, J., *Zwingli, a Reformed Theologian*, 1964

Cross, C, *Church and People 1450–1600, The Triumph of the Laity in the English Church*, 1976

Dallaway, J. (ed.), *Walpole's Anecdotes of Painting*, 1826–8

Davis, N.Z., 'Holbein's Pictures of Death and the Reformation in Lyons', *Studies in the Renaissance*, III (1956)

De Molen, R.L. (ed.), *Leaders of the Reformation*, Susquehanna, 1984

Dickens, A.G. and Jones, W.R.D., *Erasmus the Reformer*, 1994

Dickens, A.G., *The English Reformation*, 1964

Duffy, E., *The Stripping of the Altars, Traditional Religion in England, 1400–1580*, 1992

Eire, C.M.N., *War Against the Idols: The Reformation of Worship from Erasmus to Calvin*, Cambridge, 1986

Elton, G.R., *Policy and Police: The Enforcement of the Reformation in the Age of Thomas Cromwell*, Cambridge, 1972

Elton, G.R., *Reform and Renewal: Thomas Cromwell and the Common Weal*, Cambridge, 1973

Elton, G.R., *Reform and Reformation, England 1509–1558*, 1977

Elyot, T., *The Boke named The Governour* (ed. H. Croft), 1883

Erasmus, D., *Collected Works*, Toronto, 1974–

Fèbvre, L., *The Problem of Unbelief in the Sixteenth Century: The Religion of Rabelais* (trs. B. Gottlieb), Cambridge, Mass., 1982

Foister, S., *Drawings by Holbein from the Royal Library Windsor Castle*, 2 vols, New York, 1983

Foister, S., Roy, A., Wyld, M., *Holbein's Ambassadors: Making and Meaning*, 1997

Foucart-Walter, E., *Les peintures de Hans Holbein le jeune au Louvre*, Paris, 1985

Foxe, J., *Actes and Monuments* (ed. S.R. Cattley), 1837

Ganz, P., *Die Handzeichnungen Hans Holbein der Jungere*, Basel, 1937

Ganz, P., *Les Dessins de Hans Holbein le Jeune*, Geneva, 1939

Ganz, P., *The Paintings of Hans Holbein*, 1950

Glaser, C, *Hans Holbein der Ältere*, Leipzig, 1908

Grohn, H.W., *Hans Holbein der Jungere als Maler*, Leipzig, 1955

Guggisberg, H.R., *Basel in the Sixteenth Century*, St Louis, Missouri, 1982

Guy, J.A., *The Public Career of Sir Thomas More*, 1980

Hall, E., *The Union of the two noble and illustre Famelies of Lancastre and Yorke*, 1809 edition

Hervey, M.F.S., *Holbein's 'Ambassadors', the Picture and the Men*, 1900

Hillerbrand, H.J. (ed.), *Erasmus and His Age, Selected Letters of Desiderius Erasmus*, New York, 1970

Hilliard, N., *A Treatise Concerning the Arte of Limning* (eds R.K.R. Thornton, and T.G.S. Cain), Manchester, 1981

Hoak, D. (ed.), *Tudor Political Culture*, Cambridge, 1995

Howarth, D., *Images of Rule: Art and Politics in the English Renaissance (1485–1649)*

Huizinga, J., *Erasmus of Rotterdam*, 1952

Ives, E.W., *Anne Boleyn*, Oxford, 1986

Langdon, H., *Holbein*, 1993 edition

Lehmberg, S.E., Sir *Thomas Elyot, Tudor Humanist*, Austin, Texas, 1960

Lewi, A., *The Thomas More Family Group*, National Portrait Gallery, 1974

Lieb, N. and Stange, A., *Hans Holbein der Ältere*, Munich, 1960

Lloyd, C. and Thurley, S., *Henry VIII: Images of a Tudor King*, 1990

Loades, D.M. (ed.), *The Papers of George Wyatt Esquire*, Camden Soc., Ser. 4, Vol. 5, 1968

Mander, K. van, *Het Schilderboeck*, 1607

Marius, R., *Thomas More, a Biography*, 1984

Mayer, T.F., *Thomas Starkey and the Commonwealth*, Oxford, 1989

Mayor, A.H., *Prints and People, a social history of printed pictures*, Princeton, 1971

McConica, J.K., *English Humanists and Reformation Politics Under Henry VIII and Edward VI*, Oxford, 1965

McCorquodale, C., *The Renaissance, European Painting 1400–1600*, 1994

Meller, P., *Jean Clouet*, 1971

Millar, O., *Holbein and the Court of Henry VIII*, The Queen's Gallery, Buckingham Palace, 1978

Morison, S. and Barker, N., *The Likeness of Thomas More*, 1963

Mozley, J.F., *Coverdale and His Bibles*, 1953

Olin, J.C., *Christian Humanism and the Reformation: Desiderius Erasmus, Selected Writings*, New York, 1987 edition

Olin, J.C., *The Catholic Reformation: Savonarola to Ignatius Loyola, Reform in the Church 1495–1540*, New York, 1971

Os, H. van, *The Art of Devotion in the Late Middle Ages*, 1994

Ozment, S.E., *Mysticism and Dissent: Religious Ideology and Social Protest in the Sixteenth Century*, Yale, 1973

Ozment, S.E., *The Reformation in the Cities: The Appeal of Protestantism to Sixteenth-Century Germany and Switzerland*, Yale, 1975

Ozment, S.E., *The Age of Reform 1250–1550, An Intellectual and Religious History of Late Medieval and Reformation Europe*, Yale, 1980

Panofsky, E., *The Life and Art of Albrecht Dürer*, Princeton, 1955

Parker, K.T., *The Drawings of Hans Holbein in the Collection of H.M. the King at Windsor Castle*, 1945

Pettegree, A., *Foreign Protestant Communities in Sixteenth-Century London*, Oxford, 1986

Pope-Hennessy, J., *The Portrait in the Renaissance*, 1966

Potter, G., *Zwingli*, Cambridge, 1976

Roberts, J., *Holbein*, 1979

Roberts, J., *Holbein and the Court of Henry VIII*, Edinburgh, 1993

Roskill, M. and Hand, J.O. (eds.), *Hans Holbein: Paintings, Prints and Reception*, New Haven, 2001

Routh, E.M.G., *Sir Thomas More and His Friends*, 1934

Rowlands, J., *Holbein, The Paintings of Hans Holbein the Younger*, complete edition, Oxford, 1985

Rupp, G., *Patterns of Reformation*, 1969

Russell, P.A., *Lay Theology in the Reformation*, Cambridge, 1986

Scarisbrick, J., *Henry VIII*, 1969

Schilling, E. (ed.), *Drawings of the Holbein Family*, 1935

Shaw, W, *Three Inventories of the Years 1542, 1547 and 1549–50 of Pictures in the Collections of Henry VIII and Edward VI*, 1937

Smith, P., *Erasmus, A Study of His Life, Ideals and Place in History*, New York, 1962

Spitz, L.W., *The Religious Renaissance of the German Humanists*, Cambridge, Mass., 1963

Staehelin, E., *Das theologische und die gottlosen Lebenswerk Johannes Oekolampads*, Leipzig, 1939

Stechow, W., *Northern Renaissance Art 1400–1600, Sources and Documents*, Englewood Cliffs, N.J., 1966

Stowe, J., *A Survey of London*, 2 vols, Oxford, 1908 edition

Strong, R., *Holbein and Henry VIII*, 1967

Strong, R., *Tudor and Jacobean Portraits*, 2 vols, 1969

Tyndale, W., *Works* (ed. H. Walter, Parker Society) 1848–50

Villiers, G.H., *Hans Holbein: 'The Ambassadors'*, n.d.

Von der Osten, G. and Vey, H., *Painting and Sculpture in Germany and the Netherlands 1500–1600*, 1969

White, C., *Dürer, The Artist and his Drawings*, 1971

Williams, C.H. (ed.), *English Historical Documents*, 1967

Wilson, D., *A Tudor Tapestry: Men, Women and Society in Reformation England*, 1972

Wilson, D., *England in the Age of Thomas More*, 1978

Wilson, D. and Fernández-Armesto, F., *Reformation: Christianity and the World 1500–2000*, 1996

Woltmann, A., *Holbein and His Time* (trs. F.E. Bunnett), 1872

Woltmann, A., *Holbein und seine Zeit*, 2 vols, Leipzig, 1874–6

ARTICLES AND CATALOGUES

Ainsworth, M., 'Paternes for Phisioneamyes: Holbein's portraiture reconsidered', *Burlington Magazine*, cxxxii, 1990, pp.173–86

Bertström, I., 'On Religious Symbols in European Portraiture in the XVth and XVIth Centuries' in Castelli, E., (ed.), *Umanesimo e esoterismo, Atti del V convegno internazionale di studi umanistid*, Oberhofen, 16–17 settembre 1960, Padua 1960, pp.335–43

Brady, T.A., 'The Social Place of a German Renaissance Artist: Hans Baldung Grien (1484/5–1545) at Strasbourg', *Central European History*, 8 (1975), pp.299–315

Buck, S. and Sander, J., *Hans Holbein the Younger, Painter at the Court of Henry VIII*, 2003

Colvin, S., 'On a portrait of Erasmus', *Burlington Magazine*, xvi, 1907, p.67

Cust, L., 'Notes on the collection formed by Thomas Howard, Earl of Arundel and Surrey', *Burlington Magazine*, xix, 1911, pp.278–87, 323–5

'Die Familie Holbein in Basel', Basel, 1960

Dowling, M., 'Anne Boleyn and Reform', *Journal of Ecclesiastical History*, 35, 1984, pp.30–47

Exhibition of Works by Holbein and Other Masters, Royal Academy, 1950–1

Fletcher, J. and Tapper, L.C., 'Hans Holbein the Younger in Antwerp and in England, 1526–8', *Apollo*, February 1983

Ganz, P., 'An unknown portrait by Hans Holbein the Younger', *Burlington Magazine*, xlvii, 1925

Hans Holbein der Jungere Zeichnungen aus dem Kupferstichkabinett der Öffentlichen Kunstammlung Basel, Kunstmuseum, Basel, 1988

His, E., 'Holbeins Verhältniss zur Basler Reformation' in *Repertorium für Kunstwissenschaft*, 2, 1879

Holbein and the Court of Henry VIII, The Queen's Gallery, London, 1978–9

Ives, E.W., 'The Queen and the Painters: Anne Boleyn, Holbein and Tudor Royal Portraits', *Apollo*, May 1994

King, D.T., 'Who was Holbein's *lady With a Squirrel and a Starling?*', *Apollo*, May 2004

Kurtz, O., 'Holbein's Painting of Christina of Denmark', *Burlington Magazine*, xcix, 1957, pp.57–63

Leslau, J., 'Holbein and the discreet rebus', *The Ricardian*, September 1978, pp.2–14

Leslau, J., 'Further to the Holbein rebus, . . . another discreet rebus', *The Ricardian*, June 1981, pp.11–19

Morison, S., 'The Portraiture of Thomas More by Hans Holbein and After', Lecture to the Thomas More Society, 18 October 1957

Piper, D., 'Holbein the Younger in England', *Journal of the Royal Society of Arts*, 1953

Roberts, J., *Drawings by Holbein from the Court of Henry VIII*, The Museum of Fine Arts Houston, 17 May–16 August 1987

Rowlands, J. and Starkey, D., 'An old tradition reasserted: Holbein's portrait of Queen Anne Boleyn', *Burlington Magazine*, cxxv, February 1983, pp.88–92

Samuel, E.R., 'Death in the Glass – A New View of Holbein's "Ambassadors" ', *Burlington Magazine*, xcxv, 1963, p.436–41

Saxl, F., 'Holbein and the Reformation', in *A Heritage of Images*, 1970

Strong, R., *Artists of the Tudor Court*, Victoria and Albert Museum, 1983

Strong, R., 'Holbein in England – I and II', *Burlington Magazine*, cix, May 1967, pp.276–81

Trapp, J. and Shulte Herbrüggen, H., *'The King's Good Servant': Sir Thomas More, 1477/8–1535*, National Portrait Gallery, 1977–8

UNPUBLISHED THESES

Foister, S., *Holbein and his English Patrons*, Ph.D. Thesis, Courtauld Institute, University of London, 1989

INDEX